Konstantin S. Mel'nikov

Konstantin S. Mel'nikov

and the Construction of Moscow

edited by
Mario Fosso
Otakar Máčel
Maurizio Meriggi

essays by
Guido Canella
Mario Fosso
Otakar Máčel
Maurizio Meriggi
Dietrich Schmidt
Jurij Volčok

Cover
Project for the Zuev workers'
club, 1927
photomontage by S. Topuntoli

Graphic concept
Marcello Francone

Editorial co-ordination
Luca Molinari

Editing
Claudio Nasso

Layout
Serena Parini

Translations
Eva Máčel, Steve Piccolo,
Pamela Santini, Katia Golovatyuk,
Paola Giaconia

First published in Italy in 2000 by
Skira editore S.p.A.
Palazzo Casati Stampa,
via Torino 61
20123 Milano, Italy

Printed and bound in Italy.
First edition

ISBN 88-8118-539-3

Distributed in North America and
Latin America by Abbeville
Publishing Group, 22 Cortlandt
Street, New York, NY 10007,
USA.
Distributed elsewhere in the world
by Thames and Hudson Ltd., 181a
High Holborn, London WC1V
7QX, United Kingdom.

Konstantin S. Mel'nikov
and the Construction of Moscow

The European Community
The Netherlands Architecture Fund

Department of Architecture
of the Milan Polytechnic (DPA)
Faculty of Architecture
at Milan-Bovisa of the
Milan Polytechnic

Moscow Architectural Institute
(MARKhI)
"A.V. Ščusev" State Museum
of Architecture (GMA), Moscow

Technical University of Delft,
Faculty of Architecture
University of Stuttgart, Institute
of Architectural History (IDG)

*An exhibition realised
with the financial support of*
The European Community
Commission, "Project Rafael"
The Netherlands Architecture
Fund

*Responsible for the European
Community*
Otakar Máčel

Scientific Coordinator
Mario Fosso

Project and Ordering
Maurizio Meriggi

Scientific Committee
Antonio Acuto
Guido Canella
Gianni Ottolini
(DPA-Politecnico di Milano)
Max Risselada
Otakar Máčel
(Faculteit Bowkunde, TU Delft)
Aleksandr P. Kudrjavcev
(MARKhI, Moscow)
Alekasndr Šadrin
(MARKhI, Moscow)
Jurij P. Volčok
(MARKhI, NIITAG, Moscow)
Selim O. Khan-Magomedov
(NIITAG, Moscow)
Vladimir A. Rezvin
Igor A. Kazus
(GNIMA, Moscow)
Dietrich W. Schmidt
(Institut für
Architekturgeschichte, Stuttgart)

Organising Committee
Jet Christiaanse
(Qui Vive filmprodukties, The
Netherlands)
Robert Nottrot
(Faculteit Bowkunde-TU Delft)
Irina Čepkunova
(GNIMA, Moscow)
Elena Nikulina
(NIITAG Mosproekt II, Moscow)

*Models and Redrawing of them
for the Execution Models
Workshop of the DPA of the Milan
Polytechnic*
Gianni Ottolini
R. Aiminio, R. Bazzani, A. Belotti,
G. Camagni, A. Colzani,
M.T. Conidi, L. Gatti, M. Meriggi,
F. Montaldo, R. Rizzi, E. Salvadé,
F. Salvarani, A. Scaramuzzi

DPA of the Turin Polytechnic
Edoardo Baglione

Models Workshop of the MARKhI
Aleksandr Šadrin
N. Lisenko, S. Frolova,
E. Gončarova, A. Kusnecov,
A. Pankratova, A. Puckov,
V. Rjazanov, A. Romanov,
V. Šadrin, A. Zolotov

*Models Workshop of the GMA,
Moscow*
I. Terenin, D.A. Seliščev

University of Innsbruck
Erich Steiner

*Models Workshop of the TU-Delft,
Faculty of Architecture*
Robert Nottrot
B. Aslan, J. Aulman, S. Bijker,
T. Budanceva, E. Damen,
I. Klevering

*University of Stuttgart, Faculty of
Architecture and Town Planning,
IDG-Stuttgart*
Dietrich Schmidt, M. Hechinger,
J. Appel, J. Ballreich, St. Birk,
Ch. Von Buchwald, K. Filbert,
B. Frenzel, F. Friedrich,
A. Giersch, J.U. Goos, M. Gruhn,
P. Haffner, I. Hartmann,
L. Heilmeyer, Y. Jeong, J. Kübler,
M. Ledermann, C. Lembke,
Y. Maier, L. Mösche, K. Müller,
F. Reichardt, St. Rüping, A. Saile,
R. Wied

Photographs of the Models
Stefano Topuntoli
(Milan Polytechnic)
Hans Joachim Heyer
(IDG-Stuttgart)
Boris Miklautsch (IDG-Stuttgart)
Oleg Serebrjansky (MARKhI)
Hans Schouten (TU-Delft)
Hans Kruze (TU-Delft)

*Unification of the Models'
Drawings for Publishing
Computer Workshop of DPA
of the Milan Polytechnic*
Ottorino Meregalli
Erika Samsa
Albino Tomasi

Film
"Konstantin Mel'nikov"
a film by Jet Christiaanse
and Marjo Leupers
Qui Vive filmprodukties,
Amsterdam

Photographic Credits
Photographic Archives of the
"A.V. Ščusev" State Museum
of Architecture (GMA)
City Archives of Moscow (ZNDT)
Architectural Heritage Archives
of the City of Moscow (UGKIOP)

The monographic issue of the "Quaderni" of the Department of Architectural Design of the Milan Polytechnic published in January 1998, entitled Viaggio in Russia, *offers an account of the travels of several professors from the Department in the Fall of 1995 to visit the Schools of Architecture of Moscow, Nižnij Novgorod, Kazan', St. Petersburg. This was followed by the invitation of the School of Samara to participate, in Summer 1996, at the "International Design Seminar" for young architects and teachers from European schools. On this occasion Jet Christiaanse of Amsterdam and Maurizio Meriggi of Milan realised that a strong, converging interest in the architecture of Konstantin Mel'nikov had been growing for some time at both the School of Delft and the Milan Polytechnic. This led to the idea of studying the work of the Master in new ways with respect to those offered by the existing literature: for example, by reproducing the works from drawings, creating scale models, or by editing film footage of the buildings, together with archives material and interviews.*

To give substance to the project, we felt it was necessary to examine the work of the Master in its context. Hence the phrase which was to become the title of the entire initiative: "Konstantin Mel'nikov and the Construction of Moscow".

A number of different areas of interest have been combined in this project: from the Schools of Delft and Stuttgart, that of the comparison of their tradition with the experience of Soviet architecture; from the School of Moscow, that of an active re-evaluation of the works of Mel'nikov and, in general, those of avant-garde architecture in the present process of transformation of that city.

Our School was founded very recently, and therefore our interests are connected to this special condition. First of all, we are concerned with educational reform and renewal in the field of architectural design, maintaining its focus on the problems of construction on a large scale that are presently impacting the Lombardy complex. The research in progress, as documented herein, bears clear witness to the line of research we intend to follow.

Finally, the itinerary that will bring the exhibition, after stops in Milan, Moscow and Amsterdam, to other European cities, will undoubtedly help to reinforce the circuit of exchange among our Schools, permitting wide-ranging, in-depth confrontation of educational experiences and research results.

Antonio Acuto
Faculty of Architecture at Milan-Bovisa of the Milan Polytechnic

Contents

K.S. Mel'nikov, Athlete of the Heart

Reasons and Timeliness of an Exhibition

It is in the city, the place of accumulation *par excellence*, that the intellectual and artistic qualities of K.S. Mel'nikov come to the fore. It is in the city that language, the instrument of appropriation of the new in the new environment, comes up with an original expression of syntax and form of collective life. Through language the recently urbanised citizen recomposes his memory of a common origin and is absorbed in a new behaviour. He breaks down meanings and signifiers, exposing them to the trial of urban reality in transformation, and tries to master the new form of communication. If the new is represented by an environment which is itself also in transformation, as in the case of Moscow in the Twenties, after the revolution, then he is placed on a par with the other citizens, and at the same time his abilities and talents will be noticed and welcomed to the extent that he is able to make ancient values recognisable in the new forms, avoiding sentimentalism and nostalgia, indicating the path to follow. His cultural background, albeit agricultural or seafaring (also collective in nature) will develop its potential, and the encounter with productive, industrial culture will bring out the best of both values: those of an ancient myth, consolidated through fable and religion, and those of the more recently formed myth of technique, the common ground of everyday operation, aimed at founding a new common wealth.

As long as technique and form co-operate in the plastic form of the language of the architectural objects, they w evoke their past, and the space-room   ill resonate in the cinema and the th :atre of plastic images, like inhabited sculptures.[1] The encounter generates alienation, and this is simultaneously disorientation and the reason behind the freedom of the new language. The slogans applied to the works of architecture are significant. As on the frontons of temples, here writing fulfils the dual task of a typographical matrix superimposed on the typology. In contrast with simple communicative writing, the monumental inscriptions of the new collective edifices perpetually redefine the meaning of the constructed things (the objects are re-named) and make an announcement, as in a manifesto.[2]

In the convergence of men filled with a religious sense of life and a society reconstructing its bases of civilisation and its institutions through politics and ideology, the new organisation of labour through the factory provided, in post-revolutionary Russia, the most productive and fertile opportunities for K. Mel'nikov, although his idea of architecture was never productivistic nor standardised. Utilising the professional opportunities offered by the liberal policies of the union organisations, and almost 'half asleep' due to the enormous efforts made during the three years of their construction, from '27 to '29 he built seven workers' clubs, "seven different architectures by the same architect."[3]

As has often been emphasised, the path of Mel'nikov is not unlike that of many Russian artists who were his contemporaries, who found themselves in the condition to create new compositional forms in the awareness of having to find solutions to the enigma of art in history. What sets him apart, however, is that he chose to come to grips with this enigma by beginning with a poetic world that made use of 'chance encounters', accepting the challenge of each theme, case by case, while remaining faithful to his innocence as an artist, refusing to obey any pre-established aesthetic code.[4]

Like a great actor or boxer, he is not concerned with reciting or thinking up a strategy for victory, he is the character, or the athlete, from the moment he walks onto the stage or enters the ring, ready to meet the challenge of the adversary and the unexpected occurrences of the moment; like a boxer or an actor, he makes the necessary gesture in the precise moment it is required, without premeditation, nor to please himself or the audience.[5]

The exhibition of the work of K. Mel'nikov is based on the desire to reconstruct, as faithfully as possible, the form of his architecture in the context of the relations and correspondences between the works and the city. The aim is both cognitive and didactic, to provide a detailed introduction to his architecture, recognising its implicit exemplary nature and timeliness, studying it and considering it as a whole, as a diversified but unitary body of values shared by the constructed works, the designs, the utopias. At the same time, it is important to consider the fact that the ultimate reasons of these works lie, beyond their physical and spatial materiality, in their location in the city of Moscow: the historical city and that of the revolution, the ancient city and the imagined city, the city of wood and that of stone of the Thirties.

The study of the architecture of Mel'nikov offers the opportunity to observe the plan of a Moscow that is truly constructed, composed of places rather than objects and isolated episodes, inevitably catalogued in stylistic or chronological categories.

This approach is a contradiction of the custom of viewing architecture, including contemporary architecture, as a pure relic or an object of cultural antiquarianism, flattened by more or less reductive conventional formulae. Against the map of Moscow in the Thirties the works of Mel'nikov appear as places through which the city is considered and designed as a whole, places characterised and ritualised from an urban and monumental, not just functional, point of view.

This has been possible thanks to the encounter of different traditions of study, combining schools and institutions that are geographically and linguistically distant from one another in a common research, united by a shared desire and a passion for investigation. Four institutions, each with its own approach with respect to architectural design, have derived in a more or less explicit manner, through a method of historical and project-oriented study of contemporary architecture, the unitary sense of the architectural work in the construction of the city, alongside the social, technical and economic commitment of which the work is the synthesis.

Between didactic experimentation and academic tradition, the Moscow Architecture Institute (formerly VKUTEMAS), the Department of Architectural Design and the Milan-Bovisa Faculty of Architecture of the Milan Polytechnic, the Technische Universiteit Delft and the Institute of History of Contemporary Architecture of Stuttgart, together with the e A. Ščusev Museum of Architecture of Moscow, have collaborated over the last few years on a project that is, above all, cognitive and scientific in nature. Aimed at the training of young architects and the definition of a didactic curriculum, it makes use of the sources of architecture of this century, integrating studies of contemporary history, design and restoration.[6]

Philology and an archaeological vision of the architectural work in the modern city might appear to be incompatible, *a priori,* with the predominantly random, fragmentary development of the city itself; but in the case of the work of certain of the great architects of this century, they can, instead, suggest the need to offer rules and settlement strategies capable of reformulating a sense of meaning and form in the places of collective life.

The experience of historical architecture is a fundamental part of the training of the greatest contemporary architects. The architecture of F.L. Wright, Le Corbusier, Mies van der Rohe would not, in fact, be conceivable without the notion of the voyage, and that of play with the art of building of the past. Without such a background their architecture would not have been able to achieve its completeness, and the biography of this knowledge also reveals the adhesion to a principle, that of the essence of construction and its com-

position. The closer a work of architecture gets to this essence, the more it will be great, and fertile. This is the case of Mel'nikov. The form of his architecture contains both memory of the past and practical experimentation in building. Historiography has attempted to give order to this path, placing him in the corresponding aesthetic, social or ideological categories of formalism or constructivism, or viewing him as an isolated artist. But such temporary categorisation must come to terms not only with the subjectivity of the artist or the occasional reasons that prompted him to make a given work, but also with the contextual research on the project. We could put it like this: on the added value determined by his creative potential, a value that is greater in keeping with the level of figurative dissemination, apart from the usage value for the city.

As in the case of architecture of other eras, such as the baroque or, at the other extreme, that of Futurism, in that of Mel'nikov the ideological time gap seems to be bridged by the figurative timeliness of the work, full of potential repercussions in the taste and language of our time.

But beyond a knowledge of purely historical interest, or that of the iconography of a period, this exhibition is intended as

Rusakov Workers' Club, 1927: detail of the facade (photo by A. Rodčenko, 1929)

a point of encounter among contemporary architects for reasoning on the recent historical past and on the avant-gardes, beginning with a body of works that in the light of the work of analysis and reconstruction have taken on the weight and force of an anomalous architectural treatise.

Within the avant-gardes Mel'nikov does not fit into the historiographic *cliché* of an architecture of pure technique or pure ideology, and is subjected to forced grouping with the constructivists, with whom he did share certain initial premises, or with the formalists, in cases of accusation of the exercise of self-referential compositional research. In the 'group portrait' of Russian (and then Soviet) architecture in the Twenties and Thirties, Mel'nikov doesn't belong in any of the ranks, or in any definitive ideological grouping; he stands out as one of the major personalities of a figurative culture, that of Russia, to which both the European architecture and figurative arts of this century owe a great deal.

The simultaneously utopian and realistic architecture of Mel'nikov offers a vision, for European architects, of the essence of their task, rather than the nature of their craft.

Scientific Content and Program

The objective of the exhibition and the accompanying seminar is to observe the work of Mel'nikov against the backdrop and in the context of the Moscow of the Twenties and Thirties, in an attempt to render explicit, with the reconstruction in scale of architectural and urban planning models, both of constructed works and unbuilt designs, his contribution to the construction of the contemporary city and to the creation of the scenario of community and civic life in the metropolis, the new Moscow, the great Moscow.[7]

To do this, the initiative has developed the necessary collaboration between historians and architectural designers in the analysis of the materials and their interpretation for the reconstruction of the models, alongside a scientific methodology of urban contextualisation that included the graphic re-elaboration of the designs and the cartographic interpretation of the sites, with the aim of bringing out the simultaneously idealistic and practical character of the project analysed. The result is an original, in-depth documentary study, that can lead to further necessary developments both in the practice and the teaching of architectural design.

Zuev Workers' Club, 1927; section

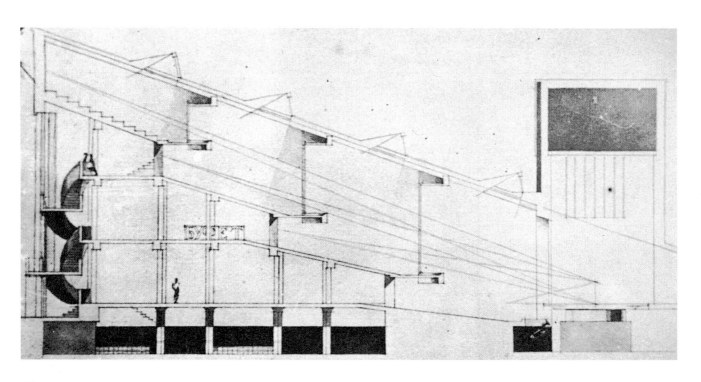

Moreover, if we consider the fact that most of the models have been the result of a didactic effort that took place in architecture schools, the primary institutional workplace for the researchers involved in the scientific committee of the exhibition, we can easily understand that in the areas of representation and reconstruction of the models the figures of the architect and the engineer, the urban planner and the historian have combined forces in an interdisciplinary effort that has brought out the complementary nature of their various roles and forms of expertise, in a unitary focus on the project. In this approach an essential contribution has been made by the work of the model-making laboratories and the teams assigned the tasks of re-drawing and construction, which rather than applying a single method in terms of choice of materials, execution and photographic documentation, have made use of their own consolidated techniques, thus rendering the collaboration among the various institutions involved more lively and stimulating.

The Exhibition

The models and the material on the panels illustrate, in documentary and thematic sections, the professional and artistic biography of Mel'nikov in the context of the transformations of the city of Moscow in the Twenties and Thirties.

Going beyond the initial impulse to organise the exhibition in chronological order, curiously enough it has been the work of Mel'nikov itself, reinterpreted and rendered explicit as a whole by the reconstruction of the models, that has suggested possibilities for groupings.

Alongside the home-studio of the architect, the models of the Zuev and Rusakov clubs, and the competition project for Leningradskaja Pravda form an introduction to the research in the area of new typologies, architectural prototypes that form the basis for the study of the functional interpenetrations and layout strategies of the rooms in the works of Mel'nikov.

In like manner, the pragmatic and utterly functional theme of the garage can be viewed in the context of the industrial reconstruction of the parts of the city of Moscow in the years of the NEP, of the First Pan-Soviet Exposition of Agriculture and Crafts, and the Sukharevskij market. Together with the Bakhmetevskij garage and the market, in the periphery the workers' clubs shine with a light all their own, representing one of the most important contributions to the self-representation of the social class of the producers on the urban scene.[8] Next to these works, the competition design for the Labor Building (1923), which contained a number of ideas that were later to be more fully developed on the theme of the section of the auditorium and the gallery.

Finally, the research on the projects for the reconstruction of the city of Moscow on the eve of the first five-year plan focuses on the two visionary designs for the Palace of the Soviets and the Commissariat of Heavy Industry, against the backdrop of the projects for the city and the Moskva riverfront developed by the Planning Office (MOSSOVET), in a monumental triangle arrangement of the centre of the city that redefines the role of the capital.[9]

Amidst the more experimental designs of his early career, which brought Mel'nikov success and fame both in Russia and abroad: the two Makhorka pavilions for the Pan-Soviet Exposition of 1923 and the Paris Exposition of 1926, and the design for the Green City in 1929 (a work from the beginning of the phase of obscurity and neglect caused by his position as an outsider), we find the complete series of the clubs and garages, in a thematic counterpoint between architecture and the city, in which the experience in Paris represents one a fundamental phase.

The overview is based on a complex, detailed narrative characterised by the exceptional nature of the works of architecture, and by the wealth of documentation on the constructed designs, in spite of the fact that the actual Mel'nikov archives of drawings are presently unavailable for direct access, due to legal difficulties.

Through an investigation that ranges from the architecture of the interiors to the re-creation of the composition of the facades and the positioning of the edifices in their original context, the narrative offers a unified overview of the architecture of Mel'nikov and of the transformation of Moscow in one of the most fertile moments of its history.

The image of the city that emerges from this exhibition is that of a settlement based on decentralisation and on the presence of many different centres positioned in different parts of the city and, for the most part, in its industrial periphery. Alongside this Moscow designed for production, Mel'nikov's project for the Green City envisions the creation of a 'New Moscow', a place of 'rationalised repose', for the creation of a new, regenerated individual.[10]

Finally, the Moscow of the Thirties, radically reconstructed in terms of planning by the program of consolidation with respect to the role and the dimension of the capital city, the Great Moscow.

The exhibition also features audio-visual materials prepared by a Dutch team, with film clips from the Twenties and Thirties, images of the present situation of the buildings of Mel'nikov in Moscow today, interviews with occidental and Russian critics, and an exclusive interview with the painter V.K. Mel'nikov, the son of Konstantin Mel'nikov, in his father's house.

But the aim of this exhibition is not celebrative. The personal and professional vicissitudes of Mel'nikov, already described with accuracy in the book by F.S. Starr, are not discussed here. Instead, the objective has been to offer criticism the possibility of new approaches, beginning with the reconstruction of the urban models and the architectural projects.

Beginning with the models of the reconstructed works and the documentary research, the aim of the seminars that accompany the exhibition will be to examine the figure of Mel'nikov, also through the testimony of those who knew him personally, as in the case of the American historian F.S. Starr, in terms of the idea of the city that emerges in his works, and the questions of a more general character posed by the architectural avant-gardes of this century in Europe and Russia on the issues of the city and the urbanisation of the territory, together with those of the modern language and its relationship with technique.

Architecture as a Life Form

In and around the Twenties the ideological siren reawakened in the artist the desire to express the new, and the contemporary Ulysses ventures beyond the Pillars of Hercules of his time, beyond the limits of a given, certain knowledge he observes the world of men with the eyes of a god-made-man, attempting to foresee the future. In this future poetry mingles with necessity, with everyday life and beauty, beyond any reasonable hope. As long as this mingling is a fusion with other men, he is welcomed and praised for the joy he is able to instil in all things. But when the titan sinks into the ideological abyss, then the poet too navigates on his wherry like the master builder atop an unfinished cathedral, before the prince banishes him forever.

This is the atmosphere and the posture revealed in the vivid autobiographical text written and rewritten by Mel'nikov from 1967 until 1974, the year of his death. Apart from the epigraphic and occasionally resentful style and tone, this text represents an exceptionally source of inspiration for those who wish to better understand the historical period in question and the city of Moscow itself, and a complement to any more or less systematic reconstruction of his work.[11] On the one hand, Mel'nikov 'scientifically' gives an order to fifty years of design activity, calling upon facts and personalities of the artistic and professional world of the Twenties and Thirties in reference to his work, leading him back in time to describe the experiences of his childhood.

On the other, the text is also a forceful poetic and cultural document, a gripping, dramatic composition, so much so that it might be worth considering using the work as the basis for a work of theatre, a film, an opera.

A similar plot involving figurative passion and historical events is offered in the invaluable work on Andrej Rublëv by Andrej Tarkovskij, masterfully illuminated in the film of the same name, rendered even more gripping and vivid by the accompanying cinematic narration.[12] The monk Andrej, a master painter of icons, is witness, in the final scene of the book, to the casting of a very large new bell for the church of Moscow. In the sequence of decisions and intuitions required to reinvent the secret of the fusion of such a large object in bronze, the gaze of Rublëv the painter, on the eve of the fifteenth century, bears witness to the trials of the relationship between the sacred figurative tradition and neotechnical ingenuity, a relationship which seems to be projected, metaphorically, into the Russia of the twentieth century, indicating K.S. Mel'nikov, architect, as one of the sublime heirs of a tradition.

The book on architecture by Mel'nikov includes such inspirational motives; it "concentrates on those places that are constant in all the times of its history, and do not depend on the material means of the composition, nor on the level of culture of the men who have built them."[13]

It has been said that the home-studio of Mel'nikov, the Pavilion in Paris, in 1925, and the Rusakov club represent the elements of a trilogy that in a more or less inevitable way has fascinated and still fascinates contemporary architects, influenced by the romantic overtones of the period, and by a lack of documentation on the rest of Mel'nikov's work.[14]

The lack of knowledge regarding his other architecture (after the reawakening of interest in the Sixties) partially caused by the public isolation of his figure and by his reluctance, during his professional and artistic career, to take univocal theoretical positions, is no longer a problem today, apart from the difficulty in abandoning the prejudices and the cultural categories of the past, and a certain convenience associated with the ordering of history in terms of schools and ideological or programmatic groupings. The work of co-ordinated research to achieve an overview and a reconstruction, as a whole, of the designs of Mel'nikov and their contextualisation, will perhaps be useful to overcome the (in many ways) ambiguous or tendentious division between Soviet architecture and European functionalism, which has all too often been one of the causes of the inconsistency, in urban terms, of many contemporary works.

The recontextualisation of the original architectonic and constructive qualities of the architecture of Mel'nikov against the background of a real city, the functional study of its parts for the realisation of the models and the reconstruction of the designs that were never built, can help us to recognise the timely character of Mel'nikov's forms, marked by an original, and in many ways extraordinary, complexity of meanings.

[1] Cf. F. Starr, *K.S.Mel'nikov, Solo Architect in a Mass Society*, Princeton 1978; for the study of the personal and professional biography of Mel'nikov, see this documentary and critical text, the most important for the knowledge of the works of the architect.

[2] On the theme of alienation Cf. M. Tafuri, *Formalismo e Avanguardia fra la NEP e il Primo Piano Quinquennale*, in Var. authors, *URSS 1917-1978, La città. L'architettura*, Roma 1979, pp. 23-25; Tafuri, analysing the work of Sklovskij, writes: "The *creation of form* as the promised land of the subjective victory over alienation, therefore: this is the latent content of the formalist analyses and the revolutionary avant-gardes. It is clear that this 'constructive' yearning, in the very moment in which it declares the autonomy of art from life, in which it asserts the need to break habitual associations, to make the usual strange, poses problems that are almost impossible to resolve. Soviet constructivism was to continuously waver between an architecture *extraneous to the everyday world* - the research of Mel'nikov—and an architecture in a *positive* dialectic with it: the research of Ginzburg, for the most part, and of Burov, Vesnin, Fridman."

[3] Cfr K.S. Mel'nikov, *Arkhitektura meij žizni. Tvorčeskaja koncepcija. Tvorčeskaja praktika (The Architecture of my Life. Creative conception. Creative practice)*, Moscow 1985, chap. XIX., pp. 80-81 "All seven of the clubs had different architectures by the same architect, and were no larger than 17,000 cubic meters. The smallest, in terms of volume, was the club dedicated to Frunze, 3500 cu-

bic meters. With the choice of the interior in three rows of balconies for three hundred spectators, the edifice of the club took on an imposing dimension. In this insertion of volumes, deception of largeness, lies my architecture."

[4] Cf. M. Tafuri, *op. cit.*, especially the remarks on the relations among the figurative arts, and between these arts and the cinema and the theatre, pp. 17-29; also see: O. Mácel, *Mel'nikov and Soviet Architecture*, in: Var. authors, *Mel'nikov, the muscles of invention*, Rotterdam 1990; pp. 25-67, especially, within the complete overview of the work of Mel'nikov, the discussion of *Visual Arts and Architecture*.

[5] For this analogy, and for the title of this introduction, I must give credit to the radio program *Appunti di Volo (flight notes)*, and in particular to a text presented in one of the recent broadcasts, F. Ruffini, *Teatro e boxe, l'"atleta del cuore" nella scena del Novecento, Bologna 1994 (Theater and boxe, the "heart athlete" in scene of XXth century)*, Bologna 1999.

[6] On this theme see the exhibition organised by the Department of Architectural Design of the Milan Polytechnic, entitled "Progetti per Milano", and its two-volume catalogue, with the "Quaderni del Dipartimento di Progettazione dell'Architettura"" n. 13-16, 18, Milano 1995-1997.

[7] The exhibition *Konstantin Mel'nikov and the construction of Moscow* is part of an initiative supported financially by the European Economic Community in the context of the "Rafael" program for the recovery of the European cultural heritage.

[8] Cf. V. Quilici, *L'architettura del costruttivismo*, Bari 1969; in particular, the chapter: *Mel'nikov*, pp. 143-153.

[9] Cf. apart from the already cited Var. authors, *URSS 1917-1978, La città – L'architettura*, Roma 1979; also: A. De Magistris, *La costruzione della città totalitaria (The construction of the totalitarian city)*, Città Studi Edizioni, Torino 1995 and the chapter: *La ricostruzione della città negli anni trenta*, in A. De Magistris, *Mosca 1900-1950 Nascita di una capitale (Moscow 1900-1959. Birth of a capital)*, CLUP Guide, Milano 1994.

[10] Cf. M. Meriggi, *The Green City*, published in this volume; in particular, the analysis of the different approaches to the theme in the competition for the Green City, in antithesis with the tradition of the Garden City, in the projects of K. Mel'nikov, N. Ladovskij, M. Ginzburg and D. Fridman.

[11] Cf. Anatoli Strigalev, (ed.), *K.S. Mel'nikov, The Architecture of my Life*, cit., manuscript written and revised by Mel'nikov between the mid-1960s and 1974, the year of his death.

[12] Cf. A. Konvalovskij, A. Tarkovskij, *Rubliev, il pittore delle icone, (Rublëv, the painter of icons)*, Rimini 1983.

[13] Cf. K.S. Mel'nikov, *op. cit.*, cap. VII: "The aim of my book is to illustrate architecture, not all the known recipes or impossible illusions, but the natural and rare, unknown sensations, but of the real world, of our senses. This book is in no way a list of constructed objects, already thoroughly, lovingly described in familiar classical treatises and contemporary treatises, that are forgotten more quickly to the extent that they depend upon fashion. This book doesn't even claim to be a monograph; there is no order either of the themes nor of the dates: in short, it is a book that is not ordinary, just as all that it illustrates is not ordinary. [...] The book does not set about discovering the laws, as it author doesn't believe in their existence. With the idea of the determination of the nature of Architecture, I demonstrate a personal attempt at concrete constructions and projects, realized, with the inclusion of the textual forms, since 1917, meaning over half a century, at the moment of the Jubilee."

[14] Cf. C. Cooke, *Mel'nikov and his critics*, in: Var. authors, *Mel'nikov the muscles of invention*, Rotterdam 1990; the writer questions the partiality of a point of view of pure solidarity with the architect in the Russian cultural and political context of the early decades of the century, favouring an analysis of the technical and constructive relevance of his work, and emphasising its naive character.

Aleksandr Kudriavcev[1]

K.S. Mel'nikov, Twenties Moscow Avant-Garde, and Modern Professional Architectural Education

The exhibition "The Architect Konstantin Stepanovic Mel'nikov and the urban development of Moscow in the 1920s - 1930s" has become a large international project, uniting the efforts of major architectural schools in four countries: the Netherlands, Germany, Italy and Russia. This is no coincidence, since in my opinion these particular countries gave birth to the new interpretation and new content of architectural design in the first decades of the twentieth century. Today, as we approach the end of this century, we have come together in order to reappraise and summarise our common legacy.

In the first third of the outgoing century the Moscow school of architecture actively participated in the professional life in the city, the project competitions and design competitions between the groups of architects, in the urban development plan 'New Moscow', and gave lectures about architectural literacy at VKhUTEMAS (Higher Artistic and Technical Workshops), VKhUTEIN (Higher Artistic and Technical Institute), the faculty of architecture of the MVTU (Moscow Higher Technical School), and at the Architectural Institute. Today all of that activity belongs to the common European cultural heritage, forming an integral part of the total architectural history of the twentieth century. This inextricable connection manifests itself in different ways. For instance, in the Jean-Louis Cohen's book *Scenes of the World To Come*, published in Montreal, Canada, in 1995 (actually a catalogue of the corresponding exhibition), which presents Moscow architecture from the Twenties- Forties as a significant influence in European architecture at that time. And the in *Deconstruction*, a book by Andreas Papadakis, Catherine Cooke, and Andrew Benjamin, published in London in 1989. This book details the organic link between the new trend in the modern architecture and the legacy of the Moscow avant-garde. During his visit to Moscow not so long ago, in the early Nineties, Jacques Derrida, one of the founding fathers of the theory and philosophy of deconstructivism, gave an interview where he touched on such topics as the general theory of form creation (the subject of the above-mentioned book) as well as the organisation of life, human existence, and Moscow in the Muscovite environment. We see this interview as a single text about a city, architecture, traditions and their birth, culture, philosophy...

It is also pertinent to note that this is not the first joint international project carried out by the participants in our exhibition. Together with our colleagues in Stuttgart and the Moscow Museum of Architecture we have organised a permanent exhibition entitled "The Russian Avant-garde I and II".

The Architectural Design Department of the Polytechnic University of Milan has published a book called *Viaggio in Russia* which documents a two-year project that took place between 1995 and 1997, presenting a report on the newly acquired knowledge about the architectural heritage and modern professional life in Moscow and other Russian cities, such as Saint Petersburg, Nižnij Novgorod, Kazan' and Samara.

Another joint project called *Rotterdam-Moscow, the architectural education in the Academy of Architecture of Rotterdam and Moscow Architectural Institute* has taken a closer look at the problems of official architectural education and professional education in general. A quick glance at the bilingual report of the project, published in Rotterdam in 1995, is all one needs to understand the role which the legacy of the Moscow architectural school of the Twenties still plays in the modern architectural education, especially in the basic programme of architectural design.

It seems to me that we managed to go even further in the current project: not only because of our joint efforts, an important fact promising in itself, but because I can also see developments in methodology, in the way this architectural legacy is being studied.

A qualitatively new trend has emerged, and I hope it will not be limited to Moscow. Moreover this is the first time a subject of architectural study has been divided into three separate elements: the first element is the personality of the Master; the second is the spatial composition, the architectural form, as documented in his projects; and the third element is the city itself in which he lived and for which he worked. The inseparability of these three elements gives us a chance, in my opinion, to re-examine an architectural creative process, which although 60-80 years old, has lost none of its relevance to the present day. It is as though this project embodies M.M. Bakhtin's *Here and Now* formula of intercultural dialogue (which incidentally, also deals with the era

which was analysed in the preparation for this exhibition) in its interpretation in terms of volume and space.

Not long before the period covered by our joint project, the Russian philosopher, theologian, and natural scientist Father Pavel Florenskij wrote: "To comprehend the world means to comprehend space." The models, integrated three-dimensional replicas of the way K.S. Mel'nikov perceived the world, are not only 'spatial projections' of the Master's two-dimensional drawings and sketches, they also span two eras: the future and the past. This accounts for the special significance of the urban development models which show how the projects and buildings designed by K.S. Mel'nikov coexisted with the development of Moscow in that time, the architect's *own* time. Especially since in the twentieth century any city, especially Moscow, with its historical past, develops very dynamically, changing literally with each new day.

In the literature (books, magazines, catalogues) of other exhibitions we can follow the changes in concepts related to the ar-

chitectural legacy of the Moscow avant-garde (including K.S. Mel'nikov) and its evaluation.

Much less is known about the development that the architectural creations of the avant-garde, including Mel'nikov's works, underwent in a constantly changing city context. Therefore historical-architectural 'cross-sections', showing the urban development situation in the areas of Moscow for which K.S. Mel'nikov designed and built, became a valuable supplement to the researcher's 'text' accompanying the project.

The triangle, Mel'nikov's favourite geometrical figure, 'works' to the full extent in the concept of this exhibition, where the vertexes of the triangle represent the creative 'self' of the architect, his creative legacy, and the city in which he created. Modelling K.S. Mel'nikov's works for this exhibition took on a specific form of educational activity, and received a fairly new interpretation. A three-dimensional structure is reproduced not only as a pure and abstract architectural form, absolute in its artistic perfection, but as an architectur-

al creation of flesh and blood with its own address, its legitimate place in the city and most importantly, with its own personality, biography and destiny. It is most probably the latter characteristic that has fed our interest in the legacy of Moscow architecture from the Avant-garde period during the last 75 years.

In the autumn of 1999 we will celebrate the 250th anniversary of the Moscow School of Architecture while two years ago was the 75th anniversary of the foundation of the VKhUTEMAS School, where Mel'nikov used to teach. Our MARKhI Institute has become successor of this school.

For us, and I hope for the rest of participants in this joint project, the preparation for this exhibition has the potential to become one of most successful ways of preserving the full value continuity of the study process and acquisition of knowledge about the legacy of the modern architecture. That is why we deemed it necessary to include the undergraduate and postgraduate students of our Institute in the modelling teams.

Central portion of the Moscow Institute of Architecture building (MARKhI), formerly I. Voroncov house, expanded in 1913-1914 by A. Kuznecov in order to house 'Stroganov' School of Industrial Arts, later University Institute of Higher Technology (MTVU)

View of the city from the roof of MARKhI towards the Kremlin

As a matter of fact, we were preparing a large exhibition and a conference for the anniversary of VKhUTEMAS. Its title *Moscow: the VKhUTEMAS Space* reflected our modern, relatively broad interpretation of space as applied to the professional and cultural legacy of the Moscow avant-garde architecture. One of independent conference's subjects was "The city and VKhUTEMAS". "Education and the city"–the union of these two concepts may open one of promising fields of study into the architectural legacy of the modern era and of mastering professional architectural skills…

This exhibition in Moscow is scheduled for the autumn of 1999. We hope that it will coincide with other events scheduled for the anniversary of the Moscow school of architecture.

As part of the exhibition "Architect K.S. Mel'nikov and Moscow of the 1920s – 1930s", which will take place in the A.V. Ščusev Museum of Architecture we plan to organise a scientific seminar, to discuss the creative work of K.S. Mel'nikov together with the value of the architectural legacy of the Moscow avant-garde, and raise the important issue of preserving the avant-garde monuments and legacy in Moscow. We would like to make this last issue central to the discussion since the state of the architectural heritage of twenties-thirties Moscow, including those protected by the state, causes serious concern about their future.

There are so many issues to be discussed: artistic and scientific as well as organisational, methodical and economic. In my opinion, it is very important that we try to connect the discussion, the interpretation and the emotional perception of those issues to the name of Konstantin Stepanovic Mel'nikov. It means that he is still actively participating and influencing the everyday professional life of Moscow architects.

"Architecture is an art which stands on the limit of the possible" Mel'nikov once wrote. An exhibition about this architect, his personality, his creative work and the city for which he did so much is also an art "on the limit of the possible".

I would like to wish the exhibition every success, and hope it acts as a source of inspiration for all the visitors in all the cities and countries it visits.

[1] President of the Russian Academy of Architecture and Construction Sciences, Academician of Architecture, Rector and head of the MARKhI department of History and Theory of 20th Century Architecture.

The fact that Delft's contribution to this exhibition consists of models of Mel'nikov's indoor car parks is quite accidental, the result of the way the bodies involved shared the work out between themselves. It is however no accident that Delft University of Technology's faculty of architecture is involved in an exhibition on a Russian avant-garde architect.

The Russian Avant-Garde and the Netherlands

For more than 30 years now a small group in Delft has been focusing its attention on Russian architecture, an exceptional situation for the Netherlands. Not that in general there has been no attention paid to the Russian avant-garde in that country, as witness the unique collections of works by Malevič in Amsterdam's Stedelijk museum and by Lisickij in the Van Abbe museum in Eindhoven. The Malevič collection was acquired as long ago as the fifties by W.J.H.B. Sandberg,[1] director of the museum at the time. Sandberg's interest in the Russian painter derived from his personal involvement in the pre-war artistic avant-garde. However, this interesting acquisition failed to encourage the study of Russian avant-garde architecture. On the other hand the creation of the Lisickij collection is an example of a 'rediscovery' in the Sixties by a younger generation that had never been a con-

temporary of the classical avant-garde. During his study of architecture in Delft, Jean Leering, the director of the Eindhoven museum, became interested in Lisickij's work and later succeeded in acquiring Mrs Vordemberge-Leda's Lisickij collection for the museum.[2] The Delft school of architecture had for years had a traditional slant. Since the beginning of the Thirties the institution had been a stronghold of the 'Delft School', a catholic grouping centred around Prof. M.J. Granpré Molière, an opponent of the functionalists of de 8 & Opbouw. After the Second World War things very gradually started to change, partly because of the appointment of J.H. van de Broek, and C. van Eesteren (1948) and later J.B. Bakema (1963) as professors. The Sixties saw the last phase of the school's transformation. Jean Leering's interest in El Lissitzky was appropriate to that period, being an example of a trend towards interest in the pre-war avant-garde. This development in Delft resulted at the end of the Sixties in the rediscovery of Russian avant-garde architecture.

Pioneering Work in Delft

An important part in this rediscovery was played by Gerrit Oorthuys, who graduated as architect in 1968. Through his family–his father was the photographer Cas Oorthuys–he had become familiar with Amsterdam's pre-war in origin avant-garde milieu. Some of those who came from this milieu, like Peter Alma, Mart Stam and Joris Ivens, even went to the Soviet Union at the beginning of the thirties to help build socialism there. This milieu formed the cultural background to Oorthuys's interest in Russian avant-garde architecture. He and his colleagues in Delft still knew little about the architecture itself, but that fact only stimulated their curiosity.

At the time we are talking about, around 1967, there was little to be known about the subject. Stalin's cultural policy, the Second World War and the cold war that followed had largely wiped out any memory of the Russian avant-garde in architecture amongst the younger generation. In the meantime a survey by Vittorio de Feo[3] had appeared in Italian, but the language barrier meant that the publication was hardly accessible in the Netherlands. Camilla Gray's[4] book on the Russian avant-garde in the graphic arts, which had appeared earlier, was more accessible, but only outlined developments up to 1922 and paid little attention architecture. Anatole Kopp's survey, *Ville et Révolution*[5] only appeared in 1967.

In that year Oorthuys and his colleagues took part in a trip to Prague, where they established contacts with students and a few members of staff of the faculty of architecture in Prague. The people from Delft tried to encourage their kindred spirits in Prague to participate in a joint project on Russian avant-garde architecture. The Czechs seemed to be interested in the subject and had the advantage of being able to manage Russian. During a meeting with the architect Jirí Hruza it turned out that he was already preparing a publication on the subject. However in August 1968 the prospects for cooperation vanished abruptly from the scene with the invasion of Czechoslovakia by Warsaw Pact forces.[6]

However, Gerrit Oorthuys and his colleague Max Risselada knew nothing of this when they left for Moscow and Leningrad in a Citroën 2CV in August 1968. But it was clear from the military columns to which they had to give way during their journey that something was going on. There were of course no Czechs to be found in Moscow, and some of them they only met later on in Switzerland as emigrants. Despite the politically unfavourable timing they collected good deal of information in Russia. Besides seeing the constructivistic buildings themselves, they met Mel'nikov, Krinskij, Rodčenko's daughter and Leonidov's son. This success was mainly due to the help and kind offices of the architect N.L. Kračeninikova of the Institute for the Theory and History of Architecture in Moscow. She it was who showed the people from Delft round what remained of the world of the avant-garde. She was in a position to consult old publications and magazines in the library of the Moscow Institute of Architecture. Oorthuys and Risselada photographed everything they could. Equipped with pictorial material and information provided orally they left for the Netherlands, where they joined with Otto Das to put together the exhibition "USSR 1917-1933, architectuur, stedebouw" at the faculty. The exhibition opened in November 1969.

The Exhibition

This architectural exhibition was designed to give a general overview, and consisted, as was usual at the early days of such 'Russian studies' not of originals but of photographic reproductions and reconstructions. So for example the model of Leonidov's Lenin library and the reconstruction of Rodčenko's 'chess chair' which were put on display were built in Delft. This piece of furniture originally formed part of the model furnishings for a working men's club as shown in Mel'nikov's Russian pavilion in Paris in 1925. This was joined in the Great Hall of the Polytechnic by the 'Tower of the Third International' which has been reconstructed in 1968 for the Tatlin exhibition in the Moderna Museet in Stockholm.[7] The only scarce originals at the

Delft exhibition consisted of material that had been collected or borrowed. An illustrated catalogue also appeared, which besides an introduction by Oorthuys presented translations of Russian programmatic texts.[8] 'Foreign specialists', i.e. Western architects working in the Soviet Union, such as Hans Schmidt and J.B. van Loghem, also received attention.[9] A lecture series accompanied the exhibition, including contributions from such new historical figures as: Berthold Lubetkin, Joris Ivens, Johan Niegeman and Peter Alma.

Looked at internationally, the Delft exhibition came at a fortunate time. The Russian architectural avant-garde was beginning to be rediscovered in Europe and the United States, stimulated by the leftward shift in politics after 1968. Two important surveys appeared on the subject, one by Vieri Quilici and one by Oleg Svidkovski[10] and Anatole Kopp's book became available in an English translation.[11] There was so much interest in the subject that the Delft exhibition went on tour, first to the Technische Hochschule in Berlin and Museum of Architecture in Stockholm, then to the United States, where it was shown in Harvard University's Carpenter Center, Princeton University's School of Architecture and Urban Planning and then in 1971 at the Institute for Architecture and Urban Studies in New York. For this last occasion an English language catalogue was published by George Wittenbron & Co.[12] As a side effect, putting on this exhibition abroad provided a series of international contacts, from Peter Eisenman to Marco de Michelis, which the school in Delft later found to be very productive.

After the Exhibition

In the Seventies and Eighties the general interest in Russian avant-garde architecture gradually moved on to more specific studies. The same thing happened in Delft, where the design issues that were current at the time determined the direction taken by those studies. In Max Risselada's group attention was concentrated on plans for urban design and residential building. Consequently in 1975 a study of the various plans for Magnitogorsk was presented at an exhibition held at the faculty, and in 1979 a publication was published that dealt with ground plans for communal housing and urbanism of the OSA group.[13] Oorthuys, who was attached to the chair in the history of architecture, retained a more general historical interest and concentrated on teaching. In collaboration with Rem Koolhaas he had prepared a monograph on Leonidov, though this was never published, and an article on Leonidov's entry to the competition held by the Ministry of Heavy Industry in Moscow.[14] The work done in the Soviet Union by Dutch architects, particularly by Mart Stam, also kept Oorthuys occupied.[15]

In 1971 Otakar Máčel was appointed to the chair in the history of architecture. His research was directed in the first instance at the development after the Russian avant-garde period, at the classicism of the architecture of socialist realism[16] and at the work of traditionalist architects.[17] In the Seventies this was practically virgin territory. Later on avant-garde subjects also attracted his attention, involving artists like Mel'nikov, Malevič and Lisickij.[18] Subsequently he regularly reviewed new literature on Russian architecture and collaborated on surveys and encyclopaedias.[19] Over the years both Risselada's group and the staff of the department of the History of architecture have regularly integrated Russian subjects into the curriculum and have improved the climate by organising excursions to Russia and putting on small exhibitions at the faculty of architecture.

Mel'nikov's works appear in the curriculum for the subject of the history of architecture for the academic year 1998-1999.

[1] For the history of this collection see J.M. Joosten, *Malevich in het Stedelijk*, in: W.A.L. Beeren, J.M. Joosten (ed.), *Kazimir Malevich 1878-1935*, catalogue Stedelijk Museum Amsterdam 1989, pp. 44-54.

[2] For the history of this collection see H. Puts, *De Lissitzky-collectie in het Van Abbemuseum*, in: J. Debaut, M. Soons (ed.): *El Lissitzky 1890-1941. Architect, schilder, fotograaf, typograaf* (El Lissitzky 1890-1941. Architect, painter, photographer, typographer), catalogue Van Abbemuseum Eindhoven 1990, pp . 81-83.

[3] V. De Feo, *URSS 1917-1936*, Rome 1963.

[4] C. Gray, *The Great Experiment. Russian Art 1863-1922*, London 1962.

[5] A. Kopp, *Ville et Révolution. Architecture et urbanisme Soviétiques des années vingt*, Paris 1967.

[6] After the invasion Hruza made a copy of his manuscript available to the Delft contingent in the conviction that it would no longer be possible for his book to appear. However, thanks to the participation of Jirí Kroha a summary in a revised formed did in fact appear in 1973: J. Kroha, J. Hruza, *Sovetská architektonická avantgarda*, Praag 1973.

[7] This exhibition was put on in September/October 1969 in the Van Abbemuseum in Eindhoven with a Dutch language catalogue (T. Andersen [ed.]: *Vladimir Tatlin 1885-1953*, Eindhoven 1969). The Delft contingent also co-operated in the preparation of this exhibition.

[8] O. Das, G. Oorthuys, M. Risselada (ed.), *USSR 1917-1933, architektuur, stedebouw*, (USSR 1917-1933, architecture, urban design) Delft 1969. This was followed by the appearance in 1970 of a translation of the 'Groene stad' (Green city) by M. Barsc and M. Ginzburg and a description of M. Barsc's Magnitogorsk plan, V. Vladimirov and M. Ochitovic (originally in *Sovremennaja Arkhitektura*, 1930, no. 1-2, pp. 17-38, 39-53).

[9] The study of the Russian avant-garde in Delft also gave a stimulus to research already in progress on the Dutch architect Mart Stam. At the initiative of Oorthuys, a Stam exhibition was held in 1969 in the faculty of architecture and subsequently in the municipal museum, Den Haag. See G. Oorthuys: "Mart Stam – overzicht van zijn werk" (Mart Stam – A survey of his work), "Bouwkundig Weekblad", 1969, no. 25; also Mart Stam, *Documentation of his Work*, London 1970.

[10] V. Quilici, *Architettura del costruttivismo*, Bari 1969; O. Svidkovski, *Building in the USSR 1917-1932*, London 1971 (this material had already been published in 1970 in "Architectural Design", 1970, no. 2).

[11] A. Kopp, *Town and Revolution*, London 1971.

[12] M. Risselada, K. Frampton, *Art & Architecture – USSR – 1917-32*, New York 1971.

[13] Fr. Palmboom, *Doel en vermaak in het konstruktivisme* (Purpose and enjoyment in constructivism), Nijmegen 1979.

[14] As far as is known, the analysis of Leonidov's projects for the proposed monograph only became available in typescript. What did appear was R. Koolhaas, "G. Oorthuys: Ivan Leonidov's Dom Narkomtjazjprom, Moscow", *Oppositions*, 1974, no. 2, pp. 95-104.

[15] G. Oorthuys, *Architetti olandesi e avanguardie russe 1919-1934*, in M. Tafuri (ed.), *Socialismo, città, architettura URSS 1917-1937*, Rome 1971, pp. 309-321; "Op zoek naar een woonwijk in Magnitogorsk" (In search of a district in Magnitogorsk), *Trouw*, Kunst & Cultuur, 29 November 1990, p. 17.

[16] O. Máčel, "De bouwstijl van het Russische proletariaat" (The building style of the Russian proletariat), *Plan*, 1975, no. 3, pp. 37-56; "Zur Theorie des sozialistischen Realismus in der Architektur", *Archithese*, 1976, no. 19, pp. 43-50; *Tradition, Innovation and Politics*, in: *Soviet Architecture 1917-1987*, catalogue the Beurs van Berlage foundation, Amsterdam 1989, pp. 15-24.

[17] O. Máčel, "A.V. Ščusev, flexibele patriarch van de Sowjetarchitectuur" (A.V. Scusev, flexible patriarch of Soviet architecture), *Wonen-TABK*, 1981, no. 16-17, pp. 18-28; "Nieuwe werelden in het voetspoor van Palladio" (New worlds in the footsteps of Palladio), *Archis*, 1986, no. 5, pp. 45-53; "Rußland – von vorrevolutionären Klassizismus zum sozialistischen Realismus", *Ars*, 1993, no. 2-3, pp. 171-178; *Die Baukunst des Plansolls. Sozialistischer Realismus als Fortsetzung der Tradition*, in J. Tabor (ed.), *Kunst und Diktatur*, catalogue Künstlerhaus Vienna, Baden 1994, vol. 2, pp. 796-803.

[18] O. Máčel, *Melnikov and Soviet Architecture*, in A. Wortman (ed.), *Melnikov the Muscle of Invention*, Rotterdam 1990, pp. 25-67; "100 jaar Melnikov" (Mel'nikov centenary), *De Architect*, 1990, no. 12, pp. 62-69; *Konstantin Stepanovic Melnikov 1890-1974*, reader module A4, TU Delft 1997; O. Máčel, "The Black Square and Architecture", *Art and Design*, 1989, no. 5-6, pp. 59-63; "Suprematismo y arquitectura", *Arquitectura Viva*, 1989, no. 8, pp. 59-63; "Proun, espacia abstracto", *Arquitectura Viva*, 1991, no. 17, pp. 33-35; "Der Traum, der Traum geblieben ist", *Werk & Bauen + Wohnen*, 1991, no. 10, pp. 10-11.

[19] Reviews of books and exhibitions on Russian architectural subjects in: *De Architect*, *Archis* (formerly *Wonen-TABK*), *Archithese*, *Bauwelt*, *Forum*, *Werk & Bauen+Wohnen*; contributions to *Sir Banister Fletcher's A History of Architecture*, London 1987; *International Dictionary of Architects and Architecture*, Detroit 1993; *The Dictionary of Art*, London 1996.

Dietrich W. Schmidt

The Legacy of Avant-Garde Architecture at Stuttgart

The Stuttgart School of Architecture 1918-1945

Following World War II architectural education at Stuttgart was substantially influenced by the modern movement. During the two and a half decades after World War I, however, rationalism and functionalism had to endure heavy attacks from traditionally-minded teachers at the Stuttgart Technical High School. The so called 'Stuttgarter Schule' (i.e. Stuttgart school of architecture), which was dominated by Paul Bonatz and Paul Schmitthenner (both members of the German Werkbund [DWB] up to 1928), pursued aims of the DWB which can best be characterised as gradual change–a reformation of architecture based on adjusting traditional values to the more rational needs of the changing society. This was a romantic pseudo-innovation, and above all a backward-looking approach which Schmitthenner traced back by to the simplicity of Goethe's Garden House at Weimar. In the Twenties and Thirties against the backdrop of the thriving industrial city numerous so-called 'country-houses' catered to the commissioners the bourgeois values of tranquillity and conventional order. An outstanding example of this type of approach is the *Kochenhof* housing estate designed by Schmitthenner, Bonatz and others in 1933.

Influences from Berlin

A contrasting set of Werkbund aims was pursued in the main by Berlin modernists like Ludwig Mies van der Rohe, Walter Gropius, Erich Mendelsohn, Ludwig Hilberseimer, Hans Scharoun and others.[1] The approach was characterised by daring new directions in architecture, in which traditional values were eliminated in favour of the values of an emerging industrialised and democratic society. Thus the architecture of their private homes no longer bore the character of a 'castle', serving to protect the private realm from the hubbub of an inhospitable and intrusive public environment. Rather the new architecture was open to its urban context in the same manner that the young Weimar Republic embraced cultural issues from abroad. From 1923/1924 on the architects, who embraced these latter convictions were organised in the so called 'Berlin Ring'[2]. They were joined by the Stuttgart modernist, Richard Döcker in 1926. It was this latter group who launched the Stuttgart functionalist housing estate 'Weissenhof', which thereby became a Berlin demonstration of modern architecture. In 1927 Mies van der Rohe contributed a design of a modern steel glass structure to a competition for a bank building facing the main station of Paul Bonatz. This stark rational design of a glass cube was not successful, however, it may have helped to make the realised building of 1931 by Bonatz more transparent. Another world famous piece of avant-garde architecture in Stuttgart beside the Weissenhof housing estate was created by Erich Mendelsohn: The 'Schockenbau', a department store built in 1926/1928 for the Schocken retail chain. It was demolished in May 1960. Each of these projects had a considerable influence on the Stuttgart architecture of the Twenties and early Thirties: In the expanding Swabian metropolis several housing estates, numerous homes, the first reinforced concrete skyscraper of the world with exposed concrete surfaces (the tower of the newspaper 'Tagblatt' by Ernst Otto Oßwald of 1926-1928), which can be compared with Noj Trockij's tower of the Narva district soviet building at Leningrad (1930) or other towers of S. Kozin or L. Teplickij for the Palace of Labour 1926, and a further department store took their cue from the two pioneering developments.

Two housing estates realised in the time of depression, 1929, as collective projects of the BDA (Bund Deutscher Architekten – Union of German Architects) by Richard Döcker, Hugo Keuerleber and Ernst Wagner deserve mention. The housing estate 'Im Wallmer' in Stuttgart-Untertürkheim and the terrace buildings 'Schönbühl' at Ostendstraße, standardised homes for low income people. Further, the terrace buildings of the 'Eiernest' extension on Karl-Kloß-Straße. 1928 by the Jewish architects Oscar Bloch & Ernst Guggenheimer reflected the esthetical effect of the Weissenhof, as well as the social responsibility of the time. Private homes of the middle class, speaking the new language, are the Kilpper house (1927/1928) and the Vetter house (1926/1927) by Richard Döcker, not to forget Döcker's own house, built in 1931. The interior function determined the outside shape. As early as 1926 the architect of the Tagblatt tower, E.O. Oßwald, erected the Freytag house on Gänswaldweg, a sharply profiled sculptural ensemble of variegated cubes. Also, Bloch &

Guggenheimer designed several elegant homes on the hillside of Stuttgart, some still existing, largely unchanged in their original configuration. Thus for example, besides seven houses on Wilhelm-Busch-Weg and Cäsar-Fleischlen-Straße (1930), the Frankenstein house of 1929 on Bopserwald-Straße exhibits the principles of Theo van Doesburg's neoplasticism. The Breuninger department store of 1929-1931, by Ludwig Eisenlohr & Oskar Pfennig, a steel frame structure of eight stories, 37 meters high, is evidently influenced by Mendelsohn's Schocken building. Large bent glass surfaces provided not only transparency of all the functions inside, but served also as an illuminated crystal at night. A terrace on top of the flat roof provided recreation facilities for the employees, thus showing the characteristic social responsibility of the epoch. While its building structure remained the same, the facades, heavily damaged during the war, were badly deformed in the late Fifties.

Modernism at Stuttgart Accompanied by Glimpses of Soviet Art and Denunciations as 'Cultural Bolshevism'

The Werkbund's influence in Stuttgart was based not only on its famous hous-

E. O. Oßwald, Offices of the newspaper Tagblatt *in Stuttgart, 1926-1928*

ing estate at Killesberg, but also on its other exhibitions. As early as in February and March 1922 Württemberg design products were shown[3] and in 1924 the exhibition "Die Form" was organised in Stuttgart, stressing the 'technical form' of a simple functionalism and the 'primitive form' under the motto 'form without ornament'.[4] Finally in 1929 the international exhibition "Film und Foto" was on display in Stuttgart.[5] It was El Lisitzkij and his wife who were commissioned by the All-Union Society of Cultural Connections with Foreign Countries (VOKS) to organise the Soviet contribution. Those exhibitions aimed at showing a new aesthetic understanding which renounced traditional perceptions of the past. Seen from the point of aesthetics the not adorned form was understood as abstract art, a symbol of the machine age and in line with the technical progress. This should be incorporated in every aspect of life, especially in industrial design, furniture, typography, graphic design, photographic art and the modern medium of film. Just as in the art of photography 'the production of false Rembrandts (or Kaulbachs)'[6] should not be the goal, in architecture, there was no room for romantic imitations

N. A. Trockij, Palace of the Soviets in the Narva district of Leningrad, 1930

of old country-houses.

In this manner progressive architectural practice in Stuttgart, influenced by the activities of the Werkbund, clashed with architectural education at the Stuttgart TH. The Weissenhof housing estate, as we know, it was not only Berlin-born, but also incorporated international ideas. Not only by the rationalist Dutch architecture of J.J.P. Oud and Mart Stam, but also by the striking Maison Citrohan by Le Corbusier (and his double house) Stuttgart was impressed. The idea of the terraced house became an issue and, in 1929 it was Richard Döcker who published his influential book *Terrassentyp*. As early as in 1926 Döcker had travelled in England, the Netherlands and the Soviet Union, seeking out outstanding works of progressive architecture for publication in his book such as e.g. the Sanatorium in Macesta by Ščusev. After 1933, however, Stuttgart architects like Schmitthenner and critics of the 'Heimatschutz' movement like Felix Schuster stigmatised this language of international architecture as 'cultural bolshevism'. The revolutionary architecture of the modern movement was now denigrated as 'building sin' which, in the opinion of the Nazis and the conservatives as well, had to be corrected. Thus the Weissenhof housing estate was to have been replaced after 1938 by a huge military complex. The project was not realized.[7]

Two examples of this cultural reaction should be mentioned: a building of a Jewish architect; and the home of a communist doctor and poet.

In 1929 the Jewish architects Bloch & Guggenheimer were commissioned to build an Orthopaedic-gymnastic institute on Zeppelin-Straße, which was completed in 1930. This elegantly terraced modern sports facility with a flat roof, large asymmetrically arranged openings in a well-balanced plain facade, and characteristic iron-pipe railings around the terraces, was converted nine years later into a conventional country house. The new owner, architect Theodor Kummerer closed the open facade with small symmetrically arranged windows of equal size with wooden shutters. He put a steep hip roof on top of the house. It was the triumph of reactionary architectural understanding and of a racist interpretation of culture, over the idea of modern living in a free society.[8]

The second example is the Wolf house of 1928-1929 on the same street by Richard Döcker. It was commissioned by the Jewish doctor and poet Dr. Friedrich Wolf,[9] member of the communist party. It is said that the Soviet writer Sergej M. Tretjakov, who had worked with S. Ejzenštejn and V. Mejerkhol'd, visited Wolf in this house. Döcker was forced to change the terraced house with a flat roof after Wolf had emigrated 1933 to Switzerland; ironically the architect mentioned on the plans "as requested by the municipal building department." A hip roof was put on top of the house in accordance with the demands of the Nazi administration. So this 'building sin' of avant-garde architecture was 'corrected' before it was destroyed during the war.

The Reorganisation of the Faculty of Architecture by Richard Döcker

After World War II Richard Döcker saw an opportunity in the destroyed city of Stuttgart, then under American military administration: in 1946 Döcker was appointed head of the Stuttgart central board of town reconstruction (ZAS) and head of the city's department of building works. One year later he was appointed professor for town planning and design of the Technical High School of Stuttgart and chairman of the faculty of architecture. With the assistance of Hugo Häring and the emigree Walter Gropius from Harvard, he established the new faculty of architecture and town planning.

In the restorative era of chancellor Konrad Adenauer and the liberal president Theodor Heuss, assistance was needed against the continuity both of inherited values of architecture and the former staff of teachers, especially against the still respected[10] old member of the Nazi party, Paul Schmitthenner, who in 1952 was honoured with the Order of Merit by Theodor Heuss. Nevertheless Döcker's enterprise was successful. However, in the chilling climate of cold war, it was natural that international modernism did not incorporate the achievements of Soviet avant-garde architecture.

So principles of the Bauhaus education like the preliminary course were now introduced at the Stuttgart faculty of architecture by Maximilian Debus, who had been in close contact to the Bauhaus. One of the first students of this school was Günter Behnisch. Beside functionalist designing, issues of organic architecture reappeared in the Fifties by Rolf Gutbrod, who erected 1955/1956 the new Liederhalle, a concert hall of flowing rooms with curved walls of concrete. The 1949 competition for this building had been won by Hans Scharoun. While the Berlin avant-garde architect failed to realise his daring and expensive design for the Stuttgart concert hall, he soon was able to carry out three high rise buildings for dwellings: the so-called Romeo and Julia flats in Stuttgart-Zuffenhausen (1954-1959) and the Salute flats in Stuttgart-Fasanenhof (1961-1963). Although architectural education in Stuttgart now was in line with the legacy of avant-garde architecture, its masterpieces in the Weissenhof housing estate now again were exposed to jeopardy. During the war 21% of the ensemble were destroyed by bombing[11]; now another 10% were torn down: the slightly damaged house no. 19 of Bruno Taut was replaced by a new structure as well as the not damaged houses no. 25 by Adolf Rading and no. 23 by Max Taut. Not before 1958, when plans to tear down the *Maison citrohan* (no. 13) by Le Corbusier became public, the buildings were officially preserved[12], those of Schneck (no. 11) and Bourgeois (no. 10) outside the official masterplan not before 1968[13]. So the restless striving for protection finally succeeded and 1981-1986 large scale restoration work was undertaken.

An even worse example of dealing with avant-garde architecture was the fate of the Schocken building in the centre of the city: despite an international campaign[14] for the protection of Mendelsohn's department store, it was torn down in 1960[15]. Teachers and students of the Technical High School led by Richard Döcker had fought a futile struggle for the conservation of this masterpiece of modern architecture against economic interests of profit then matching a fruitless project of the town to widen the street for more convenient automobile traffic.

These vain efforts for the preservation of existing architectural examples of modern thinking in the Weissenhof housing estate as well as in downtown Stuttgart may have led to disappointment and obduracy of Döcker. On the one hand he seems to become now peremptory on his experiences of the late Twenties, but on the other hand now he refuses new experiments; so his own convictions turn against him.[16] Full of bitterness Döcker resigned in 1958.

'Economic Wonder' and Students' Revolt of 1968

Furthermore now the prevalent economic values of the Sixties which generated the 'economic wonder' (Wirtschaftswunder) caused the decline of avant-garde ideas which now became a vulgarised and dogmatic economistic functionalism. Critics understood this as the bankruptcy of architecture and education, and soon the students revolted against their teachers. In 1968 they called for democratic principles of a free education and international cooperation. Under this pressure several teachers were forced to resign.

New teachers came from abroad like Horst Rittel from Berkeley and Peter C. von Seidlein (since 1974), who had studied in Chicago with Mies van der Rohe. He re-established the rigid principles of perfect quality and the inexorable ethos of working as required by his master Mies van der Rohe. Also the education of architectural history changed, when in 1970 Antonio Hernandez from Basel followed

Harald Hanson, who had kept his chair from 1938 to 1968. History of architecture now became influenced by Arnold Hauser's sociology of art.[17] Searching the roots of present understanding of architecture in the past 100 years, historical instruction for architects laid more stress upon the near past than upon the far past, like Sigfried Giedion had required since 1934.[18] So history of architecture from antiquity to the middle of the nineteenth century was taught in a general survey, whereas upon the more recent developments of the twentieth century particular stress was placed. The first person at Stuttgart University to trace the sources of modern architecture, was Jürgen Joedicke. History of architecture was taught not as a history of facts, but as a history of ideas, like Antonio Hernandez pointed out. So regarding the twentieth century the revolutionary ideas of the German Bauhaus and the international development of the modern movement came into consideration since the late Sixties, and since the late Seventies also the fulminating imaginations of the Soviet VKhUTEMAS, founded in 1920. One of the teachers there in the time from 1921 to 1924 was Konstantin Mel'nikov.

Postmodernism Reflecting Soviet Avant-Garde

While Richard Döcker in the second half of the Twenties was fascinated by the striking experiments of rationalist and constructivist buildings, now half a century later students of architecture at Stuttgart University were invited to analyse this architectural thinking of the Soviet avant-garde. Since 1976 seminars and study tours were organised. On a study tour of 1988 to Moscow the students did not only see the realised buildings of the Soviet avant-garde, but also some drawings of their unrealised projects in the Ščusev State Museum of Architecture. Furthermore the Moscow School of Architecture (MARKhI) was shown to the Stuttgart students by Leonid Demjanov. A most impressive experience was the visit of the

Mel'nikov house guided by the architect's son, Viktor Konstantinovic. Because of the fertility and profusion of ideas we tried to make the development of Soviet architecture a fixed part of historical training at our institute. Some of the results of the courses luckily could be incorporated into exhibitions. Mostly architectural models of projects, which were never realised, were on display.

The first occasion was the Tübingen exhibition "Avantgarde II 1924-1937. Sowjetische Architektur", May 15 - July 11, 1993. Among the twelve models showing various workers' clubs and the communal housing for the society 'Politkatoržan' in Moscow-Rostokino 1929-1931 by M. Ja. Ginzburg and S.A. Lisagor, there were also some ideal projects: so the one of a communal housing for Stroikom RSFSR 1930 by M.O. Baršč and V.N. Vladimirov, the one room type element of a communal housing for Gosplan RSFSR 1930 by M. Ja. Ginzburg et al., Ivan I. Leonidov's diploma at VKhUTEMAS 1927, the Lenin Institute, and the competition entry of the Leningradskaja Pravda 1924 by A. and V. Vesnin.

In 1994 eleven models of soviet competition entries of the Christopher Columbus Memorial in Santo Domingo 1929 were on display in Delft, Eindhoven, St. Gallen and Barcelona.

In 1995 and 1996 seventeen models of competition entries of 1931 for the Palace of the Soviets were on display at Stuttgart University and at Delft Technical University.

After the students' revolt of 1968, and the general criticism of functionalistic dogmatism of postmodern architecture, discussions took on a new dimension–historic issues were embraced: James Stirling, the interpreter of Mel'nikov's expressive auditoriums of Rusakov workers' club at Leicester University Engineering Building (1959-1963), won the international competition for the extension of the Stuttgart Staatsgalerie in 1977. The museum realised 1979-1984 with the great rotunda is not only a free interpretation of Schinkel's Museum of 1818 in Berlin, but a multi-coded collage of various historical elements: so we are reminded on the one hand in the back wing at Urban-Straße of Le Corbusier's principles, while on the other hand the mighty vent pipes show an homage to Centre Pompidou by Piano and Rogers. The steel-glass canopies resemble projects of the Soviet constructivism, as to be seen in some VKhUTEMAS designs. Even clearer principles of constructivism we can find in the housing complex 'Wohncity III' (1983-1987) in Fellbach near Stuttgart by the Stuttgart architect Arno Lederer. In Kemnat the architects Kauffmann & Theilig, who had worked with Behnisch & partners, realised 1989/1990 an office building that reminds us of El Lisitzkij's 'horizontal skyscraper' the so called 'Wolkenbügel'. Architectural planning seemed to break its chains of utility and feasibility by the end of the Eighties.[19] Images of early technical enthusiasm in architecture reappeared and were transformed by means of modern technology. Another example is the competition of a bank building in the centre of Stuttgart, which was won 1989 by Günter Behnisch. This bold design–unfortunately not realised–seemed to be a paraphrase on early Mel'nikov architecture: was it one of the preliminary sketches of the Soviet pavilion in Paris of 1924, or was it, more likely the competition entry of 1924 for the building of the Leningradskaja Pravda–in any case the 16 storey office building rising up to 60 meters was a steel glass structure of overhanging floors around a common core. Though being three times higher than Mel'nikov's structure and not revolving around its core, at least the impressive sculptural shape owed quite obviously to the belief in technical capacity, which was a characteristic issue of avantgarde architecture in the time between the two World Wars. 65 years later it seemed possible to realise the daring ideas of the early Twenties. Economical reasons like in the Twenties and new ecological reasons, however, ruined the bold project in Stuttgart.[20]

1 Bruno and Max Taut, Otto Haesler, Hugo Häring.
2 Other members were Otto Bartning, Adolf Meyer, Wassili and Hans Luckhardt, Heinrich Tessenow, Ernst May, Adolf Rading, Karl Krayl, Peter Behrens, Hans Poelzig.
3 'Werkbundausstellung württembergischer Erzeugnisse'.
4 June 29 - July 31, 1924 (cf. Joan Campbell, *The German Werkbund. The Politics of Reform in the Applied Arts*, Princeton University Press, Princeton, New Jersey, 1978).
5 Organised by Gustav Stotz May 18 - June 26, 1929. (See: *Die Form*, 1929, pp. 95, 123, 177, 277-79, 365-369).
6 Walter Riezler in *Die Form*, 1929, p. 366.
7 Competition of the 'Generalkommando V' with entries by P. Schmitthenner et al.; not realised because the Generalkommando was to be moved after 1941 to Strassburg.
8 Cf. D.W. Schmidt, *The Bloch-Tank House in Stuttgart by Bloch & Guggenheimer. Modern Architecture Reshaped after 1933 into a Traditional 'German Home'*, in DOCOMOMO Conference Proceedings, Bratislava 1996, p. 245 –248.
9 Dr. Friedrich Wolf (Neuvied, 23.12.1888 – Lehnitz, 5.10.1953); emigrated before March 5, 1933 to Switzerland and later to the Soviet Union; wrote in 1935 the social critic drama *Professor Mamlock*.
10 1949 member of the Bavarian Academy of fine Arts, 1952 honourable citizen of Kilchberg, 1954 honourable member of the German Academy of urban planning, 1957 honourable member of BDA, 1964 Great cross for distinguished services of the Federal Republic of Germany.
11 So the 7 houses nos 16 and 17 of Gropius, no. 18 of Hilberseimer, no. 20 of Poelzig, nos 21 and 22 of Döcker and no. 24 of Max Taut.
12 On August 28, 1958.
13 On October 25, 1968.
14 The campaign was started on July 19, 1959 by the Department of Architecture of the TH-Stuttgart and was vividly supported by Reyner Banham, Johannes J. P. Oud, Pier Luigi Nervi, Bruno Zevi, Ernst Neufert, Richard Neutra, Ludwig Mies van der Rohe, Walter Gropius and last but not least by the widow of the architect, Luise Mendelsohn.
15 Approval of demolition on November 11, 1959; begin of demolition works May 2, 1960.
16 Cf. D.W. Schmidt, *Vom pathetischen Aufbruch in die Moderne zur Stagnation im Dogma. Theoretische Anmerkungen zum Wandel von humanen Architekturvisionen. In Richard Döcker (1894-1968). Ein Kolloquium zum 100. Geburtstag. (Reden und Aufsätze Nr.53)*, Stuttgart 1996, p. 52 ff.
17 A. Hauser, *Soziologie der Kunst*, München 1974.
18 Cf. S. Giedion, *Kunsthistorischer Unterricht an der Technischen Hochschule*, manuscript of July 18, 1934; the same, *The Life of Architecture, 1st lesson at Harvard University*, November 15, 1938; the same, *1st lesson at Yale School of fine Arts, October 27, 1941* (as quoted by S. Georgiadis, *Geschichte für Architekten – Der Fall Sigfried Giedion*, in D.W. Schmidt (ed.), *Festschrift zum 70. Geburtstag von Antonio Hernandez*, Stuttgart 1994, pp. 31-39).
19 Cf. D.W. Schmidt, *Architektur im „Wilden Süden"– Junge Beiträge*, Wiesbaden 1993, pp. 85 ff.
20 For stylistic consultation I want to thank Dr. Romin Koebel, MIT.

Guido Canella

Avant-Garde as Allegory

Mel'nikov's house-studio, 1927-1929

Sketches drawn by Mel'nikov for his own house in the early Twenties

Beginning with the Middle Ages the cultural revolutions of the Occident have originated in cities, while in the Orient they often developed within a fluid, unresolved relationship between the city and the countryside. This aspect is accompanied by another fundamental component of inspiration, without which we cannot fully understand the trajectory of Russian art. This is the component which a scholar of Slavic art, Michael Alpatov, has described in an essay[1], where he asserts that the representational technique of the icon, which does not use perspective, does not depend upon a factor of delay with respect to western figuration, but on the use of a different symbolic code, a different model of reference of reality. In fact a famous art historian, Erwin Panofsky, speaks of *perspective as symbolic form*[2]; or of perspective not as a technical procedure aimed at achieving a more faithful simulation of the real, but as an artifice, a linguistic algorithm. In this view, with perspective our Renaissance is seen as adopting a closed, secular model, even when dealing with religious subjects; a hierarchical model inside which, at least at the outset, the criteria of symmetry is connected. All this is absent in the Slavic, Russian, Byzantine, orthodox figurative tradition, as this tradition represents almost exclusively religious images which tend, so to speak, to overlook the geo-metric rules of vision and even the laws of gravity.

At the beginning of this century Moscow was still the terminus of the countryside, rather than a driving factor for the increase of new relationships of production. Thus the rural world remained an incisive force in Russian culture, even when the avant-garde began which preceded the First World War. Painters like Larionov, Gončarova, Burljuk, Malevič depart from academicism, adopting a fable-like figuration of the rural world; just consider the animals and tools that levitate in the paintings of Marc Chagall. And it is undoubtedly the tradition of the Russian icon, more than an overlapping of experiences between the Orient and the Occident, that is decisive in the leap from the figurative to the abstract: while Vasilij Kandinskij pursues it through immersion in German Expressionism, emigrating to the West, it is precisely with Kazimir Malevič that a rapid, drastic passage happens from Cubofuturism to the 'point of no return' of Suprematism, with an acceleration and a radicality that, perhaps, not even the abstraction created by distilling German Expressionism can equal, although sustained by the intellectual and moral reason of an extraordinary historical circumstance.

And what is true for painting, literature, music, at times is also true for architecture.

In Russian architecture, that frees itself from academicism after the October revolution, the entire decade of the Twenties is crossed by a vein of internationalism, a sort of adaptation, although with reservations, to the Esperanto of the functionality and figurative radicality in progress in the West, which in the past I have had occasion to call *Euroconstructivism*[3]. For example, in the correspondence between Moiseij Ginzburg–leader of the OSA (Association of Urbanist Architects), and founder of the magazine 'SA: Sovremennaija Architektura' (Contemporary Architecture)–and Le Corbusier, we can see that, in spite of the polemics, which from the Soviet side in those years judged the development of the Modern Movement in the West as being based on utilitarian motivations, the main ideological motive of Ginzburg and the OSA remains precisely that of the economy. In fact the international isolation of the Soviet society, which in those years, at least in virtual terms, was positing claims of equality, social progress, technological advance, cannot be separated from the base of relationships of production; the poetics of the OSA was based on this sort of 'utopian materialism', or the Soviet typological and figurative expression closest to modern Western architecture.

But the poetics of Mel'nikov has little in common with these motivations and this inspiration, to the point that it cannot be fully understood unless it is isolated from the overall context of the Soviet architecture of the time.

Mel'nikov was born in 1890, to a family of peasants. His father left the village and ventured to Moscow, where he became a functionary of the railroad, while simultaneously conducting another activity, that of the collection and sale of milk, with the help of the young Konstantin Stepanovič. Therefore it is probably that his arrived in the city still armed with a mental scenario in which the village is surrounded by a limitless horizon. And, once he became an architect, we can imagine that the ideological and political contro-

versies regarding the destiny of the big city involved him only in part, because we should not forget that the personality of Mel'nikov preserved those traits of individualism, egotism and pride of a personality formed in the country, reliant only on his own will and his own hands. If anything, an excess of imagination thrives inside him, so that his 'city of the future' is conceived like a Kremlin in its typological and figurative syncretism, certainly an alternative both to the traditionalist city of the Academics and the functionalist city of the Constructivists. Traditionalism, in fact, is the ultimate claim of nationalism, which will be reinforced with the construction of Socialism in a single Nation and which also runs, poorly disguised, through the success of the avant-garde: in practice, beginning with the Thirties and the first five-year plan, a classicist restoration was imposed.

In the period that extends from 1917 to 1921, during the so-called 'Communism of war', under the effects of the world war that had been lost and the civil war in progress, the population of Moscow and the large cities diminished dramatically, with thousands of deaths due to starvation. In fact it was only with the advent of the NEP–the New Economic Policy in effect from 1921 to 1928–that the Soviet Union was able to establish a sort of market economy with embryonic forms of capitalism, a certain influx of foreign investment and, as a result, a revival of production and settlement in the cities. In spite of all this, during the Communism of war the relationships of intellectuals and artists with the western world continued. And it was precisely in the radicalism of the avant-garde that the heroic phase of the Revolution managed to identify a new communicative value, a new symbolic and figurative code of political propaganda, both for the formation of a new society, and for the 'white' counter-revolution, as is demonstrated by the Constructivist graphics of Aleksandr Rodčenko and El Lisickij in those same years. These were the years in which the Soviet government

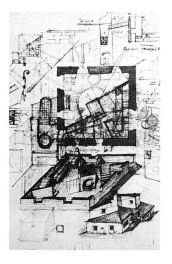

Sketches drawn by Mel'nikov for his own house in the early Twenties

Comparison between the icon Saint Boris, Saint Vladimir and Saint Gleb with battle scenes (beginning of the sixteenth century, Moscow, Tret'jakov Gallery) and the painting by Paolo Uccello, Battle (circa 1456, London, National Gallery). Excerpt from M. Alpatov, Le icone russe. Problemi di storia e di interpretazione artistica, [Russian icons, problems of history and artistic interpretation], Einaudi, Torino 1976, plates 183, 184

Church in the Voronet
monastery, Rumania, 1488.
View from southeast
and entrance to the church
on the south facade

attempted a daring, original policy of mass acculturation, especially with respect to the strong resistance in the countryside, using the city as a vehicle to hypothesise a possible horizon of progress, with which to mobilise the creativity of intellectuals, artists, architects and schools. This led to the use of slogans and avant-garde graphics to go beyond the paternalistic fatalism of the czarist era, rooted in illiteracy and religious iconography, and the orientation toward dynamic means of communication, like trolley cars and trains, capable of crossing the large cities and the great expanses of the Russian countryside. And this was the same direction for the orientation of architectural renewal.

Nikolaj Ladovskij is one of the key protagonists of Russian avant-garde architectural culture in this period, because he was the main force behind the VKhUTEMAS, the school of architecture inaugurated after the revolution, in 1920, combining elements from different backgrounds (from the academies of *Beaux-Arts* to the technical schools), and setting up different courses of training. The idea behind the initiative was to eliminate academic teaching, of which Ivan Zoltovskij, a great lover of the Italian Renaissance, born in the mid-1860s and a famous architect during the *ancien régime*, was the most talented, erudite and open-minded representative.

The VKhUTEMAS was created one year later than the German Bauhaus, and followed its development in parallel, becoming an even more complex melting pot of components, poetic tendencies, personalities, but also a tangle of contradictions, interferences, polemics, fully reflecting the clashes in progress in the world outside the school, of a cultural density comparable to few other periods in the history of architecture. Perhaps this situation can be compared only to what took place during the Weimar Republic, but the Soviet experience involved an even more feverish level of ideological ferment; we must remember that in this period intel-

lectuals and artists were attempting to make intuitions, statements, expressions correspond to the directives of the new Soviet power, whose ideology was still being constructed.

In the VKhUTEMAS Ladovskij interprets the analytical-deductive line of didactics, a radical alternative to that of the academic tradition, but also distant from that of functionalism. And this leads to the department guided by Il'ja Golosov and Konstantin Mel'nikov, with a more operative orientation. But it should be noted that with respect to the experimentalism of the Bauhaus, already virtually oriented toward industrial reproduction, the research conducted at the VKhUTEMAS still contained a matrix of formal asceticism, still imaginative at the outset, that reminds us of the research of contemporaries in the field of painting.

The critical contributions on Mel'nikov are not very extensive. Fredrick Starr–the most complete biographer in the west,[4] like Khan-Magomedov in Russia[5]–tends to attribute the influence for his works to certain western precedents, narrating that Mel'nikov had encountered Mendelsohn in Moscow, and hypothesising that for the Rusakov Club the architect was inspired by one of Mendelsohn's sketches for an industrial complex, dated 1914. He also states that in order to develop his own language, Mel'nikov looked for stimuli in western architecture magazines, that were available in the Soviet Union at the time. Yet it seems improbable that the linguistic results of Mel'nikov could descend from Expressionism, as the critics would often have it, because I feel they are the result of different premises. The common aspect, if anything, is a spiritualism that, while in the Expressionists has an apocalyptic sense, in the case of Mel'nikov is condensed in a narrative montage, the legacy of a sort of religiosity and mysticism that are irrepressible, even after the Revolution, as components of the ethnic, cultural, linguistic essence, and of the construction, of the identity of a nation.

In the designs of Mel'nikov the recurring

environmental archetypes are places frequented–the church, the tavern, grain silos, the *isba* cabin–, but there are also the figurative archetypes of certain work tools: the hammer, the sickle, the axe, the wool-winder, the knife, and even that sort of conveyor belt that cuts across the facades of his designs in diagonal. These are tools or elementary mechanisms that can be found on the table or in the yard of a family of Russian peasants or in the workshop of a craftsman, and that return to the surface in the dreams (or the subconscious) of Mel'nikov, becoming terms in his vocabulary. In the subsequent passage from the vocabulary of memory to the syntax of composition, we can suppose that the school of arts and crafts, which he was encouraged to attend by an employer-patron aware of his talent, played a part; a school where he refined his training in the operative sense of building. It is precisely this versatile approach to technique that can be seen in all the different phases of Mel'nikov poetic itinerary: that of wood, lasting until the mid-Twenties, with the *pavillionaire* type of construction; then that of brick, which in some cases, through simulation, seems to lean toward the use of reinforced concrete and steel (a desire that could have been satisfied by the wealthy clients for the Parisian projects that were never built); a mixed technique that gradually becomes more complex, as if pursued by the 'presto con fuoco' of inspiration.

If we compare one of the first projects by Mel'nikov, for a complex of communal dwellings, with the very famous design for the Monument of the Third International by Vladimir Tatlin, both from 1919, we can see, in allegorical terms, the respective extremes of the country and the city the separate the path of modernity in architecture. In contrast with the futurism of Tatlin, the future vision of Mel'nikov appears to be cut out with scissors with equally well-sharpened blades: one formal-figurative in character, the other functional-behavioural. The first tends to detach itself from his recent academic training in the reduction of the archetype of the rural or suburban house (overhanging pitches, large arch to mark the collective accessway, small openings for internal climate control, etc.). The second attempts to circumscribe in the closed layout, with an oval courtyard, the typical site of collective life in the country or the suburb, all designed for ease of construction, with normal materials and techniques.

In a project four years later, for a complex of houses for workers on the Serpukhov Ulitza in Moscow, the first for which Mel'nikov obtained official recognition, he continued with the research on the overall layout. In this case he begins with a plaza where four towers for individual dwellings are arranged in an *exedra*, connected by a closed accessway above a portico, connecting them to the community services centre. The plaza is like the palm of a hand, with extended fingers, the volumes of the two-storey buildings for family dwellings, each with an independent entrance, to protect the traditional autonomy of the peasant families that moved to the city to work in industry. The theme of the relationship between the private bedroom cell and the spaces of collective life–examined here in the towers for the single occupants–was already a focus of Soviet design research, and was to be realised five years later by the functionalist architects of the OSA, in the *Dom-kommuny* (communal house) by Moisej Ginzburg.

With the works in wooden carpentry the ascending phase of Mel'nikov's career begins. At the Agricultural Exposition in Moscow in 1923, one of the first representative projects of the NEP, designed by Žoltovskij, Mel'nikov was assigned, as a relatively secondary theme, the construction of the 'Makhorka' pavilion, for a popular brand of tobacco. Here we can already observe his way of interpreting the Constructivist dictates, aimed more at separating than incorporating, at not enclosing the volume of the construction within its structural alignments. For example: the extraction of the bolted that leads to

N. Gončarova (1881-1962), Mowing, *1910*

D. Burljuk (1890-1920), The bricklayer, *1913*

M. Chagall (1887-1985), I and the village, *1911*

the overhang of the upper level; or the free positioning of the window frames, either rectangular or circular; or the introduction, perhaps for the first time, of the diagonal, which was to become a sort of signature, not as the best layout solution but, on the contrary, as the necessity to adapt the functioning of the building to a predetermined scheme.

The same is true of the Sukharevka Market, which Mel'nikov built in Moscow in 1924, where the planimetric composition uses the oval, the diagonal, sawtooth patterns (which also recur in the roofing), transcribing and reordering the accumulated, random aggregation of the typical Russian market. This violation of the orthogonal scheme of the functionalist model, by then universally employed, and also by the architects of the OSA, both in the layout and in the elevations, would seem once again to be based on the good common sense of the country, where things are built in keeping with a state of necessity and following the practices of experience, without marked distinctions between the interior and the exterior of the construction; insubordination, therefore, especially with respect to an abstract reason of urban economy, which in building proceeds within the geometry of the repeatable type. Is this not, perhaps, the same duality between rationality and narrative that was evident at the origins of the avant-garde in painting, and which, now in terms of a confrontation between the functional and the figurative, is also reproduced in Soviet Constructivism?

The project by the Vesnin brothers, fifth in the ranks of the competition in 1923 for the Building of Labour, to be built in the heart of Moscow, is indicated by architectural historiography as the moment of the birth of Constructivism. For the remaining 45 competitors, it is said that they responded to the appeal of Sergej Kirov (the administrator who was mysteriously killed in 1934), who in a speech in 1922 described the event as an opportunity to prove to the world that the 'semi-Asians' of the USSR were capable of beautifying their land with the 'enchanted' palace of the workers and the peasants: a monument that the enemies of Socialism weren't even capable of dreaming about. Probably the words of Kirov did influence, in general, the folkloric orientation of many of the proposals; but, in my opinion, Mel'nikov's was not among them. He seems to interpret these urgings as an encouragement for the pursuit of an original Soviet architecture, free of Occidental influences; a path capable of making use of the local tradition, and thus an emancipation from classicist culture and from that of bourgeois avant-gardism. In fact, with respect to the neo-Byzantine archaicism of the winning project by Noi Trockij and the mechanicist symbolism of that of Il'ja Golosov (fifth place), the 'deconstructivist' design by Mel'nikov–especially for us today–appears extraordinarily advanced, with precocious compositional mastery, because it contains, in an already quite developed form, nearly all the typical elements of his subsequent poetics: exploded design of the layout, tumultuous convergence of conical volumes, a rising crescendo, saw-tooth diagonals, etc. An unexpected appearance that was to unfold with even greater inventiveness in the design, in 1931, for the Palace of the Soviets.

If we compare the design for the Building of Labour in 1924 with those of approximately the same period for the ARCOS headquarters in Moscow, where the whole is controlled almost by a classical aplomb, and of the competition for the Moscow facility of 'Leningradskaja Pravda', where Mel'nikov seems to want to challenge functionalist Constructivism on its own turf–in a competition won by the project of the Vesnin brothers–, making use of the rotating dynamism of the Tatlin's futuristic Monument of the Third International, the compositional mastery achieved in this phase becomes even more evident. These variations of Constructivist timbre seem to be the result not of a temporary disorientation of inspiration, but of the curiosity to test, with a certain technical virtuosity, his capacity to translate his imagination into figures. The project for the ARCOS headquarters can prompt reflection on the influence of the architecture of Constructivism in general, and that of Mel'nikov in particular, in the Occident. The stereometric articulation of solid and empty parallelepipeds and cylinders, the anchoring at the base of the domed element, the facades divided by horizontal bands cut into squares and rectangles, are features that were later to be reinterpreted in a figurative breakthrough developed in architecture before and after the second world war (among others, for example, with Giuseppe Terragni and James Stirling).

For the Exposition of Decorative Arts in Paris in 1925 Le Corbusier built the Pavilion of 'L'Esprit Nouveau', but the atmosphere of the Exposition, with its classicist, eclectic and, at best, Déco works, was also disturbed with provocations of modernity by the Pavilion of Tourism by Robert Mallet-Stevens. Yet the greatest curiosity, both in aesthetic and political terms, was aroused by the Pavilion by Mel'nikov. This French adventure was a launching pad for his success; and the reasons he obtained this commission can be identified above all in the originality of the proposal, but also in the lack of available resources, and his talent for worksite intervention, as a kind of architect-carpenter, that permitted him very rapidly to take risks other more famous colleagues would never have attempted. The success achieved by the Pavilion, although it was opened after the beginning of the Exposition, opened the way into the Olympus of international architecture; in Paris Mel'nikov became friendly with Mallet-Stevens, and perhaps with Tony Garnier, and Auguste Perret, the dean of modern French architects, kidnapped him with a car to take him to see his *atelier*–as Mel'nikov recalls in *The Architecture of my Life*, his autobiography, with its significant title.

After the triumph, Paris seemed to want to put such originality to the test, com-

missioning him to design a garage for two thousand cars, built over the Seine. Mel'nikov's response, in its provocative daring, seems to be a challenge to Le Corbusier himself. And in the wake of criticism regarding the extraordinary dimensions of an overhang, he ironically added a crutch to the drawing, with the features of Atlas.

After his international success in Paris Mel'nikov met with greater recognition in his homeland, and was commissioned to design two garages, which he finally managed to build in Moscow. Reference has correctly been made to the rectangular plan of the Manege, which he transcribes in rhomboidal form in the Leyland bus garage; and to the layout of a nineteenth-century depot for locomotives, that he reworks in the other garage, for trucks, on Novo-Rjazanskaja Ulitsa.[6] Nevertheless, while it is true that Mel'nikov basically continues to cultivate the mystique of a capital city seen from the country, it is also true that at this point, in passing from the use of wooden carpentry to that of large metal trusses and structural walls, he feels obliged to recall the respect for that classical formulary learnt during his training in Moscow, and of which the works of Žoltovskij were still the finest examples. But the metaphor of the classical order adopted by the master is further transfigured, allegorically, in harsh solid geometry; for example, in the access portals protruding from the facade beneath the large tympanum and, on the other side, in the large exposed masonry blocks perforated by portholes, alternating at rhythmical intervals, like a massive order, with full-height glazings.

Is this more refined building technique or elementary, almost archaic construction, in the case, for example, of Mel'nikov's ability to achieve, in masonry with courses of mortar, an effect of drapery or weaving, in which to cut out large round eyes? The fact is that Mel'nikov is not afraid of appearing insufficiently 'modern' or 'constructivist' in making use of a mixed technique, like that of the countryside, in

K. Malevič (1878-1935), Dynamic suprematism, *1916*

40

Railway carriages painted for the Bolshevik propaganda

which brick, mortar, wood are treated with equal dignity, raw materials to which he attributes equal representative importance with respect to composite materials like reinforced concrete and steel. Thus the refusal to pursue technical and typological solutions as an end in themselves, or dictated by preconceptions and procedures that are not those functionally involved in the assembly of the figure. In short, for Mel'nikov the construction of architecture is, first of all, figuration, the opposite of technical exhibitionism.

The rise and fall of the role, and as a consequence of the typology, of the 'workers' club' calls for a separate discussion. Here it is sufficient to point out that its historical precedents can be seen in the glorious 'house of the people' that accompanied the formation of the Labour Movement in the more industrialised European nations, and how in the Soviet Union its fate–like that of the 'house-commune'–went hand in hand with the ideological crisis of the regime between the last phase of the NEP and the beginning of the first five-year plan. In Moscow alone there were over 800 workers' clubs, most created in existing buildings, with the task of keeping the working masses united and politically oriented. In 1926, through a series of competitions, an attempt was made to develop a design for a standard workers' club. While the *atelier* of Aleksandr Nikolskij in Leningrad–famous for the design of the 'standardised school for 1000 students', illuminated by shed roofing, like a factor–developed a prototype that could be defined as 'cubist', the solutions proposed by the members of OSA–Ginzburg, Andrej Burov, the Vesnin brothers and others–generally tended to make use of the 'S' or swastika layout which, since 1925, had been internationally consecrated in the new headquarters of the Bauhaus of Dessau, designed by Gropius. The prototype presented by Ivan Leonidov stood out from these, with a linear arrangement and transverse main volumes with an ogival section, that already seems to incorporate a value oriented toward dis-urbanism.

During the second half of the Twenties the polemics among the various groupings of Soviet avant-garde architects became more bitter. In 1926 a schism led to the detachment from the ASNOVA (Association of new architects)–whose theorists were Ladovskij and Nikolaj Dokucaev, and whose most creative hands were those of Mel'nikov and El Lisickij–of the OSA, whose press vehicle was the magazine *SA*. While Aleksandr Vesnin was the spiritual leader, Ginzburg attempted to achieve legitimacy for the cultural line of the group, if not official recognition, defending it on several fronts: at times with silence (the name of Mel'nikov never appeared, not even once, in *SA*), at times by seeking a distance from Western avant-garde culture (as in the case of the above-mentioned correspondence with Le Corbusier in 1930). For his part, in his memoirs, Mel'nikov paid back the architects of OSA (including his friend Il'ja Golosov), sparing only Aleksandr Vesnin, whom he considered as the other authentic modern Russian architect, apart from himself, of course.

The solution proposed by the architects of OSA for the theme of the workers' club is substantially institutional in character, as it is wholly contained in the functional planimetric diagram. While that of Mel'nikov is an interpretation, which we are tempted to call 'Stanislavskijan', linguistically but also behaviourally wholly identified with the theme. His workers' club is the modern condensor of an ancient life of association, still timely and therefore destined to consolidate itself, virtually, in the incubator of a future collective life.

I have already spoken of how the design process of Mel'nikov justifies figurative intuition in terms of typological invention; as, for example, when the mobile walls in the Club Rusakov enable three rooms to be reconfigured in a single graded seating area. Although building proceeded with rather primordial techniques in the Soviet Union between 1927 and 1929, Mel'nikov minimises the problem of the

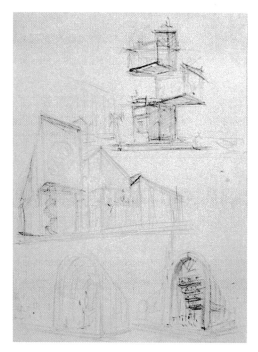

overhang, which in this building reaches about four meters, declaring that it is "a solution utilised, by now, all over the world." If anything, his creativity seems to have been stimulated by the extraordinary result of the deceptive proportions, the out-of-scale appearance with respect to the true size. Mel'nikov was later to speak of 'Homeric violence', probably in reference to the blinding of the Cyclops. In fact, the subsequent closure of the large windows, that allows the light to enter the club, represented the moment in which it was reconverted for the new cultural function of the so-called 'cultural entertainment of the masses', when the screening of films took the place of active discussion and grassroots democracy, and the state-produced cinema was used to produce a cultural standardisation: no longer a culture built from the ground up, place by place, but a culture imposed from the top down. Thus the transparent essence of the workers' club, which created a direct relation between dwelling and workplace, outdoors and indoors, light and darkness, was to be reduced to meet the needs of a rigid political line, which in typological terms led to the replacement of the workers' club with the cultural centre. Nevertheless it was precisely this theme that gave rise to the great but unfortu-nately short-lived professional success of Mel'nikov in his homeland as well, and to an extraordinarily anomalous typological and figurative phenomenon within the panorama of Soviet Constructivism. Many municipal and industrial labour unions turned to him for the design of their clubs; in just three years, from 1927 to 1929, Mel'nikov was able to build six such facilities. He also designed a seventh, the Zuev Club, which was built, instead, by his older friend Il'ja Golosov. The unbuilt design by Mel'nikov is composed of a series of five cylinders arranged in a linear pattern as in an internal combustion engine, glazed and partially interlocking; while the design by Golosov has a rather conventional rectangular plan, with a cylindrical corner tower for the stairs (often cited in a controversy of influences with respect to the Novocomum of Terragni). And–in spite of the fame achieved in time, practically equal to that of the Club Rusakov–perhaps Mel'nikov was correct when he observed that Golosov had reduced his five-cylinder organism to a single cylinder, in a marginal position, making it if not precisely decorative, essentially a signal, a mere landmark.

The sequence of the clubs built by Mel'nikov is full of invention and creativity, because each opportunity is treated as a separate case, for a new figurative solution. It is here that he begins the construction of his virtual Kremlin, creating triangular relations, erecting in the periphery of Moscow a series of epic characters for which he rehearses, with overall and detail solutions that alternate from case to case, a syncopated recital, which is not above making use of revisitations of the past; for example, in the Club of the Rubber Industry, where a lunette, with a pincer-like staircase, is superimposed on the convex facade with giant pilaster strips alternating with full-height glazings.

When criticism, on both the aesthetic and the economic fronts, began to intensify, Mel'nikov too tended to limit himself to the rectangle and, perhaps, to dust off the two axes of symmetry, as in the Club Svoboda, leaving the spatial counterpoint up to a higher facade relief and to the incisive role of small added volumes.

It is only in the small scale of the Club Frunze (3500 cubic meters, as opposed to an average of about 15,000 for the clubs) that the composition of Mel'nikov appears in a functionalist version. In the Club Burevestnik of the Chemicals Union, also commissioned to Mel'nikov in 1929, the rectangular layout is accompanied, again in a lunette arrangement, by a lobed tower, glazed and inscribed in the circle of the roofing, containing rooms that could be subdivided by means of mobile walls; a tower that tends to play a signage role,

Labor Palace in Taskent.
1932-1922 competition project

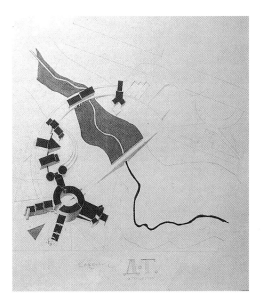

contradicting, to be honest, the criticism he had made of Golosov regarding the Zuev Club. While in the Club Pravda in Dulevo, one of the first, dating back to 1927, the exploded layout is overlaid with a large cylinder containing a gallery, that overlooks the hall below, trapezoidal in form, but ready for transformation into an autonomous room when necessary.

In the city of Mel'nikov's dreams the workers' club could also be a sort of transfiguration of the village tavern, where the rural community met to share their problems and age-old expectations; because Mel'nikov's idea of democracy could still refer to a sort of 'rural collectivism'.

While in this period in the Soviet Union few things were actually built, the quantity of designs is excessive, especially because of the many different competitions; in like manner, the critical debate was lively and heated, because architecture was seen as a powerful medium of mass communication, on a par with film and certainly with literature, given the widespread illiteracy inherited from the prerevolutionary society. In 1930 the critic Nikolaj Lukhmanov published *The Architecture of the Clubs*[7], in which he praises the role played, and above all the interpretation given by the poetics of Mel'nikov; while in a subsequent publication in 1932, on *10 worker's clubs in Moscow*[8], works built by different architects are analysed by different critics, who focus on functional shortcomings, construction errors, cost excesses, aesthetic ambiguities. No club meets with their approval, and while those by Mel'nikov meet with particularly harsh disapproval, the others too–including one by the venerable Vesnins–are treated with equal severity.

The young Mel'nikov in the photographs of the period looks a bit like Charlie Chaplin, with his regular facial features, small moustache, striped trousers, the white handkerchief in the breast pocket of the jacket, the gaiters. We mustn't forget his humble origins, that can explain a certain forced elegance, that becomes a way of asserting his right to belong to the caste of the architects, who were still mostly from bourgeois families. The last photos often show him wearing a white knitted skull-cap that gives him a hieratic look, against the backdrop of his home-studio on Krivoarbatskij Lane, in the historical Arbat quarter, repeatedly re-designed and finally built at the same time as the workers' clubs, and utilised almost as an experimental testing ground for the other designs. In 1973 the English writer Bruce Chatwin visited the house, and wrote a description of it in an interesting encounter with Mel'nikov.[9] The two partially interlocking cylinders that make up the house communicate a solemnity similar to a place of worship–museum, temple, mausoleum?–, which is anything but funereal; in fact, the cult of Mel'nikov is, if anything, that of the family, as is appropriate for someone who comes from the country. Certain ingenious technical devices are applied here, with craftsmanlike skill: the framework of bricks laid in a curved pattern, with a diagonally crossed honeycomb structure, that permits the creation of a series of stretched hexagonal windows; or the system of the floor slabs, composed of a *plancher* of wood with interlocking boards, dividing the cylinders into four levels, up to the top level used for the studio. Light plays a dominant role, decisive for the interiors space, which is permeated by a joyful sacredness, where the concave masonry walls are perforated by about sixty windows, creating a variable flow of light in keeping with the movement of the sun during the day. Even the base of the bed, attached once and for all in masonry, in a solemn position–throne, altar, sarcophagus?–, seems to allegorically immortalise the ancestral sense of continuity between slumber and death.

The theme of the 'Green City' is all that survives of the defeated utopia of the 'disurbanist' urban planners. In fact the idea was no longer to develop an alternative to the growth of the large cities, but simply to create a settlement model for regenerating vacations and rest for tired workers.

This was a theme that the progressive societies of the time had to emphasise, if only to demonstrate that the focuses of Socialism were different from those of Capitalism. In fact a couple of years later in Spain, in the final phase of the democratic regime before the civil war and the Francoist invasion, the rationalist architects of the GATPAC came to grips with a similar theme, designing the *Ciutat da Rapòs i de Vacances* on the Catalan coast. In 1929, for the competition promoted by the newspaper *Pravda* for the 'Green City', a sort of garden-city for repose for 100,000 workers, at a distance of 30 kilometers from Moscow, the winning projects were those of Ladovskij (the founder of ASNOVA), Ginzburg (the leader of OSA), Fridman and Mel'nikov. I have already spoken of how he found himself working in a socialist society, not through his own political orientation: in contrast with Majakovskij, who from the outset was a Bolshevik by conviction and the poet of the city par excellence, Mel'nikov arrived without ideology, armed only with an individualism that led him to proceed by trusting his own instinct and a wisdom acquired through direct experience. And yet, in contrast with the other competitors who have abandoned, to a great extent, their avant-gardism, aware that the times were changing, his proposal is the most socially radical he had ever produced, so much so that it seems to enter an Orwellian world, or a collectivist behavioural mechanism that borders on obsessive planning of individual life.

The proposal of Mel'nikov, differently from the others, that focus on the single-family house and private means of transport, is based on public transport and collective living and, in general, on a far-sighted ecology (closeness to nature, circulation of air in the spaces, wind energy, etc.) aimed at the physical and psychic regeneration of the worker through slumber. His Laboratory of slumber, in a building with two wings, and the floors of the dormitories inclined like ramps, has a name based on a play on words between the

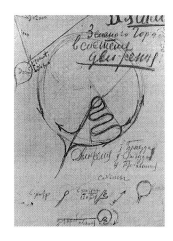

Sketch of the railway circulation system for the 'Green City', 1929

terms for sleep and for music. And when, in his old age, he wrote *The Architecture of my Life*, he began precisely with the temporal arc of a day in the country, asking: "Why do I no longer rise in the morning, when dawn begins?". I like to think that Le Corbusier, in the competition for the Palace of the Soviets, the most 'constructivist' design of his career, took the Solar Pavilion of the Green City of Mel'nikov into account.

Because this project by Mel'nikov has been widely criticised, and even mocked by Ginzburg, it is worth examining two questions, here, that directly concern his poetics.

The first has to do with eccentricity in architecture. I do not believe that in the figuration of Mel'nikov there is an intent to *épater le bourgeois*, also because the landscape of Moscow and the other Russian cities, still in the years of the NEP–it is described very well by Angelo Maria Ripellino in two excellent essays[10]–is very different from that of the occidental city. The Soviet city appears as a large, hungry belly that receives everything and digests it, in a historical situation of ferment that takes the place of the earlier doldrums of Oblomovism. In contrast with the western capitals developed over the course of at least one century, Moscow was still a historical settlement surrounded by wooden constructions, through which the countryside penetrated the city, with the first industrial structures popping up here

and there, and therefore the question of eccentricity was very pertinent, particularly in the case of every new construction, regardless of its style.

The second question has to do with parody in architecture. For this argument, it suffices to think of how paradox marks the course of the fable, from *The Nose* of Gogol' to the devil in *The Master and Margarita* by Michail Bulgakov. In like manner, in the case of Mel'nikov, if we wish to speak of parody it is certainly not a question of irony; if anything, we are faced with true mimicry, drawn from the bizarre and from wit, of the sort often found in the behaviours and the languages of the countryside, expressively taken to the point of caricature or the grotesque, where the paradox allegorically conceals ancient folk wisdom.

Many years ago I proposed[11] that the revolutionary origin of the architecture of Boullée and Ledoux could be traced back to the phase before the French Revolution, or to the confrontation between the Mercantilists and the Physiocrats, where the former were in favour of the hegemony of the city, and the latter in favour of the economic dominance of the country. In this dualism the poetical conception of the two French architects seems more inspired by the Physiocratic perspective of a city-capital, condensed in large monuments, but relegated to an exclusively representative, institutional role. On that occasion, on the theme of revolutionary architecture, I suggested a comparison between certain works: on one side those of Boullée and Ledoux, on the other those of Tatlin and Leonidov, as expressions that, in the analogy of certain characters of dilated formal decisiveness–sphere, cone, spiral–, seem to embody a certain disurbanistic vocation.

In the Soviet Union, from 1928 to 1932, or in the years extending from the end of the NEP to the middle of the first five-year plan, a confrontation-clash between opposing political factions was underway, with different visions in the macroeconomic and macrourbanistic fields: be-

Sketch of the People's Palace, 1932

Architectural fantasies –
Urban landscapes with
K.S. Mel'nikov's projects
and buildings, 1964

tween those who sustained that the advent of the Soviet regime constituted, in itself, a guarantee of the transformation of the large city from capitalist to socialist; those who asserted that the Soviet society should abolish the big city, as a typical expression of capitalistic concentration, through the decentralisation in small and medium-sized settlements; and those who went so far as to hypothesise infrastructures and industrialisation that were not aggregated around residential centres, but scattered throughout the territory, spread out to redeem the countryside. And all this is quite similar to the conflict between the Physiocrats and the Mercantilists.

Nevertheless, in the comparison I suggested at the time, with the term "revolutionaries" I did not necessarily mean architects fully involved in a political ideology, but rather architects poetically stimulated by a movement that would subvert the traditional order of the city. For example, if that of Tatlin can be considered an experiment *in vitro* for the future city, in line with the literary revelations of Černyčevskij or Khlebnikov, when they hurdle the conflict between city and country in the mythical vision of a castle of glass[12]; and if the projects of Leonidov remain the most rigorously disurbanistic in a socialist utopia that is not within reach of the society and the Soviet city during those years; the research of Mel'nikov, and above all in the last, marvellous designs, is perhaps less rooted than any other in

ideology, because the virtual design of his city appears, by then, to be constructed by means of monumental landmarks, similar in this to the urban order Moscow was to adopt after the second world war, but with an allegorical thrust of very different poetic quality.

The competition in 1931 for the Palace of the Soviets to be built in Moscow near the Kremlin offers a particularly significant opportunity for an assessment of the state of architecture on an international level, not unlike other major competitions such as, for example, the one in 1922 for the headquarters of the *Chicago Tribune*, or the one in 1927 for the League of Nations building in Geneva. The competition was held in phases, and in the first invitational phase twelve architects were called upon: only three Russians (Žoltovskij, Krasin, Iofan) and nine foreigners, including three Germans (Poelzig, Mendelsohn, Gropius), two Frenchmen (Perret, Le Corbusier), three Americans and Italy's Armando Brasini. In this first phase the greatest impact seems to be that of Le Corbusier, with a design that is one of my personal favourites, because it manages to filter and restore, in synthesis, the essence of the finest period of Constructivism. But the traditionalist academic component, constrained but not eliminated up to this point, as I said, returns forcefully to the limelight here, taking advantage of the particular character of the theme.

Žoltovskij, as we know, was an architect who performed with great mastery in all the various phases of his career–classicism, modernism, restoration–and here again he displays a sort of alienating detachment from the classical order, a detachment that other academics, and not only among the Russians, have almost never been able to achieve. Boris Iofan was born in 1891, one year after Mel'nikov, and was trained in the wake of Žoltovskij. But, at least in the first phase, his design is only partially based on the organisation defined by the master, purifying it of all stylistic and decorative concessions, except for the tower with a telescopic section, topped by a large statue which, in the case of Iofan, is supposed to represent a worker holding the torch of his emancipation. This design follows precisely that path of mediation, of compromise, the effect of the inclinations of the new ideological developments on culture, including architectural culture, in the middle phase of the first five-year plan. In 1932 the second phase of the competition was open to all participants, and 160 projects were submitted; the jury, composed of 70 persons, assigned the victory to the project by Iofan, while making a series of recommendations for modifications. As an emblematic parameter regarding the subsequent development of the project, we can select the height of the statue of Lenin, stipulated by Stalin himself in place of the statue of the liberated worker; the height was defined as 50-75 meters at first, then 80 in 1934, 100 in 1939, and finally reached an overall altitude, with the building-pedestal, of 220 and then 415 meters, because it had to be taller than the Eiffel Tower (300 meters) and the Empire State Building (407 meters).

Mel'nikov was the only Soviet architect of international renown who was not invited to take part in the first phase of the competition. He contributed a design for the second phase, a sort of counter-proposal, which was not taken into consideration, and was compared to the delirium of a visionary, and seen as an affront to the very theme of the competition. Even more surprisingly, the infinite accounts of the competition, which have been written ever since, and even very recently, systematically overlook his entry, considering it (correctly perhaps) impossible to judge, meaning that the only place in which it is critically discussed is the monograph on Mel'nikov by Frederick Starr in 1977. Starr interprets the main elements of the composition–the two semi-cones, one standing on its base, the other on its point–as a symbolic gesture in which Mel'nikov wished to illustrate, in the first, with the pyramid of the Pharoahs, the stratification of the social classes that continued until the last phase of Capitalism and, in contrast, in the second, the reversal of the situation thanks to the advent of the Soviet state. This project is undoubtedly difficult to interpret, because the allegorical transfiguration interacts here with the symbolic importance of the theme, giving rise to a dramatic cosmogony of the parts, that cancels out both the courtly component and the tectonic component of the monumental complex. Thus the figurative result manages to overwhelm any possible symbolic assumption regarding the theme, making it utterly implicit, latent. As if Mel'nikov, in this case, had made use of the pantograph to release, in the free sculptural de-formation, the exploded diagram of his own compositional dynamic. The first of the two semi-conical volumes is inclined, aiming the perspective effect towards infinity, while the second frays out against the sky, almost like a gigantic plant, in which the natural appearance is dramatically transfigured into a sort of liberating shout-gesture.

As confirmation of the fact that in modern architecture, just as in the architecture of the past, there is a recurring presence of certain rhetorical devices, we must acknowledge that in spite of the theme and the markedly celebratory intentions, the competition managed to produce three very different yet fascinating design works, because apart from those of Le Corbusier and Mel'nikov, the design by Ginzburg, in my opinion, also achieves a degree of expressive force that never appeared in his other works, before or after the competition.

The competition for the Palace of the Soviets marked the beginning of the decline of the professional career of Mel'nikov in the Soviet Union, although his fame continued to grow abroad. He was already present with works at the Fourth Triennial in Monza in 1929, and at the Fifth Triennial, inaugurating the Palazzo dell'Arte in Milan in 1933, one of the eleven solo exhibitions dedicated to the memory of Antonio Sant'Elia, featuring the works of the acknowledged masters of international modern architecture, was set aside for Mel'nikov: the others were Perret, Le Corbusier, Lurçat from France; Gropius, Mies van der Rohe, Mendelsohn from Germany; Hoffmann and Loos from Austria; Dudok from Holland; Wright from the United States.

The project submitted in 1929 in the competition for the Monument to Christopher Columbus in Santo Domingo is, perhaps, already the beginning of the phase in which Mel'nikov, aware of his waning status at home, hopes to extend his activity abroad. A dream that was not to be. In this competition, and perhaps it is no coincidence, Leonidov was also among the competitors; he had been trained at the VKhUTEMAS under Ladovskij, but now officially was a part of the OSA, where nevertheless the comrades were forced to defend his figurative extremism against accusations of abstraction and formalism. While the figuration of Mel'nikov was based on the addition of formal elements released from their original symbolic value (cone, spiral, wings, blades, etc.) and re-semanticized in the allegorical ensemble of the whole, the figuration of Leonidov stopped short at the signs of a virtual "Morse code" of architecture, almost echoing the state of these elements in the title of the ninth *Bauhausbucher* that Kandinskij wrote in 1926: *Point Line Surface*.

The conclusive phase of Mel'nikov's poetics, by now sustained by the experience of many years, still keeps alive the impulse of innovation, both in terms of figurative inspiration and typological revision. If anything this innovative drive is accentuated, with a certain de-compositional virtuosity, thanks to the expansion of the scale, through the use of the pantograph. So much so that we are tempted, paradoxically, to turn to recent deconstructivist research as a way of giving greater credibility to the last creative period of Mel'nikov, which has for the most part been ignored, both by his contemporaries and by the subsequent historiographers of the Modern Movement.

In 1931, before the design for the Palace of the Soviets, Mel'nikov participated in the competition for the MOSPS Theatre in Moscow. In this design we see the recurring elements of his language: de-composition in explosion of geometric solids, diagonals, etc.; but in this case the diagonal takes on the aspect of a sacred flight of steps, as at Delos, and that of the two cylinders arranged with a horizontal axis seems to tumble toward the ground, outlining the semi-volute of a cyclopic Ionic capital. This dominant volume functions as a stage apparatus for the most important of the three spaces set aside for the performances. And on the convex side of the vertical stage space opens, vertically, the extension of the stage toward the exterior, in such at way that the real city can be used as a backdrop, or the structure can become a sort of balcony-megaphone to broadcast the performance out into the city. Making a comparison with the organisation of the 'Totaltheater', designed five years earlier for Erwin Piscator, we can note that in the design by Gropius the typological and figurative emphasis is on the introversion of the device of maximum multi-functional impact in the relation between the performance and the spectator; while that of Mel'nikov has a dual value: the first, as we have said, is extroverted; the second, based on the internal typology, limits the technical set possibilities of the three stages, differentiated in form and size, positioned at the edge of the hall, utilising the mechanism

A. Rodčenko, Crisis, photomontage, 1923

of rotation of the amphitheatre of the spectators to maintain the traditional frontal relationship between the stage and the audience.

Mel'nikov–an architect of international renown, the equal in the world of Le Corbusier and a few other names, featured in all the most important events and publications on architecture–at this point finds himself in a condition of alienation and ostracism, and in order to survive he is forced to combine his salary as a teacher with the pay he receives as a designer in a state technical office, where he is assigned the most conventional, routine tasks. All that is left for him is to design things on his own, participating in major competitions, although he knows he cannot possibly win them.

The project he submitted in 1932 in the competition for the Palace of Culture of Tashkent, which still features the exploded approach in the plan, has an unusual smoothness in the facades; the interlockings, the diagonal, the relief design on the facade of the Inturist garage are also more timid, resigned, in his last official work, built in Moscow in 1934, but only partially, and with major modifications. When ideological orthodoxy was directed against all intellectualism, in general, and particularly against all that remained of the Constructivist avant-garde, accused of formalism and bourgeois utilitarianism, Mel'nikov may well have wondered, justifiably, why his poetics could not be accepted in the Soviet society of the time, whose cultural policy, by then decisively directed toward the so-called 'Socialist realism', called for a return to the tradition and a clean break with respect to western influences; he may well have wondered why, precisely during the phase of the construction of the socialist city, his architecture was not taken into consideration, in spite of the fact that he had remained distant from any technical or functionalistic extremes and, especially in the last phase, had attempted an utterly original reinterpretation, full of allegory and representative impact, of the age-old Russian

ethos, multiethnic, polarised between the city and the country.

The competition in 1934 for the headquarters of the Commissariat of Heavy Industry on Red Square in Moscow, offers a full interpretation of this phase of ambiguous cultural transition. The Vesnin brothers submitted a design with the collaboration of Ginzburg, and the latter submitted another, with the collaboration of the Vesnin brothers: functionalist constructivism, tormented by the need to adapt, borders on caricature, at this point. Instead, the opportunity was confronted by Mel'nikov and Leonidov, two opposite poetic temperaments, two diverging figurative paths, but also two extraordinarily coherent exponents of a Russian avant-garde architecture removed from occidental influence. Neither Mel'nikov nor Leonidov appears as a case of complete ideological-political identification, and yet they do not attempt to retreat from the challenge of a coherently different architecture, necessarily the expression of a country which had become, for better or worse, socialist. Perhaps what the two had in common was the element of the allegorical transfiguration of a Russian-Byzantine tradition of the icon, based on the experience of life in the country, the village, the city, that might be compared to the theorising of Gramsci's 'nazional-popolare'.

While in the figuration of Leonidov the constructivist approach seems to be liquefied and recongealed through distillation in an alchemical composite, with reflections of the transparencies of Tatlin, but also of the mirages of Černjčevskij and Khlebnikov, in the figuration of Mel'nikov the constructivist order is broken down into a series of geometric, plastic, even sculptural scores, and re-orchestrated as in a Piranesian melodramatic complex of exceptional vigour and architectural originality, which in spite of its indubitable rhetorical content, based on allegory, excludes any concession to stereotyped celebration, as can be seen, for example, in the crescendo of the arches, introduced for the first time, and here epically crushed by the ascending diagonal that revises the classicist borrowing. I mention the vision of Piranesi because there is a text by Ejzenštejn from 1946-1947[13], translated in Italian with the title *Piranesi o la fluidità delle forme* with an introduction by Manfredo Tafuri, in which neither Ejzenštejn nor Tafuri mentions Mel'nikov. And yet, as an approach to this last design, and perhaps to the entire poetic path of Mel'nikov, I believe there is no better guide than this text by the great Russian director.

Thus in 1934, precisely with this competition, what might have been the opportunity for the apotheosis of a Soviet way of avant-garde architecture, an original way because rooted in the context, just as the North American architecture of Wright or, later, of Kahn was rooted in its context, with the discovery of the roots and motivation of pre-Columbian civilisations and the new frontier of the pioneers, was lost.

When in 1946 the threadbare ideology of Andréj Znadov definitively descended on the scattered remains of the avant-garde and the intellectuals and artists who had taken part, the few survivors of death and the gulags wandered through the streets of Moscow, like the 'dead souls' of Gogol, and the constructivist architects still working made their compromises with the new directives of the Party, tossing in arches, pilaster strips, columns, pinnacles or, like Ginzburg, going to the coast of the Black Sea to design houses and hotels based on an ambiguity between modernity and regionalism. With Leonidov by then reduced to silence (he was to pass away in 1959), Mel'nikov was the only one who did not surrender, even in his last designs: he continued, undaunted, to design for himself, or perhaps for 'future memory'. One of his last efforts is a series of sketches for the Soviet Pavilion at the World's Fair in New York in 1962, where perhaps he hoped to be able to relive the happy days of the Exposition in Paris.

I would like to conclude by quoting from a passage by Ripellino[14]: "Everyone has his favourite era, his personal 'âge d'or'. Henry Miller in A Devil in Paradise complains that he was not able to live in Paris in the days of Apollinaire and Rousseau. I would have liked to live in Moscow, at the time of Mejerkhòl'd." But those days, I might add, were also the days of Mel'nikov.

[1] M. Alpatov, *Le icone russe. Problemi di storia e di interpretazione artistica*, Turin 1976.
[2] E. Panofsky, *La prospettiva come forma simbolica e altri scritti*, Milan 1961.
[3] G. Canella, *Moisej Ginzburg o dell'eurocostruttivismo*, introductory essay in M.JA. Ginzburg, *Sull'architettura costruttivista*, edited by E. Battisti, Milan 1977.
[4] S.F. Starr, *Melnikov. Solo Architect in a Mass Society*, Princeton, New Jersey 1978.
[5] C.O. Khan-Magomedov, *Konstantin Mel'nikov*, Moskva 1990.
[6] S.F. Starr, *op. cit.*
[7] N. Lukhmanov, *Architektura Kluba*, Moskva 1930.
[8] *10 Rabočich Klubov Moskvy. Architektura Klubnogo Zdanija*, edited by V.S. Kemenov, Moskva 1932.
[9] B. Chatwin, *What Am I Doing Here*, London, 1989.
[10] A.M. Ripellino, *Majakovskij e il teatro russo d'avanguardia*, Turin 1959; *Il trucco e l'anima. I maestri della regia nel teatro russo del Novecento*, Turin 1965.
[11] G. Canella, *Un ruolo per l'architettura*, Milan 1969; republished in *Per un'idea di città*, Venice 1980.
[12] G. Canella, "Attesa per l'architettura sovietica", in *Casabella-Continuità*, no. 262, April 1962.
[13] S.M. Ejzenštejn, *Piranesi o la fluidità delle forme*, introductory essay by M. Tafuri, in *Rassegna sovietica*, vol. XXIII, nos 1-2, January-June 1972; republished in M. Tafuri, *The Sphere and the Labyrinth. Avanguardie e architettura da Piranesi agli anni '70*, Turin 1980.
[14] A.M. Ripellino, *Il trucco e l'anima*, cit.

Jurij Volčok

**Architect K.S. Mel'nikov:
A Dialogue with the City**

What did Moscow look like in the early Twenties, and what did people think about the city? Let's listen to the words of those who lived there at the time:

In 1928 a Russian art critic, professor A.A. Sidorov wrote about Moscow: "Caught between Europe and Asia is the city of Moscow—city of the Tsars, Byzantine heiress, bearer of the fantastic idea of the 'Third Rome'. In the 18th and 19th centuries, in the era of the Russian emperors it was a wonderful provincial town, with its own flair, introverted and slightly lazy. Just before the revolution it grew to become a large industrial city, the centre of liberal intelligentsia and political opposition, the home of private art collections in which Matisse and Picasso sat next to ancient religious icons. Then came the Moscow of those terrible first years after the revolution—demolished, hungry and savage, close to death. And, finally, the Red Moscow of today, the Soviet capital, a conflux of boundless energy. Of all cities Moscow is perhaps the one which brings out the most contradictory feelings inside us. Does Moscow have a face? A thousand faces? Or no face at all? Moscow has been called the heart of Russia for a considerable time now. She has suffered a great deal but managed to retain her dynamism and vitality. It is not easy to uncover the core of her restless heart. And so Moscow has remained enigmatic."[1]

"Caught between Europe and Asia...": this should not be understood as the concept of Eurasianism as proposed by L. Gumilev in his reflections on the place of Russian culture in world history. Professor Sidorov is talking about something else. He offers his own clue to help solve the 'mystery' of Moscow, a city where in his time, the urban (European) and the rural (Asian—according to his interpretation) lifestyles coexisted in a natural way. From that time onwards, a 'wonderful provincial town' had to attract the 'conflux of energy' essential for a capital city and acquire a 'new face' or a 'thousand faces'.

This latter idea of Sidorov coincides in a surprisingly exact and concise way with writer Michael Osorgin's perception of Moscow, expressed in the opening sentence of his novel *Sivcev Vražek* (the name of a street in Moscow close to Arbat): "In the boundless universe, in the solar system, on the planet Earth, in Russia, in Moscow, in his study in a corner house on Sivcev Vražek Street, in an armchair there sat a scientist—the ornithologist Ivan Alexandrovic."[2]

Here the author gives the 'exact co-ordinates' of a specific location in the city, which represent one of the 'thousand faces' of Moscow, and we cannot comprehend this face without thinking about a real Ivan Aleksandrovic, living at this particular location. He lives there, inside the building, within 'his own study', his own home, his own personal place in the city.

But apart from the fact that both texts obviously date from the same period, what do they have in common as far as their vision of the city is concerned?

Both books are characterised by a fairly *detached view of the city*, since they speak to a reader who has little knowledge of the real life of Moscow and who is not in daily contact with it, and yet still needs to understand the 'life and fate' (quoting another author, Vassilij Grossman, who wrote about Moscow later in the Forties and Fifties)[3] of the new Russian capital which was by then a completely different urban cultural context than other European cities such as Berlin and Paris (the cities where the two above mentioned books were published).

One specific feature of this detached approach should be emphasised: both authors show (as does Sidorov in his photo documentary about Moscow published in Berlin) or describe (as does Osorgin in his novel about the city which he was forced to leave in 1922) the city in which they lived.

Although they lived in a city steeped both in the legacy of history and the visions of a great future, the authors only depict the city in which they lived, so their stories are neither an historical narrative, nor a semi-fantastic utopia. Unlike numerous examples of both these genres dating from the same period, these texts reveal the absolute balance between past and future, crystallising a particular moment in time. In order to properly understand the architectural problems and to immerse ourselves in the professional realities of urban planning in Moscow during the Twenties and Thirties it is important that we should comprehend the problems of this time in all their diversity, and also try to look at the city with the same detached attitude that had become a logical element in the architectural profession at that time. "In the boundless universe, in the solar

system, on the planet Earth, in Russia, in Moscow, in his study in his own house on Krivoarbatskij Lane (a street adjacent to Sivcev Vražek in Arbat) there sat an architect Konstantin Stepanovič …"

Mel'nikov himself could not have given a better definition of his Place in Moscow. Even Osorgin's style of writing is similar to Mel'nikov's,[4] aptly reflecting the latter's perception of himself. Mel'nikov displayed his 'signature' in big letters on the façade of his house, right above the front door, advertising the importance of his name, his personality, his profession, his creative "self" in the scale of the letters he used for the address of his House.

This similarity was a result of many influences, the most pertinent of which was the fact that K.S. Mel'nikov was very introverted and reserved in his social life, but amazingly open, daring and uncompromising as an artist. At a first glance these character traits seem to be mutually exclusive, but their polarity forms the basis for the professional, creative contact between the architect and the city.

However, this complementary nature of Mel'nikov's creative and social character is also reflected by his Arbat address. A modern researcher, professor G.S. Knabe, referred to the similarity between Mel'nikov's character and the positive characteristics of "Arbat society in the 1920s and 1930s."[5]

In his opinion, it was in this very area of the city that the Moscow lifestyle of the era was being created. Arbat, being the most 'Muscovite' area of the city, possessed all the qualities which made Moscow a capital city.

And I think that Mel'nikov quite naturally participated in the cultural life of his age by deciding to build his house on one of the Arbat lanes. The same logic lead him to pick out Arbat Square amongst all the city squares to be redesigned as part of the 'New Moscow Plan'; the architect considered Arbat Square a part of the city and at the same time his "property", "his own" address in the city (in the boundless Universe...), an extension of his own House. The diversity of contrasting relationships between not just the Muscovite, but the Arbat inhabitant and the city as a whole determines the "central place" of architecture in these relationships (and, according to G. Zedelmeier in a broader context, between culture and civilisation, or in the context of urban development, between urbanisation and de-urbanisation). Mel'nikov adds another aspect to these relationships, a well-chosen definition of which was given by Vjačeslav

Ivanov in his article *Byronism as phenomenon of the Russian spirit*, first published in 1916: "...In Byron's day, man as a political or 'urban' creature, had found three solutions for the possible unification of people, and all these alternatives have since demonstrated the unfeasibility of their practical implementation ... the theocratic ideal of the Middle Ages; ... the national state; ... the revolutionary guillotine. ... England [of the Byronic age] was such an 'ambivalent assembly', including both 'vigorous attack' and 'rigorous repulse', and created the basis for the Byronic idea of freedom as a question of self-assertion and self-determination of the human existence in its most pure and real form, crystallized and abstracted from the historical features of continental life."[6]

By substituting Twenties and Thirties Moscow for Byronic England, and using the term "continental life" to describe European culture and architecture, we can create a comprehensive overview of Mel'nikov and his creative activity.

Ultimately, it was K.S. Mel'nikov—a peasant's son, who considered the seven-

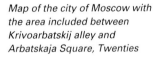

Map of the city of Moscow with the area included between Krivoarbatskij alley and Arbatskaja Square, Twenties

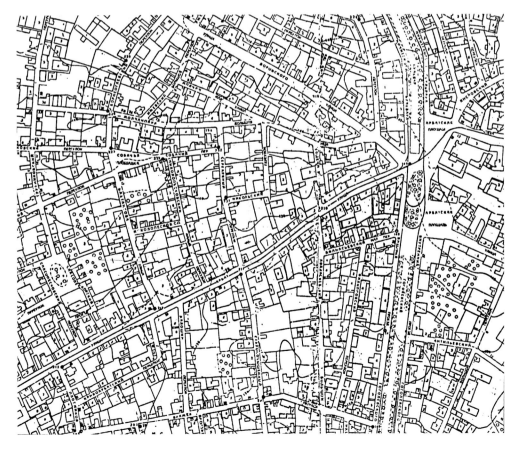

teenth century the most significant in Russian history, who had ancient icons on the walls of his modern house (in twentieth-century Moscow), who did not lack a sense of national pride, and who experienced the heavy strike of the 'revolutionary guillotine'—who was to become the Lord of Soviet Architecture in the Twenties and Thirties.

In spite of the collectivist nature of the architectural profession and life in general in Moscow in those years, Mel'nikov could afford to retain his own creative self, expressing it in various ways.

This diverse, impulsive and refined professional relationship between the architect and his design activity, perceived through his own Self, can be compared to the way the philosopher and writer Andrei Belyj[7] perceived himself, who, incidentally, grew up and spent most of his life in a house on the corner of Arbat Street and Denežnyj Lane.[8]

Self-sufficiency, individualism and perfectionism prevented Mel'nikov from joining any professional associations. The artistic organisations of the day did not meet Mel'nikov's professional requirements.

His only partner in discussion, reflection and co-production, with whom he could be on equal terms as far as understanding was concerned, was the city itself: to be more accurate, the contemporary city as defined by art critic Sidorov.

With this in mind, it is quite logical that Sidorov was one of the first critics who noticed Mel'nikov's work and wrote about it in the press.[9] This is yet another example of the dialogue between the architect and the 'mysterious' city of Moscow.

In 1925, the first Russian translation of C. Sitte's *City Planning According to Artistic Principles* appeared. This work was first published in Germany in 1889 and was virtually a classic by the Twenties; in France it was translated as early as 1902, while in the author's home country Germany it ran into five editions between 1889 and 1921.

Although this book on the artistic perception of the city was translated and published in 1925, Sidorov had already recognised Mel'nikov as a great artist as early as 1924. Thus the need to create a concept for the city of Moscow as a unified whole, and as an object of artistic activity, became even more acute.

However, there were many reasons for this need, some of which stemmed from the uneasy coexistence between the urban and rural lifestyles in the new Russian capital.

This gave rise to a quite sincere confidence, or at least hope, that many problems related to the urbanisation of the city could be solved with the intervention of art and culture.

Against this background, Howard's idea of a 'garden city', already well known in pre-revolutionary Russia, acquired a new meaning: the proletarian, Soviet garden city with green suburbs became a manifestation of the 'garden city' idea.

All layers of society were involved in discussion on this topic, including school students and adolescents. The information campaign under the slogan "Each citizen shall have a clear idea of his or her city" even spread to the countryside. This campaign served a real purpose: to cultivate urban social habits among the peasants who had become first generation city

Mel'nikov on the roof of his house in Krivoarbatskij alley, late Twenties

Project for the arrangement of Arbatskaja square, 1931; view from Arbat street (model by A. Šadrin with V. Rjazanov, 1999)

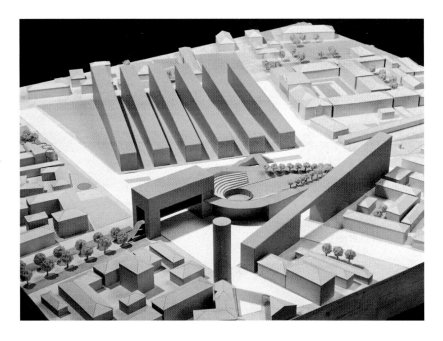

dwellers. Its significance can hardly be overestimated taking into account the doubling of the urban population by the end of the Twenties.

This need to acquire a new understanding of a city ("studies of a city are the sign of our time, characterised by the development of public thought"—as was said at the time) created a context where the professional debate of the day was between urbanists, i.e., those who defended urbanist tendencies, and de-urbanists. Although if one looks at a list of those who participated in the initial discussions, it is quite clear that the main 'actors' in the debate were like-minded in their understanding of the basic principles of architectural art, no matter how polar their opinions might seem. The majority of them were active participants and leaders in the constructivist movement.

In 1930, for example, the Vesnin brothers proposed urbanisation projects (urban development concepts for Kuzneck and Stalingrad).

At the same time, the project developed by M. Ginsburg and M. Barsc for Magnitogorsk was based upon the diametrically opposed idea of de-urbanism which the architects actively supported and promoted.

Thus within the confines of constructivism, its many leading practitioners managed to demonstrate the wide variety of possibilities their "general line" still offered, and they considered participation in the debate a means to "sharpen" the "laboratory" technique of architectural design they claimed to have discovered. The architect I. Leonidov was not involved in the discussion about the problems of coexistence between urbanist and de-urbanist trends, moreover, in his Magnitogorsk project he attempted to resolve the irreconcilable conflict, combining the merits of both of these approaches in urban development.

Even the name [the country of] 'Magnitogor'e' given to Leonidov's project suggests reconciliation: an end to debate. The future belonged neither to a city nor to a village, but to a 'village-city' which from that time onwards would be transformed into the 'garden city'.

Both deep in meaning and rich in artistic inspiration this position is fundamentally close to Mel'nikov's way of looking at the city in its modern context, using architecture to bring about perfection. From this point of view, Leonidov turned the city of Magnitogorsk into the country of Magnitogor'e, and in the artistic mind of Mel'nikov, who also avoided participation in any sort of debate, the city of Moscow became the country of Moscovia.

Even the names of the 'Devič'e Pole' (Maidens' field) and 'Sokolničeskoe Pole' areas where Mel'nikov chose to build his famous workers social clubs, the 'Kaucuk' social club on Pljuščikha and the Rusakov club, show just how comfortable Mel'nikov felt working on such 'border' territories, regardless of whether they were in the centre or on the outskirts of the city.

The idea of designing a city space as if furnishing a house was inspired not so much by an obedience to the given situation, as by a hypersensitivity to the reality, by an immediate desire to refine and perfect it. "A city street with continuous lines of buildings on either side allows the creation of *a compositional image of the street,*

Novo-Sukharevskij Market, 1924; view from the Sukharevskaja tower (model by A. Šadrin with A. Puckov, 1999)

of its 'interior'" (printed in bold by K.S. Mel'nikov).[10]

This 'interior' approach which sees the city from the inside, as if it were the inside of a house, seems to reconcile many conflicts, or, to be more precise, discrepancies between the European (using Sidorov's definition) understanding of the creative possibilities of architectural form and Asiatic lifestyles, which dictated the urban reality. This approach allowed Mel'nikov to free his creative work from any limitations of debate, whether within the architectural community or from within himself, and from any form of excessive self-control and self-censorship, those tendencies which often push the artist towards professional compromise when it comes to the creation of architectural forms.

Mel'nikov's theory of the urban interior was based on the interior of his own house, his natural habitat. Its design was based on a peasant's *izba* (Russian peasant cottage), and slowly but surely (judging by the architect's sketches), with more and more conviction, moved towards its eventual circular shape - an ideal shape which spoke volumes to the author.[11] This is the shape which symbolised the maximalist character of the period of transition from optional, incidental features of the compositional solution in the given city environment to an absolutely clearcut, self-assured perfect solution.

Mel'nikov's house consists of two interlocking cylinders—shown on the plan as two rings metaphorically joined together to represent a marriage union. One ring is the space for the architect himself, for his study, the other ring contains the living areas for the architect's family.

In the logic of this concept, the diamond-shaped windows, not so much in a strict geometrical sense as in impression, symbolise an unstable, fairly tense relationship between the Master and the world. It is no coincidence that in nearly all the photographs of Mel'nikov in his study, he is sitting with his back to these windows. Mel'nikov was inwardly focused in a par-

ticular sense of this word: he concentrated on his own interior. Another photograph shows Mel'nikov on the balcony of his own house dressed as if he were about to go out to the theatre: here he belongs not to himself, but to the House and to the city at the same time. It looks as though he is sitting in a theatre box, an appropriate analogy in this case, and perhaps Mel'nikov would have agreed, as at the height of his career he always dressed impeccably.

In fact most Moscow architects in the Twenties and Thirties were dandies, dressing to the latest fashion, which at that time meant the European fashion. Even so, Mel'nikov stood out because of the perfect, almost theatrical way in which he dressed, never without a white handkerchief in the top breast pocket of his coat. As part of the city interior he felt himself both at home and on stage.

This duality of consciousness and perception of the self, when one feels protected and at home, and yet at the same time vulnerable as if facing an audience on a stage, accurately describes the nature of the dialogue between the architect and the city itself. On the one hand, its space could be adjusted to make it comfortable and habitable, while at the same time its imperfections had to be recognised and improved in order to remove the sense of

Novo-Rjazanskij truck garage, 1926; plan and view of the roof structure designed by V. Šukhov (photo by A. Rodčenko, 1928)

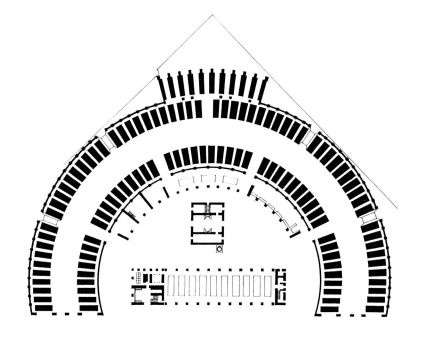

discontent which arose when one became aware of the drawbacks of the urban reality.

Another characteristic feature of the dialogue between the architect and the city was the way in which Mel'nikov not only felt for the city emotionally and considered it as an object on which he could apply his professional skill and effort, but the way he also studied the city carefully, its structure, forms, details, architectural methods and techniques. He allowed himself to be educated by the city. I like to think of him as a grateful partner in the dialogue, eager to participate in any form of joint creativity.

It is possible to follow a footpath that starts from the architect's House and runs along Arbat Street to the square of the same name, before turning left to the boulevards, where it crosses Tverskaja Street and Puškinskaja Square (here Mel'nikov's *Leningradskaja Pravda* building and the *Izvestija* apartment blocks can be seen), and then descending to Trubnaja Square. Finally a sharp turn to the right and upwards towards Roždestvenka leads past the monastery and ends at the Architectural Institute.

This route is interesting because it passes through a veritable catalogue of Moscow architectural history, while at the same time giving a good look at the 'Arbat society' of the city.

In Mel'nikov's Arbat Square project he designed the square as the central focus for the Arbat society. Parallel rows of apartment blocks emphasised the urban character of the area. Perhaps the housing estates Mel'nikov built in the Sretenka and the Serpukhovskoj Val districts of

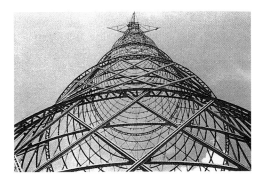

V. Šukhov, Tower of Sabolovskaja radio, 1922 (photo by A. Rodčenko, 1929)

Moscow served as prototypes (again in the centre and at the edge of the city).

With this in mind it is important to note that in the early Twenties one of the streets in the vicinity of the Serpukhovskaja Zastava (one of the streets closest to the city limits) was renamed the 'City Street'.

There is no need to dwell on the social reason for renaming streets in Moscow and other towns and cities of the Soviet Union which took place at that time because the symbolic character is quite obvious. The trend was similar to Mel'nikov's approach where compositional solutions and city areas were starting to be combined in his creative work. Mutually complementing and supporting each other, they often give him the solution to a design concept.

The site chosen for Mel'nikov's model workers' dwellings lies at the junction of Serpukhovskaja Street and Ščipkovskij Lane, not far from City Street. Also in the same area is the Sukhov radio mast, designed by the engineer V.G. Šukhov, whose authority was uncontested by Mel'nikov and with whom he eagerly collaborated.

It goes without saying that Mel'nikov did not intend to copy the layout of the city or simply to interpolate it into a new situation. The Master reconceived elements of the city structure, giving each particular element its own significance from the artist's point of view. It can be clearly seen in the exhibition models of both the Arbat Square reconstruction and for the living quarters on Ščipok.

Mel'nikov's familiarity with the Sretenka area and the adjoining Kolkhoznaja Square also provided him with inspiration for new designing ideas. The layout of the Sukharevskij market shows a "tight packing" of lanes crossing Sretenka Street almost piled on top of each other. Curiously, one of them, the nearest to the marketplace, is called the 'Last Lane', even though this Last Lane runs up to the very centre of the city, while on the other hand City Street is almost at the city limits. In this way the structure of the urban fabric was being gradually evened out.

Perhaps the semicircular shape of the central building of the city hospital on Kolkhoznaja subconsciously suggested the design solution for the Novo-Rjazanskij car parking facility. But even here Mel'nikov's row of associations is more rich and profound.

On the plan of the city one can clearly see geometrically identical semicircular shapes of workshops situated next to Moscow's main railway stations (Kurskij Station for example). Mel'nikov combines these two elements, and as a result the bus garage, normally a quite prosaic utilitarian building, acquires an additional quality once only found on city estates, at one time the most influential type of housing in 19th-century Moscow from an architectural point of view.

Without stressing this association, the architect leaves it as another of those city mysteries Sidorov spoke of. This mystery reveals itself only to the 'enlightened' or sometimes not at all, remaining the 'secret' of the private relationship between the architect and the city. And this is not the only example of the confidential relationship

Mel'nikov's buildings enjoy with elements of the urban structure that were symbolic to him.

Particularly the site chosen for the Rusakov workers social club in Sokol'niki, which can be seen on the map, was intimately connected with the initial design for the Resurrection Church nearby on Rusakovskaja Street designed by the architects P.A. Tolstykh and L.A. Lozovskij in 1911.

The Church was initially designed to face eastwards (as was the workers social club). But in 1913, during the implementation of the project (to celebrate the 300th anniversary of the Romanov royal family) the main facade was made to face parallel to the street. Mel'nikov's social club looks as if it has turned to face away from the Church, but in the mind of the architect, it conducts an incredibly intimate dialogue with it.

The architect was convinced that all his work, including the workers social clubs, would become the catalyst for the intensive construction of new public centres in the city. The logic of such thought is shown in his design for the space 're-served' for public use near the Rusakov

Kaučuk Club, 1927-1929; view of the building with Devič'e field in the forefront (model by A. Šadrin with S. Frolova, 1999)

workers social club, which combined many features of his unrealised projects.[12] A similar idea is 'encoded' in a different way in Mel'nikov's solution for the exterior and the roof of the workers social club on Pljuščikha. This design creates an 'urban landscape' consisting of 'tightly packed' urban housing, typical for Moscow.

It is as though Mel'nikov was inviting architectural development of the Devic'e Pole area according to the 'laws' of urban life, which would make the 'city fragment' represented by the workers social club, more extended, significant and completely urban in its appearance.

I also think that the classic 'Mel'nikov diagonal', realised to its full extent in the Paris pavilion, was born out of his dialogue with the city.

The transparent structure of the Šukhov tower not only influenced the structural design for the walls of Mel'nikov's own house, but also taught him to see through the structure of any building as if it were transparent.

The structural system of a house, a building which represented the 'anatomy for an artist' helped Mel'nikov to assert himself in many specific solutions related to architectural form and to elaborate his own 'trademark' techniques for the creation of forms and volume-spatial structures.

The diagonal technique used in his designs was perhaps 'hinted' at by a tenement building built at the turn of the century on Roždestvenka opposite the Architectural Institute. Its 'sheared' facades seem to 'ask' to be unfolded by breaking the single-plane structure in two pieces to create the idea of that type of passage common on nearby Kuzneckij Most and the Petrovskij Linii.

It might have only been a mere suggestion, a 'working hypothesis', but it is quite consistent with the creative quest of the architect.

In this case the dialogue between the architect and the city becomes naturally integrated into the logic of the cultural dialogue concept that was elaborated by the

View of the roof of the entrance (photo by A. Rodčenko, 1929)

philosopher and cultural scientist M.M. Bakhtin at around about the same time.[13] Mel'nikov's work shows us that architecture in the Twenties and Thirties were part of the most significant trends of that era in the sphere of human knowledge and creative work.[14]

Mel'nikov immersed himself in the culture of his day. He worked with the real facts of the contemporary city, simultaneously entering into dialogue with it, pushing back the barriers of time, part of the inherent power of architecture.

We therefore considered it important from a methodical point of view that this exhibition of his work should contain detailed reproductions of particular urban development projects, especially those which are part of the models. The models and drawings are 'cross-sections' in time, covering three to four time periods. The first model shows the state of the urban development in the Twenties, an era which directly preceded the birth of new architectural ideas. The second model shows how Mel'nikov's projects interacted with the existing environment, taking into account all the urban development transformations included in the project. The third model shows how the city looks today.

Drawings have also been made for the late Thirties-Forties. This period saw significant changes in the concept of Moscow's reconstruction and the beginning of implementation of structural reforms, envisaged by the General Plan of 1935.

The exception is the project for the Bakhmetevskij car garage. An abundance of archive materials allowed us to make 'additional reproductions' showing the different design variants Mel'nikov worked out, as well as the situation immediately after the main building had been constructed.

For projects that were actually built, such as the Bakhmetevskij car garage and the Rusakov and Kaučuk workers social clubs the 'reproductions made at the moment of construction' show 'cross-sections' of the buildings, which allow us to distinguish the newly structures from their surroundings.

Mel'nikov's urban development projects are shown in the context of the whole city, including all urban development factors which we think influenced the character of his architecture.

We used fragments of geodetic surveys of Twenties, Thirties, Forties, Seventies, and Nineties, supplemented by materials from the CA NTD archive in Moscow to help us make the models as accurate as possible. In our models we tried not only to reconstruct the architectural situation which existed in any one particular area at the time of Mel'nikov's professional dialogue with the city, we also wanted to show the difference between the beginning and the end of the twentieth century.

That is why the main dividing lines between the various city districts are not the streets (which are only sketched) but the fences that at one time formed the boundaries between the various city estates, which were far more important at the beginning of the century.

In order to give an integrated impression of the development, we decided not to visually mark Mel'nikov's projects. They exist within the context of the entire urban fabric. The model of the centre of Moscow, showing 'big projects' of K.S. Mel'nikov, provides food for thought not only concerning the way the General Plan of 1935 attempted to deal with urban reconstruction, but also with regard to current problems and perspectives of architectural design in the historic centre of the city.

[1] Alexis A. Sidorow, *Moskau*, Berlin, 1928, p. VII.

[2] M. Osorgin, *Sivcev Vražek*. The novel was written in exile and published by the editing house of the 'Moskva' bookshop in Paris in 1929. The quotation is taken from the book: Mikhail Osorgin, *Vremena*, ed. Rossijskaja kniga, Ekaterinburg 1992, p. 3.

[3] The creative career of the writer Vassilij Grossman, including the history of publication of the novel *Zizn' i soud'ba* (Life and Fate) see in particular: Semjon Lipkin, *Life and fate of Vassily Grossman*, Moskva 1990.

[4] This is shown by Mel'nikov's own writings collated in the book *Konstantin Stepanovic Mel'nikov*, Iskusstvo, Moskva 1985. Compiled by A.A. Strigaljov and I.V. Kokkinaki.

[5] See G.S. Knabe, *Arbat society and Arbat myth* in the coll.: *Moscow and Moscow text of the Russian culture*, Moskva 1998.

[6] Vjaceslav Ivanov, "Byronism as phenomenon of the Russian spirit", in *Rodnoe i Vselenskoe* (Native and Universal), Moskva 1994. -pp. 270-271.

[7] See: Andrei Belyi. *Symbolism as understanding of the world*, 1994.

[8] G.S. Knabe, *op. cit.*, p. 146.

[9] On 13 September 1924 , A.A. Sidorov published his notes on the work of Mel'nikov's, who in his opinion "seems to be one of those artists who in the very near future will be largely responsible for the appearance of USSR cities." Quoted from the book cited by A.A. Strigaljov and I.V. Kokkinaki. p. 159. On 19 April 1944 ?. A.A. Sidorov completed his statement concerning the work of Mel'nikov, he wrote in particular that the Master "had always been one of those architects who worked with enthusiasm and success on the solutions of the problems concerning the 'practical architecture' itself," *ibid.*, p. 227.

[10] Quoted from: A.A. Strigalev, I.V. Kokkinaki, cited collection of works., p. 140.

[11] Many sketches by K.S. Mel'nikov, including the sketches mentioned here, for the project of his own house were included in the book by S.O. Khan-Magomedov *Konstantin Mel'nikov*, Moskva, 1990.

[12] See S.O. Khan-Magomedov, *op. cit.*, p. 252-253.

[13] See M.M. Bakhtin *Problems of Dostoyevskij's poetics*. Moskva 1979.

[14] See L.M. Batkin *Italian humanists: style of living, style of thinking*. Moskva 1978, and V.S. Bibler *From science studies to the logic of culture. Two philosophical introductions to the twenty first century*, Moskva, 1991.

Maurizio Meriggi

Mel'nikov's Design for the City of the Future.
An Itinerary in the City of Moscow

"The architecture of the future
Walls, apart from their solidity and
thermal characteristics, govern the
penetration of light, without
window frames any longer: gentle,
the light is directly spread, without
the possibility of knowing how or
from where.
For suburban houses, where the
buildings have more corners, a less
transparent material is used, while
for urban rooms a more transparent,
monolithic material is selected. This
is not glass, but a material that
supports all the weight of the
construction. Walls without doors, a
unit, beautiful, majestic."
K.S. Mel'nikov, 1944[1]

"The city of the future
The city street entirely immersed in
greenery and only for pedestrians.
The street for vehicles below (not
requiring the plowing of snow,
protected from ice), further down—
moving sidewalks, and even further
below—more rapid transport.
The houses are inclined, and a
curtain for aerial accessways is
attached to the sloping part; devices
can dock on the skeleton of the
houses.
There is a hospital city, a city of
meat, on the snowcapped peaks of
the city stand illustrious men, a
pantheon city, a city of ethnography,
each state constructs the national
city, the capital."
K.S. Mel'nikov, 1944[1]

In the work of K.S. Mel'nikov, does a recognizable project for the future city exist?

While it has been easy for critics - because the graphic and literary documentation permits it—to see Mel'nikov as the artist-architect, the dreamer, who offers us a glimpse in his notebooks of a rough, original idea for the modern city, and therefore to unhesitatingly respond positively to the above question, until today it has been very difficult, if not impossible, for architects - at least for those who are not Moscovites—to fully comprehend the elements through which this project can become intelligible and communicable. We have had to rely on the intuitions that the evocative capacities of each of the works of this master of modern architecture, albeit on paper or in stone, is capable of suggesting in the emotional sphere.

Perhaps it is precisely here that the difficulties in comprehension begin: the narrative ability of the hand of Mel'nikov tends to convince us that in each case each work is unique, abstractly posited in an ideal space, that of the extraordinary imagination of the master.

The work reconstructed in this exhibition is the result of an attempt to go beyond the mere suggestions evoked by the writings and works of Mel'nikov, or of the desire to understand more, to manage to associate the magic of his architecture with a real scenario. The entire exhibition is organised with this objective: to attempt as far as possible to contextualize his designs in a real situation.

The following notes propose an itinerary that does not claim to be exhaustive; it serves for orientation, drawing attention away from the pages of the catalogue to certain panoramic vantage points from which to get an idea, if not of the project, at least of the *mise en ensamble* of the landscape that is produced by the association of the works of Mel'nikov with the 'natural' characteristics of the edification of the city of Moscow which, in my opinion, constantly represented, for the master, the real site of his dreams.

The City: A Forest and a River

Two designs developed, significantly enough, one for an international exposition in which the image of the new Russia after the revolution was to be officially presented, the other for a large European metropolis, reflect more than any others an accentuated programmatic character, to the point of representing a sort of manifesto of the city designed by Mel'nikov during the course of his striking artistic career: the pavilion of the USSR at the International Exposition of the Decorative Arts in Paris in 1926, and a bridge-garage for the city of Paris for 1000 taxis, suspended over the Seine.

In an interview for the magazine *Le bulletin de la vie artistique* on the USSR pavilion, reacting against the accusation of formalism implicit in the questions of the interviewer, Mel'nikov responds: "…This glass box is not the result of an abstract idea. The idea came from life itself, I have adapted to the circumstances. First of all, I began with the position of the lot assigned to me—the lot is surrounded by trees: it was necessary that my little house could be striking through its irregular masses of colour, its height, the artistic conception of the form. My tools were very humble ones: this determined the choice of the materials. I wanted the pavilion to be air and light, as much as possible: this is my personal preference, but I believe it also reflects the preferences of our entire people. Walking alongside the pavilion not all the passers-by enter. But all of them, in one way or another, see what is on display inside my pavilion, thanks to the glass walls and the staircase, that opens to encounter the throng, passing through the pavilion, permitting the visitors to observe the pavilion from above. Where the surfaces that cross one another above are concerned, they will surely disappoint the lovers of completely closed roofs! The roof is no worse than any other: it is composed in such a way as to allow air to enter while offering protection from the rain, that cannot enter at any part.

But don't you think that the abundance of glass and this strange roofing make your pavilion too light?

But you are not saying that you would prefer something heavier. And for what possible reason should a temporary building be given the false attributes of the eternal? My pavilion doesn't have to remain standing for the entire life of the Soviets; it merely has to stay up until the end of the exposition. In short, the definition of the colours, the simplicity of the lines, the abundance of air and light of this pavilion, unusual features which may or may not please the observer, come from my country. But hasn't it even occurred to you, for God's sake, that I have intentionally constructed a symbol?"[2]

The edifice of the pavilion is positioned (and hidden) in the clearing of **a forest** in the Parisian exposition park. The design of the building—as its architect states in the interview—is based, first of all, on this environmental context, which is exploited to represent, in the fiction of display, the *natura agri* of the Russian territory ("I wanted the pavilion to be air and light, as much as possible: this is my personal preference, but I believe it also reflects the preferences of our entire people.")

The mass of the garage for 1000 taxis is suspended on a bridge that crosses a river—the main generating element of the *forma urbis* of Russian settlements.[3] The garage is constructed by raising the flow of the vehicles crossing the bridge by means of a series of ramps that enter the half-glazed, half-opaque volume of the parking garage. The architecture of the building is based on the combination of two elements of a contrasting nature; the lightness and dynamism of the ramps are contrasted by the heaviness of the caryatids of the Atlasses who, with their feet resting on the two banks of the river, struggle to support the overhanging volume of the garage.

Both these designs are developed starting with a shared concept of architecture that is found in all of Mel'nikov's work.

On the one hand, the architecture is a

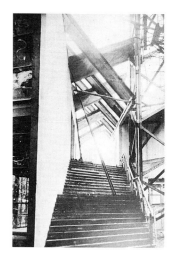

Soviet Pavilion at the Paris "Exposition Internationale des Arts Décoratifs et Industriels Modernes" in 1925; view of the diagonal ramp

light *diaphragm* that regulates the exchanges between interior and exterior: in the pavilion, the alternation between glazed and opaque surfaces of the walls, and the shifting of the pitches of the roofing that cover the ramp give rise to an intermediate space, both a projection of the interior toward the surrounding nature and vice versa; in the garage on the Seine, which was to have been built in correspondence to each of the bridges, the pattern of the ramps that provide access to the different completely open and suspended levels of the building make it a sort of semi-transparent wing behind which, through the rapid flow of the traffic, one glimpses the different spans that compose the landscape of the city.

On the other, the architecture is **a device** that orients and organises the flow of air and light, but also and above all of people and things, in the environment: the staircase in the air in the clearing in the woods of the park in Paris stretches outward to grab the audience and carry it into the centre of the volume, in a position that allows the observer to see all the spaces of the pavilion as well as the surrounding nature; the ramps of the garage gather vehicle traffic from the street, channelling it into the air in the eddy of the rising levels, forcing pure movement to materialise in the elevation of an edifice.

Architecture for an Urbanised Countryside

The suspension between a landscape based on scattered settlements, made of light, precarious wooden architecture, and one with the distinctive signs of a metropolitan dimension, with intense vehicle traffic presented in Paris by Mel'nikov with these two buildings reflects the structural condition of Moscow in the Twenties—a city with a dual soul.[4]

On the one hand, the centre of Moscow has all the typical characteristics of a middle-class metropolis of the late 1800s, with a well-consolidated centre bordered by two tree-lined ring roads, dominated both by grandiose monumental complexes—the Kremlin, the Church of Christ Savior—and by the imposing buildings along the squares and the main arteries—such as the classic example of the *neo-Russian* GUM department stores on the Red Square, with the glazed shopping galleries; on the other, there is the Moscow of an archipelago of suburbs, arranged along waterways and positioned around a historical nucleus, with fortified monasteries and factories at the centre, representing not so much a series of outposts of the city in the country as an incursion into the city of the boundless Russian countryside.

Within the archipelago a rail network is inserted composed of a ring segment that connects the radial segments that terminate in the city, with nearly ten large stations, with lines arriving from the other major cities of the Union. A dense array of small stations along the ring and the radials already allowed this rail network to function as a metropolitan and regional transport system as well.

The first Master Plan for the city in the 1900s—the 'Novaja Moskva' plan directed by two of the masters of the pre-revolutionary era, A. Ščusev e I. Žoltovskij.[5]—attempted to address this dual nature of Moscow. It proposed: a thinning out of the centre with the conservation of the major monumental complexes of the past and the confirmation of the role of this part of the city as the metropolitan centre; for the concentric outskirts, the construction of an immense garden-city—contained within the ring of the rail line and separated from the industrial zones—which would extend from the suburbs into the heart of the city.

Given this context and utilising the indications of the two projects Mel'nikov developed for Paris, it is possible to begin to visit the spaces of this city according to a guiding scheme.

Reform of the fabric of the peripheral zones

The environmental dimension evoked by the pavilion in Paris, and the fluvial land-

Project for a thousand-taxi garage on a Seine bridge in Paris, 1925 (model by D. Makarov, photo by O. Serebrjanskij)

scape that can be glimpsed in the perspective drawing of the garage both return in the panorama of the First Pan-Soviet Exposition for Agriculture and Crafts, on the banks of the Moskva, on the site of today's 'Gor'kij' Central Park of Culture and Rest.[6]

We must imagine, behind a bridge-diaphragm, an expanse of wooden buildings, farms and cultivated fields, windmills and silos, which nevertheless take on the appearance of great classical edifices—triumphal arches, pantheons, temples. In the back of the exposition, near the river, stands the pavilion of the Makhorka tobacco factory—a bundle of three wooden buildings, interlocking in and on one another, a composition of three large pitched roof surfaces oriented in different directions, that gives the edifice a levitating movement that coincides with the itinerary for the visit to the pavilion/factory.

The transformation into a modern industrial settlement of that special type of rural/semi-industrial periphery known as the *sloboda*[7] is the theme on which Mel'nikov focuses in the projects for the workers' quarter on the Bol'šaja Serpukhovskaja, and for the Sukharevskij Market.

These works are proposed as realistic forecasts of the transformation of the landscape of Moscow had the city continued to develop in the form of the archipelago of towns connected by the rivers and by the various infrastructures.

In the small workers' housing estate on the Ulica Bol'šaja Serpukhovskaja (a radial street for the city of Serpukhov, southeast of Moscow), the layout of the complex designed by Mel'nikov orders a series of linear village-streets[8] in a fan pattern within the trapezoidal lot. These rows characterised by a broken profile due to the diagonal orientation of each housing unit with respect to the internal street, are arranged in keeping with both the alignments on the edges of the block and the visual perspectives offered by the irregularity of the street grid. In corre-

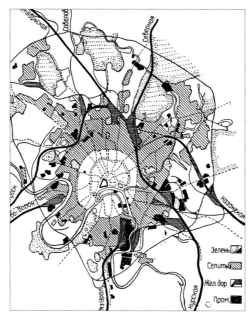

P. and B. Gol'denberg, schematic plan of Moscow in the 19th-20th century, 1935; industries are in black, parks are dotted areas, the central area is in white, railways are marked with a thick line, the streets with a dashed line

spondence to the ends of the village-streets on a curved connection drive, a series of common houses are positioned, multi-storey buildings with lodgings for single workers. The arch defined by these buildings, connected to each other by a raised passageway, is completed by a complex with a detailed plan and volumes, for collective services and a library, facing onto a clearing with a variegated form, on the corner of the parallelogram. The Novo-Sukharevskij Market takes on the form of a small city, a town located inside the historical city, so much so that the individual wooden shops are organised according to a scheme similar to that of the family residences in the project for the Ulica Sepukhovskaja, in rows, here with a composite scheme of fan-shapes with three converging axes forming a crossroads where the masonry building of the Café-Restaurant and the administration is located.

In linguistic terms, the designs are based on a reworking, using the vocabulary of the avant-garde, of the figurative repertoire of the traditional landscape of Russian settlements, but conducted according to above all a typological principle, that applies the geometric reason of traditional Slavic decoration to generate new architectural devices and figures capable of flexible insertion in the mutable, delicate semi-urbanised fabric of historical

Moscow, introducing modernisation without upsetting the balance between the metropolitan dimension and that of the countryside scattered throughout the city.

New monuments for the centres

The two designs for the centre of the city developed in this period, one for the Palace of Labour in the labyrinth of squares that extends between the Kremlin and the Bol'šoj Theater, the other for the building of the *Leningradskaja Pravda*, on Puškin Square, use the panoramic itinerary as a strategy: in the Palace, whose typological layout is indifferent to the morphological condition of the site, the three auditoriums are freely arranged in a mixtilinear pattern, each in pursuit of its own frontal positioning and orientation with respect to the three squares, while they are connected by a system of ramps and raised accessways that wind between the buildings, providing well-selected views; in the Leninpravda the theme of the spiral winding of the accessway and that of rotation are even resolved by means of a mechanical device that permits the different planes to be oriented, at will, toward the panoramic views of Puškin Square and Tverskaja Street.

In the corpus of the work of Mel'nikov the theme of the city centre was to remain rather marginal, and above all none of his works on this theme were ever built; the periphery of Moscow was the true focus of his experimentation.

At the ends of the street-villages of the workers' housing complex on the Bol'šaja Serpukhovskaja, and at the centre of the convergence of the rows of shops in the Novo-Sukharevskij Market, we find buildings that are not particularly large, but which in contrast to the minute scale of the ordinary fabric of the rows of izby-houses and izby-shops appear quite monumental: the collective services building and common house in the first, the cafe-administration building in the second.

It was beginning with what has been developed here that Mel'nikov went on to create his designs for the garages and workers' clubs in the second half of the Twenties, two other elements which, together with the residential fabric and the religious monuments of the pre-revolutionary era, were to define the new architectural image of the Muscovite *sloboda* of the period.

New monuments in the industrial sloboda

Before analysing some of these buildings it is necessary to focus on certain aspects that set them apart from other works of the same period, including those of avant-garde architects, still present in the fabric of the Moscow periphery.

Around them we find the formation of small neighbourhood *architectural ansambl*[9] based on a singular principle of monumentality, the complete opposite of that of the so-called 'Stalinian' Moscow, characterised by a stylistic uniformity in the architecture.

As the reconstructed urban-scale models presented here demonstrate, in the parts of the city that gravitate around the works of Mel'nikov the monumental effect is not so much, or not only, the result of the architecture of the new buildings in itself, or of their interaction with an environment specifically reconfigured to contain them, but rather of the interaction they establish with the reality of the surroundings.

From this point of view these buildings are true monuments—in the etymological sense of the term—on the condition of a nonjudgmental view of the Muscovite urban landscape, without avoiding or demolishing the less praiseworthy parts of the context—a practice, on the other hand, that was widespread in the reconstruction of the city in the Thirties-Fifties. Located in parts of the industrial periphery of Moscow that are very different from one another, the edifices of the garages and the clubs by Mel'nikov tend to impose a new order upon each of the areas, exploiting various presences, without any ideological judgements regarding their quality, making use of both contrast and assonance as compositional factors. In the two examples that follow, we can observe the use of contrast, in the first, and assonance, in the second.

Triangular plazas
The 'classicist' monumental footprint of the parking area-*stables* for Leyland buses, Garage Bakhmetevskij, occupies an entire large block, at the edge of the *val* (*bastion*—a further ring road on the city of the former embankments that enclosed the city).

The inclination of the front and rear of the building with respect to the sides and the streetfront facilitates the movements of entry and exit of the buses.[10] Nevertheless, thanks to this off-axis arrangement and the axis of the volume of the *stables* in diagonal with respect to the block—with a solution similar to that of the Pavilion in Paris, with an alternated pitched roofing to indicate the diagonal passage inside the building—three trian-

gular plazas are formed around the garage, offering three partial views of the garage with respect to the orthogonal street grid. The composition of the plaza on the long side is characterised by a long, unified elevation—horizontally defined by the level of the eaves and the large skylights on the roof, and vertically marked by the combination of the rhythm of the skylights with that of the lateral access doors—that faces a discontinuous frontage of residential buildings of different types (from the *izba* to the town house to the multi-storey building) all aligned with the street; the third side is closed off by the volume of the administration building on the corner of the block.

The composition of the most courtly of the plazas, the one in front of the garage, is characterised by: an elevation of the building constructed as a direct citation of the facade of the large neo-classical Stables edifice that dominates the plaza on the northern side of the Kremlin—Manežnaja Square—with the large oblong tympanum, supported by a pseudo-colonnade composed of portals with splayed jamb/columns and surfaces in glass brick/intercolumns; the unitary character of the figure of the large tympanum is countered, on the other side of the street, by a regular series of *izbas*, while the end of the administration building closes the third side of the triangle.

The reconstruction effected here, based on the original unbuilt design, features, to the rear, the oval volume of the workshop, distinguished by the elevation that accentuates the horizontality of the form, in relation to the rear elevation of the garage-stables, that is composed of a series of portals that measure and accentuate the variability of its vertical development; on the third side of the plaza the entrance gate is positioned.

Apart from an instinctive preference for the figure of the triangle often mentioned by Mel'nikov, this example of the triangular plazas—like others found in his work, such as Arbatskaja Square or the

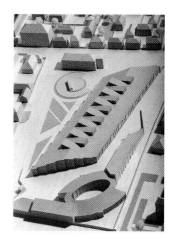

Bakhmet'evskij garage, 1926; view of the model (model by A. Šadrin with A. Puckov)

View of the facade of the building

system of plazas that is formed around the complex of the Commissariat of Heavy Industry—also reveals the application of a precise strategy used to represent, in the composition, the picturesque quality and variety, but also the fragility and lightness of the edified environment of historical Moscow.[11] This approach is even clearer in the following example.

The centre of a 'street-village'

The clubs of Mel'nikov are all built using the same principle—the system of rooms that can be separated or combined in different configurations using mobile diaphragms. In this manner the theatrical space of the club is not separated from the other spaces of the building; it can be integrated with them according to utilisation requirements, creating a variable indoor landscape that could assume different forms in keeping with two principle modes:

– with a system of rooms composed of spaces that are connected to one another but on different levels, and divided by vertical mobile partitions—this is the case of the Rusakov, Zuev, Frunze and Pravda clubs;

– with a system of rooms composed of spaces that are connected to one another on the same level, and divided by mobile partitions, or are placed on atop the other and connected by movable floors—as in the Burevestnik, Svoboda, Gor'kij and Kaučuk clubs.

The reason behind the construction of the workers' clubs was to create a connection between the different moments in everyday life (byt, in Russian), and in particular in the passage from the collective dimension of factory work to the individual dimension of family life in the home.

Thus the position and the choice of the 'typological device' is very important.

Let us examine the Burevestnik club, for the interesting characteristics of the site of the club with respect to the overall character of the Muscovite *sloboda*, and for the clarity of the solution with respect to the context.

A. Betankur, Manege, Moscow, *1817*

On the long narrow lot perpendicular to a street at the edge of the large urban park of Sokol'niki[12], a street with a significant name, 'vegetable garden street' (*Ogorodnaja*), the Burevestnik club stands in front of the leather factory of the same name, beside which there multicoloured brick complex, the 'Makaronnaja fabrika'.[13] The latter features a frontal courtyard bordered by a modern house that contains the administration and the gatekeeper's room, along the street, and a sequence of silos, in the back of the courtyard.

The profile of the club, that follows the long sides of the lot, cuts back on the short side facing the street to form a small triangular plaza, with a cylindrical glazed five-lobed four-storey volume for social activities and the club library. If we add the segment of the street in front to this triangular space, we have an even larger area whose architectural definition involves the complexes of the two factories mentioned above.

The system of rooms of the club is developed starting from the wall at the end of the building facing the street, along the longitudinal axis of the lot, in a sequence of spaces: the hall of the theatre, with lateral stepped tiers, in direct continuity with the gymnasium, separated from it by a mobile partition. Both, in the design, were to be connected to a swimming pool below by means of the removal of the central part of the flooring (a mobile floor slab), permitting the organisation of activities that could shift from one space to the next with great ease.

When all these different environments—the courtyard of the 'Makaronnaja fabrika', the complex of the Burevestnik factory, the segment of Ogorodnaja Street, the triangular plaza, the five-lobed tower and the sequence of internal spaces—are seen in a single scheme, a unified composition takes form. This is achieved not only through the reciprocal equilibrium of the dimensions in the layout and in elevation among the various elements and spaces, but also through an orchestration of the new figures in contrast or assonance with the pre-existing elements in the surrounding context.

Thus, in the middle of the street-village of Ogorodnaja Street, a complex (*ansambl'*) takes form based on the minute dimensions of the architecture of this country road placed in the industrial *sloboda* of the Sokol'niki quarter.

The 'Green City'

A synthetic image of how the Moscow of those years could have developed, maintaining its characteristics of discontinuity and heterogeneity of panoramas, and the fusion of the edification with the natural landscape and its hills, woods and rivers, can be seen in essence in the project for the 'Green City'.

The competition for the design of a settlement for vacationing and relaxation called the 'Green City'[14] held by the municipal authorities and the trade union associations of Moscow in 1929 was an opportunity for a number of architects of the Soviet avant-garde to formulate a hypothesis of radical reform of the city. These architects saw the theme of the competition as that of the creation of a newly founded city, in the true sense of the term, which would be developed based on totally innovative criteria in terms of the positioning of activities, the typology of the buildings for the various functions, and the relationship between the edified and natural environments.

For Mel'nikov the project represented an opportunity to demonstrate, to the municipal and union clients financing the undertaking, how to build a new settlement beginning not with an abstract, a priori scheme, but with the concrete experiences conducted in the suburbs of Moscow on the level of settlement management and the construction of the urban landscape.

Clearly identified and enclosed within the figure of a perfect circle, subdivided into specific sectors with a well-defined geometrical centre, the 'Green City' of Mel'nikov is suspended between a health care facility and a city for mass tourism.

This new city is imagined as a transfiguration of the real Moscow in the landscape of the countryside, to be located at a distance of about 30 kilometres to the north-east of the rail line around the city; the Green City would also be circled by a rail line, of the same diameter (about 10 kilometres). This is the specular copy of Moscow, in all aspects: just as the real Moscow is the city of industrial production, the new Moscow is the city of production of repose for the inhabitants of the real city; in both the cities the areas set aside for production are located along the rail line and served by it; in both the circumferences formed by the infrastructures a centre is constructed—the political centre of the Kremlin in Moscow, the Institute for the Creation of the New Man in the Green City; just as the real city is divided into sectors by radial arteries, so the Green City is divided into sectors that are based, instead, on environmental characteristics (wooded parkland, agricultural parks, park sector for the raising of livestock, zoological park, children's sector); in the former, the residential peripheries are ordered in *sloboda*, while in the latter the residential units for repose are positioned in *sloboda* composed of the alignment of large edifices in series along an axis.

In the 'Green City' of Mel'nikov we find listed and re-proposed, in a new variation, all the typologies he had developed for the buildings he built or designed in Moscow during the Twenties.

In the following comparison we can see an almost immediate formal and typological correspondence between the buildings of the 'Green City' and those of Moscow:

– in the large collective edifice of the Station-kursaal the space is bordered by two concave symmetrical surfaces, the roofing and the tiers, with a section similar to that of the Svoboda and Burevestnik workers' clubs;

– in the buildings for hotel facilities (zone hotels), the internal environment of the rooms is constructed to maximise the

Burevestnik Club, 1929; montage with the ulica Ogorodnaja [Gardens street] (M. Meriggi)

View of the square facing the building with, on the background, the 'Makaronnaja fabrika'

Project for the 'Green City', 1929; settlement scheme and its location in relation to Moscow

passage of the sun's rays by means of a diaphragm wall, with a system that is different from the one Mel'nikov used for his own house, but conceptually analogous;
– in the buildings for the lodgings of the resident personnel of the 'Green City' the typology of the village-street is used, as in the design for the workers' housing on Ulica Serpukhovskaja, with the variation of an indoor street;
– in the buildings called 'Sonnaja-Sonnata', on a formal plane there is an apparent similarity to the figure of the front of the Bakhmetevskij Garage (with the slumberers taking the place of the buses). The city seen up to this point has all the characteristics of an urbanised countryside: this can be seen in the stylistic character and the compositional procedures, based on a 'ruralisation' of the typical figures of the architecture of the city and a monumentalization of those of the architecture of the Russian countryside. Accepting this logic of inversion found in the entire design, we could speak of an 'ideal country' rather than an 'ideal city'.

In the itinerary, up to this point, we have attempted to show the visitor to the Moscow of Mel'nikov how, from the idea of architecture based on the concepts of *diaphragm* and *device* of the two 'manifesto' works—apparently decontextualised—of the Pavilion in Paris and the Garage-bridge, not only edifices but also a series of urban landscapes take form, interacting with the context/environment of Moscow. We have also seen, in the 'Green City', in a refined form of the city—identified only by the design of the infrastructures, the natural landscapes, the subdivisions—the re-composition of the works of architecture and corresponding urban landscapes that characterise the Moscow of the Twenties in Mel'nikov's vision.

It should also be emphasised that the description of the transport modes in his idea of a future city— "…The city street entirely immersed in greenery and only for pedestrians. The street for vehicles below (not requiring the plowing of snow, protected from ice), further down - moving sidewalks, and even further below—more rapid transport"—can combine perfectly with the design of the transport networks for the 'Green City'.

What remains to be clarified is the configuration of a part of the city regarding which the designs of the first half of the Twenties, and that of the 'Green City', tell is little or nothing: the centre.

What is concealed behind the star at the centre of the 'Green City'?

Just what is the Institute for the change of the individual (for the construction of the new man)?

Considering the fact that during the same months in which Mel'nikov was working on the project for the vacation and rest settlement he was also developing his design for the Monument to Christopher Columbus, the mysterious institute could have resembled the mysterious beacon of the monument. But this is pure speculation. Most of the designs developed by Mel'nikov in the Thirties involve the centre of Moscow, and an analysis of these works as a whole may lead to a hypothesis with which to give form to the vision: "on the snowcapped peaks of the city stand illustrious men, a pantheon city, a city of ethnography, each state constructs the national city, the capital."

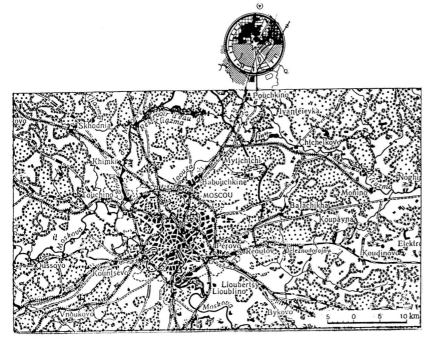

The 'Ansambl'[15] City: The End of the Moscow of the Twenties, the End of the Architecture of Mel'nikov

The work of Mel'nikov in the first half of the Thirties took place in a political, structural and cultural framework that was completely different from that of the Twenties. The composite municipal administration in which representatives of the trade unions, co-operatives, political associations (like the Komsomol) played key roles had been completely replaced, and the administration of the country and its capital was concentrated in the hands of the Party leaders.[16] Beginning with the results of the first phase of the competition for the Palace of the Soviets, the attitudes and orientations of the new administration in the areas of architecture and urban planning also became clear: the city of Moscow was to explicitly display the characteristics of a capital city, not only of the USSR, but of the entire world proletariat.

In keeping with this role, architectural culture was ordered to conform to a conventional code—that of classicism—within which to develop proposals, and a well-defined *forma urbis*—radial, concentric - within which to design "Squares and main roads"[17]. It should also be added that in this context there were two new themes for Moscow - the construction of the riverfront and the subway system.

On the organisational level the design of the city was divided among a certain number of *Ateliers of urban architectural design* within the Mossovet[18], under the supervision of different masters from different generations, including Mel'nikov. During the second half of the Thirties, after the definition of the regulatory plan of 1935 that organised, in a coherent design, many of the proposals developed by the ateliers of the Mossovet, Mel'nikov was 'fired', so to speak, and removed from the scene due to a lack of commissions. In the two-volume publication that contains the projects developed by the various ateliers, in the section on atelier N. 7, directed by K.S. Mel'nikov, there is an editor's note—the only such note in the entire publication—that expresses disapproval, disavowing any responsibility for the projects published, with a severe critique—formalist, inadequate, erroneous projects.[19]

This unfortunate destiny, when observed today, appears quite enigmatic: we have seen, in fact, that in principle the 'urbanistic' position of Mel'nikov was fully in line with the radial-concentric *forma urbis*[20]; at first glance, the forms of his designs in the Thirties manage to create an original equilibrium between adhesion to a classicist code, monumentalism, iconophilia (the sculptures inserted in the buildings) and adaptation to the new scale of design of the city; in his designs for the Palace of the Soviets, for Arbatskaja Square and for the Narkomtjažprom he is one of the first architects to comprehend the possibilities for design below ground level offered by the construction of the subway, inserting stations, utilising forms that grow up from below, entire parts of the underground edification. In substance, his architecture never assumes a stance of radical opposition with respect to the new themes, or at least his opposition is no more pronounced than that of other architects who continued to work later (like, for example, his ex-colleague Il'ja Golosov).

The historical documents available to us

View of the center of Moscow with works by K.S. Mel'nikov (model by A. Šadrin with E. Gončarova, A. Pankratova, A. Romanov), Arbatskaja square (1931), the Peoples' Palace (1931-1933), the Narkomtjažprom (1934), the Labor Palace (1923), the Gončarno-Kotel'niceskij riverside (1934)

to date cannot explain, in a convincing manner, the reasons behind the *affaire Melnikoff.*

The model presented here, with the reconstruction of his projects in the centre of Moscow, may offer an explanation. The model has been conceived to illustrate, with a shift of scale, the same elements of overall composition that characterize the landscapes he created in the designs for the clubs, the market and the garage (presented here with urban-scale models). In substance, having already encountered many situations that reveal Mel'nikov's sensitivity to pre-existing environmental elements—even the smallest aspects of the delicate settlement fabric of Moscow—the makers of the model have decided to represent the real Moscow of the Thirties, with its true characteristics such as relatively low density of edification, the conspicuous presence of monasteries and churches that were later demolished or removed from the urban landscape, the tangle of small streets and alleys of the historical city. The model shows how the *the snowcapped peaks* of his works of architecture function perfectly in the contrast with the surrounding fabric, and how each of the objects and complexes designed, each absolutely independent of the others, tends to reinforce the archipelago structure of the city, with independent, distinct parts capable of coexisting to give rise to a unique, heterogeneous, variegated landscape, full of contrasts, like that of the Moscow of the Twenties. On the other hand, the same works of architecture are not capable of interacting with the structure of the city outlined in the new plan: the 'ansambl' city', a unitary object constructed by means of the application of a rigid grammar of urban composition that produces redundancy and co-ordination among the various scales.

Although it still existed, physically, in the Thirties, the Moscow of the Twenties was conceptually finished, wiped off the map of the city the new plan was preparing to build. In substance, we are inclined to believe that the problem of the *affaire Mel-*

nikoff lies in a basic incompatibility between his project for the future city and the future city that was taking form.

Although Moscow continues today to display that majestic elegance, in its centre, created by the builders of the 'ansambl' city' between the second half of the Thirties and the post-war reconstruction, nevertheless in its overall structure, in its green peripheral areas, in the mingling of the landscapes created by its hilly topography, with its subways and labyrinths of underground passageways through which over five million Muscovites move every day, something of the idea of the city expressed in the quotation that introduces this itinerary seems to survive.

This is why we have decided to entitle this exhibition on the work of this master of modern architecture "K.S. Mel'nikov and the Construction of Moscow".

[1] Published in K.S. Mel'nikov (ed. A. Strigalev), *Arkhitektura moej žizni. Tvorčeskaja koncepcija. Tvorčeskaja praktika (The Architecture of My Life. Creative conception. Creative practice.)*, Iskusstvo, Moscow, 1985, pp. 136-137.
[2] In *Le bulletin de la vie artistique*, no. 11, 1925, pp. 231-233.
[3] This is the position of the scholar of the Russian landscape, historian of art and European civilisation Ivan Grevs (1860-1941). On this theme, see also the essay by D.S. Likhacev, *L'immagine della città*, in idem, *Radici dell'arte russa. Dal Medioevo alle avanguardie*, Milan 1991, pp. 331-357.
[4] On the literary documentation of the image and nature of Moscow in the Thirties see the essay included herein by M. Meriggi, *Moscow 1922-1929. Urban landscape and city management.*, and its notes.
[5] On this subject see the essay included herein by Ju. Volčok, Ju. Kosenkova, *Moscow 1922-1929. The New Moscow Plan.*
[6] For an iconographic source see the illustrations to the essays included here by Ju. Volčok, *The Muscovite competitions of the 1920s*, and by M. Meriggi, *Urban landscape*, cit.
[7] In an imprecise translation the term means *suburb*. On this subject see the note no. 19 in the essay included here by M. Meriggi, *Urban landscape*, cit.
[8] The typical settlement of the Russian and Slavic countryside in general, with a very widespread bibliography. For a synthesis see the chapter *"L'abitazione"* and the relative sources in the volume by E. Gasparini, *Il matriarcato slavo. Antropologia culturale dei protoslavi*, Sansoni, Florence, 1974, pp. 115-166.
[9] The term utilised here—*ansambl'* (ensemble), the phonetic Russian transcription from the French—, is used here in the Russian form because in the artistic disciplines, and in architecture in particular, it has taken on a specific, more complex meaning, coming to identify a particular compositional procedure based on co-ordination and repetition; the literature on this

theme is very widespread; the reader can refer to the doctoral thesis of M. Meriggi (prof. G. Canella), *Affabulazione e montaggio. Il progetto dell'angelo e del diavolo nella città e nell'architettura russa e sovietica*, IUAV, Venice, 1996 and the essay by M. Meriggi, *Viaggio in Russia*, in idem (ed.) , *Viaggio in Russia*, monographic issue of the magazine *QA*, no. 21, 1998, pp. 8-21.

[10] A precise reconstruction on the functioning of the building is included here in the profile on the model of the Garage Bakhmetvskij prepared by O. Máčel and R. Nottrot. Also see the essay included here by O. Macel, *The indoor car park as a commission.*

[11] On these characteristics see the essay by P. Muratov, "Krasota Moskvy" (The Beauty of Moscow), in *Moskovskij ežegodnik*, 1909, 10 october, pp. 49-56.

[12] A reconstruction of the characteristics of this quarter of Moscow is found in the profile included here on the *Club Rusakov. Sokol'niki district historical development* prepared by Ju. Volcok and E. Nikulina.

[13] For iconographic reference see the illustrations included here in the essay by M. Meriggi, *Urban landscape,* cit.

[14] See the essay included here by M. Meriggi, *The 'Green City'*.

[15] This is the form assumed by Moscow with the plan of 1935 and the post-war reconstruction. On the concept of the *ansambl'* see note 9. On the characteristics of the Soviet '*ansambl' city*' see, in particular, the volumes by A. Bunin, M. Kroglova, *Arkhitekturnaja komposicija gorodov (The architectural composition of the city)*, Moskva, 1940 and Ju. A. Egorov, *Ansambl' v gradostroitel'stve SSSR (The ansambl' in urban planning in the USSR)*, Moskva, 1961.

[16] See T. J. Colton, *Moscow. Governing the socialist metropolis,* Belknap and Harvard, Cambridge - London, 1995.

[17] This is the title of one of the chapters of the manual by A. Bunin, M. Kruglova, *Arkhitekturnaja komposicija*, cit.

[18] On this subject see the essay included here by Ju. Volcok, *Moscow 1932-1940 The Architectural Planning Workshops of Moscow City Council (MOSSOVET).*

[19] *Ibidem.*

[20] This can also be seen in the proposal he developed in a consultation requested from the leading architects of Moscow on the theme of the city's urban form, published as a response to an investigation by the magazine *Kommunal'noe khozjaistvo* (The municipal economy), no. 6, 1929, pp. 24, 31.

The Indoor Car Park as a Commission

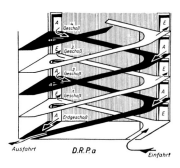

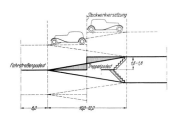

G. Müller, double spiral ramp in the "Garage for a large city" in Berlin, 1937; scheme and section

Despite the avant-garde's fondness for and adoration of cars in the twenties, indoor car parks play no part of any significance in the work of modern architects. Seemingly this sort of commission had little appeal. The only two recognised examples, Auguste Perret's Renault garage in the Rue Ponthieu in Paris (1905) and Matté Trucco's Fiat factory in Turin-Lingotto with the test circuit on the roof (1926-1928) were not really indoor car parks at all. The Fiat factory, with its ramp, most closely resembled an indoor car park.

Mel'nikov's works, which included five garages, remain an exception. Indoor car parks as a distinct building type hardly appear in histories of modern architecture, which makes Mel'nikov exceptional in another way, largely because of the expressiveness of his car park designs. Although indoor car parks had already been designed and built before the First World War, it seemed that their architectonic quality was such that there was no reason to include them in any of the histories of architecture. Given this lack of interest, the attention that engineers have paid to the subject is quite disproportionate. A possible example is the project for an indoor garage on the Saldenstrasse in Berlin-Charlottenburg, carried out by Luckhardt & Anker. The project was treated in detail in Georg Müller's German publication on garages (1925), but hardly at all in A.

Wendschuh's monograph on the Luckhardt brothers.[1] The next design for an indoor car park by the same architects–the Wender garage in Berlin–was of greater architectonic interest, and was given appropriate attention in the Luckhardt monograph, though in 1925 Georg Müller dismissed it as already outdated.[2]

The development of indoor car parks is inseparably linked with the growth in the use of the car, so that it is hardly surprising that most patents relating to indoor car parks come from the United States. Ever since the First World War the problem of parking in major cities has led to the idea of storing cars in separate buildings. It is likely that one of the first multi-storey car parks in continental Europe was the Bellevue garage in Berlin Moabit. This garage was five storeys high and had a capacity of 200 cars parked on six levels (including the basement).[3] The vertical construction is typical of indoor car parks in large cities; single-storey garages at street level take up too much space, and are mainly used for buses, trams and lorries. These kinds of car sheds or depots for public transport vehicles were built in practically all large towns.

Garaging Systems and the Appearance of the Indoor Car Park

The biggest problem with an indoor car park constructed vertically is what do

about the differences in level. There are two main solutions, a lift or a ramp. Both solutions probably go back the same length of time and were applied from the time that indoor garages first began to appear: even the Bellevue garage in Berlin had a lift. Sometimes the two systems were combined (e.g. G. Müller's Bondy garage in Prague, 1928). There are a number of versions of the lift system using mobile bridges or turntables (Rota-floor), but these are less important when considering Mel'nikov's indoor car parks because the Russian architect never used lifts in them. The ramp system also comes in a number of versions: the single straight or spiral ramp, the double spiral ramp, the Josline ramp and the d'Humy ramp. With a single ramp, ascending and descending vehicles use the same route. With a double spiral ramp, completely separate circuits are provided for ascending and descending traffic. The first time this system was applied was in 1924 in the Postgarage in Budapest. The Josline ramp somewhat resembles the previous example, but keeps the traffic on each floor at the same level, with an inner ramp for departing traffic and an outer ramp for arriving traffic (e.g. the Motor Mart Garage, Boston, 1926-1927). Easily the most frequently applied system was the d'Humy ramp, named after the Belgian F.E. D'Humy, a resident of the United States. His system

involved two carriageways constructed in such a way as to be separated vertically by half a storey. This system is efficient and easy to apply to a variety of different floor layouts. The application of these kinds of ramps has led to a great variety of constructional techniques for building indoor car parks. The capacity the car park is intended to have, the shape of the available plot and the shape of the ramp and the way it is integrated into the structure as a whole, could provide a basis for further categorisation.[4]

For single level car parks the only things that matter are the horizontal circulation and the way they connect with the surrounding streets. The way they connect can make it possible to have several entrances and exits, so making better use of the available floor area and allowing internal traffic to follow a more straightforward route and move more quickly (separation of traffic flowing in different directions, limitation of turning manoeuvres etc.).

Before the Second World War indoor car park architecture had a heterogeneous appearance. If their exteriors were not completely utilitarian, they reflected the architectural conventions of the time for commercial buildings ranging all the way up to the skyscraper (e.g. the Kent garage in New York). Sometimes car parks formed part of a building with a different

E. Bagetti, Automobile House in Rome, 1928; view of the building

View of the double spiral ramp

purpose, such as a department store or an office, which made them architectonically subordinate to the whole. Nor should it be forgotten that civil engineers were the ones who generally took the lead in designing indoor car parks, and if an architect was involved it would only be as the designer of the external elevations. This even happened to Mel'nikov on two occasions. Yet there are exceptions. The Wender garage (1924), by the Luckhardt brothers and Anker, mentioned above, was a homogeneous design in which the ramps determined the form of part of the external elevation. Another striking example was Laprade and Bazin's Citroen garage in the Rue Marboeuf in Paris (1929). This was an example of a modern structure with a transparent glass frontage that was bound to attract the attention of passers-by, and was a conscious attempt by Citroen to present its cars as a modern and advanced means of transport by providing them an architectural setting which was itself modern and advanced.[5] A few other designs, such as Jan Greve's Torengarage in Den Haag (1928-30),[6] Hermann Zweitgenthal and Richard Paulick's Kant garage in Berlin[7] (1930) and Eugenio Miozzi's Autorimessa in Venice (1935),[8] can serve as examples of indoor car parks designed with some attention to architectonics. Sometimes indoor car parks illustrate the different directions in which architecture is moving in a single country. So for example the Venetian Autorimessa was designed in the spirit of Italian rationalist architecture, with no ornamentation whatsoever. The ramps are accentuated by transparent vertical side walls contrasting with the horizontal elevations containing the parking places. As against this E. Bagetti's Casa dell'Automobile in Rome[9] (1928), now demolished, looked like an eclectic palazzo, that could equally well have housed a completely different activity. But the mock historic frontage concealed a double ramp constructed in reinforced concrete.

Mel'nikov's Car Parks

It is probably an accident that Mel'nikov became a 'car park specialist', triggered by the commission given to him by the city of Paris in 1925. This precedent gave Mel'nikov the courage to start another–successful–indoor car park project on his own initiative, a year later in Moscow. This made him an indoor car park specialist. In the literature on Mel'nikov references to these projects properly draw attention to his extraordinary architectural vocabulary. Apart from general approval[10] little is said about the principle underlying his garages, so that it is not easy to make a proper comparison and judgement of Mel'nikov's solution against other projects.

Mel'nikov designed a total of seven car park for five different locations, four of which were actually built. His work included two different versions of an indoor car park in Paris (1925), a municipal bus depot for Leyland buses (1926-1927), two versions of a garage for goods vehicles (1926-29) and frontages for indoor car parks for Intourist (1933-1936) and Gosplan (1934-1936)[11], all in Moscow. The Gosplan garage is not included in this exhibition. In 1927 Mel'nikov submitted an application for a patent on a parking system. The essential feature of the application was the traffic flow in a single level car park. Cars would drive in through the entrance and park next to one another in a row. Subsequent rows would have the same width as the first but would always be separated from one another by traffic lanes. On departure the cars would never need to reverse but would always be able to drive off in the direction of the exits, which were located at an angle of approximately 127 degrees to the parked cars. The number of rows would have to be the same as the number of entrances. The scheme was identical to the one used in his design for the bus depot on the Bakhmetevskaja ulica in Moscow. The patent application was rejected.[12] The reasons for the rejection are not known, but the most usual reason is that the patent office finds that the subject of the application is not patentable or that the invention is not original.

[1] For Luckhardt & Anker's car park project, compare G. Müller, *Grosstadt-Garagen*, Berlin 1925, pp. 98-103 and A. Wendschuh (ed.): *Brüder Luckhardt und Alfons Anker. Berliner Architekten der Moderne,* Berlin 1990, p. 297.

[2] A. Wendschuh, *op. cit.*, pp. 196-197; G. Müller, *op. cit.*, p. 52. The older Luckhardt monograph only mentions the Wender garage (U. Kultermann, *Wassily und Kans Luckhardt. Bauten und Entwürfe*, Tübingen 1958, pp. 52-53).

[3] M.E.H. Tjaden, "Het garagevraagstuk in de grote steden" (The problem of garaging in major towns), *Het Bouwbedrijf*, 1927, p. 328. Tjaden was director of the Building Inspectorate, Amsterdam.

[4] For ramp systems and the various constructional approaches to multi-storey and single level car parks, see G. Müller, *op. cit.*, 1925; G. Müller, "Het garage-probleem in de grote stad" (The problem of garaging in city centres), *Het Bouwbedrijf*, 1929, no. 15, pp. 291-298 (lecture by G. Müller, translated by M.E.H. Tjaden); H. Conradi, *Garagen*, Leipzig 1931 (Kleingaragen, Hallengaragen, pp. 5-87, Großgaragen, pp. 5-104; in the series *Handbuch der Architektur*, IV, 2e Halfband, Heft 6a en 6b); G. Müller, *Garagen in ihrer Bedeutung für Kraftverkehr und Städtebau*, Berlin 1937.

[5] Although this garage is more a showroom for a car dealer, it has the characteristics of a car park. The building made a great impression at the time. In his book Maurice Casteels gave the illustrations of this garage the subtitle *Gebäude wie dieses können späteren Zeiten einen Begriff von unserer Zivilisation geben. M. Casteels: Die Sachlichkeit in der modernen Kunst*, Paris-Leipzig 1930, p. III. See also S. Giedion, "Architecte et construction, reflexions à propos du magasin d'exposition Citroën, rue Marbeuf", in *Cahier d'Art*, 1929, pp. 475-481; H. Conradi (Großgaragen), *op. cit.*, pp. 31,32,54; G. Müller 1937, *op. cit.*, pp. 135, 143, 145, 174, 263.

[6] R.L.A. Schoemaker, "De grote-stads torengarage in den Haag" (The city centre multi-storey car park in den Haag), *Het Bouwbedrijf*, 1930, no. 24, pp. 476-481; H. Conradi (Großgaragen), *op. cit.*, pp. 40-42; G.Müller 1937, *op. cit.*, pp. 117, 142; P.A.M.-Griffioen, *Herbestemming van de 'Torengarage te Den Haag'. De eerste parkeergarage in Nederland* (Rezoning of the 'Torengarage' in Den Haag. The first multi-storey car park in the Netherlands), report part 1, Research into the history of the building and the techniques used in its construction. Doctoral thesis, Department of Building Technology and Processes, faculty of civil engineering, TU Delft 1996.

[7] H. Conradi (Großgaragen), *op. cit.*, pp. 37-38; H. Johannes, *Neues Bauen in Berlin. Ein Führer mit 168 Bildern*, Berlin 1931, p. 28; G. Müller, 1937, *op. cit.*, pp. 106, 119, 122, 123, 204205, 262; R. Rave, H.-J. Knöfel: *Bauen seit 1900 in Berlin*, Berlin 1981, no. 35.

[8] U. Nebbia, "Autorimessa a Venezia", *Casabella*, 1934, no. 83; "Autorimessa a Venezia", *Architettura*, 1935, no. 1, p. 24; G. Müller, 1937, *op. cit.*, pp. 118, 119, 134, 139-142, 145, 203, 265; P. Maretto, *Venezia. Guida all'architettura del XX secolo*, Genua 1969, p. 100; S. Polano, *Guida all'architettura italiana del '900*, Milan 1991, p. 220.

[9] G. De Cupis, *La "Casa dell'automobile"*, Rome 1929; H. Conradi (Großgaragen), *op. cit.*, pp. 33-35; G. Müller, 1937, *op. cit.*, pp. 119, 134, 137, 138, 262-263; P.O. Rossi, *Roma. Guida all'architettura moderna 1909-1991*, Bari 1984, p. 53.

[10] See S.O. Khan-Magomedov, *Konstantin Mel'nikov*, Moskva 1990, pp. 103-118.

[11] Starr dated the Gosplan garage 1929; see S.F. Starr, *Mel'nikov. Solo Architect in a Mass Society*, Princeton 1978, p. 260.

[12] For the shortened original text of the patent application, see K.S. Mel'nikov, *Opisanie sistemy garaza architektora K.S.Mel'nikova*, typescript dated 15 April 1927, in A.A. Strigalev, I.V. Kokkonaki, *Konstanin Stepanovic Mel'nikov. Mir khudoznika*, Moskva 1985, pp. 181, 282.

Dietrich Schmidt

**From People's House to 'School of Communism':
Houses for Training Programs and Recreation
The Development of the Soviet Workers' Clubs**

Origins and Cultural Situation

The soviet workers' club served as the already in the empire of the Tsar existing *maison du peuple* (People's House, Russian: *Narodnyj Dom*) as a facility of cultural entertainment and recreation after every day work, and as an institution for the instruction of workmen. In the time before the revolution, education features faced especially the needs of technical instruction.[1] Immediately after the revolution the *narodnyj dom* was also to overtake the function of political agitation. It was to become, as Anatole Kopp wrote, a 'social condensor'. This is why there is a close connection to the 'Proletkult' movement of the leftist Bolsevics Bogdanov, Gor'kij and Lunačarskij. One of the aims of the 'Proletarskaja Kultura' was to change the egocentric individual of the capitalist society to a well-informed combatant for a socialist society, combining the needs of the individual with those of everybody.[2] This ideological aim of educating workmen matched a pragmatic intention in the young Soviet Union: The enormous rate of 80% analphabetism had to be lowered. This was done partially in the workers' clubs. These ideals of reforming society and education made the People's *House (narodny dom)* become a symbol of the new and better society, desired by many a progressive architect.[3]

Visions

Thus the cubo-futurists expressed their visions of international brotherhood and amicable arrangement of people in the Živkulptarkh project of the people's commissariat of education 1919-1920, called 'temple meeting point of people'. After the end of the civil war in 1922, and encouraged by the recovering economics during the NEP period, architects turned back to the real needs of the labouring class and developed a type of workers' club. There were numerous competitions and scheme projects.

Programs of the Building Type

Lenin's wife, the pedagogue Nadezda Krupskaja, had published already her programmatic article "How a workers' club should be", in 1918, in the magazine *Proletarskaja Kul'tura*. She described here the program of rooms: A hall for meetings and performances, a canteen, lavatories and closets for the working clothes, a library and a reading room, a tearoom. All this was provided also in the philanthropic *maison du peuple* of the 'ancien regime'. New, however, in the program of the socialist politician were the so called 'circle rooms' for political discussions and instructions. These rooms, by the way, were not only devoted to politics, but also to music, literature and fine arts, so the workers' club should be a political workshop and a cultural one as well. On the X congress of the KPR (B) in March 1921, the trade unions are defined as 'schools of communism' (*Škola Kommunizma*);[4] this ideological propaganda formula appeared six years later on the facade of Mel'nikov's Rusakov-club.

Progressive artists like El Lisickij had a slightly different meaning: the workers' club for them should be a workshop creating a new type of man. Its architecture was to express the new age. El Lisickij called the club a 'social power-station' respectively a 'high school of culture'.[5] Here "all periods of life of the labouring masses" should find "recreation [...] after the daily work." But the proletarians also should be "educated as collective people and their interests in life" should be "widened". El Lisickij pointed out: "The decisive moment of the club is, that the masses should be self-acting here and not congregating from outside to entertainment." (Especially this ideal, we must say, was not often realized.) El Lisickij's opinion regarding the formal shape of the workers' club was: "If the private home aims the effect of utmost Puritanism, here in the public home, the utmost luxury should be accessible for everybody."

Regarding the sociological purposes of the clubs there are differences in the opinions of the idealistic-thinking architect and of the pragmatic people's commissar Anatolij Lunačarskij. While El Lisitzkij desired: "The task of the clubs is to make men free and not to suppress them as formerly was done by the church and the state."[6], Lunačarskij claimed in 1927 not emancipation but education: "political mass work, military-patriotic, moral and aesthetic education [sic], scientific atheistical propaganda, sports and arts."[7]

The Architectural Development of the Workers' Club

According to El Lisickij we can distinguish four different categories of workers' clubs:

– smaller types in collective houses,
– clubs of factories,
– clubs of trade unions,
– clubs for villages or town-districts.

The typology of the soviet workers' club was developed mainly either by real competitions or by abstract scheme designs, so for example, projects for 500 or 1000 people. A lot of abstract projects were devoted to the metal workers, because of their economic importance in the little industrialised country. The important auditorium owed much to the typology of the theatre.

An early example of a competition is the one of the *narodny dom V.I. Lenin* 1924-1925 in Ivanovo-Voznesensk. Among the participants I.A. Golosov, Krinskij & Rukhljadev, G.G. Vegman & V.A. Krasil'nikov, and Belogrud', G.B. Barkhin's entry won the first prize. Another important competition was the one of 1925 in Leningrad for the house of culture in the Moscow-Narva-district with the participants Ščuko, Trockij, Gegello and Dmitriev; the changed project of the winner Gegello was realized in 1927 and later was called "Gor'kij Palace of Culture". Two dissimilar principles of designing evolved: on the one hand, the stereometrically differentiated sculptures of the constructivists (Pen, Golosov, Leonidov, the Vesnin brothers, Vladimirov et al.),

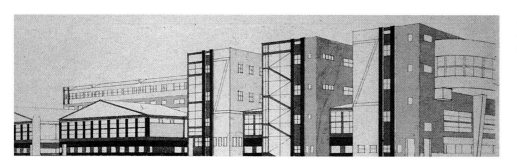

I.A. Golosov, Competition project for the "V.I. Lenin" People's Palace in Ivanovo-Voznesensk, 1924

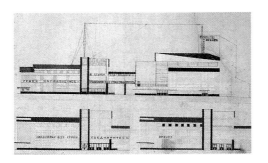

avoiding symmetrical structures, because of the dissimilar importance of the building's units depending on their different usage. Thus, this was a functionalist principle. On the other hand, the compact composition of a generally symmetrical macro-structure, preferred also by Mel'nikov, as to be seen in the Rusakov-club, the Kaucuk-club, the Frunze-club, the Pravda-club and the Gor'kij-club. In other words, two competing architectural opinions of a structure articulated by its visible functions, and one of a monumental structure articulating more the social importance of the whole building. The workers' clubs of the early Twenties often were housed in existing buildings; so for example the "Club of the Red Putilover" in Leningrad was the former Kamennij-Church, brilliantly converted by the constructivist Aleksandr Nikol'skij in 1925-1926. After 1925, the first new workers' clubs are realised, from then on arising throughout the whole Soviet Union in large quantity. As V.S. Kemenov says, in the year 1931, 34 millions of rubles were spent by the trade unions to build workers' clubs and palaces of culture.[8]

The Contribution of Konstantin Mel'nikov

The most well-known examples are the six clubs of Mel'nikov, all realised within the span of three years between 1927 and 1929, five of them in Moscow and one in Dulëvo. These clubs soon got nicknames, a clear sign of public attention; they were frequently discussed in numerous articles and books of the time in Moscow,[9] and some of them even abroad.[10] Looking for the reasons for this great reputation not only in Russia, where Lukhmanov claimed in his book about *The Architecture of the Clubs*,[11] that only Mel'nikov was able to realize a typical architecture of workers' clubs, we find two explanations: At first there is the always individual solution of his buildings. Their expressive quality of design is easily imprinted on the memory and cannot be confused with another. Secondly Mel'nikov developed new spatial solutions in the sense of El Lisickij's "transformable rooms, providing different ways of using and moving." This gives his clubs a formal quality as well as a functional one. It is this combination of emotional and rational values, the impressive designed shape and the often logical organised functions, that imprinted the Mel'nikov clubs on the collective memory of architectural criticism. So in the expressionist sculpture of the *Rusakov-club*, called by Nikolaj Lukhmanov 'the magaphone at Stromynka'[12] and often compared to Mendelsohn sketches, the inner functional elements of the building like stairways, auditoria and stage, form the outside shape. The three cantilevered auditoria could be separated from the main hall by vertically semi-revolving partitions, thus providing smaller assembly rooms. So the whole structure seems to match constructivist principles; as a lot of photographs of the

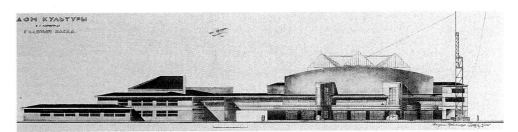

club of Mel'nikov stemmed from the constructivist Aleksandr Rodčenko, this building often was misinterpreted as an example of constructivist architecture. However, if we look upon the symmetry of the plans and the main facade, we can distinguish a more formalist aproach instead of a constructivist one. Different from the 'functional method' of constructivist designing, the symmetrical shape was primary in Mel'nikov's design method and the different rooms had to fit into this shape, so they were secondary. The prismatic structure of the shed-roofed *Frunze-club* attracted public attention by its elegant typographical layout of the facades formerly telling the purpose of the building in the eloquent way of the advertising boards of the Roaring Twenties. The contemporary critics compared its symmetric front elevation to a granary and its side elevation to an aeroplane, thus indicating the importance of industrial values for architecture.[13] Inside this small building, vertically sliding walls served to separate the first and second balcony from the parquet.

A similar construction system was proposed by the architect in the preliminary design of the *Svoboda-club*, an elliptic tube like a traditional Russian water tank put between two cubes at the ends, and thus being a piece of architecture *parlante*: The products of the Svoboda factory were rubber boots for working in the water. This symbolism, however, was not understood as it seems: The building was nicknamed 'cigar of freedom'. Its main auditorium could be divided in two by one vertically sliding wall working like a guillotine: In the centre of the building

the heavy sliding wall should be moved up and down between two lattice masts. This obviously caused functional problems in the entrance zone as the masts stood directly in front of the main doors. So in the solution of the realised version of the building, later called *Gor'kij-club*, the sliding wall was not moved vertically but horizontally. Nevertheless this functional element still articulates in the facades outside.

The system of horizontal sliding walls was also used in the *Burevestnik-club,* where the main auditorium hall could be connected with the sports hall in the back, thus enlarging the usable space. The street frontage is dominated by a four-story glass tower of five cylindrical elements, housing the circle rooms. This impressing form caused the nickname 'cage of parrot'.[14] Behind this imposing sculptural effect, the rectangular structure of the club itself becomes, aesthetically seen, less important. In both clubs a small swimming pool below the main hall was proposed by Mel'nikov, but never realised due to economic reasons and the lack of sewerage.

A major leitmotif in Mel'nikov's architectural vocabulary (consisting of primary geometric forms) is the circle, providing more than only the option of formal uniqueness; it is an outlook on the architect's understanding of the contribution of architecture to society. Mel'nikov obviously disliked the socialist kind of rationalism using rectangular cubes as devices for achieving order and discipline in the new socialist society. The system of orthogonal order for him meant, beyond the practical needs of order, also

P. A. Golosov, Competition project for a workers' club with 500 seats, 1927

regimentation and control of the individual. This was not so different from the Tsarist regime, and Mel'nikov, who was striving for emancipation and responsibility of the individual, rejected this kind of repressive order. As a result, he often used variations of this allegory of individuality, not only in his unrealised projects like the public housing projects of the Mossovet (1929), the dynamic Columbus memorial lighthouse for Santo Domingo (1929), the Frunze-military academy (1930), the Palace of Soviets (1931-1932), the Palace of Culture for Taškent (1933) or the *Zuev-club* (1929), but also in the realised ones. So, for example, in the double cylinder of his own house (1927) and in the functional truck garage at Novo-Rjazanskaja ulica (1927). By means of this functionally-organised building, we learn that not in any case the circular scheme was used only in a symbolic way.

The floor plan of the *Pravda-club* in Dulëvo is also based on circular elements: so the multifunctional stage, which can be attended from inside and outside is semi-circular and the auditorium's balcony is a full circle. This, however, restrains the visibility of the stage from the lateral seats of the balcony. Both the rounded stage building as well as the upper auditorium articulate as cylindrical elements rising above the overall flat structure of four protruding wings, featuring a human body as in Renaissance times: an "ancient device to stress the role of the individual amid Russia's dawning Cultural Revolution."[15] By this floor plan with the four symmetrically wings protruding into the natural surrounding the building is in-terlocked with the landscape. The people using this facility liked it, and according to Khan-Magomedov they nicknamed it 'star of the chemists'. And indeed the building's functional organisation was convenient, though the symmetry of the plan seems strained: the entrance embraced by two wings, called the people inside, where a clear structure without long corridors welcomed them. Nevertheless this bright structure with large windows did not match functionalist principles: so rooms of different purposes like the foyer to the left and the sports hall to the right had the same size. And the central rotunda of the upper auditorium was not of a central importance, because it was used only in case the auditorium downstairs was too small. So this building, too proves that for Mel'nikov the aspects of form were more important than those of functionality.

The esthetical order of the *Kaučuk-club* also owed much to classical features. Located at a street corner, it is erected on a sector of a circle. So on the one hand, the convexity of the main facade seems a logical answer to the urban situation. On the other hand, it articulates the bent rows of the auditorium behind it. So the building's partly circular shape is based on functional features. The strict rhythm of vertical stripes of windows from the bottom to the top and the centralised entrance[16] give the structure a somewhat classical order. The vertical pieces of wall seem like pilasters of a colossal order, but without capitals and bases. However, it was no longer the same stark neo-classical order of the doom time of the *ancien régime*[17], but it offered a wide spectrum

A. Vasil'ev, A. Ponomarova, schematic design for a type B club for workers in the metallurgical industry, 1928

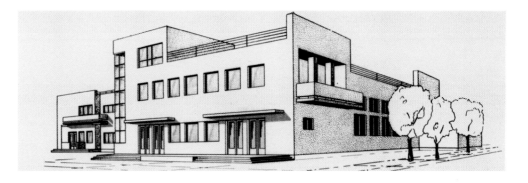

of expressionist perspectives (like the battered ramps of the entrance) and functionalist ideas as well: Not only the large windows and the roof platform are modernist features; inside the structure Mel'nikov planned, as in other clubs, flexible sizes of the auditorium providing the option of different usage. Here the proposed separation of rooms should work by moving the central floor up and down. (This technically difficult and expensive plan, however, was not realised.)

Some Constructivist Examples

All these Mel'nikov clubs belong to the second category of factory clubs. Also Vjaceslav Vladimirov's *Proletarian-club* for metal workers of 1927-1928 at the chaussee Enthusiastov (now called 'Kompressor'), Semën Pen's *Rotfront-club* for printers at Krasnoproletarskij street and Il'ja Golosov's *Zuev-club* at Lesnaja street are of this category and time in Moscow. The latter one was the result of a competition Mel'nikov had participated in, without success. All of these architects were members of the constructivist union OSA. Beside Ginzburg and Leonidov, who never actualised a workers' club, the main protagonists of constructivism were the Vesnin brothers. For Baku and its region they planned four workers' clubs, three of them being realised: in Surakhany north east of Baku 1928-1932 by Aleksandr, Viktor and Leonid; in Baku-Černygorod (the centre of oil industry) 1929 by Aleksandr and Leonid; and the *V.I. Lenin-club* in the European district Bailov on the south coast of Baku 1929-1931 by Aleksandr and Leonid. The workers' club for Stepan-Rasin-Town, planned in 1932 by the three brothers, was not built. The structures of all of them owed much to the Islamic architecture of the country with their white flat cubes around an inner courtyard; however, not imitating the traditional ornamentation of the surfaces. In Moscow, their *Dom Politkatoržan* in Vorovskij street, planned for the Union of political exiled people of the Tsar regime, could

be realised only in parts, because the union was dissolved during the building process in 1931-1935. Later on it worked as *club of actors*. All of these clubs are plain examples of the constructivist method: according to the different usage, grouped elements are built together ('con-structed'), depending on the rational organised functions; so the shape outside is defined by the functions inside. The thereby articulated architectural sculpture remains functional even if it is only a torso, as to be seen in this example.

Larger Examples – Palaces of Culture

The larger clubs are called, according to their widened program, Palaces of Culture. On the one hand, the club architecture of the socialist society now reaches the goal of El Lisickij: to provide for everybody the "utmost luxury" and "recreation after the daily work for all periods of life of the labouring masses". On the other hand, in the early Thirties a general change of the use concept becomes indicative, showing the tendency of political disengagement; emancipation and education of workmen in the sense of the *proletarskaja kultura* movement, dissolved in 1932, are disregarded as anachronism after the consolidation of the political system. The demand for a revolutionary consciousness degenerates to a mere phrase. Thus the other goal of El Lisickij lost its importance: "...that the masses should be self-acting and not congregating from outside to entertainment." Workmen contributing actively to cultural processes were disliked in the period of Socialist Realism, so the intercourse with culture degenerated to a

P. A. Golosov, schematic design for a type G club for workers in the metallurgical industry, 1928

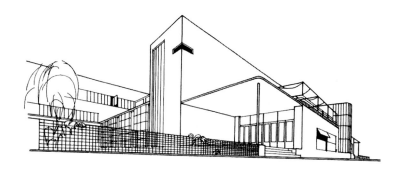

I.A. Golosov, Zuev workers' club in Moscow, 1927-29 (model by M. Ott, H. Schule, R. Schule)

Vesnin brothers, House of the former political detainees, 1931-35 (model by I. Boyd, Ch. Thum, K. Voelz)

mere reception; respectively consumption of it. The windows of the assembly rooms are closed by masonry because they no longer serve for discussions but only as a cinema. Excepting the still constructivist *Palace of Culture in the Proletarian District,* erected after a great competition in 1932-1937 on the ground of the Simonovskij monastery by the Vesnin brothers, or the *Gorbunov Palace of Culture* 1930 by Jakov Kornfel'd, the stagnant understanding of culture now becomes evident also in the architectural vocabulary.

A well-known example is the *Palace of Culture Hammer & Sickle* of 1929-1933, by Ignatij Milinis, a partner of Ginzburg. During the construction period the formerly constructivist project was adjusted to the taste of Socialist Realism: it was decorated with pseudo rustic-work, the partly open ground floor with Corbusier pilotis was closed by plastered masonry, and instead of the elegant roof platforms, the structure was covered with a hip roof behind gables. The maxim of Ginzburg, that the architect should not ornament but organize life, had been perverted.

[1] For more information about the previous history of *maison du peuple* see: D.W. Schmidt, *Der sowjetische Arbeiterklub als Paraphrase des deutschen Volkshauses,* in Schädlich, Schmidt (Red.), *Avantgarde II 1924-1937. Sowjetische Architektur,* Stuttgart 1993, pp. 76-80.
[2] A. Kopp, *Town and Revolution,* London 1970, p. 115.
[3] Cf. Bruno Taut et al. in Germany.
[4] Cf. E. Hösch, H.-J. Grabmüller, *Daten der sowjetischen Geschichte. Von 1917 bis zur Gegenwart,* München 1981, p. 46.
[5] El Lisickij, *Russland. Die Rekonstruktion der Architektur in der Sowjetunion,* Wien 1930.
[6] El Lisickij, 1929 *Rußland: Architektur für eine Weltrevolution,* Frankfurt 1965, pp. 25-27.
[7] Cf. *Great Soviet Encyclopedia,* Washington 1974, p. 326.
[8] V.S. Kemenov (ed.), *10 rabočikh klubov Mokvy,* Moskva 1932, *Introduction.*
[9] Cf. K.N. Afanas'ev, V.I. Baldin et al. (eds), V.E. Khazanova, *Iz istorii Sovetskoj Architektury 1926-1932 gg. Dokumenty i Materialy. Rabocie kluby i dvorcy kultury,* Moskva 1984.
[10] Cf. M. Ilyine, "L'architecture du club ouvrier en U.R.S.S.", *L'Architecture d'Aujourd'hui,* no. 8, 1931. pp. 17-19 and Leonie Pilewski, "Neue Bauaufgaben in der Sowjetunion", in *Die Form,* no. 9, 1930.
[11] N. Lukhmanov, cit., Moskva 1930.
[12] N. Lukhmanov, cit., Moskva 1930.
[13] V.S. Kemenov (ed.), cit., Moskva 1932, conclusion.
[14] According to Nikolaj Lukhmanov, cit., Moskva 1930.
[15] F. Starr, *Melnikov. Solo Architect in a Mass Society,* Princeton 1978, p. 163.
[16] Similar to the second variant of his Diploma 1917.
[17] Cf. his student projects of 1914-1916 and the administration building for the A.M.O. automobile factory, 1917.

Kostantin Stepanovič Mel'nikov
(1890-1974)

The works of the Soviet architect Konstantin Stepanovič Mel'nikov, which used to be the subject of fierce discussions in their time, are seen today as brilliant examples of Soviet architecture in the Twenties. Mel'nikov contributed to the design and construction of new types of building, launched numerous totally new compositional ideas, and influenced the development of modern architecture not only in Russia but throughout the world as a whole. Mel'nikov was born in Moscow on 22 July (3 August) 1890 into a working-class family, descendants of peasants from the province of Nižnij Novgorod. At the age of 13, after having spent 4 years at a local parish school, he was placed as an office boy in a firm of heating engineers called 'Trade House Zaleskij i Čaplin'. One of the proprietors—a well-known Russian heating engineer V.M. Čaplin—having noticed the artistic talent of the boy, helped him to prepare for entrance examinations to the Moscow School of Painting, Sculpture and Architecture (in 1905) and supported him later during his years of study. This same Čaplin influenced his final choice of profession by insisting that Mel'nikov continue his studies in the architecture department after he had completed the School's painting department programme in 1913. Mel'nikov was taught painting by S.V. Maljutin, K.A. Korovin, and N.A. Kasatkin. In his later work as a

painter, Mel'nikov always remained faithful to the teachings of these great masters. In architecture his teachers were F.O. Bogdanovič, S.V. Noakovskij, and I.A. Ivanov-Schitz. Mel'nikov's academic designs, carried out on actual commissions, always combined the functional aspect with the features of a particular historical design form, and were marked by the feeling for style that was emphasised by all his teachers. Even in his student days, Mel'nikov designed the facades of the AMO car factory (now ZIL), under the leadership of A.V. Kuznezov and A.F. Loleit.

In 1917 Mel'nikov received his architect's diploma. After the October Revolution, as one of the 'Twelve Masters', he joined the architectural workshop of the Moscow City Council (Mossovet) led by the 'Senior Masters' Žoltovskij and Ščusev.

Owing to the economic hardship and lack of any construction in these years, the workshop could not offer practical work to young architects, however, it provided them with a sort of further education, where they could carry out semi-didactic projects and compete in the art of graphic and technical analysis of the monuments of world architecture. During his work in the Mossovet workshop Mel'nikov drafted the plan for the Butyrka district as a part of the 'New Moscow' city plan. He also developed a project for the living quarters of the Moscow psychiatric hospital and a number of other projects. With the psychiatric

hospital project Mel'nikov bade farewell to the Classical style. Though he retained the feeling of deep gratitude towards his teachers of these years, Žoltovskij and Ščusev, his own creative career followed a new direction.

From the very first years when Soviet architecture started to take shape, Mel'nikov's creations stood out for their monumental planning and spatial solutions, an individual approach to functional usage, and his own original signature. Mel'nikov's practical activity corresponded to his own thesis: "Creation is there, where one can say: It is mine."

Mel'nikov's designs received public attention during the first major post-revolutionary Moscow competitions of 1922-1923 (model dwellings for workers' districts of Moscow, the Palace of Labour etc.). The small specialised Makhorka pavilion he designed for the first "All-Russian Agricultural Exhibition" was perceived by the public as a programme manifesto. From that time onwards the architect's work enjoyed publicity: he received interesting commissions (design for the Novo-Sukharevskij market project in 1924, among others), and, moreover, he was invited to participate in commission competitions along with acknowledged masters. In 1924-1925 he won three competitions in succession. The subjects of the competitions were: a design for the sarcophagus for the Lenin mausoleum (implemented), a

On page 84:
*Mel'nikov in his studio in 1927
(portrait by Henri Cartier-Bresson)*

*Mel'nikov in front of the stair to the
"Makhorka" pavilion, 1923*

*Mel'nikov's exhibition sector at the "5th
Triennale" of Milan in 1933*

*Mel'nikov with his wife Anna Gavrilovna in
front of his house-studio under construction,
1927*

design for the Moscow branch of the newspaper *Lenigradskaja Pravda*, and finally a design for the Soviet pavilion at the "Paris International Exhibition of Decorative Arts".

The Soviet pavilion, built in 1925, revealed a new concept in exhibition architecture. In the same period Mel'nikov constructed a complex of sales kiosks in Paris, exhibited his previous projects and designed two projects for multi-storey car parking facilities on request of the Paris city council (the daring compositional concept of one of them anticipated Western architectural thought by 30 years). In this way Mel'nikov's work became known to the international architectural community and from now on his name would arouse an unceasing interest. The architect participated in international architectural exhibitions in Warsaw in 1926, in New York in 1927, and in 1933 he was invited, along with prominent architects of various countries, to contribute an exhibition of his work to the 5th Triennale of decorative arts in Milan.[2]

In the second half of the Twenties, Mel'nikov designed a number of car parking facilities, workers social clubs, exhibition pavilions, his own house, standard apartment houses, the monument to Christopher Columbus in Santo-Domingo and many other buildings. Most of his designs during this period were implemented (four car parking facilities in Moscow, six workers social clubs in Moscow and

surrounding area, his own house, the Soviet pavilion for the exhibition in Thessaloniki, etc.). This productivity meant that Mel'nikov became one of the innovative architects of the Twenties, building far more than others did. However, a significant number of these buildings were of a temporary character.

In the early Thirities Mel'nikov proposed a number of large-scale urban development projects (the experimental recreational 'Green City'; the reconstruction of Arbat Square; the replanning of the Lužniki district, of the Central Park of Culture and Recreation (Gorkij Park) and the embankments; as well as the projects for the MOSPS Theatre, the Narkomtjazprom Building on Red Square, the Soviet pavilion for the 1937 Paris Exhibition). He also headed the Seventh architectural workshop of the Mossovet.

All Mel'nikov's works—no matter how different they were, even when they had the same function, like clubs or car parking facilities—bore common features. In the opinion of their author, the architect must not accept the functional assignment as given, without the chance to make changes. He was convinced that the specific character of the architect's profession allows it to develop and deepen the function originally described as a scheme; this creative principle nourished many of his innovative ideas. Many buildings designed by Mel'nikov have a multifunctional solution.

Since in Mel'nikov's eyes architecture was an art form with high emotional impact, he tried to use architectural forms to affect the viewer, to steer human emotions using architectural plastics, spatial solutions, volume proportions, light, and by changing the onlooker's perspective during their passage inside and outside the building.

Mel'nikov's creations are generally characterised by a dynamic expression. The architect's favourite techniques include cantilever forms, activation of diagonal axes in two and three-dimensional spaces, contrasting interpretations of same or similar forms ("symmetry beyond symmetry"), and the application of non-trivial plane and solid figures relatively uncommon in architecture (triangle, parallelogram, arc, parabola, cylinder, cone etc.). The dynamic of his designs is not only expressed in his original use of volume and space, i.e. by means of form, but also by a real and effective motion: the architect proposed to introduce rotating architectural structures (the designs for the building of *Leningradskaja Pravda*, the Columbus Monument, the MOSPS Theatre) and the transformation of interior spaces using mobile diaphragm walls (the designs for workers social clubs). In fact Mel'nikov became one of the first architects in the world to propose and develop both of these concepts. Because he regarded technology, no matter how advanced, as a mere tool in

the architect's hands, Mel'nikov created many examples of innovative spatial structures (the car parking facility over the Seine in Paris, the Svoboda factory workers social club, his own house, the pavilion for the New York Exhibition and many other projects). His works are marked by sharp artistic expression, bold and unexpected forms, and romantic inspiration. The author himself liked to give symbolic interpretation to his designs.

Although clearly an individual, Mel'nikov was at the same time a typical representative of Russian post-revolutionary art and Twenties Soviet architecture, or to be more exact, of the innovative 'Moscow school'. Owing to their revolutionary and unique individual character, the architect's works always provided rich material for the artistic debate of that era. He participated in ASNOVA (The Association of New Architects): members of this group (including Mel'nikov himself) were sharply criticised both by the Constructivists (OSA) and by VOPRA (The All-Union Organisation of Proletarian Architects) members for their preoccupation with the artistic aspects of the architectural structure and for their interest for the laws of creation and perception of architectural forms.

The revival of the Classicist legacy, which started in the Thirties, created a permanent negative attitude to Mel'nikov's designs. Though Mel'nikov's designs of this transition

period made some attempt to enrich architectural volumes, making them more plastic and decorative by introducing sculpture, ornaments and other decorative details (widely used by most architects of this time), he never returned to the principal of copying the 'eternal classical forms' he had once studied so keenly in his school years, and which the younger generation of architects was hastily trying to learn. The architect was forced to retire from designing and teaching activities. During this period he took up painting, but some years later he started teaching again.

In the post-war years Mel'nikov participated in several architectural competitions (including 'The Pantheon' in 1953, the Monument to the 300th anniversary of the union of Russia and the Ukraine in 1954, the Palace of the Soviets in 1958, the Soviet pavilion for the New York World's Fair in 1963, the children's theatre in 1967). In the same period he continued to teach, something he had done from as early as 1921 in the Vkhutemas school of architecture. He was granted the titles of Doctor of Architecture and Honourable Architect of the Russian Soviet Federative Socialist Republic. In 1965 Mel'nikov's works were displayed in a large solo exhibition.

K.S. Mel'nikov died on 28 November 1974.

Although Mel'nikov was not a frequent speaker at public artistic forums or in the media, he was not one or those architects who consider the graphic language of their profession the only means of self-expression. As early as the Twenties Mel'nikov delivered reports on topical questions to ASNOVA and INKhUK (texts have been lost). Some of his published articles included contributions to discussions organised by the magazine *Arkhitektura SSSR*. Especially significant are Mel'nikov's texts directly related to his designs: the commentaries, newspaper articles and notes published later, which have the character of a programme and an autobiography at the same time. In Mel'nikov's last years his most prominent literary work was a voluminous autobiographical manuscript.

All Mel'nikov's literary creations, like his architectural endeavours, are marked by unique thought, non-standard form, expression and polemic. His style is not a calm, impassive narration, he speaks with ardour and assertiveness, trying to capture and convince the reader. His language, which at times intentionally breaks with stereotypical usage, can be paradoxical, challenging, and sharp. Aphorisms belong to his favourite verbal tools of expression. At the same time Mel'nikov makes much use of metaphors and puns (words which sound the same but have a different meaning). The sentences sometimes contain a certain internal rhythm, emphasised by text effects applied to individual words and lines, such as a different typeface, underlining, paragraph layout and even colour-marking. All this is reminiscent of the desire "to control the eye like a musician controls the ear" inherent in Mel'nikov's architecture.

[1] Text published in the book *Masters of Soviet Architecture on architecture* (Mastera Sovetskoj arkhitektury ob arkhitekture), Moskva, 1975, vol. 2, pp. 154-161.
[2] The 5th Triennale included 12 personal exhibitions: 1 - A. Sant-Elia, 2 - Ch. Le Corbusier and P. Genneret, 3 - A. Loos, 4 - E. Mendelsohn, 5 - L. Mies van der Rohe, 6 - W. Gropius, 7 - W.M. Doodock, 8 - G. Hofmann, 9 - F.L. Wright, 10 - A. Lurce, 11- K.S. Mel'nikov, 12 - O. Perret.

The Cylindrical House-Studio of 1927

"In 1927, when I decided to build in the center of Moscow, my intention was neither to be controversial nor was it an attempt to please a way of life that all believe to have in common. It served as a personal declaration of the profound meaning such a gesture has for each one of us. A house with the inscription: ARCHITECT KONSTANTIN MEL'NIKOV.*

Our house, like a solo performance, proudly resounds amongst the confusion and clamour of the disproportionate piers of the capitol. Through a supreme sense of balance and a steadfast tension, it tunes itself in order to listen to the pulse of modernity.

I am alone, but not lonely. I am protected from the din of a great city by the inner vastness of the individual. Now I am 77 years old. I am at home and the silence attained clearly holds within its depths the memory of the distant past."

K.S. Mel'nikov, 1967

A work of absolute uniqueness for the construction scene in Moscow, the House-Studio seems to summarise the contrasting tones of Soviet architecture from the late Twenties. From this standpoint, the *cilindričeskij dom* appears, perhaps, as more innovative, while at the same time remaining faithful to the registers of urban change characterised by limited resources and independent construction, than many other well-known experiences of that time which were proposed in the name of a 'new', 'rational', 'contemporary' concept of living.

The building's conception was carried out over a long period of time and was influenced by the architect's personal experiences as well as by the profound transformation of housing concepts and organisation during the first tormented historical phase of Soviet Russia. The idea of a personal dwelling, of a house of one's own— *dlja sebja*—took shape for Mel'nikov in the early, extremely difficult, post-revolutionary years. Years that were marked, in the collective psychology, by poverty and community housing, the so-called *velikij peredel*. Terms such as 'compact' *uplotnjat'* and 'expel' *vyseljat'* became, for the majority of the population, a tragic reality.

The project's first layout foresaw a modest building with a square foundation on two levels derived from constructions which traditionally—it is said—characterised the urban Russian image. Following the *izby* building tradition, the entire composition was centred around the *russkaja peč'*, the Russian stove. Its placement impressed upon the structure the diagonal movement which would inspire the play on volumes in the tobacco pavilion at the "Soviet Agricultural Exposition" and would remain a reoccurring element in the poetry of his projects. A second version, with a circular plan, anticipated, albeit in rudimentary terms, the key to the final project. The fascination with the elementary quality of the 'circular form' and its possible derivatives was certainly not an original idea at the time. This is shown in the student research conducted in VChUTEMAS for the studios of Krinskij and Ladovskij as well as the presence of the cylinder form in Russian architecture at the beginning of the century: an example of these being the extraordinary Čaev house designed by A.P. Apyskov.

These initial ideas would find their practical expression after a few years in a general, social and economic context and the architect's personal situation would also radically mutate them. Meanwhile, Mel'nikov's career took an extraordinary turn, perhaps even unexpected, which was aided by the remarkable response to the Soviet Pavilion constructed for the 1925 "Decorative Arts Exhibition" in Paris. Starting with the commission for the Leyland bus garage on the Bakhemet'evkskaja ulica, Konstantin Stepanovič had become a forerunner in Moscow's arduous professional arena. Unlike many of his colleagues, he made no effort to pursue useful affiliations. After attaining a more solid economic position, thanks to city and the Regional Council of Unions (MOSPS) commissions, Mel'nikov had by then identified the final composition key for the House-Studio as seen in the request presented to the authority of the Khamovniceskij central district in the summer of 1927. Moving from the circular plan, probably drawn up in 1922, Mel'nikov transferred the generating element of the new variation, elaborated on between 1926 and 1927, from the 'hearth'—destined to remain a fundamental element of interior design in the form of a stove whose important mark is still visible today—to that of the overlapping couple of cylinder bodies explicitly alluding to the poles of the domestic nucleus. This solution made full use of the particular conformation of the available lot which was narrow and long. In the project submitted to the district authorities, which did not yet foresee the practicable terrace, the cylinders were of the same size. In the final lay-out the diameter of each remained the same whereas they differentiated in height. The anterior volume, dominated in the front by an impressive window which revealed and illuminated the high-ceiling of the living room (*gostinnaja*), was lower than that of the volume in the back.

This second volume was characterised by a constellation of hexagonal openings that filtered the light into different 'private' areas as well as into the studio creating an extraordinary chiaroscuro effect inside. Even the distribution of the rooms within the two cylinders illustrated the symbolic key of the composition which boasted domestic intimacy and isolation from 'the deafening noise' of the world outside. This distribution was dictated by the prevailing principle of axial symmetry and permeability. The only exception, not by chance, can be seen on the ground floor, destined, obviously, to mediate the relationship between outside and inside, between the collective space and family life. Arranged diagonally, the first cylinder contained the kitchen, the dining room, the entrance hall and a short hall providing access to the bathroom, the children's playroom and his wife Anna Gavrilovna's *tualetnaja komnata* which were located in the volume at the back where the sleeping quarters were housed on the second floor. More than making reference to the images of the American silos that fascinated the European avant-garde so much, this 'puristic' combination of cylinders could plausibly be a reference to elements in sacred architecture (if one thinks to the Cathedral of the Assumption in Vladimir). The symmetrical composition gives a classical tone which was intended perhaps to echo, although in a radically different

context but not less tormented than the situation after the 1905 revolution, certainly not in the forms, but the underlying intentions of the project for the second Šekhtel' house. Equally noticeable, on the other hand, are the similarities with the 'monumental' cadences from another work by Šekhtel': the Derožinskaja House on Kropotkinski jpereulok. The relationship between innovation and tradition appears in all remaining aspects of the work interested in constructing an active dialogue with that 'modernity' towards which the 'avant-garde' articles and projects pushed in order to amplify the radical

slogans of the Soviet cultural 'revolution'. The "innovative" structural solutions were interestingly described by Nikolaj Lukhmanov in the article he inaugurated in the pages of *Stroitel'stvo Moskvy* (no. 5, 1929) providing a comparison of opinions on *cilindričeskij dom*—an original interpretation of the brick wall. Konstantin Mel'nikov arrived at such solutions working with traditional building techniques that were still being used and which were derived from uses dating from the distant past. Nor is it of little importance that the architect attempted to probe into the meaning of 'social' through the

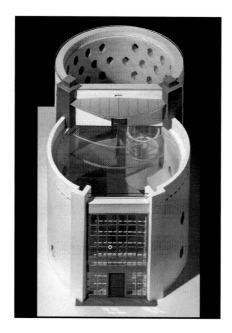

View of the model
(realised by E. Baglione, 1998)

solutions carried out in the project for House-Studio. Urged on as he was by the debate on mass housing taking place in the Soviet press, he developed two proposals for collective housing based on different combinations of cylindrical bodies. In one of the solutions the idea of a sequential placement of the volumes on a circular plan was taken up again. This had already been seen in the project for the Zuev Club and then later, between 1931 and 1932, it was further developed in the competition for the Frunze Military Academy in Moscow. Although these projects were not carried out, the idea of the Cylinder House, by itself, was developed further in the early Thirties. In fact, the architect Kalmykov presented his ideas in *Arkhitektura SSSR* (no. 5, 1933), the new journal from the Union of Architects (SSA) which had just been founded after the break up of various professional associations. Among the series of hypothetical solutions were prefabricated houses based on a circular plan with hexagonal openings designated for the "settlements of people in central Asia." Although the unfolding debate about Soviet architecture excluded any kind of urban development, that just a few years prior would have been considered feasible in Moscow, the experimentation which had thus far been carried out was proposed again for the forced industrialisation of the USSR. This was directed primarily towards the remote Soviet territories in

the east where collectivism was favoured.

Introducing Kalmykov's article, A. Bunin affirms, without mentioning Mel'nikov, that "the questions raised—the construction of buildings using local materials within a seismic zone, issues regarding the settlement plan in both industrial and agricultural areas and the ideas of a national architecture—contribute in making this first phase of design for new types of housing extremely valuable..." The building characteristics and the context out of which his projects developed was to heighten the contrasting opinions which were provoked in architectural circles. Some analysed and observed his work precisely because of its 'demonstrative' nature—this being an 'individual' characteristic which would also, through typological and building choices, delineate a socially acceptable course of action in a phase marked by the growing need for housing. At the same time the work became the object of heated criticism from certain avant-garde circles where the basis and purpose of all research about housing could only be collective in nature and whose developmental trajectory was tied to the undisputed dominion of the industrial process. While Lukhmanov's 'villa-house' in Krivoarbatskij aroused "particular interest", A. Karra and V. Smirnov gave the title "an experiment without principles" to the *cilindriceskij dom*. This was an understandable contrast

of opinions. The months when Mel'nikov started work on the job site coincided with publications in important journals like *Sovremennaja Arkhitektura* (Contemporary Architecture) and *Revoljucija i kul'tura* (The Revolution and Culture), alongside *Stroiltel'stvo Moskvy* (The Building of Moscow) which hosted a 'platform' of discussions on the House-Studio, where proposals for 'provisional' or 'community' housing increased and the 'type solutions' for 'collective' living were compared. It is not surprising, therefore, that the work, for its many 'innovative' aspects on the level of pure spatial conception, came to be seen as having a conservative approach with respect to projects like the *Perekhodnyji dom* of Narkomfin-NKF of M. Ginzburg, I. Milinis and S. Prokhorov, or even the impressive *Dom-kommuna* of M. Baršč and V. Vladimirov designed for the Strojlom of RSFSR. It was oriented towards affirming 'retrospective' values and themes which, at that time, part of the Soviet avant-garde negated in the most absolute terms completely agreeing with the politics pursued by the regime.

Alessandro De Magistris

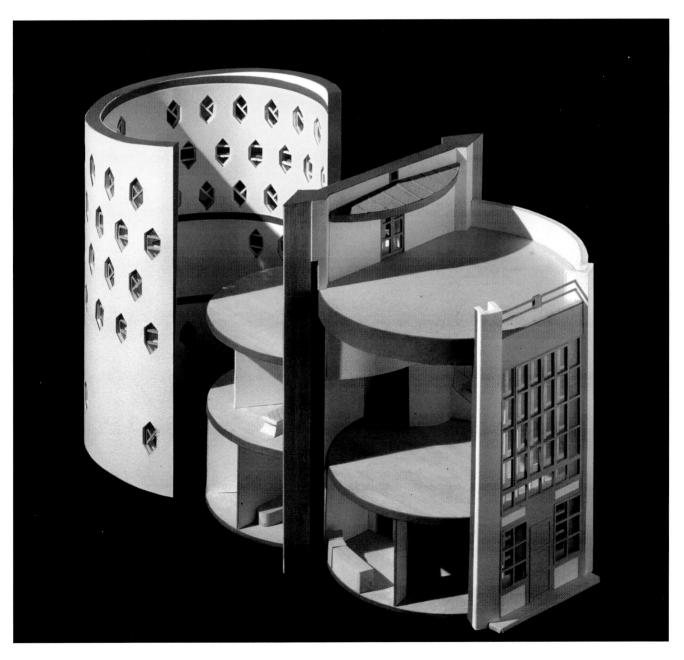

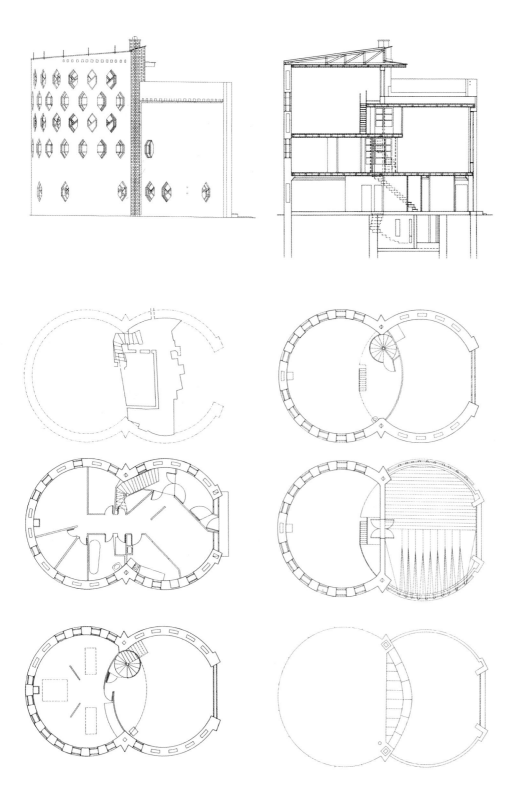

*Mel'nikov's house-studio, 1927
(taken from A. Gozak, Ju. Pallasma,
The Mel'nikov House)* scale 1:300

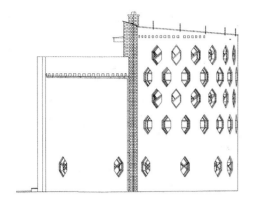

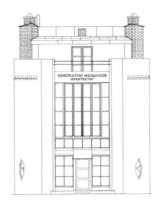

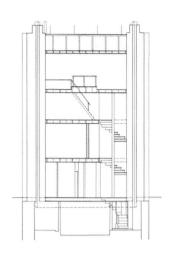

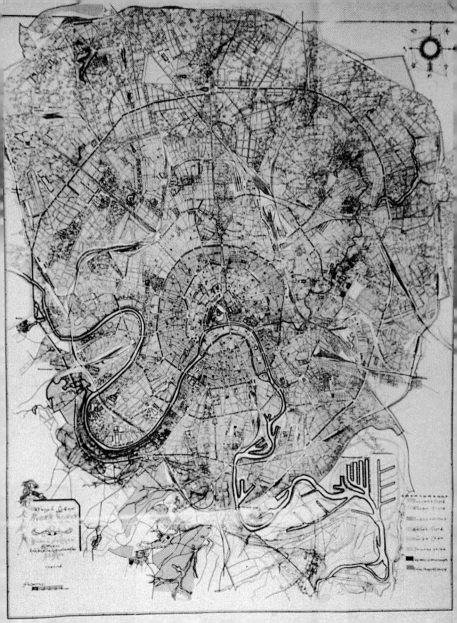

Architecture for an Urbanised Country-Side:
Moscow between the NEP and the First Five Year Plan

The 'New Moscow' Plan

A characteristic trait of the late twentieth century has been the close attention paid both to the social history of Russia and to her urban construction history with regard to the large and small historical towns, to the historical-cultural value of the municipal fabric, to the prognostic planning potential of building on historical territories, and to the possibilities of their preservation and reconstruction.

In 1997 Moscow marked its 850th anniversary. This event naturally sharpened interest in the city's historical-architectural heritage. Moscow's city organism has been built up over the centuries as an irregular, logically planned system organically linked with the city's topography. Having arisen in the area between the rivers Moskva and Neglinnaja, the city gradually acquired a complex, branched structure in the course of the centuries. However, its basic individual character has been preserved: the combination of ring roads, which appeared in the place of former fortifications, and radial roads, which converged on the main and dominant architectural feature—the Kremlin.

The Kremlin is the architectural centre; it dominates the whole territory of the Belyj Gorod (White city) and Moscow beyond the river; on the periphery of the city it was supported compositionally by ensembles of monasteries around which were united significant 'knots' of city building. The large-scale hierarchy of this multi-centred system was complemented by a multitude of small suburban centres. The whimsical picturesqueness of Moscow's city landscapes in the eighteenth century was tactfully complemented by classicist ensembles which did not destroy the fabric of the city but only underlined the "unity of stylistic variety" so characteristic of Moscow. In the first half of the nineteenth century Moscow was still to a large extent able to conserve its patriarchal character, including in itself spacious areas of flower and vegetable gardens. But already within a few decades it had changed beyond recognition, having entered the ranks of the greatest cities of the world and occupying the eighth place in speed of growth. The intensive building of railways, factories, mills and profit-making houses significantly changed the face and the structural lay-out of the Russian capital.

The expansion and building of the city in this period often took place without the participation of planners or city architects, but only on the basis of commercial considerations. There was no common blueprint for the reconstruction of Moscow. The city authorities bought up private plots and houses to straighten out and broaden the roads, a process that dragged on for decades. Industrial and workers' regions did not, as rule, correspond to sanitary norms, and the problem of transport became more and more urgent. In 1911-1912 the city Duma made attempts to solve these problems. Several variations of projects for a metropolitan line were worked out, and a plan was accepted for the building of twenty housing estates within the city limits for the settlement of 36,000 workers. The realisation of these undertakings was hindered by the outbreak of the First World War.

In spite of the unregulated nature of the approach to problems of city administration, in pre-revolutionary Russia there was an active development in the science of urban construction, which increasingly involved the adjacent spheres of transport, water and canalisation, sanitation and hygiene, planting with trees and gardens, etc. At the beginning of twentieth century quite a powerful and self-sufficient school of urban construction thought was created. It put forward a number of major theoreticians, such as V.N. Semenov, L.N. Benua, I.A. Fomin, M.G. Dikarskij, G.D. Dubelir, etc. In their works the city was interpreted as a complex social organism, which existed in inseparable connection with the particularities of territory and landscape. Special attention was devoted to the problem of the growth of the city, the increasing role of the suburbs, the transport system and the planting of trees and gardens. Russian city-builders had their own reading of the ideas of the English theoretician,

On page 96:
AV. Ščusev, "Novaja Moskva" plan, 1923

View of the city from the Sparrow Mountain, early Thirties

View of the city towards the southeast, with the Slaughterhouse in the foreground, 1914

AV. Ščusev, Plan for the Khamovičeskij district, 1922

E. Howard, on garden cities. First of all, they were attracted by the idea of the elastic plan, which permits the perception of the city as a continuously developing organism. In reaction to Howard's schema, V.N. Semenov came to the idea of the multi-centred city, to the understanding of the city as a single, harmoniously functioning organism. Also not without importance for the Russian city-builders were questions of urban aesthetics, and the importance of including architectural monuments in construction.

Thus the revolutionary government which came to power in October, 1917 had a significant base in the theory of urban construction for the realisation of its grandiose plans for the transformation of cities in accordance with the task of building a society that would be in principle new. It seemed that the abolition of private possession of land, the nationalisation of industry and the removal of the social stratification of the population would finally permit the avant-garde ideas of world urban construction thought to be realised in life. Besides, this was a task of exceeding complexity insofar as everything was changed: the bases of social organisation, way of life, familial-legal relations, clothing, tastes, aesthetic preferences. One of the most important professional tasks for architecture became that of catching certain viable tendencies in the confused representations of the

future and giving them the opportunity to develop.

The first post-revolutionary years were marked by an enormous upsurge of interest in urban construction, and in a very varied range of contrasting suggestions—from idyllic little houses surrounded by nature to fantastic settlements hovering in the air. New aesthetic ideas were worked out, in particular, in projects for the festal decking-out of cities. This was done with the active participation of the most outstanding architects and artist. The most evidently basic tendencies of this time in the reconstruction of existing cities can be discerned in the project for the re-planning of Moscow. The elaboration of this plan began already in 1918 in a specially created workshop attached to the Moscow Soviet. The workshop was led by the recognised authorities of pre-revolutionary architecture—the academic I.V. Žoltovskij and A.V. Ščusev. K.S. Mel'nikov co-operated with this workshop, together with such masters as S.E. Černysev, N.V. Dokučaev and N.A. Ladovskij.

The workshop had as purpose the elaboration of a plan for the reconstruction of Moscow, taking into account the new social bases of the construction of life. In the first studies, created in the summer of 1918, there were already apparent those principles which later became the basic content of the 'New Moscow' plan: this was the joint work of urban architects and engineers,

transport workers and power engineering specialists; the striving to abolish the contrast between the centre and the suburbs; the creation of new blocks with beautiful, hygienic living quarters; the planting of trees and gardens in the centre; and the removal of factories, mills and dumps beyond the borders of the city. The territory of the city was clearly divided into industrial, commercial and sports zones, and residential garden cities. Thus the new administrative centre was planned to be on the Leningradskoe sosse. Zarjad'e represented the commercial centre, Khamovniki region—the educational centre, and Vorob'evy hills—the sports zone. The basic industrial zone with the port and workers' settlements was placed on the south-eastern border of the city.

In the project for the re-planning of Moscow, the Kremlin was given the role of a museum and the main historical centre of the city. The image of the new Moscow was not imagined by the authors without the active inclusion of architectural monuments into the new construction. The project was often criticised for its 'museum' approach to the reconstruction of the city, but the architects' position remained unbending. Replying to criticism, A.V. Ščusev wrote in 1925: "It is necessary to fight against the old structures, but amidst the old rubbish we must also be able to see what is valuable, so that it should not perish together with the rubbish."

P.A. Golosov, Plan for the Suščevsko-Mar'inskij district, Twenties

N.Ja. Kolli, Plan for the Rogočeskogo-Simonovskij district, 1920

L. Lisickij, Scheme for the center of Moscow with the localization of the 'Horizontal skyscrapers' system, 1924

L.M. Poljakov, Plan for the Presneskij district, 1920

E. Norbert, Plan for the central area of the city, Twenties

"Pan-Soviet Exhibition of Agriculture and Craftsmanship" in 1923 (reconstruction by I. Khadina, 1952)

The actual value of the heritage was understood in the project of the New Moscow not only in its architectural-aesthetic aspect, but also in its urban construction aspect. The ring-and-radial plan of the capital that had evolved in the course of history was interpreted in the light of the latest attainments of the theory of city-planning. It was proposed that the development of the city in the future would not only "abrogate", but would still more emphasise its historical structure. The plan envisaged four ring motorways, three of which would be existing ring motorways broadened and reconstructed. In addition, a new 100-metre-wide ring road was planned; it would unite amongst themselves the suburbs of Ostankino, Sokol'niki, Baumanskij district, Moskvoreč'e, Vorob'evskoe sosse, Fili, Serebrjannyj Bor, Petrovsko-Razumovskoe. It was proposed that new residential areas, planned on the model of the garden cities, be placed on these territories. It was calculated that only three million people could be accommodated on the territory of the existing city, while the population of Moscow was projected to reach five million by 1950. It was proposed that the excess population be mainly accommodated in the new residential areas in the north-west, north and north-east of the city.

The main centre of Moscow was surrounded by a series of secondary suburban centres. The ring-radial plan was emphasised by large buildings for public purposes around the Sadovoe Kol'co ring and the Circle Railway with a broad ring of greenery just behind it. The park zone went from the green ring towards the centre of the city in several deep wedges. The realisation of the plan of the greening of Moscow began already in 1922-1923.

The ring motorways divided the city into zones with differing building heights, becoming lower as one went from the centre to the periphery. In the first zone seven-storey buildings were allowed, in the second—five-storey buildings, the third began to be constructed mainly with three-storey buildings, while the suburbs had one-to-two-storey buildings. However, by 1924-1925—the time when work on the project came to an end—the idea for the construction of the centre underwent some changes. The project began in the years of the civil war and collapse, when a massive outflow of people from the cities was observed. The transition to the new economic politics at the beginning of the Twenties led to an enlivening of city life and a growth in population. Therefore Moscow, too, which had originally been planned as a city of few-storeyed buildings, became somewhat larger in scale. Now, in the centre and some of the other regions, it was permitted to build isolated tall buildings placed at rare intervals amidst a great quantity of greenery. In developing the idea of the Moscow plan a 'horizontal skyscraper' project

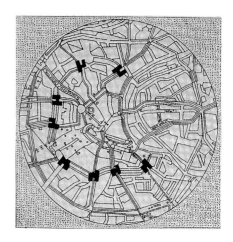

was created by L. Lisickij—large, horizontally extended building raised off the ground on three vertical supports. In placing eight such buildings at the intersections of the ring and radial motorways, the author was interpreting them as high reference points emphasising the ring-radial structure of the city. Under the 'horizontal skyscrapers' were put the metro stations, which were given the role of the main form of city transport in the 'New Moscow' plan. From the plan of the new city there began a search in Soviet architecture for solutions to the problem of the city's high silhouette; this became one of the main artistic tasks of the following years.

Although the historical centre had received considerable attention in the project for the re-planning of Moscow, nevertheless it suffered significant changes. Red Square was linked with a group of central

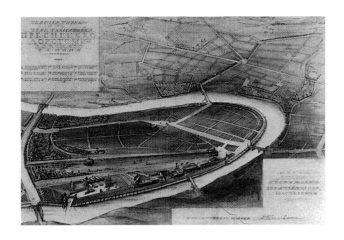

squares—Theatre Square, Revolution Square, Okhotnyi rjad, and was united by a boulevard with the square at the Rumjancev museum. Okhotnyi rjad, being built over by shops and eating-houses in a disorderly fashion, was doomed to disappear, and its place, very close to the Kremlin, it was proposed that a majestic symbol of the new life be raised—the Palace of Labour (later the hotel 'Moskva' was built on this spot). In the programme for the competition for the project of this building (1922) it was emphasised that its architecture had to blend with the existing building. A large number of projects were submitted for the competition (K.S. Mel'nikov also took part in the competition); these demonstrated a significant range of aims—from a striving to repeat the stylistic particularities of the surrounding buildings to a play of contrasts in forms and scales. The projects for the Palace of Labour, though never realised, nevertheless had a substantial influence on the whole following development of Soviet architecture, opening the theme of the mutual relationship between the city and the country's 'main building'.

Within the framework of the 'New Moscow' plan a series of other competitions were conducted: for projects for new bridges in Moscow (1920), the All-Russian stadium (the International Red Stadium) on Vorob'evy hills (1920 and 1924), the Reconstruction of Soviet Square

(1923), the planning of the All-Russian agricultural exhibition (1922-1923), the competition for projects for the overall building of zones with model houses for workers (1922), in which K.S. Mel'nikov also took part. According to the 'New Moscow' plan he also drew up plans for the Butyrka region and Khodynka field (1921-1923).

The forming of the Soviet urban construction school, whose beginning coincided with the first post-revolutionary years, was from its first days marked by several characteristic features. First of all, there was the striving for the centralisation of the administration of the urban construction process. Already in December, 1917 the Higher Soviet of

the people's economy was organised. It contained a special "Subsection of publicly useful state buildings", and in May-June, 1918 the Committee of state buildings was formed, one of whose main tasks was putting in order the building of cities on the territory of the whole country.

The second characteristic was the striving to include as much territory as possible in one urban construction plan; this striving proceeded from the opportunities to develop the people's economy by plan. The first to approach the idea of regional planning in real earnest was the architect B.V. Sakulin, who in 1918-1922 worked out a project for an agglomerate consisting of Moscow and its satellite towns, which would encircle the capital in

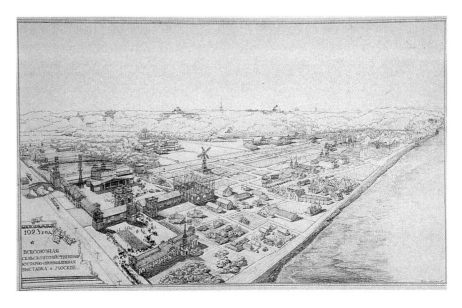

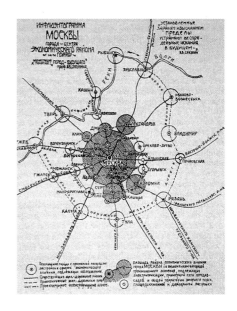

three rings. The first ring was composed of workers' settlements; it was planned to move factories and mills out there. The second ring included in itself the towns of Voskresensk, Podol'sk, Zvenigorod, Nara and others near Moscow. The third ring included Klin, Dmitrov, Aleksandrov, etc. At the expense of these towns, which would develop their own industry, the author's conception was that Moscow should be converted mainly into a scientific and cultural centre. The old city, in B.V. Sakulin's opinion, was a closed city in the social and territorial senses, and its separate parts did not mesh well with each other. The city of the future would be an open system with practically limitless possibilities of development. Sakulin applied the same system of greening the city as in the 'New Moscow' plan—a broad green strip beyond the Circle Railway, with broad wedges entering into the centre of the city.

Externally, Sakulin's Moscow agglomerate system was reminiscent of E. Howard's conception, but, as the author himself pointed out, its aim was different. Howard's scheme was hostile to the great city, but here a system was envisaged giving influence to the great city ('influentogramma') and the opportunity to relieve it; it was a scientifically based system for the development of the great city. In correspondence with the scientific spirit of the time in Russia, Sakulin's urban construction theory would

contain attempts to apply mathematical methods for the harmonious construction of space in the project for the Moscow agglomerate. In particular, he created a model tracing out Moscow's motorways and a project for the capital's metro on this foundation. After the First World War, the first regional planning schemes were worked out in England, Germany, France and Holland. However, one of the biggest of these, the plan for the Ruhr region, encompassed only 3.5 thousand square kilometres, while B.V. Sakulin's project encompassed 90 thousand square kilometres. In 1922, on the basis of the State plan for the electrification of the country (GOELRO). B.V Sakulin published his project for settlement on the European territory of the USSR encompassing an area of one million square kilometres.

The Moscow agglomerate project was worked out four years earlier that the project for the Doncaster region created by P. Abercrombie and T. Johnson in 1922, which was considered a classic. Another characteristic of the Soviet urban construction school that had already appeared early on was its striving to find a single system of settlement and types of settlements that would universal for the whole country. This poured out into a discussion on garden cities which flared up on the pages of newspapers and magazines in 1922-1923. This discussion's

understanding of the idea of the garden city was quite different from E. Howard's schema. In the forefront were the tasks of the collectivisation of everyday life and the transformation of the garden city from an adjunct of the great city into an independent settlement. In the discussion there emerged the outlines of those vexed questions which were very fully discussed in 1929-1930 in the polemic between the urbanites and the de-urbanites. But already one could observe the tendency to abstraction with regard to the problems of urban construction, and the construction of universal schemes which bore no relation to the character and idiosyncratic particularities of each city.

The 'simple life' solutions to the task of urban construction did not fail to tell on the project for Moscow. Thus in 1925 Professor S.S. Šestakov created a project for Greater Moscow which was at first glance similar to B.V. Sakulin's, but which differed from it in the lesser degree to which the system of satellite cities was worked out, and in the schematic character of the territory of Moscow itself, which took scant account of its complex historical structure.

E. Howard's ideas, which were directed against the great city, were transferred in a mechanical way to the planning of the Russian capital. Meanwhile, building continued in the real-life city of Moscow, but in quite a disorderly fashion. A.V. Ščusev wrote

about this with anxiety in 1926: "We see haphazardness and lack of co-ordination on a massive scale only because each commissariate and each trust builds in its own way, linking and co-ordinating only the practical and economic aspects of the question."

In December, 1926 a policy for the industrialisation of the country was proclaimed; investment in building began to increase rapidly. This to a large extent facilitated the separation of the practice of the building of cities from the theoretical urban construction quest. In a social-cultural respect society was moving forward to that moment at the end of the Twenties which is habitually called in Soviet history 'the great cross-roads'. The creative tolerance which was characteristic of the post-revolutionary period was more and more replaced by ideological intolerance and tension, which in the future had a negative influence on the destinies of many architects, including K.S. Mel'nikov.

Jurij Volčok, Julia Kosenkova

The Moscow Competitions of 1922-1923

The years 1922 and 1923 were ground-breaking for the understanding of the architectonic principle of avant-garde art: in painting, in literature and in architectural creativity. These years are no less important for the formation of the urban way of life and the creation of an urban culture in the country at large, and, most importantly, in the capital.

It is not simply that Moscow's population grew rapidly from 1921 onwards; what is also important is that this growth was due to an influx of peasants who were newcomers to city life.

The third component of the new creative atmosphere of those years was the renaissance of a full-scale professional life, which embraced also the construction industry. Clear evidence of this is seen in the multiplicity of competitions in these and the following years.

The themes of the competitions, which were announced in these two or three crucial years for the future of architecture, eloquently convey the spectrum of social and professional preferences in these years. In 1922 the Moscow Architectural Society (MAO), under a commission from the Moscow Council, announced a competition "for the design of an integrated model housing estate of workers' houses." On 1 October the same year the MAS set up a special commission to elaborate the rules of a competition for the Palace of Labour, and on 24 October, in collaboration with the main exhibition committee of the "All-Russia Agricultural and Trade & Industry Exhibition with a Foreign Section", the MAS announced an open competition for the design of a general plan and of separate exhibition pavilion buildings. K.S. Mel'nikov was an active participant in all three competitions.

The sequence of these competition schemes was itself very interesting to analyse, since it reveals the logic of the realisation of the architects' creative efforts produced, on the one hand, by the new design challenges facing the profession, or, more exactly, a new social interpretation of their essence, and, on the other hand, by the need to make sensible use of highly diverse urban land: workers' districts, the city centre and a landscaped park. Even the programme of the competition contained a twofold challenge: the erection of a structure and the town-planning of the surrounding district. Thus, the competition for the design of model housing for workers had a double objective: the creation of a new type of workers' housing block and the detailed planning of two areas of Moscow designated for housing development under the 'New Moscow' reconstruction plan.

One of the two areas designated for housing development was located between the Simonov Monastery and the Kamer-Kolležskij Val in the northern sector of Lenin (formerly Simonov) Sub-district (Rogoze-Simonov district). The other is along Greater Serpukhov Street and the 1st and 2nd Scipovo Lanes (Zamoskvorečkij District).

The success of this competition -and of the subsequent competitions- was in part due to the fact that the Moscow Council's architectural

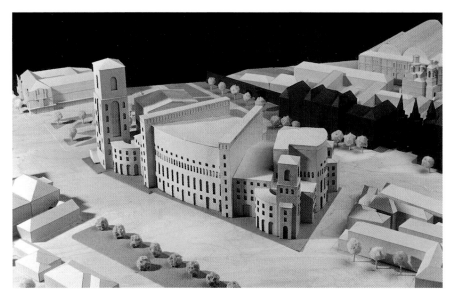

workshop, where the 'New Moscow' plan was created, and the MAS, were both under the same director, A.V. Ščusev. For this reason the staging of open competitions by a public organisation was regarded as an active way of engaging professional architects in the planning and execution of a new general plan for the city.

The competition for the design of workers' housing contained general elements which had been adopted for the Moscow reconstruction plan. For example, the ground area to be developed was not to exceed 30%—the same proportion as was stipulated in the reconstruction plan guidelines, which provided for exactly this density of development in the designated zones[1]. The competition programme specified elevations, in the Simonov zone, equivalent to 2-3 storeys, and in the Serpukhov—3-4 storeys. This was also in keeping with Scusev's ideas on the character of the development plan for Moscow and on the gradual lowering of the roofscape along the radii from the city centre outwards to the periphery, where the maximum elevation was three storeys.[2] The competition programme stipulated that the apartment-block developments should include 75% family accommodation and 25% single-person units. The estate also contained buildings for residents' meetings, an estate management office, a medical centre, a garage for three cars, a laundry-house and a

series of outhouses.

It is important to mention that the programme included the provision of a number of service facilities, both for communal house-maintenance and for social purposes. The site therefore had to be designed not only on spatial criteria, but also with social facilities provided in keeping with the new social order.

In 1924 M. Ja Ginzburg gave the following assessment of the competition programme: "The positive merit of the 'workers' model housing project' is that it has allowed the architect to think on a more modern scale. This project also incorporated an overall intention, i.e. the creation of a multiplex housing block incorporating most of the social functions in a communal plan. Thus, instead of small detached houses, yards and gardens, there was now scope for creating new estates of mass housing-blocks with huge internal courtyard-garden areas, play areas and a number of social facilities (a meeting hall, a reading room, a health centre, a nursery school, a creche and others)."[3]

The submission of designs was scheduled for 10 January 1923, and more than 50 entries were received. They generated an astonishing amount of interest. The exhibition of competitors' projects, which was staged inside the MAS building, attracted a large number of visitors and provoked discussion and exchanges of views—some of them diametrically opposed—and it was

clear that the competition appealed to much more than narrow professional interests.

A.P. Ivanickij wrote of the competition: "Russian architecture faces a new-and difficult- challenge. We must therefore expect mistakes and mishaps, disagreements and differences of opinion on seemingly uncomplicated issues. It is equally to be expected that the social side of the project should excite public interest and a thirst for more information."[4]

For their competition entries, the architects had drawn up a general plan of the site, and also some examples of dwelling units. For all their diversity, the winning designs had certain features in common. They all shared a particular zoning arrangement in relation to single and family occupancy. As a rule, the family blocks were grouped separately from the hostel-style dwellings for single persons. The buildings designated for social use are usually placed in the geometrical centre of the site, or form the centre-piece of the composition. In all the designs there is a strong emphasis on green areas.

In some of the Simonov site designs—those of L.A. Vesnin, S.N. Ridman, M.P. Parušnikov, A.S. Fufaev, and E.I. Norwert—elements of the traditional circumferential style of development have been preserved. But the majority of the designs show diversity of compositional method. The residence blocks are placed asymmetrically, leaving both wide

Competition project for the Labor Palace by A.E. Belogrud, A.A. Vesnin, I.A. Golosov, K.S. Mel'nikov, 1923 (model by A. Šadrin, A. Ermakova, A. Zolotov)

open areas and compact, intimate yards. In some designs the centrepiece is a large internal green area around which groups of residential blocks are placed: this is the solution adopted by L.A. Vesnin (the Simonov site), E.I. Norwert, (Simonov and Zamoskvorečkij sites), the Golosov brothers (Zamoskvorečkij), Belogrud' (Zamoskvorečkij, a non-prizewinning design), and in Ridman, Parusnikov and Fufaev's project (Zamoskvorečkij).

The design by K.S. Mel'nikov, which won second prize for the Zamoskvorečkij project category, is significantly different from the other entries. His three-storey serrated-plane residence blocks fan outwards from the main area, where the communal and social facilities complex is situated. Several four-storey blocks for small families stand adjacent to it, interconnected and adjoined also to the communal/social block on the first floor level by a covered walkway. S.O. Khan-Magomedov rightly considers that, since the assembly hall was the nucleus of the communal/social block, it may be regarded as Mel'nikov's first club building, and the whole complex—as one of Soviet architecture's first commune-blocks.[5]

The competition for the Palace of Labour became one of the most popular in the history of Soviet architecture. It resulted in the jury awarding prizes and commendations for 25 design projects—about half the number of entries. Unfortunately, not all the prizewinning project files were preserved, and therefore many of their authors remain unknown, the designs having been exhibited, under the competition rules, under code names.[6] In all the surviving designs there are quite elaborate plans relating to a large social facilities building; in varying degrees the entrants have integrated this with the surrounding residential development. The competition also yielded stylistically new solutions, notably in the entries by the Vesnin brothers and those of I.A. Golosov and K.S. Mel'nikov. It proved to be a rather more complex matter for the contestants to formulate their attitude to the overall town-planning intention for the central area of Moscow. For example, a contestant whose design was exhibited under code-name 'Gamma' wrote: "The designated development area, surrounded on three sides by squares and Tverskaja Street, which are fairly spoiled and lacking any overall integrity, calls for a building that is dominant, solid, compact, and in no way obtrusive by its silhouette (without large protuberances or variations of height, etc.), so as not to amplify, by its irregularities and disturbing shapes, the ugliness which we already see there."[7] In an explanatory note under the code-name 'Proletarian' we read "...the design is not intended to stand frozen

View from the Moscova at the îPan-Soviet Exhibition of Agriculture and Craftsmanshipî in 1923 with, on the right, the îMakhorkaî pavilion by K. S. Mel'nikov

View of the Novo Sukharevskij market by K. S. Mel'nikov, 1924

View from the Moscova of the MOGES thermal energy plant (I. Zoltovskij, 1928-29, photo by A. Rodcenko)

Detail of the power plant

in time, but so as to reach forward, with all its parts, towards the prominent main entrance, the main mass of which moves, as it were, towards the central tower, and the whole building tends dynamically from the Kremlin toward the city, its entrance facing towards Theatre Square."[8]

Apart from Mel'nikov's design, the town-planning model replicates the competition entries of the Vesnin brothers, Golosov and Belogrud', and this enables us to perceive graphically the diversity of approaches towards architectural interpretation of Moscow's historical town-planning heritage in the early Twenties.

The competition for the construction of the "All-Russia Agricultural Exhibition" is also directly linked to the elaboration of the 'New Moscow' plan. It may be seen as an example of the merits of town-planning.

The competition to design the exhibition was directly connected with other works involved in the reconstruction of Moscow: "One should mention the programme of large-scale work which will unfold in the immediate future," A.V. Ščusev wrote, "namely: 1) the rebuilding of the worn-out Crimea Bridge, 2) the Moscow River bridge along Titov Avenue, whose function will be to complete the circular tramline route C, bringing to life the run-down riverside part of Khamovničeskij district on the left bank, and finally, two bridges beside the Bab'egorsk

dam across the Strelka which close the tramline route A circuit. All three works are fully part of the proposed renewal plan for Moscow, and for this reason the city of Moscow stands to gain enormously from the construction of Exhibition Moscow."[9]

According to the All-Union Central Executive Committee's decree of 19 October 1922, the possible venues for the Moscow exhibition were: "the square of allotments near the Crimea Bridge, the area of part of a garden adjacent to the Golicyn Hospital, and the whole area of the Neskučnyj Garden." The choice of venue was undoubtedly influenced by the Moscow reconstruction project, which had by then entered its final planning stages.

The site was located right on that green wedge of land which links Neskucnyj Garden with the city centre. While the other sites earmarked as probable exhibition venues—Sokol'niki, Petrovsko-Razumovskoe—already boasted large numbers of trees, the Neskučnyj Garden area was nothing more than a dumping ground near which stood two unfinished apartment blocks and the 'Bromley' plant.

Thus, a large area of the city became green and pleasant during the construction of the exhibition.

The competition programme incorporated the idea of a functional connection between separate groups of pavilions, their logical organisation, and also the need to take account of

the relief of the designated site. The deadline for submission of entries was 24 November 1922.

In parallel with the open competition, designs for the general plan were commissioned from P.A. Golosov, I.A. Žoltovskij, I.A. Fomin, S.E. Černysev and V.A. Ščuko.

The competition programme expressed clearly the social orientation of the exhibition, and how greatly it differed from its pre-revolutionary antecedents at home, as well as from contemporary ones abroad. The main idea behind the exhibition was to promote the nascent socialist agriculture, the progressive developments in agricultural buildings, and the exchange of professional experience. The exhibition was to have represented literally all branches of agriculture and the crafts industry. It was no accident that the scientific education pavilions became its centrepiece. The programme also placed heavy emphasis on questions of cultural education; a theatre and a cinema screen were included into the design. The main visitor to the forthcoming exhibition, the peasant-farmer, must be able to gather from it not only particular knowledge, but also an idea of the diversity of the cultural life of the capital.

In the first half of December the jury examined both the competition entries and the commissioned designs (with the exception of the design by I.V. Žoltovskij, which was not

submitted), and concluded that not one of them was capable of implementation. Early in January 1923 Žoltovskij's draft was accepted as the basis for the general plan.[10]

The designs for the "All-Russia Agricultural Exhibition" are representative of the leading trends in Soviet town planning which had emerged by the middle of 1922. First and foremost it highlighted the clear differences between the Petrograd and Moscow schools of town planning. All the Petrograd architects—V.A. Ščuko, I.A. Fomin, N.E. Lanser and A.A.Ol'—demonstrated in their designs a striving towards an ensemble style of planning, symmetry of composition, and strict academic monumental forms.

The Moscow school's designs, however, display a more picturesque, essentially rural character. The general plan submitted by I.A. Golosov, for example, is reminiscent of the layout of a rural development with garden, typical of the new villages being designed in large numbers by Soviet architects at the time.

The Moscow school's designs also clearly reveal experience in planning model housing developments for workers. In particular, one can clearly discern the design intention in the project by Pantelejmon, one of the Golosov brothers, in their joint competition entry for the residential development in the Zamoskvorečkij district.

One acknowledged deficiency common to all the designs was that they paid too little attention to the role of the River Moskva. The most satisfactory design in this regard was that of I. Žoltovskij, and it was he who, in February 1923, was commissioned to design the general plan of the exhibition and its most challenging structures, including the Main Pavilion and the arch at the central entrance.[11]

The epic which was the construction of the "All-Russia Agricultural Exhibition" featured K.S. Mel'nikov's work too: his 'Tobacco' pavilion, which, together with 'The Saw' in Zamoskvoreč'e and his design for the Palace of Labour, became notable landmarks in his creative portfolio in the first phase of Soviet architectural history, and an undeniable contribution to that heritage.
Jurij Volčok

Urban Landscape and City Management
In the first half of the Twenties, in the image of the city of the "thousand and thousand cupolas",[12] the installation of the Soviet government and the new urban administration in Moscow were accompanied by projects conceived, both in form and substance, as temporary presences, with a demonstrative, propagandistic function—illustrations of how the settlement could change thanks to the new regimen of the society and of life. In these projects, that represent the

debut of avant-garde Soviet architecture on the urban scene, it is imagined that the countryside, taking on the signs of technological modernisation, penetrating the city of stone would gradually alter its appearance, introducing a sense of open space and its own architectural image.[13] The "Pan-Soviet Exposition of Agriculture and Crafts", featuring works by both the masters of the generations preceding the revolution and the newer talents, had the appearance of a segment of urbanised, industrialised countryside that had somehow been transported by the Moskva directly into the heart of the city, in an illustrative demonstration of the contrast between two alternative settlement models.[14]

The same subject returns in the projects by Mel'nikov examined here, for the competition for workers' housing on Ulica Serpukhovskaja or the Sukharevskij market, which reinterpret the settlement typologies of the Slavic tradition (the linear village) using the language of the avant-garde, and in the two pavilions for the Makhorka factory in 1923, and for the government of the USSR at the Paris Exposition of 1925, based on a reworking of the forms and compositional procedures typical of Russian vernacular wooden architecture.

The site of the exposition of the city of the future included different areas of the city, from the riverside Exposition grounds to the streets and

squares of the centre, in which settings were created for the propagandistic celebratory demonstrations of the new regime.[15] The theatrical sets erected in the city, to enliven and transform it, in the absence of concrete construction, often became the focus of architectural work, in the context of competition: the projects of Mel'nikov presented here for the Labor Building and the Moscow headquarters of *Leningradskaja Pravda* were theatrical set-pieces, works somehow destined to put the city itself on stage—with a set design that is arranged around existing monuments, in the Labor Building, or with a series of rolling platforms to offer varying views of the busy urban setting of Strastnaja Square.

In the second half of the Twenties the various actors in the transformation of the Soviet settlement manifest their activity in the city with projects that, although still linked to a certain extent to the requirements of propaganda, have a more peremptory and permanent character.

In the mixed context of a city still predominantly built with the typologies of rural residential architecture, in the midst of churches with gilded and blue cupolas, and gentrified *usad'by*, the Kremlin and the monasteries, the streets of the affluent centre and the streets lined with the wooden *izby* of a countryside that penetrated into the heart of the city,[16] three new settlements stood out

with great clarity.
The first was located on the Moskva, where the new presences began to transform the zone from a historical industrial district into a monumental centre.[17]
The second was in a triangle between the Kremlin, Ulica Tverskaja (later Gor'kij) and Ulica Mjasnickaja, where the citadel of the new Soviet government was being built, with ministries, headquarters of new economic agencies and the state administration.[18]
The third, crowning this nucleus of monuments and officialdom, took on the form of another city, built with the budgets of the trade unions and co-operatives, grouped around many different centres represented by factories, warehouses, garages, services, or consolidated suburban nuclei.
The latter—historically peripheral because far from the affluent centre, but the focal point of the relations between the city and the country, with its *sloboda*[19] that represent the effective extension of the countryside inside the city—was to become the main gravitation zone for the migratory influx of workers brought to the city between the years of the NEP and those of the first five-year plan.[20]
This is the area of most of the construction in the Twenties which, with the exception of a few exemplary medium-sized housing complexes for workers, involved the building of

facilities for leisure time activities: sports, culture, and the workers' clubs.[21]
The workers' clubs built in the period 1927-1929 by order of the trade unions of the capital represented one of the key factors for the development of Soviet architecture in the Twenties, both due to the participation in their design of the masters of the Soviet avant-garde,[22] and for the importance of this theme in the construction of the city during those years.[23]
The workers' clubs in Moscow represented a combination of two fundamental requirements or aims. The first was in keeping with the need to implement a political and cultural program: to provide, in a fully accessible way, services for workers designed to encourage free time activities that could become a focal point in the social fabric of the neighbourhood, a connection between collective life, in the factory, and individual life, that of the home and family, while educating a community of people recently transplanted from the country to the city regarding new behaviour patterns based on collectivisation, on the one hand, and the use of new technologies on the other.[24]
The second was based on the need to manage the productive settlement as a whole, without being able to count on the implementation of complex, large-scale programs of edification. This situation was resolved by means of isolated interventions in the

neighbourhood fabric, aimed at giving the new centres both a symbolic and a physical value as focal points for development.

In the context of this program, the architecture of the workers' clubs was an opportunity for experimentation with new typologies, both for the creation of particular spaces in conformity with activities based on new types of behaviour and new forms of entertainment,[25] and in terms of the construction of the urban landscape. These buildings, only occasionally seen as part of an organic program of renewal and reform of the zone,[26] combining with a variegated system of pre-existing structures, led to the formation of the new centres of the Moscow of the 'industrial reconstruction' during the years of the first five-year plan.

Although the question of the location of the club buildings in the neighbourhood is addressed in the specialised literature of the day only sporadically, focusing only on the alternative between a location close to the workplace or another close to the place of residence of the workers,[27] in reality the panorama of the clubs in Moscow is less banal; in fact, an analysis of the various cases reveals that while there is a frequent use of a frontal positioning of the club with respect to the factory—as in the clubs by Mel'nikov, Burevestnik and Zuev—more often these 'new neighbourhood centres' were located in the vicinity of a more complex

series of important pre-existing facilities—churches, parks, hospitals and other services, as in the two parts of the Moscow periphery that gravitated around the Rusakov and Kaučuk clubs, reconstructed here.[28] Thus segments of urban landscape were constructed whose composition is activated thanks to certain formal qualities of the club buildings, like the out-of-scale character of all the clubs by Mel'nikov, which becomes functional for a composition based on contrasts with open green areas, the continuity of the dense, minute fabric of the *izby*, the variety of the linguistic timbres of the architecture of the Moscow periphery.

Designed in keeping with a methodology that identifies, 'case by case', the typological choices and formal configurations of the building, the eight clubs designed by K. Mel'nikov in 1927 and 1928, radical departures with respect to the standardised canons established in the competition guidelines for the standard clubs,[29] tend to address a more complex theme, seeing the organism of the club as a device[30] capable of responding to precise internal functional requirements while also acting as focal points for the assembly of the different settings of the urban landscape in which they are inserted.

At the end of the Twenties, with the beginning of urban planning and the debate on urban policy, the experience of the workers' clubs came

to an end. These buildings continued to be built in Soviet cities, but in a very different administrative, political and cultural context.

In the Moscow built in the years to follow, with the progressive concentration of the administration of the city and the absorption of local and municipal authorities and entities into that of the state (when they were not totally replaced by it),[31] architecture was assigned the task of working on a different theme—that of the capital city[32]—which was formulated according to criteria that made the experiences and compositional procedures developed in the construction of the clubs in the suburbs of Moscow seem obsolete and ineffective.

Maurizio Meriggi

[1] CGALI (Central State Archive of Literature & Art), f. 964, op. 3, d. 66, sheet 9 rev.
[2] *Ibid.*, sheet 6.
[3] *The Artist and the Viewer* (Khudoznik i zritel), 1924, no. 1, p. 58.
[4] *Arkhitektura*, monthly journal of the Moscow Architectural Society, 1023, no. 3-5, pp. 35, 37.
[5] S. Khan-Magomedov, "Clubs Today and Yesterday", in *Decorative Art* (Dekorativnoe iskusstvo), 1966, no. 9, pp. 2-6.
[6] See: *From the history of Soviet architecture 1917-1925*, pl. 53.
[7] CGALI (Central State Archive of Literature & Art), f. 686, op. 1, d. 20, sheet 113.
[8] *Ibid.*, sheet 98.
[9] See: *The Construction Industry* (Stroitel'naja promyslennost'), 1923, no. 2, p. 7.
[10] CGANKh (Central State Archive of the Economy), f. 480, op. 6, d. 10, sheets 25, 33.
[11] For more detail on the building design for

View of the club for Zuev city hall workers (I. A. Golosov, 1927-29) with, on the background, the tramway depot, Tenth

View of the club for Proletarij workers in the metallurgical industry (V. Vladimirov, 1927) with, on the background, the Compressor factory

View of the ulica Ogorodnaja (Gardens), club for Burevestnik workers in the leather tanning industry (K.S. Mel'nikov, 1928-1930); "Makaronnaja fabrika" complex in front of the club, Tenths

the exhibition, and generally on the theoretical and cultural heritage of Soviet town planning in the years 1920-1925, see the works of M.I. Astaf'eva-Dlugac, in particular her PhD research article "The development of theoretical ideas and principles in Soviet town planning immediately after the revolution (1917-25)". It was her untimely decease that prevented her from contributing to this edition. We dedicate this text to the memory of one of the leading researchers in the architecture of Moscow from the Twenties to the Forties.

12 The image is utilised by Mikhail Bulgakov in the article "Sorok sorokov", published in the magazine *Nakanune*, April 1923.

13 This notion comes from the utopian novel by the agrarian economist and author A. Čajanov, *Putešestvie moego brata Alekseja v stranu krest'janskoj utopii*, Moscow 1920, in which he describes a Moscow of the future that is completely melded with the countryside. In the society imagined by Čajanov the technological revolution has reached the point of being able to control the climate for purposes of agriculture. Many copies of this book were published, and it was quite popular in the early Twenties.

14 Again it is Michail Bulgakov who observes: "...The squama of the Moskva divides two worlds: on one of the banks small single-storey houses, red and gray, the usual open, welcoming air, while on the other stands the city-pavilion, jutting out, jagged with roofs and summits, pointed..." From a report on the "Pan-Soviet Exposition of Agriculture and Crafts", entitled "Zolotistyj gorod" (The city of gold), published in *Nakanune*, September-October 1923.

15 On the Plan of monumental propaganda and the installations for political demonstrations in Moscow in the Twenties, see the wealth of photographic documentation in V. Tolstoj, I. Bibikova, C. Cooke, *Street art of the revolution*, Thames and Hudson, London 1990.

16 An exceptional traveller offers us an image of this world at the end of the Twenties, start-

ing with the character of the streets of the urban network of the city: "There is something unique about the streets of Moscow: the Russian village hidden inside them. When you pass through one of the doors of the city (they usually have a wrought iron gate, but I have never seen one closed), you find yourself at the edge of a sort of district. In front of you opens a wide, spacious farm courtyard, or a village; the terrain is hilly, children play on sleds, there are shelters for firewood, tools placed in corners, scattered trees, wooden staircases that give the backs of the houses, which from the street are citified in appearance, a rural look. In these courtyards there are often churches, just as in a large village square. Thus the street dilates to become countryside. (...) As in every other city, Moscow too constructs, with names, a little world inside itself. There is a club called 'Alkasar', a hotel named 'Liverpool', a 'Tirol' inn. (...) In no place does Moscow appear to be the city itself, it all looks like periphery. (...) On the streets of the outskirts, alongside wide avenues, peasant houses alternate with Liberty-style villas or the sober facades of eight-storey buildings." From W. Benjamin, *Moscau*, 1925-1930. For an analytical overview of architecture in Moscow from the Twenties see the various guides to the contemporary architecture of the city, especially those of A. Latour, *Mosca. Guida all'architettura moderna. 1890-1991*, Zanichelli, Bologna 1992 and of A. De Magistris, *Mosca 1900-1950. Nascita di una capitale*, Clup, Milano 1994.

17 The edifice that best represents this trend is the MOGES heating plant built in 1928-1929 by I. Žoltovskij on the island of the Moskva, almost directly facing the Kremlin. Beginning with this same period, other heating plants were built on the riverfronts - such as that at Krasnopresnenskaja—and large industrial complexes like the ZIS (later ZIL) automobile factory, expanded between 1928 and 1938, also facing the river, in front of the Danilevskij monastery.

18 During the Twenties in this part of the city

were realised: Centrosojuz building (All union co-operative agency), Le Corbusier with N. Kolli, 1928-1935; Gostorg building (State Trade agency), B. Velinovskij, M. Barsc and others, 1925-1927; Koždindakata building (Leather Union), A. Golubev, 1925; Narkomzem (People's Commisariat of Agricolture), A. Ščusev, 1928-1931; NKPS building (People's Commisariat of Telecomunications), I. Fomin, 1929-1934; URSS State bank, I. Žoltovskij, 1927-29; Dynamo sports Association building (Army sport association), I. Fomin, A. Langman, 1928-1929.

19 We can provide the definition of this type of settlement according to B. Dal', *Tolkovyj slovar' zivogo velikoruskogo jazyka* (Unilingual Dictionary of the Living Russian Language), Sankt Peterburg-Moskva, 1882: "slobodà synonym of svoboda (*liberty*); (...) villages of free persons; suburban settlement, suburban village, suburb; outside the city walls, type of township (...) large village with more than one church, a market or fairgrounds, or seat of the local government, a sort of capital of the rural area; also an industrial village, where the peasants almost never plough; slobodka (diminutive) found in large sectors of the city where both peasants and middle class people live, with zones for the cultivation of cereals and small agricultural enterprises (kulaki)."

20 Dates on the demographic dynamic and industrial reconstruction of Moscow are in T. Colton, *Moscow. Governing the Socialist Metropolis*, Belknap Press of Harvard University Press, Cambridge – London 1995. See in particular the chapter "The Urban NEP".

21 The clubs, by far the qualitatively most important intervention, represent centres of regrouping of the Soviet society, whose origin and spread, functional program and typology, evolution and story have been fully illustrated in the introductory essays. See in particular the essay published herein by D. Schmidt, *From People's House to "School of Communism". Houses for training programs and recreation.*

22 The importance of the experience of the

workers' clubs and the cultural buildings in Soviet architecture is emphasised in the recent book by Vigdaria E. Khazanova, *Klubnaja žizn' i arkhitektura kluba*, Rossijskij Institut Iskusstvoznanija, Moscow 1994, retracing briefly all the architecture of the masters of the avant-garde, from this particular point of view.

[23] Cf. with reference to the role of the clubs in the construction of Moscow, A. Ikonnikov, "Moscow. Dialectic: center and periphery", in *Zodiac*, n. 13, March-August 1995.

[24] This program is illustrated in the volume by the critic N. Lukhmanov, *Arkhitectura kluba*, Moscow 1929, especially in the chapters: "The functions of the club", "The problems of comfort", "Industrialization and culture".

[25] The volume by V. E. Khazanova, *Klubnaja žizn'*, cit., offers a wide overview of the artistic phenomena and the spread of the use of new instruments of mass communications, and of the prevailing cultural interests in Soviet society in the Russia of the Twenties; according to the author, the avant-garde theatre, cinema and radio, on the one hand, and new forms of collective behaviour, on the other, are the phenomena that had the greatest influence on the development of these new typologies.

[26] The most complete realisation, from this point of view, is not found in Moscow but in Leningrad, with the centre of the Moskovskij-Narvskij quarter, with a long, large space surrounded by a single grouping of buildings: the Gor'kij cultural building, the Mass kitchen, the 10th of October school, the residential complex on Ulica Traktornaja, the district Soviet headquarters, all built between 1925 and 1930.

[27] In a partial way, the question is discussed case by case in the volume edited by V.S. Kemenov, *10 rabočikh klubov Moskvy (10 workers' clubs in Moscow)*, 1932. A more detailed debate on the role and positioning of these edifices in the fabric of the Soviet city took place, beginning in 1929, around the competitions for the new industrial cities, in which the club was utilised as a node of relationships, including physical ones, in the composition of the settlement. See the volume by V.E. Khazanova, *Klubnaja žizn'*, cit. p. 113-119. In Moscow in the Twenties there were also housing complexes with related workers' clubs, theatres and cinemas—as in the housing complex on Ulica Sabolovska by N. Travin of 1927, the building on the riverfront by B.M. Iofan of 1928, and the commune buildings by M. Ginzburg, M. Barsc and I. Nikolaev built in 1928- 1930—although in these cases we are dealing with parts of the edification that do not fully correspond to the function of the workers' club. The question of the composition, as a whole, of the club with the rest of the settlement and the positioning of the building in the city is systematically analysed in the fourth section of the volume by various authors *Arkhitektura rabočikh klubov i dvorcov kul'tury*, Gosudarstvennoe Izdatel'stvo literatury po stroitel'stvu i arkhitekture, Moskva, 1953, pp. 59-70, which at the height of the era of Socialist Realism totally censures the Moscow clubs of the Twenties. The Kaučuk and Zuev clubs appear only in demonstrative schemes of possible locations of the edifice with respect to the block, considering the following options: on the street, corner, freestanding, ensemble, landscape.

[28] See the herein published texts on the urban developpement of the areas nearby the Kaučuk and Rusakov clubs.

[29] On the question of the standardised clubs cf. the essay by D. Schmidt, *From People's House to "School of Communism"*, cit., published herein.

[30] On the question of Mel'nikov special approach to clubs design see the essay by M. Meriggi, *Mel'nikov's design for the City of the Future. An itinerary in the City of Moscow*, published herein.

[31] Cf. T. Colton, *Moscow. Governing*, cit. and in particular the chapter "Stalin's Moscow".

[32] On this theme cf. the profile that follows, by Ju. Volčok, *The Architectural Planning Workshops of Moscow City Council (Mossovet)*.

Works from 1922 to 1929

Competition Project for the Complex of Model Dwellings for Workers' on Bol'saja Serpukhovskaja Street, at the First and Second Scipkovskij Lanes

"…The contemporary atom burns down cities, but in accordance with my first, 1922 project, this is my motto for the Architecture of narrow streets, where the person has acquired for himself the kingdom of respect, love and veneration."
K. Mel'nikov, 1967[1]

"The competition has opened—the first All-Russian competition, declared by the Moscow Soviet and the Moscow Architectural Society in 1922, for the architecture of model dwellings for the workers of Moscow.
To the novice the competition looked liked a temple of supreme justice. I was in a quandary—to enter or not to enter? I had enough only for some English Whatman paper, I brought it and put it on a workers' board. On the walls of the exhibition of projects I didn't find it and I was surprised on seeing the board deposited separately on an armchair. I was afraid to go up to the huddle of quarrellers. On the day that the results of the competition were confirmed, the hall was overflowing with people angry at the ungainly appearance of the solitary board. They demanded that it be removed from the competition. But when the envelope was opened with the motto 'Atom' I did not recognise my name, which had been pronounced in my presence publicly for the first time. In the jury's protocol, the reviewer Ivanickij wrote: 'The author of the project decided to

make his own original plan of the buildings, he had the thought of constructing separate flats for families, and he has solved this task successfully. Every flat has a separate entrance and its own little garden. For single people separate blocks connected by an overhead gallery with a restaurant and club have been planned. Both in their general conception and individually these have been worked out successfully, if we do not consider the complex form of the corridor and its broken line. However, this can be easily removed. There is a formal violations of the requirements of the competition in that a park and fruit garden have been built. The facades of the buildings are too boring and monotonous in form. The project is original and is worthy of special attention, although there is a violation of the programme.' … My first motto—'Atom'. I believed in the mysterious will of the architect to move the expanses of our feelings, to bend the primitive straight line of the Universe into the enchanting jaggedness of the 'Saw'. The task involved planning flats for families of two types: one type with individual housekeeping and the other with communal, and bed-sits for single people. It was required that public buildings for cultural and everyday needs should be placed on the territory of the plan. This subject was worked out in two rounds, and those taking part in the second … were

composed of people who received prizes."
K. Mel'nikov, 1967[2]

"… My project under the motto 'Atom' (nicknamed 'Saw') was given a prize and was sharply different from the others in its architectural composition. Its basic idea was the maximal isolation of individual use of all types of residents, both families and singles. The family blocks consisted of each unit occupying one 'tooth' of a saw and with each flat having its own plot of land attached right next to its entrance. The single people's flats were strung on the overhead elevated gallery, which connected them with the central block of the hall-restaurant and the other cultural-recreational rooms…"
K. Mel'nikov, Sixties[3]

The area
The plot which was set aside in 1922 for the building of the model houses for workers was situated in a historical area—Zamoskovoreč'e beyond the Sadovoe Kol'co (Garden ring)—and faced onto Bol'šaja Serpukhovskaja street. For a long time this region had been considered to be on the edge of the city: here in the seventeenth-century numerous settlements bordered on spacious meadows, pastures, kitchen-gardens and plough-land. The role of centres of composition and meaning was originally played by the Danilov and Donskoj monasteries. At the

end of the eighteenth and beginning of the nineteenth centuries there began a gradual development of industry.
At the end of the nineteenth and beginning of the twentieth centuries the building density in the area was quite low, with wooden housing prevailing. Many plots were leased out, which did not favour the forming of stable compositions.
An important city-building role was played in the region of Bol'šaja Serpukhovskaja street by the bell-tower of the church of the Ascension, which was built in the 1840s. Thanks to its height, it could be easily seen from distant parts, and it compositionally united a building region that was quite varied in character.
The price of land in this region was not high. This helped some rich merchants to buy up many small yards for the building of charitable institutions, a phenomenon that developed on a massive scale in Moscow at the end of the nineteenth and beginning of the twentieth centuries.
For the first competition for the siting of model homes for workers, a plot was chosen where a hostel of the Ljapiny merchants had been situated in 1885 with free flats for 'women learners' (students) and widows. The area of this basic plot was increased by adding several properties to it. The whole existing complex of buildings was designated for development. In the project presented by K.

On page 112:
Soviet Pavilion at the Paris "Exposition Internationale des Arts Dècoratifs et Industriels Modernes", 1925

Competition project for workmen's study houses on Bol'šaja Serpukhovskaja street, 1923

Reconstruction of the Twenties competition area with the localization of the actual project (Ju. Volčok, E. Nikulina)

View of the model (realised by A. Šadrin with V. Šadrin)

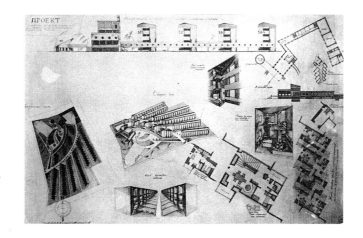

Mel'nikov to the competition, in addition to solving the basic problem of creating comfortable flats for workers corresponding to the hygienic norms of the time, architectural problems were also solved. Thus the plot set aside was treated as a quarter surrounded on all sides by streets. In siting the blocks of flats, the particularity of the city-building situation was taken into account, together with the original fan-like distribution of streets and lanes, which created a spatial opening up of the area in the direction of the Serpukhovskaja zastava. Apparently the role of the bell-tower of the Ascension church was also taken into account in the compositional structure of the complex; in this direction the inner space of the courtyard was opened up. The project received the second prize.

The first prize in the competition was awarded to the project of S. Černyšev (with the participation of N. Kolli). However, it was never realised. The plot was built on in the second half of the Twenties with standard residential houses. In the planning process several existing blocks were used, while the church building that was constructed at the beginning of the twentieth century next to the hostel, was refitted as a club. The plot has been preserved as built up at the end of the 1920s, with certain changes, to the present time.

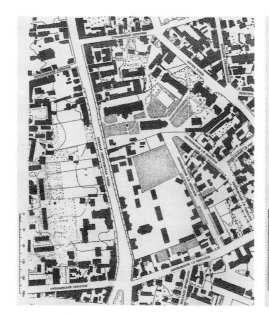

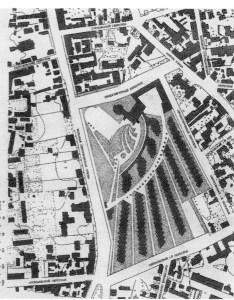

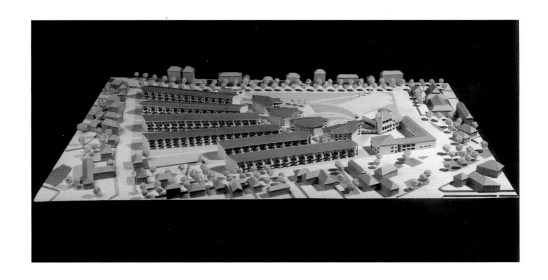

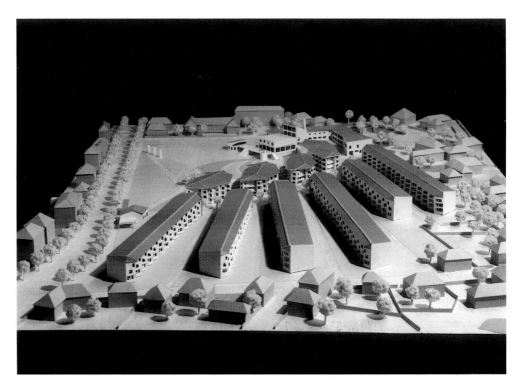

Mel'nikov's project

By contrast with the existing chaotic building of the plot, Mel'nikov's model complex looks like an integral organism, with the draught plan clearly and artistically conceptualised. There is enough energy (in Mel'nikov's understanding of the word) in this small complex to organise the spatial expanse of the city between the Paveleckaja and Serpukhovskaja squares. The drawing of the plan is to a definite degree immersed in the surroundings. In spite of the fact that the new composition deliberately invades the historic milieu and offers to change and reconstruct everything, at the same time it follows the planned rays of the Bol'šaja Serpukhovskaja and Ljusinovskaja streets, which radiate from the square on the Sadovoe Kol'co (Garden ring). These rays are supported in the project by the lines of houses opening out from the round square like a fan, with a detached sculpture as the compositional centre of the complex.

The vertical line formed by the church nearby was carefully preserved by the author. On it there opens out the great public zone of the complex, forming an axis towards Serpukhov square that opposes the rays of houses. The work on the architectural model brings out Mel'nikov's use in the workshop of axial constructions, rhythm and repeated contrasts. These classical methods in the composition allowed him to create a complex structure full of tension but at the same time balanced and integral. The dynamism of the fan-like distribution of houses was calmed by the identical repetition of blocks. Their movement from the tense bow of the alley was offset in the drawing by a spiral of public gardens heading towards the sculpture. The general dynamism of the fan was balanced by the calm, almost square, enclosed 'peace' of the public centre in the corner.

In the model the shapes of the pitched roofs have been interpreted by the authors insofar as the archive materials do not permit us to recreate them with sufficient authenticity. The colour in the buildings of the complex is also conditional and helps to bring out their horizontal mood. The situation is not quite clear with the newly laid streets restricting the building plot. On the model the old building that remains is shown without changes, without its architectural merging with the new streets. A new marking out of the streets was not proposed as a competition task. K. Mel'nikov extended the competition programme in his project.

Juij Volčok, Elena Nikulina, Alexander Šadrin

[1] From K.S. Mel'nikov, *Arkhitektura moej žizni. Tvorčeskaja koncepcija. Tvorčeskaja praktika*, Moskva 1985, p. 84.
[2] *Ibidem*, p. 72-73.
[3] *Ibidem*, p. 153.

The Competition Entry for The Palace of Labour in Okhotnyj Rjad

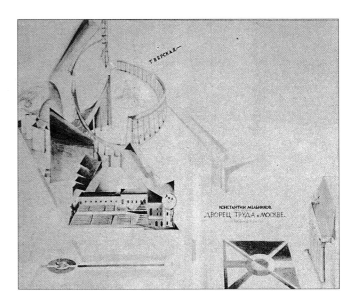

"In the excitement of my Saint's-day celebration I penned the design for the building of the Joint-Stock Company 'Arkos' and boldly submitted it for the Palace of Labour design competition. The Palace project was a large, ambitious theme, embracing the development of the very heart of our beloved Moscow. Three of her celebrated squares—Theatre Square, Resurrection Square and Okhotnyj Rjad Square—would be home to three lecture halls of my Palace, resembling a family of mammoths.

These days you cannot find auditoria without sound systems which stifle the soul of the voice, and up to now people have not known of my design, dating back to 1923, which included a hall with eight steeply rising circles so that a soloist could be heard by audiences of thousands without any need for amplification. This and the subsequent competitions squeezed that frail creature—Architecture- out of the prize stakes, and, like bush fires, were lost to memory, right down to the huge drawing boards on which the completed drafts had lain ... In order to direct the delegates quickly and easily to their allocated seats, without subjecting them to the jostling and confusion of the entrance foyer, each circle was provided with its own stairway and entrance, cloakroom, buffet and so on. Access to the lobby was possible on one side via a

hanging gallery, and on the other by half-landings on the stairways. The shape of the auditorium was dictated by the need to concentrate the speaker's voice, which is contained inside the focus of the parabola. The delegates' seats were felt-lined and upholstered in leather, to dampen the sound. The arrangement of the auditorium into tiers meant that it could be cleared in one minute. ... My presence at the competition went unnoticed, and my work, which culminated in the gleaming parabola of the crystal hall on the corner of Theatre Square and Okhotnyj Rjad, was not appreciated. So what on earth were the prizes in this competition being awarded for?—I ask myself."
K. Mel'nikov, 1967[1]

Okhotnyj Rjad Area Historical Development

For the 1922 competition for the design of the Palace of Labour, it was proposed that a block should be constructed in the immediate vicinity of the Kremlin—in Okhotnyj Rjad. This area is one of exceptional urban-planning significance, being located inside the ring of central squares which encircles the Kremlin and Kitaj-gorod.
The squares took shape during the eighteenth and nineteenth centuries in the area of the solid line of fortifications which, in the fifteenth and sixteenth centuries, had been marked out for defensive purposes around

the walls of the central hub of the city. The defence positions ran along the Neglinka River, which flowed along the westward line of the city's fortifications.
According to decrees on the regulation of the city, the fortifications were not to be built on. These prohibitions, however, were constantly being flouted. A trading area sprang up on the Neglinnaja adjacent to Kitaj-gorod. Under Tsar Boris Godunov a stone bridge was built across the River, leading from Red Square to Tverskaja Street. Numerous small shops started to appear near the bridge. Trading activity, which had been expanding inside Kitaj-gorod, was taking over the space along its walls. The shops were removed in 1707 during the construction of supplementary earthworks around the fortress walls by order of Peter I. By the middle of the eighteenth century these fortifications lost their defensive significance and were gradually dug up.
In the classicist period the spaces occupied by the defence positions began to be put in order. It had hitherto been defined by the natural landscape and the spontaneously expanding trade.
The site occupied later by the Manege was at that time occupied by the Hay Market, where firewood was sold, and sod, which was needed for building. The market gave its

name to Mokhovaja (sod) Street, which ran along the western boundary of the chain of former defence positions. This street became one of the most prestigious at the time. It was here that, in earlier times, the courts of the nobility were situated. And it was on Mokhovaja Street, in the second half of the eighteenth century, that, by order of Catherine II and following the design of the architect M. Kazakov, the construction of the university was begun.
Along the bed of the Neglinnaja several ponds were formed. Here there still existed an extensive garden dating back to Ivan the Terrible. According to the Projected Plan for the City of Moscow (1775), which defined the main directions for the transformations to be made in the classicist period, the bed of the Neglinnaja became enhanced, transforming itself into a system of ponds and canals. A park zone was taking shape. Two regular squares were becoming delineated: Okhotnyj Rjad and Mokhovaja. (At this time the structure of the residential blocks of Okhotnyj Rjad had taken shape, in the place where trade, mainly in poultry and game, had been carried on).
The project was never brought to fruition. At the end of the eighteenth century the Neglinnaja ponds were drained, and in 1817-1819 the river-bed was enclosed in an underground

Competition project for the Labor Palace, 1923; perspective view with, on the foreground, Teatral'raja square

Views of the Okhotnij Rjad area, Tenths

Reconstruction of the Twenties competition area and localization of the project in the area (Ju. Volčok, E. Nikulina)

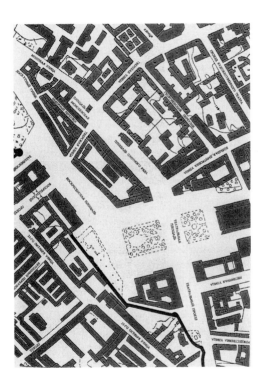

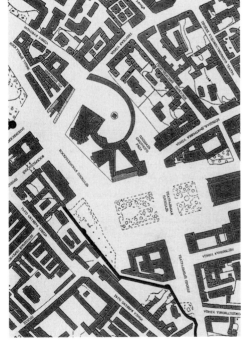

culvert.

This was the period when a new scheme for creating the central squares and improving the general area abutting up to the Kremlin walls and Kitaj-gorod. On the site of the largest pond and Voskresenskij Bridge, Voskresenskaja Square (now Revolution Square) was created. Along the Kremlin walls the Aleksandrov Garden was laid, for public recreational purposes, and the site of the old 'Moss' market was given over to the building of the Manege, to the design of A. Betankur. In 1821-1825 the architect O. Beauvais created a design for Theatre Square, which embodied the ideas of the regular classical ensemble, the compositional *leitmotif* of which became the Bol'šoj Theatre, built in 1825. However, even this project was not fully realised. Construction on the square continued throughout the nineteenth and twentieth centuries. In the 1820's and 1830's saw also the laying out of Okhotnyj Rjad Square, which was surrounded by commercial premises. It included the site of the Moiseev Monastery, demolished in the eighteenth century, to the south of Tverskaja Street (opposite where the National Hotel now stands).

The ancient, highly ornate Church of Paraskeva Pjatnica was preserved. The church was built at the end of the seventeenth century, funded by V. Golicyn, Empress Sofia's

lover.

The development of the structure of the central squares continued to progress in the late nineteenth and early twentieth centuries.

Between 1874 and 1883, W. Sherwood and A. Semenov, an engineer, built the Museum of History, which was to become one of the main features of the development of Red Square; at the same time it completed the perspective of Tverskaja Street. The building was executed in the style of ancient Russian architecture and was typical of the stylisation which permeated the arts in late nineteenth-

century Russia. The years 1890-1892 saw the construction of the city Duma (subsequently, the V.I. Lenin Museum), designed by D. Čičagov, a prize winner in two earlier special competitions. It was erected on the foundations of the old Mint building, which had stood there in the 1730's. From the closing years of the nineteenth century onwards, architecture underwent a change of style, and a new type of administrative and commercial building started to appear. It was multi-storey, and with visibly enlarged proportions of the main articulations. This style of

construction had originally begun in Kitaj-gorod, but by the early 1900's it had spread to the central squares. On Theatre Square in 1899-1905, V. Valkott and L. Kekusev saw their design for the grandiose 'Metropol' complex come to fruition, comprising a modern hotel, shops, offices, a cinema, cafes and restaurants for the enjoyment of the public. This building greatly changed the scale of development projects for the future composition of the square.

The thrust towards redesigning the old city squares, which was first manifested in the Palace of

*View of the model
(realised by A. Šadrin with
A. Ermakova, A. Zolotov)*

Labour design competition in the early Twenties, was a natural progression from the transformations begun in the late 1880's.

However, the radically altered social situation greatly complicated the work of the urban planners and architects, in relation to both the 'New Moscow' scheme as a whole, and the designs entered in the competition.

Nonetheless, in both the formulation of the task and in a number of the designs we may observe the continuation and development of the trends established in the design of the 'Metropol' complex.

The competition rules required that the proportions of the building should be in harmony with the neighbouring squares and streets, and especially with Theatre Square and the theatres themselves. The squares surrounding the Palace of Labour must bear the imprint of the architect and an opulent appearance in keeping with its purpose, but expressed in simple contemporary forms and without reference to any specific style from a previous era. It was permitted, in cases of special necessity, to cross this line to the extent of adding small decorative features to the design.

The entire site allocated for the Palace of Labour construction, hitherto occupied by small shops, was designated for demolition.

The area surrounding the Palace of Labour site may certainly be called diverse, in the way it had come to be filled in the course of its history. On one side there was Theatre Square, with its organised, classicist formulation, and on the other, Tverskaja Street, compositionally linked with the Museum of History building, which completed its perspective. The extensive facades of the new complex were to look out over two other squares: Voskresenskaja Square (latterly, Revolution Square), which was fairly small, and where the main building was the city Duma, while the space in front of the Kitaj-gorod wall was used as a public garden; and then Okhotnyj Rjad Square, once astir with trade activity and now still, in spirit, very much a market place, but already on the way to becoming a road-traffic artery.

Mel'nikov's Project

The design by K. Mel'nikov placed the accent on creating a new spatial layout that would blend with the diverse surroundings.

He rejected the idea of designing the building as a block which would simply fill up the available space within the boundary lines.

The architect endeavoured to include the city dynamically in the structure of the new complex, so as to make the spaces of the internal and external squares of the Palace of Labour complex flow smoothly from one to the other, to the mutual enhancement of both. An exception was made for Theatre Square, where the compositional structure demanded greater conformity with the rules of a regular city. Mel'nikov's structure, as we know, was not even considered by the competition organisers. In fact, not one of the prize winning designs ever saw completion.

In 1931 a competition was launched for the design of a new hotel which, it had been decided, would be built in place of the Palace of Labour, and the block was partly demolished in connection with the construction of the first line of the Moscow Metro system.

In 1932 the building of the hotel Moskva began, following the design of L. Savel'ev, O. Stapran and A. Ščusev, but was interrupted by the war and not completed until the Seventies, by the architects I. Rozin, D. Solopov et al.

At the end of the Thirties a long-standing structure between the Moskva hotel and the Manege was dismantled, and Manege Square came into being.

In recent years a large shopping centre has been built here, to a design by M. Posokhin and D. Lukaev, making use of the subway area. On one level of the centre there is an archaeological museum, with exhibits including fragments of Voskresenskij Bridge, which spanned the Neglinka, linking Red Square with Tverskaja Street in times of old.

The model gives us a clear idea of the first professional attempts by an architect to define the principles of the new architecture in urban design. The proportions of the auditoria are strictly in keeping with their location. The Small Hall has its facade set towards the State Duma, while the portal of the Large Hall closes the vista of the main thoroughfare—Tverskaja Street—and forms the square. The third hall is orientated towards the Bol'šoj Theatre and resembles the building opposite in such a way that together they form a kind of gateway on to Okhotnyj Rjad. The open amphitheatre of audience seating opens out on to Theatre Square, which the design architect envisioned as a scene of mass rallies. At the same time, the low-rise, zigzag-shaped buildings blend with the small-scale surrounding constructions. The model also shows how the varied colour-scheme of the buildings matches the surrounding environment. For example, the facades looking on to Red Square feature more red. The progressive character of the design dictated that, compositionally, the model of the Palace of Labour should echo the constructivist sculptures of the period. The composition of the Palace has the dynamism of the spiral of a radio mast. Its web-like

designs contrast strikingly with the colossi of the vaulted halls. The whole complex gives a feeling of space opening out from the halls into the internal courtyards, streets and squares, and at the same time outwards to the surrounding city.

The Palace is so varied in its forms and in contrast to the external environment, that it is perceived not so much as a separate entity—a composition of space and scale- but rather as an integral, self-sufficient fragment of a city of the future. At the same time it is quite strictly harnessed to the main existing urban *leitmotifs* in the historic centre of Moscow. It transpires that the Paraskeva Pjatnica Church, which was being demolished under the 'New Moscow' scheme, falls inside the boundaries of the semicircular *piazza* formed by the open colonnade in Mel'nikov's design. In one version of the hypothetical alternative designs for the scheme, it has been retained and stands centrally in the square, in the place of a designated monument.

Jurij Volčok, Elena Nikulina, Aleksandr Šadrin

[1] From K.S. Mel'nikov, *Arkhitektura moej žizni. Tvorčeskaja koncepcija. Tvorčeskaja praktika*, Moskva 1985, p. 73.

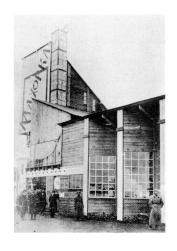

"Design specifications for the 'Makhorka' Pavilion"
Assignment: to construct a factory with an exhibition room; site area 60 square sazen[1]; cubic volume from 150 to 200 sazen; construction material rigid wooden structure.

Data
Passage of the product through consecutive sieves. Light weight (sieving) equipment. Light weight product.

Design Solution
Vertically positioned scheme for the passage of the product through different processing stages.

Exhibition conditions (external)
From the main entrance visitors are routed along the riverbank. Sharp incidence of angled surfaces and gradual condensing of space at the pavilion entrance. The open spiral staircase forms a vertical line (rhythmically, i.e. moving down and nearer).

Exhibition conditions (internal)
One-way passage of visitors. Certain production elements can be exhibited. A broken horizontal line and unequal spaces in vertical direction. Difference (contrast) between spaces of the different pavilion sections.

Result – Expression
In spite of the minimal size of the building (a kiosk type), the composition techniques allow us to achieve considerable space:
1. The visitor takes a 1/5 of versta[2] route through the pavilion; changing perspectives occupy the are of 60 sq. sazen and a height of 4 sazen.
2. With the same data, the impact area affecting the visitor is 200 sq. sazen.
3. The large spaces only reach the height of 9 sazen.
4. Vertical alignment of tobacco production equipment allows drag conveyers to be replaced by gravity feed.
K.S. Mel'nikov[3], 11 December 1923.

"About the 'Makhorka' Pavilion"
The Makhorka pavilion of the All-Russian Tobacco Syndicate, situated within the Agricultural Exposition at the Krimskij Bridge in Moscow, was my first work. The assignment envisaged the building of a mechanised factory, including a greenhouse and an exhibition room, on 270 square metres. According to the technical design, the equipment was to consist of several horizontal drag conveyors. I proposed my own system, with conveyors to be replaced by gravity feed, i.e., vertical movement of the product during processing.
My first treatment of a production route in such an arbitrary way convinced me of the fact, that if architects, when designing a building, looked critically upon engineering data, it would benefit the engineering itself. From a one-storey building, conceived by my process engineers, Makhorka developed into a whole concept of separate spatial units, with cantilever drops of huge dividing walls and transparent glazing without angle structural support. The pavilion architecture was based on the natural process, following the flow of the internal life of the building. The construction of the pavilion has outlined the architectural and design techniques which are characteristic of modern construction, such as cantilever systems, stairs, angle glazing and a sloping exterior."
K.S. Mel'nikov[4], Sixties

The 'Makhorka' pavilion: the first design proposal of Mel'nikov ever to be built
In 1923, the complex of the All-Russian Agricultural and Cottage Industries Exhibition, the first large-scale exhibition of achievements of the Soviet Republic, was built on an area previously used as a rubbish dump on the embankment of the Moskva River. A.V. Ščusev and I.V. Žoltovskij were appointed project managers. They invited their workshop employees to participate in the design process. From Saint Petersburg came V.A. Ščuko, who was charged with the construction of the Foreign Section, consisting of several buildings. Many VKhUTEMAS professors, Mel'nikov among them, took part in the project development. Mel'nikov, being the youngest project participant, was given the task of designing one of the less important pavilions. The Makhorka syndicate was an industrial pavilion for which no architects were engaged at all.
Mel'nikov created a composition of small wooden deal-clad sloping-roofed structures, which, in combination with such architectural details as a spiral staircase, a glass-enclosed elevator belt, and the graphic designs on the walls, gave the building a highly expressive character. Mel'nikov himself considered the alteration of the original production process, as proposed by the tobacco syndicate, as the main advantage of his proposal. The architect substituted so-called drag conveyors by gravity-fed vertical conveyors. This allowed him to build a complex, dynamic and multi-space pavilion instead of a simple utilitarian barn. Faced for the first time with the construction of an exhibition space, Mel'nikov used spatial techniques in this design which he would apply repeatedly in his future creative endeavours. The architect combined the diverse spaces so as make best use of the visitors' flow through the building. In his evaluation of Makhorka, Mel'nikov specified the technique which enabled him to reach the desired effect:

*View of the "Makhorka"
pavilion, 1923*

*View of the model
(realised by I. Terenin)*

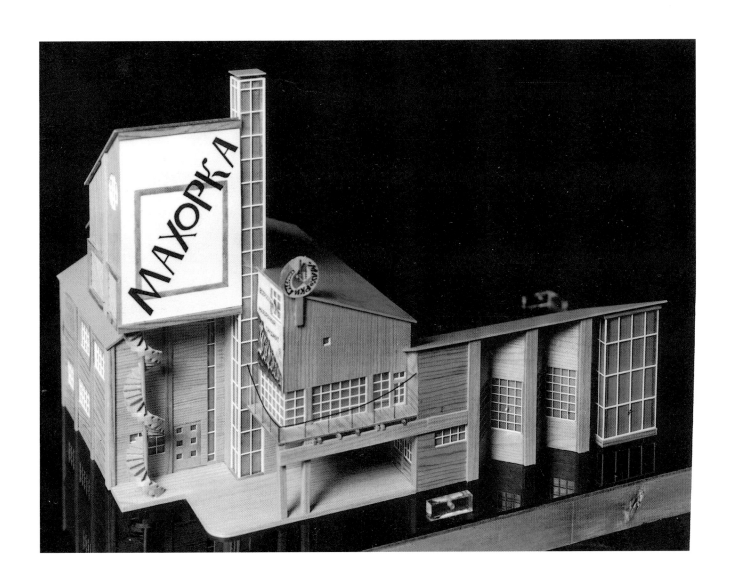

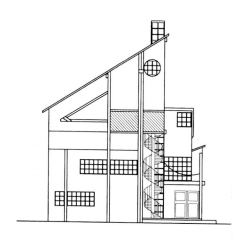

'Makhorka' pavilion, 1923
(re-drawn by A. Tomasi)
scale 1:300

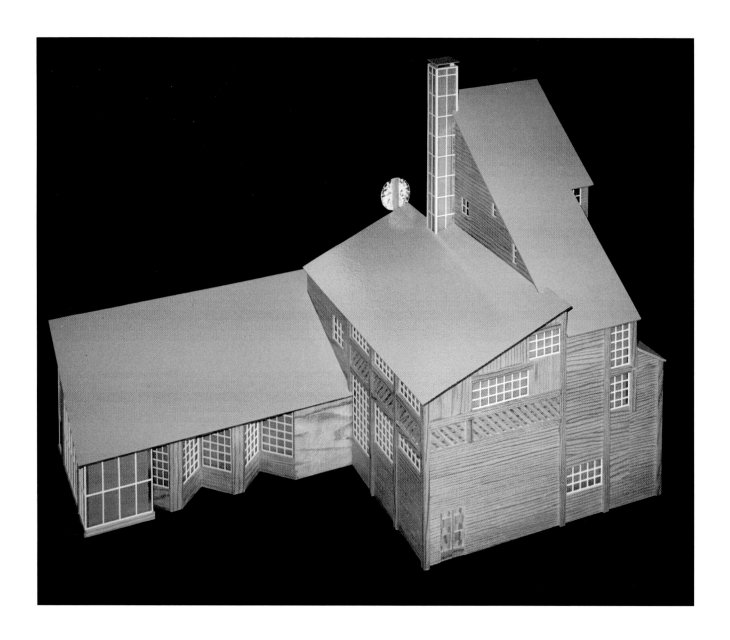

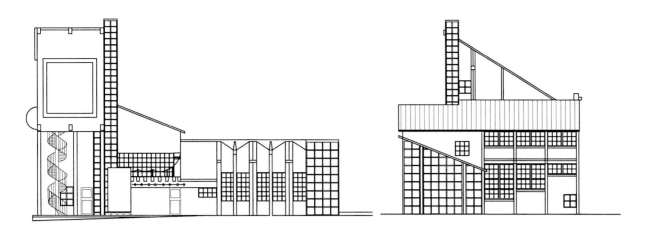

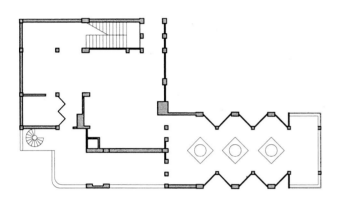

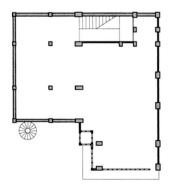

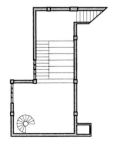

expression. Features of this technique were: a long 1.5 mile visitor's route and the 200 square sazen impact area. In this way, the architect whose initial assignment was to build a small (kiosk-type) structure, created a visitor flow scheme (having changed the production process of the building owner), and thanks to this scheme, achieved the maximum architectural impact on the viewer. Makhorka was but an initial step in this direction. Mel'nikov's desire to 'guide' his viewer through and around architectural space found greater expression in the 1925 Paris pavilion, and later in the seven workers' social clubs designed by him in Moscow. The architectural community of the Twenties was unanimous in calling Makhorka the most artistic and innovative exhibition pavilion.

The model of the Makhorka pavilion was made in 1982, commissioned by the A.V. Ščusev State Research Institute of Architecture for the festival "The days of the Russian Federation in Italy".
Irina Čepkunova

1 Russian measure of length, equivalent to 2.13 metres.
2 Russian measure of length, equivalent to 1066,79 metres.
3 From K.S. Mel'nikov, *Arkhitektura moej žizni. Tvorčeskaja koncepcija. Tvorčeskaja praktika*, Moskva 1985, p. 155.
4 *Ibidem*, p. 156.

The Novo-Sukharevskij Market

"(…) Near Sukharev Tower the new merchants bravely took their fate in their hands and built the impressive 'Novaja Sukharevka' market on a huge earmarked site inside the neighbouring block. (…) The construction of the market began under the state-funded Moscow Communal Management scheme, but, under the influence of the non-state funded tower, the merchants fell in love with architecture. (…) In the midst of all the surrounding visual delights rose the monumental building of the Committee with its tavern-style saloons, and the fervent passion of the famous Sukharevka had once more returned, in architectural form, to Moscow. My departure from the country did not inconvenience the builders. (…) From Paris I sent back a sketch of the market's colour scheme: a bouquet of flowers for each row and for every type of trade. But when I returned in 1926, the whiteness of January had shrouded both the New Economic Policy and my patrons in permanent snow, and forced architecture to transfer its attention to other projects, at home or abroad."
K.Mel'nikov, 1967[1]

Sukharevskij market site developpement

The site designated for laying out the Novo-Sukharevskij market in the Twenties is located in the block of land which abuts on to the Sadovoe Kol'co (Garden Ring) and which looks on to Sretenka—one of Moscow's historic trading streets.

The area close to Sretenka, in terms of the city's layout, is characterised by relatively early residential occupation. There were numerous settlements here from the earliest times, especially military ones. In the sixteenth century, in the immediate vicinity of the Novo-Sukharevskij market site stood the Nikolaevskij (St. Nicholas) Friary; it was on a high elevation, between two hollows formed by the River Neglinnaja and an unnamed stream, both of which flowed through the vegetable gardens towards the Sretenka. In 1547 the friary burned down, and was never restored. The site was later occupied by the Church of St. Nicholas, which remained there until the Thirties.

Unlike the majority of blocks in the Sretenka area, the market site was particularly spacious. The residential courtyards of the settlers ran along the streets and alleys, but the courtyards themselves were not built on, and were apparently used for tillage or for cattle-pasturing, since both were a regular feature of life in the settlements. The layout of the block which had formed in the seventeenth century has survived several centuries. In 1701 the Sretenskij Gate was replaced by the Sukharev Tower, where Russia's first school for the training of naval officers was opened. The tower became encircled by a large unplanned market, which became a natural completion of Sretenka Street, already by then a trading area fully occupied by trading-stalls. In the eighteenth century the interior courtyard area was being used for vegetable-growing, but in the 1740's it was taken over by the silk factory. Even so, the interior area was still not built on. In the process of the area's evolution through the eighteenth and nineteenth centuries, the building plan along the boundary lines of the block was altered, and even up to the early Twenties its central part remained in use as vegetable gardens, which belonged, at this time, to the Gethsemane Brotherhood of the Troice-Sergiev Monastery. In the early years of this century the block was considered unprestigious and undesirable as a place of residence, being so closely located to the market. This situation was exacerbated by the fact that the 'vegetable-plot economy' in the centre of the site was being run in the old way and had created many additional inconveniences for the local residential population. In the Tenths the city authorities prohibited the further use of the area for vegetable-growing, and this had the effect of stimulating the construction of large blocks of apartments for rent in the Sukharev Square area. This period saw the construction of one of Moscow's first cinema buildings.

The urban-regulation measures of the Twenties and the desire to achieve unimpeded traffic-flow along the city streets resulted in the closure of the Sukharev Tower market and the removal

View of the Novo-Sukharevskij market and of the coffee-bar building, 1924

View of the market on the Sadovoe kol'co in front of the Seremetevskij hospital and of the Sukharevskaja tower, Tenths

of the trading site to the centre of the block which abutted on to the Sadovoje Kol'co (Garden Ring). By this time some warehouses and only one residential rent-block had been built along the inner boundaries of the area in question. A large proportion of the area remained vacant.

Mel'nikov's design
Having analysed the planning situation and the distribution of properties, Mel'nikov decided to provide through-access from the streets to the market-place via Tupoj Lane, which led off Sretenka, and two narrow estates from the direction of Malaja Sukharevskaja Square and Bol'šoj Sukharevskij Lane. The central entrance to the market was from Sukharevskaja Street, at an angle to the existing line of buildings.
In this way, the market ended up being well integrated with the evolved layout of the block, and provided an organic in-fill of the 'compositional gap' in its centre. At the same time, thanks to street-trading—an everyday city activity—the new market succeeded in completely integrating the block into the developed city complex which Sukharevskaja Square was to become in the Twenties.
In the Thirties the timber buildings were gradually demolished. Up to the present, only the central administrative block has remained intact.
The area has now, once again,

been excluded from the general fabric of the city and is host to unplanned buildings.
On the backcloth of Twenties urban planning, the model of Moscow shows the pattern of construction in those years: the Sukharev Tower was still standing, the avenue had not yet become a wide circular thoroughfare lined with large buildings.
The site for redevelopment is bordered by dense housing construction and long, low-rise—mainly office—buildings. The entire new market complex may be seen as a city within a city, in terms of both the use of the land and the modern-style planning solution radically different from traditional planning convention.
The baroque ellipse of the

market's centre layer gives the trading area a compact scale, since it is similar in size to the original residential area.
On its south side, it is set off by unobtrusive rows of trading stalls. The radiating lines of stalls are moderated by the strict geometry of the overall solution. The dominant point of the largest building—the only original building still standing, which is at the power-supply centre of the complex— harmonises all its parts into a single whole.
An artistic compositional idea is not the sole objective of a designer's work, since it is naturally linked with functional development criteria.
The entrances to the market-place, which define the directions of the compositional

axes, face towards the adjacent side-streets and thoroughfares across the reconstructed site and channel the flows of traffic and people in an organised way.
Jurij Volčok, Elena Nikulina, Aleksandr Šadrin

[1] From K. S. Mel'nikov, *Arkhitektura moej žizni. Tvorčeskaja koncepcija. Tvorčeskaja praktika*, Moskva 1985, p. 74.

Reconstruction of the Novo-
Sukharevskij market area before
and after the realization of the
project (Ju. Volčok, E. Nikulina)

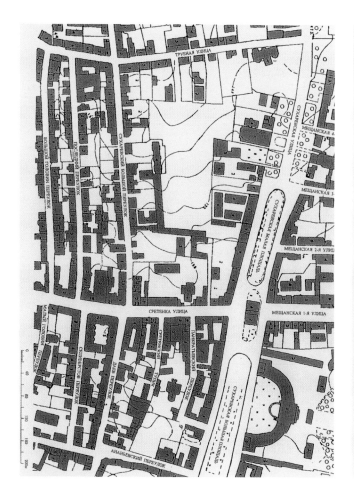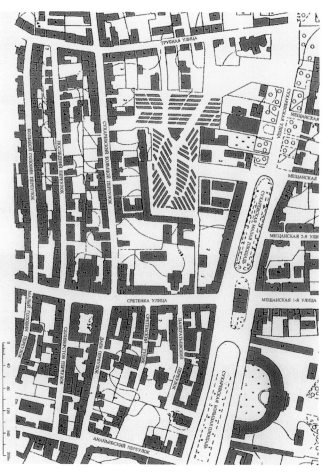

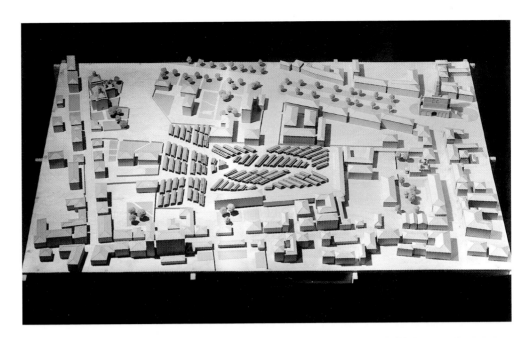

**Leningradskaja
Pravda**

"I designed this five-storey building as a light steel skeleton construction in order to get a firm conviction that the idea of the 'Living Architecture'—which occurred to me and struck me as well—is feasible. The pavilion of the Moscow branch of the 'Lenpravda' newspaper had, without doubt, some advertising elements, and this prompted me to bring the advertising actions in the organism of the building itself.
The round static core (with a staircase and a lift) threads the beads of floors, which can rotate in any direction with the resulting endless play of different architectural shapes—the so far unexplored power of the architectural dynamics.
The plan shows the facade with the floors unfolded into a full angle of rotation."
K.S. Mel'nikov, 1924[1]

Utilising these annotated comments by K.S. Mel'nikov *a posteriori* to his design for the Leningradskaja building, and the representation of the edifice in the only existing drawing—the elevation—two separate reconstruction hypotheses have been developed: the first by Otakar Máčel, Robert Notrott in the model realised at the Faculty of Architecture of TU-Delft, the second by Erich Steiner in the digital model realised in the Faculty of Architecture of the University of Innsbruck.
M.M.

Reconstruction by O. Máčel and R. Nottrot
Mel'nikov's design for the Moscow branch of the Leningrad paper *Leningradskaja Pravda* was a project for a closed competition held on 16 July 1924.[2] Apart from Mel'nikov, the other participants were Ivan Golosov and the brothers Alexander and Viktor Vesnin. The chosen location was a small 6 x 6 plot on Strastnaja square (Puskin square). The task was concerned less with providing comfortable offices for the editors of the newspaper than with 'expressing the agitative character of the building'.[3] In other words, the building was required to serve as visual propaganda.
As was characteristic of the pioneering years of the new Soviet state, the participating architects self-confidently equated this visual propaganda with their avant-garde architectural idiom. In their eyes the new architecture represented the new social order, agitation by political iconography, in a way that would never have occurred to them later, in the era of socialist realism. Consequently they each submitted entries with a definite individual character. Mel'nikov himself wrote later that the exercise developed into an architectonic duel with the Vesnins.[4] It seems that as far as he was concerned the entry sent in by his colleague Golosov, with whom he taught at

VKhUTEMAS, did not really count.
The project by Alexander and Viktor Vesnin is the best-known entry to the competition. An industrial-looking building, with constructional elements deliberately displayed as design features—a shaft derrick and visible moving lifts. This was the Vesnins' second important 'romantic constructivism' project, the successor to their Palace of Labour project.[5] Il'ja Golosov's entry was based on a floor plan of two squares superimposed at an angle of 45 degrees to one another, so creating and eight-point star. The structure erected on this base was prism-shaped, broken only by a cylinder-shaped volume at first floor level. A narrow, postmodern-looking vertical disc and a projecting vertical addition on one side of the volume gave the building an asymmetric look.[6] Finally Mel'nikov submitted a single drawing showing a building with five storeys, each positioned differently.[7]
The basic idea of Mel'nikov's entry was a fixed round core containing a spiral staircase and a lift, with five floors arranged round it. The ground floor was conceived as fixed, the four upper floors as moving round the core. This is why at first sight his drawing seems asymmetrical, because he was trying to show the different ways in which two floors could be set relative to one another.

How the floors were supposed to be turned is not entirely clear. Only one vague provisional sketch is known still to exist, which shows three volumes turning. The building was conceived as a construction of steel and glass. The visible constructional elements and the diagonal external staircases for each floor relate this design to 'romantic constructivism'. Although the drawing is graphically unimpressive, Mel'nikov's design is the most advanced of the three entries. The projects by the Vesnins and by Golosov look much better as drawings, but apparently Mel'nikov thought that the principle of his design would be decisive, not its presentation. While a sense of movement and dynamism was expressed in the Vesnins' design by 'illustrating' movement and hinted at by Golosov by the use of expressive forms,[8] Mel'nikov conveyed it literally (if conceptually). He himself referred to it as 'living architecture',[9] in the same way as he was later to refer to the moving walls in his clubs as 'living walls'. This may indicate that Mel'nikov, in contrast to his colleagues, saw movement not as a rendering of mechanical inspiration but by analogy with a living organism.
His design for a moving building did however fit into the short-lived tradition of dynamic constructivist architecture that had developed in the

*Area of Puskin square where
the building was to be erected*

*Competition project for the
Moscow offices of the*
Leningradskaja Pravda
newspaper, 1924

meanwhile, beginning in 1919
with Tatlin's Tower for the
Congress of the Third
International. As examples of
what the movement actually
achieved in architecture, one
might mention stage settings by
Alexander Vesnin and Ljubov'
Popova, or A. Exter, B. Gladkov
and V. Mukhina's *Izvestia*
pavilion at the All Union
Argricultural exhibition held in
Moscow in 1923.[10] At the
beginning of the Twenties,
movement, actual or conceptual,
was seen as representative of
the dynamism of the new era, so
that Mel'nikov's design
represented the propagandistic
aspect of the new society in the
architectonic style of the day.
The Novo-Rjazanskaja indoor
goods vehicles park, the
Bakhmetevskaja bus depot and
the Intourist indoor car park can
all be seen in built form. The
reconstructions of these
buildings were based on
comparisons between the shape
as drawn and the shape as built.
The indoor car park in Paris and
the *Pravda* pavilion exist only as
drawings and are therefore
interesting to model. In these
cases it is hardly appropriate to
describe the process as reconstruction. The buildings are
in fact constructed, albeit to
scale, directly from the
drawings. It is a rewarding
business, because the result it
will lead to is unknown, a
surprise. The single drawing that
Mel'nikov provided of an
elevation of the *Pravda* pavilion

Views of the model
(realised by R. Nottrot with
J. Aulman)

makes a challenging starting point for research into and construction of a model. Mel'nikov's own notes and notes made by Frederick Starr, who had met him, provide a little more help, though still inadequately. "The five-storey building is presented as a construction of light steel ribs, to pass on the conviction that the plan could actually be put into practice. My mind is filled with the fascinating notion of 'Living Architecture' (...) A static round core (staircase and lift shaft) surrounded by floors which can simply rotate in any direction: the endless magic of a wealth of architectonic silhouettes... the still unknown force of architectonic dynamics. The elevation is shown on the drawing with the floors fanned out to make a complete circle"[11], wrote Mel'nikov. Starr refers us to a previous sketch which appears on the same sheet of paper as a perspective view of the Makhorka pavilion. Could it be that the spiral staircase that he used in this pavilion and against which he once posed for a photo was his inspiration for these rotating floors? The American historian also tells us something about the shape of the floors: "The design—for which unfortunately only one preliminary sketch and one drawing survive - was based on a series of identical glassed-in units that were to be stacked one on top of the other to form the sculptural whole. In the

earliest sketch, these units were to be trapezoidal in plan, while in the more definitive drawing they are lozenge-shaped."[12] Literally any form could be hidden behind the elevation as drawn, unless a particular concept is assumed when working out the floor plans. A first attempt at interpretation assumed five identical floors in an arrangement which seen from above resembled a pentagon or five-point Soviet star. This failed to produce a result which agreed with the drawing of the elevation. In subsequent researches it was found more useful to assume that the ground floor had a different shape from the others. In the end, working on the basis of four identical floors rotated in four directions at right angles to one other, it turned out that the simple drawing of the elevation was actually highly refined. The floors, piled on top of one another, between them show all the elevations which go to make a single floor. This may also explain why Mel'nikov's competition entry consisted of no more than a single drawing. It is also important to realise that at the beginning of this century architects often let themselves be specially inspired by industrial products. When it turned out that in the final model as seen from above the general offices in the Pravda tower assumed the shape of a ship's propeller, this was very much in tune with the spirit of the age.

The rotation of the floors seems possible because of the way they are arranged round an axle, a cylinder in fact. This cylinder was most probably intended to contain a staircase and a lift, with the stairs spiralling round the lift shaft. The floors appear to be supported by steel trusses, arranged around the central cylinder. In the drawing these trusses are shown to be either straight or curved. They do of course curve round the cylinder, but even the glass elevations on the first and second floors still show slight curves. In the model these parts of the elevation are translated into glass elevations which are also curved in plan. In the drawing the glass elevations on the third and fourth floors are provided with straight trusses. Working on the principle that curved trusses indicate a curved section of the elevation, it follows that the sections of the elevation in which the truss is straight also follow a straight line. If the straight elevations in the floor plan of a floor stand out radially from the cylinder and the curved elevation flows tangentially from the cylinder, this turns out to leave room for the missing piece of elevation, visible in the drawing on the first and fourth floor, the part of the elevation with no trusses. This arrangement seems to provide an alternative way of constructing the elevation as drawn. Anyone who is more familiar with Mel'nikov's drawings knows that once in a

while he allowed himself minor structural faults for the sake of a 'pretty picture'. The small differences between Mel'nikov's drawing and the newly constructed version may therefore possibly be explained as Mel'nikov's 'poetic licence'. In earlier attempts to achieve complete correspondence between the original drawing and the reconstruction, the floor plan turned out to assume a geometry that might well be termed 'imperfect'. During the investigation Starr's assertion that the different units were identical was taken seriously, but considerable doubt was cast on the 'precision' of Mel'nikov drawing.

On further analysis of the result a number of problem areas came to light concerning the building's 'dynamics'. Rotation of the floors relative to one another turned out to be less straightforward than one might at first have thought. One might well wonder what inspirations Mel'nikov had had during the design process. The position of the internal stairs turns out to create a 'dead' angle, within which rotation is impossible. The entrance from the office wings to the staircase is blocked by the stairs through an angle of about 90 degrees. The stairs outside the building act in a similar way. Two floors can be rotated relative to one another only as far as the external stairs allow. It is possible to affect the angle through which a floor can

be turned by making the stairs that run along the curved elevation movable, so that the angle between two floors can be increased by 'gliding' along the elevation. During the research the idea of the external stairs 'gliding' round the curved parts of the elevation was eagerly accepted and was viewed as supporting the decision to make these elevations curved. Mel'nikov's drawing gives too few indications of the shape of the ground floor. In the reconstruction the cylindrical core is continued down to ground level, so determining the shape of part of the rear elevation. The external stairs are extended by an extra flight curling round the core on the ground floor. The facade to the ground floor, following Mel'nikov drawing, has a small relatively heavily proportioned section on the left with a larger more fragile-looking section on the right. The section of the facade on the left has a 'weight' that may perhaps indicate the basic shape of the floor plan: a rectangular space, on to which the more transparent part of the building is built, as represented by the fragile right-hand section of the facade in the drawing. The width of this built-on section is the same as that of the head elevations of the individual floors.

Because deducing colours from black-and-white illustrations is always bound to create uncertainty about the 'correct'

colour, the model is finished in grey, and so is limited to indicating the shape that emerged from the research.
Otakar Máčel, Robert Notrott

Reconstruction by E. Steiner
This non-realised competition design for a Moscow-branch of the newspaper *Leningradskaia Pravda* is a rare example of 'kinetic architecture'.
In contrast to many examples of utopian designs at that time, it would have been possible to construct the building by contemporary technologies. Quotation by Mel'nikov: "Onto a round, static core (with elevator and staircase), the floors are arranged, with its free and independent revolving in any direction you like."[13] While Mel'nikov was integrating his idea of the revolving units, as a synonym for technology, motion and power directly into the building, he created an "architecture organism" showing the spirit of the revolution.
Our reconstruction of the project is based on the following principles assunti.
1) *Static System*. Steel frame-overhanging girder. The cantilevered storeys are held and stiffened on both sides with

these girders on the central tower. Specific feature: The truss joists of the steel frames are formed straight on the one and parabolic at the other side of these units. Since the diagonals are connected close to the window raster and because of the windows are not showing any shortening on the whole length-side of the unit, I would say that a bending of the truss joist in a second level is impossible, excepting the tower area.
2) *Materials*. Floors in glassed-in steel frame; tower in steel-concrete (bending stress). If it were a steel-construction you would see the joints of the metal sheeting on Mel'nikov's drawing.
3) *Scale-definition*. From sizes of people, railings, rooms and stairs.
4) *Ground projection of Mel'nikov's drawing*. Each top view of the floors shows oblique-angled shaped trapezoidal units, on the one longitudinal side tangential and on the other side in a more central direction to the core.
5) *Definition of the window-modules*. Frontsides: the intimated ellipse on the second floor is resulting as a circle in the front view; that means that

from the height of this ellipse you get the horizontal size of one window; by addition of these modules, the whole length of the frontside will result. Lengthsides: both lengthsides from each of the rotating units are varied in length as a result of the different numbers of windows; the lenghtside on the third floor appears nearly without a shortening, so that you can get a window-module for these sides of the units.
6) *Doors*. Quotation by Mel'nikov: "The view is drawed in the full rotation of the circle."[14] That means to us, that this original drawing from Mel'nikov shows a very specific situation. A situation of a limiting state regarding the revolving units. From this state it is possible to recognise the movement of direction from this specific situation and also you can fix an approximate area of door-openings from the core to the units.
7) *Stairs and elevator*. Outside stairs: they are constructed in the computer-space and changed as long as they are corresponding to the stairs on the original drawing. The result is that the stair near the second floor is outside this unit but if we look carefully at the drawing, a

tall shadow around the ellipse on the frontside, offers us the possibility of an overhanging landing for this stair. The stair to the top of the fifth floor creates an unexpected problem. Completing this stair, following the original drawing, it intersects this revolving unit. Logically, the stair should be near the railing. There are two possibilities concerning the reconstruction. The first one is to accept this as a deliberate action of the architect, or second to assume that it is a big drawing-mistake. We decided the first, because you cannot see the outside stairs of the ground floor and the fifth floor, I constructed them with the main design in mind. The 'chimney' on the top of the building height without antenna (22.37 meters), locates the position of the elevator.

8) *Bearings*. Mel'nikov intimates a thrust bearing and casters on the underside (bottom) of the storeys as a protection against overturning. These casters could also be a primitive drive-system.

9) *Ground floor*. For this storey the drawing shows the less indications concerning the probable shape. After a first rectangular variation, we decided to take over the principle of the oblique-angle shape. On account of the suggested landing base on the right part of the front side, and because of the differing facade design and the letters (*kontora* = office),we interpretate this area as a protruding-entrance.

Epilog – Knowledges
The rotation of the units is limited by railings, outside stairs and by the door-openings into the tower. We can also say that it was not desired, as a result of statically—and designing considerations, that all the units are positioned congruent on top of each other. The modest polychrome version of my photorealistic pictures refers to a colour-scheme that Mel'nikov developed for his 'torgsektor sale kiosks' (Paris 1925).

Acknowledgements
For their friendly support during our work, we would like to thank Professors Rainer Gräfe of Innsbruck University and Leonid Demjanov of the Moskow Architecture University.
Erich Steiner

[1] From K.S. Mel'nikov, *Arkhitektura moej žizni. Tvorčeskaja koncepcija. Tvorčeskaja praktika*, Moskva 1985, p. 158.

[2] C. Cooke, I. Kazus, *Soviet Architectural Competitions 1924-1936*, London 1992, pp. 11-12, 18-21.

[3] N.P. Bylinkin, A.V. Rjabusin (ed.), *Istorija sovetskoj arkhitektury (1917-1954)*, Moscow 1985, p. 54.

[4] K.S. Mel'nikov, *Arkhitektura moej zizni*, cit., p. 73.

[5] See S.O. Khan-Magomedov, *Alexander Vesnin and Russian Constructivism*, New York 1986, pp. 123-125, 127-128; A. Kopp: *Constructivist Architecture in the USSR*, London-New York 1985, pp. 44-46.

[6] See S.O. Khan-Magomedov, *Il'ja Golosov*, Moskou 1988, pp. 114-115.

[7] See S.F. Starr, *Melnikov. Solo Architect in a Mass Society*, Princeton 1978, pp. 70-72; S.O. Khan-Magomedov, *Konstantin Mel'nikov*, Moskva 1990, pp. 67-68, 76,78. The illustration of the design as given by Starr differs in detail from the accepted version; it seems to have been copied (possibly by Mel'nikov himself).

[8] In his preliminary designs Golosov considered giving the facade two ascending diagonal bands, suggesting a dynamic driving force, S.O. Khan-Magomedov, 1988, *op. cit.*, p. 115.

[9] K.S. Mel'nikov, *Proekt pavil'ona gazety 'Lenpravda' v Moskve*, typescript 1924(?), in Idem, *Arkhitektura moej žizni, op. cit.*, p. 158.

[10] Chr. Lodder, *Russian Constructivism*, New Haven-London 1985, pp. 166-168, 170-180.

[11] K.S. Mel'nikov, *Arkhitektura moej zizni, op. cit.*, p. 158.

[12] S.F. Starr, *op. cit.*, p. 70.

[13] K.S. Mel'nikov, *Proekt pavil'ona gazety 'Lenpravda' v Moskve, cit.*, p. 158.

[14] *Ibidem*.

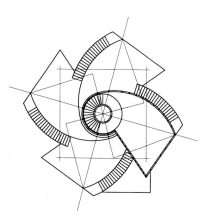
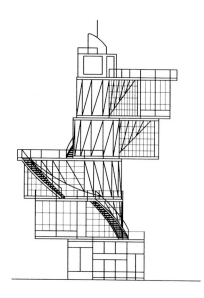
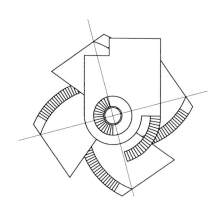

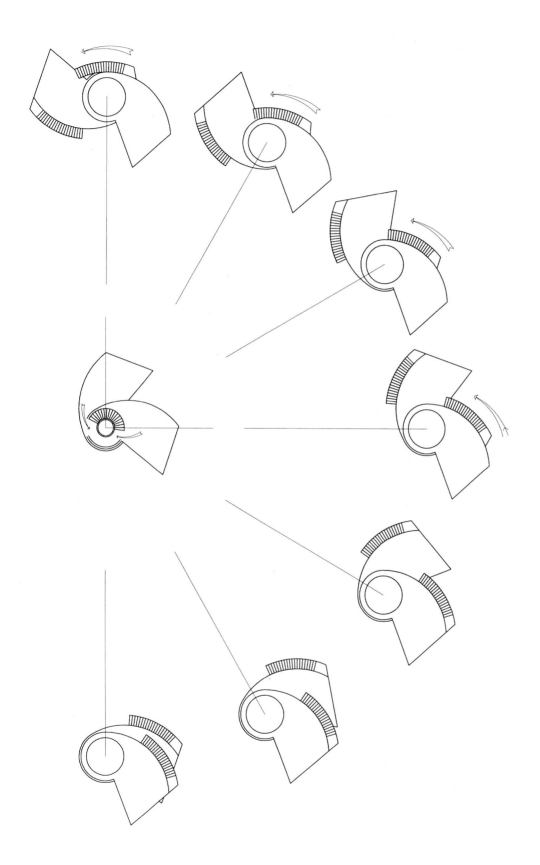

Leningradskaja Pravda, *1924*
(digital model by E. Steiner,
re-drawn by J. Aulman)
scale 1:300

The Pavilion of the USSR at the "International Exhibition of Contemporary Decorative Arts and Industry" in Paris

"When I was working on the Soviet pavilion for the Paris exhibition of 1925, the task that was given me came down to exceptionally laconic, yet very concrete formula: 'It is necessary to construct a pavilion.' A plot of land was also indicated to me. That was almost the sum of it. I clarified what was to be displayed in the pavilion, in what quantity, etc., and I made detailed calculations, but could not find a solution to the task. Then, when completely diverted from the results prompted by the calculations, I quite unexpectedly even for myself received the solution to the pavilion that I had been looking for. It even changed my original 'calculations' to a certain extent … I had finished the pavilion at the Paris exhibition and the 'Makhorka' pavilion at the Agricultural exhibition in Moscow in 1923 right up to the poster on the wall and the coat of arms over the entrance to the exhibition—without any finishing touches or retouches."
K.S. Mel'nikov, 1933[1]

"The light from above was designed without glass and without cascades. Daylight freely penetrated in rays from various corners; it played on the red planes, and the red colour was reflected on the visitors—they all went red, whether they wanted it or not. The inexplicable, which is the true product of architecture, was hidden in the opposing combinations of the homogeneous masses of the pavilion."
K.S. Mel'nikov, 1967[2]

"The territory on which we were building the 'red pavilion' was not only small (29.5 by 11 metres), but also to the highest degree unsuitable for building. The square was crossed by tram lines, which it was forbidden to remove, in accordance with the conditions laid down by the Parisian authorities. Consequently, the dimensions of our building were limited not only in the horizontal, but also in the vertical plane. It was impossible to put a foundation under the building because of the tram lines. One had to think that many would gloat over the fact that the Soviet Union 'is not putting down roots' in the literal sense of the word. Well, we had only just accomplished the revolution, we were young, and we could shrug off the difficulties.
England and France constructed luxurious structures—not pavilions, but real palaces. The Italian pavilion was like that of a shopkeeper who had struck it rich. This was the tradition of many French exhibitions, and the pavilion was often officially called 'The Palace of Arts', ' The Palace of Electricity'.
We—the Soviet people—hated everything in architecture that reminded us of palaces. This applied not only to the exhibition, but to all architecture throughout the world. We were creating 'anti-palace' architecture. So we renounced the closed-in spaces that reminded us of palace suites and the expanses of walls which closed in the narrow world of palace life; we strove to join the interior with the exterior, considering this to be democratic…
Alexander Rodčenko was the pavilion's main artist. We understood each other, were quick on the uptake, as they say, for Rodčenko considered exhibition compositions to be a variety of architecture. My struggle in architecture was with 'the palace', while his struggle in exposition was with 'the shop' , for previously every exhibition was no different from a large shopping arcade."
K.S. Mel'nikov, 1966[3]

Immediately after the establishment of diplomatic relations between the 'red' USSR and France at the end of 1924, the USSR was invited to take part in the International exhibition of decorative arts, which was supposed to open in Paris in the spring of 1924. The organisation of the pavilion was entrusted to the Exhibition committee formed in association with the Russian Academy of artistic sciences, which began its work on November 13, 1924. Immediately a competition for sketches of the pavilion was organised. Insofar as the president of the committee was the people' s Commissar for Enlightment N.A. Lunačarskij, a convinced supporter of classicism in architecture, besides the Muscovite architect-avant-gardists—the Vesnin brothers, M.Ja. Ginzburg, I.A. Golosov, N.A. Ladovskij, K.S. Mel'nikov, N.V. Dokučaev, V.F. Krinskij and a group of graduates of VKhUTEMAS—orders were also given to the traditionalist academicians I.A. Fomin and V.A. Scuko from Petrograd. Evidently warning of the possibility of protection being given to the 'classics' by the people' s commissar, L.B. Krasin, an authoritative statesman who was at that time the Soviet ambassador in France, in a letter to A. Lunačarskij warned him: it is necessary ' at all costs to avoid our being reproached for wanting to show off the artistic achievements of the previous epoch. Let out exhibition be boor or insufficient, but it must unfailingly be ours, Soviet."[4] The organisers of the Soviet pavilion set out from the idea that "all countries attach enormous significance to the exhibition and have been preparing for it for a long time without sparing expense, so that they will furnish their premises in a rich and luxurious manner. Our aims and our approach is completely different: we attach a political and commercial significance to the exhibition … We are not intending to compete in luxury with the foreign states, but we still hope to show what new things we have done in this period and in what these new things have found their expression … It has been decided … to make a powerful exhibit out of … our pavilion, too; it would reveal, on the one

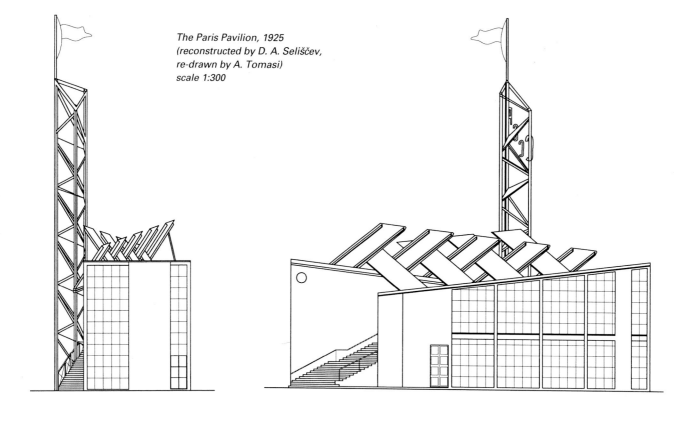

The Paris Pavilion, 1925
(reconstructed by D. A. Seliščev,
re-drawn by A. Tomasi)
scale 1:300

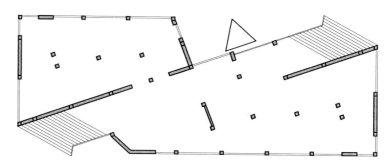

hand, our architecture, and on the other—our national creativity and culture."[5]

The competition was opened on November 18, 1924 for one month. The Exhibition committee presented the principled requirement that "the pavilion must express the idea of the USSR", " from the outside it must be original and must be distinguished in character from the usual European architecture."[6] On December 18, 1924 a special commission (N.D. Bartram, Y.A. Tugendholdt, D.P. Sterenberg, B.V. Šaposnikov, E.E. Arkin) with the participation of Lunačarskij and Majakovskij reviewed the sketches presented. The Vesnin brothers and the graduates of VKhUTEMAS did not present projects. The second and third prizes were won by Ladovskij and Ginzburg respectively.[7] Mel'nikov's project was recognised to be the best. It

was offered to him that he present a project by December 30 that had been reworked in accordance with Lunačarskij's comments. This final project was approved by the Exhibition committee on January 6, 1925. On January 11, 1925 the newspaper *Izvestia* no longer spoke about the 'classics', but informed its readers: "As a result of a closed competition to which the best young architectural talents were invited, the Committee accepted the project for the pavilion of the USSR belonging to Architect Mel'nikov. This pavilion, being light in structure, reflects the idea of the USSR as a workers-peasants' state and a union of separate national republics. Architect Mel'nikov is going to Paris, where he will immediately set about constructing the pavilion." An area on the Prospect Cour-la-Reine, two blocks away from the

Alexander III bridge, opposite the Grand Palais exit, at the main entrance to the exhibition, was assigned for the building of the pavilion. Just next to the USSR's pavilion was Italy's, on the other side of it was Norway's, and not far away—England's. The overall effective area of the pavilion was foreseen by Mel'nikov's project—the building blueprints had been made by the engineer-architect B.V. Gladkov—as 380 square metres (including 125 square metres for passages), of which the area of the ground floor was 231 square metres and of the first floor—149 square metres. The opening of the Paris exhibition took place on April 28, 1925 at three in the afternoon. Among the national pavilions the Soviet pavilion was the only one which deliberately used the innovative language of architecture and art for the creation of its artistic image. It

stood out sharply amidst the eclectic styles of the pavilions of other countries. The volumetric composition of this light wooden frame construction represented a rectangular, two-storeyed construction, cut through diagonally by a broad open staircase lea ding to the first floor and covered by an original spatial structure—two rows of flat, mutually intersecting slabs Most of the area of the external walls was glazed, which permitted people to see the exhibits of Gostorg, Gosizdat and the exhibit devoted to the various nationalities of the USSR from the outside, without going into the pavilion. Beside the staircase there rose a triangular wooden mast, which was crowned by the symbol 'USSR' and the red flag—signs of enthusiasm for heroic activity. The façade planes of the walls and the structural elements of

140

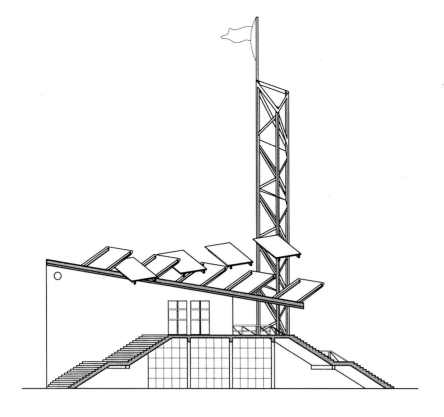

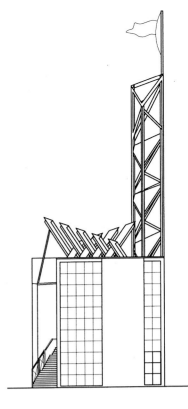

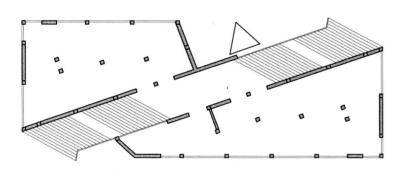

the pavilion and the tower were coloured, in accordance with the sketches of the main architect of the pavilion, A. Rodčenko, in red and grey. All the wooden parts were prepared in a factory, they were gathered in one place and raised by girders on cranes without scaffolding. The mast was built in the same way—in two stages: first two thirds, and then the rest. Thanks to the fact that all the structural elements had been prepared in the factory, the pavilion was assembled by nine workmen in a little more than a month.[8]

Mel'nikov's Soviet pavilion, which was counted worthy of the Grand Prix in Paris, became one of the first substantial innovative works, not only of Soviet, but also of world architecture in the twentieth century. Le Corbusier 's opinion is well-known; he used to say that the Soviet pavilion was the only pavilion at the

exhibition that was worth looking at. Through the language of its artistic forms its architecture proclaimed the new striving— both social and aesthetic—of socialist society. In the "Explanation of the works of the architect K. Mel'nikov", note was made of the symbolic expression of the union of nationalities in the very architecture of the pavilion: "The Union of Republics is expressed in the structure of ceiling, consisting of elements that mutually support each other."[9]

After the completion of the work of the exhibition, the USSR pavilion was given to the Council of workers' syndicates of Paris and put in a new place in another region—on the Avenue Maturennes Moreau. But later it was dismantled. Several attempts have been made to recreate it in Paris, but without success to this day.

In 1996, in the Moscow Institute of Communal Economy and Construction (MIKKHIS), in which the Professor Emeritus and Doctor of Architecture K.S. Mel'nikov had in the course of sixteen years (from 1958 to 1974) passed on his knowledge and creative experience to students, the question was raised concerning the recreation of the distinguished monument of architecture that was now lost in one of the parks of the city of Moscow. In connection with this various factual graphical material was investigated: project solutions accomplished by Mel'nikov and published in the native and foreign press, models preserved in the A.V. Ščusev State Museum of Architectural Science and Research (GMA), archive material given by the families of K.S. Mel'nikov and A.M. Rodčenko, and also site photographs of the pavilion. It

was noted that Mel'nikov had, in the process of building, introduced a serious of changes into the work which had not been recorded by him in drafts and were not illumined in the literature or in existent models (that were made later).

As a result of a comparative analysis of project solutions and realised spatial, architectural planning and structural solutions (according to archival photographs, and taking into account the witnesses of contemporaries and relatives of Mel'nikov and Rodčenko), it was established that the constructed pavilion differed from the original project conception in various ways.[10]

For the working out of the corrected project materials, taking into account the above-mentioned changes, a geometrical analysis of the spatial-planning and structural solutions of the pavilion was required, since the blueprints known in the literature had not been parameterised. With the aid of large-scale transformations in accordance with the existing graphical data (facades and plans), a geometrical database on the structure was obtained, allowing one to reproduce any project document. On the basis of the geometrical modelling, both the previously known and unknown forms of blueprints were completely parameterised on an IBM computer: the main, rear and side facades, the plans of the ground and first floors, the diagrams of the positioning of the assembly-constructed elements of the ground and first floors (new), a section of the building, a plan of the roof (new) and a plan of the tower (new). A three-dimensional computer model of the pavilion was formed.

A model of the pavilion on a scale of 1:50, which guaranteed fidelity in the transfer of spatial-planning, geometrical, colour and other characteristics, was worked out, taking into account all the changes introduced by Mel'nikov into the structure in nature. It was stipulated that the model's roof should be detachable to permit a view of the interior.

The author and leader of the project for the recreation of the pavilion was Professor V.N. Semenov (deputy head of the MIKKHIS faculty, director of the SIUP Centre), the research, elaboration and execution of the model were performed by the construction engineer D.A. Seliščev. The computer modelling of the blueprints of the projects was carried out by the technician-architects N. Bočarova, T.V. Volkova, E.G. Kuznecova and A.K. Mukhametdinov, the consultant was the engineer P.V. Belenkij. The consultants on the reconstruction were the president of the KM-Centre I.A. Kazus' (deputy director of the A.V. Ščusev GMA) and the president of the scientific-method council of the KM-Centre, candidate of architecture S.G. Petrov (deputy head of the department of the A.V. Ščusev GMA).

Igor A. Kazus', Vadim N. Semenov

[1] From K. S. Mel'nikov, *Arkhitekturnoe proektirovanie (Architectural Planning)*. 1933 in *Mastera sevetskoj arkhitektury ob arkhiteture*, Moskva, Iskusstvo 1975, vol. 2, p. 171.
[2] S.O. Khan-Magomedov, *Konstantin Mel'nikov*, Strojizdat, Moskva 1990, pp. 82-102.
[3] B. Brodskij, *Khudožnik, gorod, celovek (The Artist, The City, Man)*, Moskva 1966, pp. 15-16.
[4] Karpova, P. *L.B. Krasin*. Moskva 1962, p. 181.
[5] Rjazencev, I. *Iskustvo sovetskogo vystavočnogo ansamblja 1917-1970 (The Art of Soviet ExhibitionEnsembles, 1917-1970)*, Moskva 1976, p. 25.
[6] V. E. Khazanova, K.N. Afanas'ev, *Iz istorii sovetskoj arkhitektury, 1917-1925: dokumenty i materialy*. Moskva 1963, p. 190.

[7] *Ibidem.*
[8] *Kraznyi zurnal* (Red Magazine), 1925, no. 12.
[9] Rjazancev, *Iskustvo sovetskogo vystavočnogo ansamblja 1917-1970*, cit., p. 305.
[10] In particular: 1. a podium was raised from all four facades; 2. a window frame was installed on the façade 1-15 under the staircase (on axes 5-6); 3. two round windows were installed on the facades 1-15 and 15-1 on the walls (on axes 1-2 and 15-14) on the first floor; 4. on façade 15-1 a two-storeyed window modulus (on axes 10-9) was replaced by a blind pier; 5. on façade 15-1 a door was installed in the blind pier (on axes 9-8); 6. on facades I-A and A-I blind piers (on axes Zh-D and B-G) were extended to the level of the roof; 7. a door was installed on the plan of the ground floor along facade 15-1 (on axes 9-8); 8. internal supporting columns were installed on the plan of the first floor along transverse axes 3-3, 7-7, 9-9 and 14-14; 9. the dimensions of the doorway on the plane of the first floor (on axes 8-9) were corrected; 10. above the staircase only nine mutually intersecting panels of ceiling were raised instead of ten; the panel of the extreme left of the tower was not installed; the spatial position of the panels was changed (made more precise); 11. a prop was made for the panel on the extreme right of the mutually intersecting panels above the staircase; 12. the 'hammer and sickle' emblem was installed on the extreme right of the mutually intersecting panels over the staircase; 13. on both sides of the flights of stairs on the staircase the first three steps were filled out with 'runners'; 14. the position and quantity of the uprights on the staircase banisters were changed(made more precise), as was the geometry of the banisters; 15. banisters were installed on the blind walls along the flights of stairs. The following changes were introduced into the construction of the tower: the cross-section of the three props had a trapezoid shape instead of the project's rectangular shape; the cross stays of the tower were attached above the props; the six triangular diaphragms were upholstered along the perimeter with boards and formed a box shape turned over from bottom to top; six vertical board-brackets were attached above the cross stays from the two sides along each prop; instead of the projected continuous diaphragm there was a crowning tie consisting of boards along the sides of the props; the composition of the 'USSR' symbol was corrected; a mast with a red flag was raised on the tower; all the facade planes of the pavilion, and also the surfaces of the structural elements, the mutually intersecting panels and the mast, were coloured in red and grey.

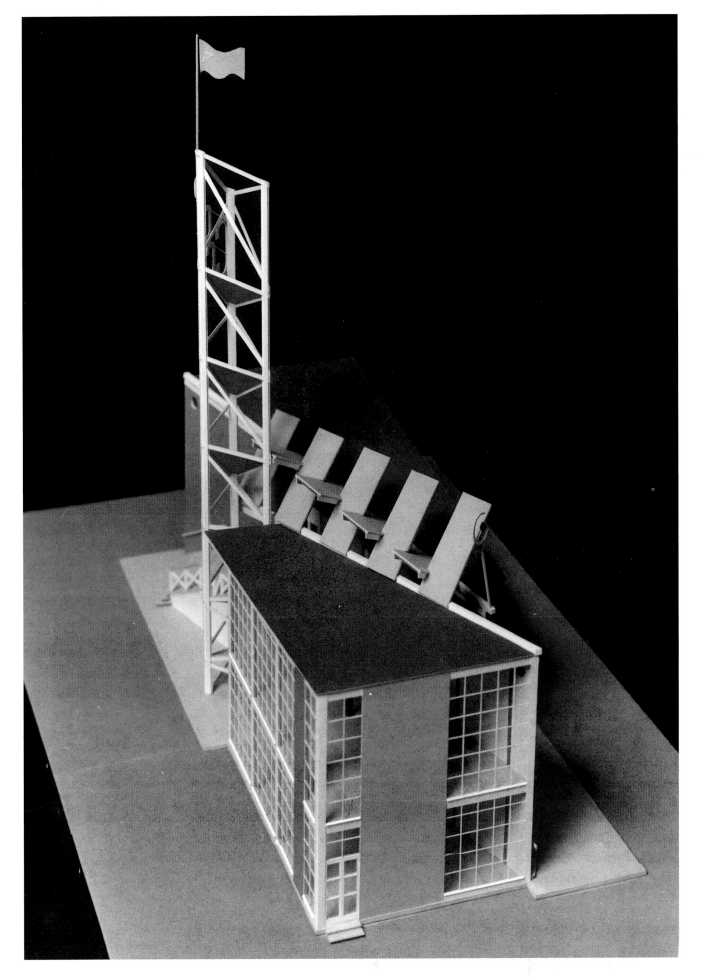

Garage, 1925-1927

**Indoor Car Park
Paris**

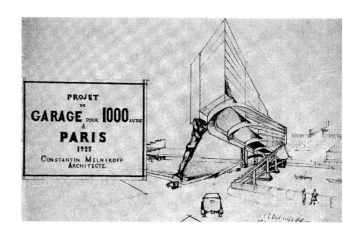

The success of the Soviet pavilion at the "Exposition des Arts Décoratifs" brought Mel'nikov an unexpected commission from the city of Paris, a design for an indoor car park for taxis with a capacity of a thousand vehicles. It is not known who precisely was the initiator of the commission. With the permission of Leonid Krasin, the Minister of foreign trade, who was staying in Paris at the time, Mel'nikov started work on this project in the summer of 1925, during his holiday in St. Jean de Luz. He prepared two different versions of which seven drawings are known in the literature. Neither version was realised.

Apart from the drawings already mentioned, no other source material is available. The first of Mel'nikov's own writings on this project date from the sixties and were published in part in a shortened form. His autobiographical work *Arkhitektura moej žizni*[1] (Architecture of my life), completed in 1967, contains a few remarks on the indoor car park project. There also exists a typescript *Stroitel'stvo garažej*[2] (The building of garages), bearing the date 29 October 1965, which contains information about his indoor car park projects in Moscow and Paris. In the autobiography Mel'nikov lists a few general principles which applied to the project. The requirements for ascending and descending

vehicles were first that their paths should not cross, second that the gradients should be the same, third that the bends should have the same radius and fourth that there should be the least possible number of bends. He also went on to mention the utilisation of the whole available floor area for parking, traffic lanes consisting entirely of ramps and a total height which should equal the height of the vehicles.[3]
The first version,[4] of which four drawings are known, was conceived as a detached, 10-storey high square, 50 metres by 50 metres, with a frontage designed as a grid made up of square elements. Four of these square elements were left open in two different places, allowing people outside to see two bits of the ramp. In this way Parisians were granted a fleeting glimpse of the ascending and descending vehicles. In his monograph, Starr compared the composition of the frontage to an Art Déco perfume bottle.[5] The system of ascending and descending seemed very advanced for its time but was not completely clear. Mel'nikov spoke of four non-intersecting spirals, which would seem to indicate a twofold application of a double spiral ramp, but the available drawings are too abstract and seem to contradict one another.[6] The four ramps would have had to cross the parking floors in such a way that the floor space available for

parking would have come to much less than Mel'nikov indicated in his plan. Cars were to park on the parking floor in single or double diagonal rows, which would have made for easier manoeuvring on the part of the drivers but would have reduced the parking capacity. The diagonal parking arrangement was known in 1925, as was the double spiral ramp, but the doubling of this arrangement of ramps was new. The only question is whether this system could actually have worked in the commission as specified.
The second version was an elongated volume with its centre resting on two supports, suspended above a bridge over the Seine. The ramps were designed to wind around the two long elevations and provide a spectacular view of arriving and departing vehicles. But it was not only the movement of the vehicles which was intended to contribute to the image of the dynamism of metropolitan life. Its concept was so daring that the building itself embodied a dramatic gesture. The suspended points of access from the bridge and the way they were continued in the diagonals of the ramps on the side walls gave a very exciting total impression. An additional feature was that the block was not completely rectangular but sloped gradually downwards towards the centre at the top and upwards away from the

centre at the bottom. This enormous projection appears to have worried the clients, so Mel'nikov decided to add an Atlas figure to each extremity of the building to provide extra support.[7] It seems an ironic gesture on the part of the architect to allow a building conceived in concrete to be supported by naturalistically executed male figures taken from ancient Greek mythology. There exists a rarely displayed drawing of this project which still lacks the telamones.[8] Although Mel'nikov was never one to shrink from a dramatic gesture in his work, such an emphatically displayed piece of architectonic tightrope-walking is striking but not the only one of its kind. In Moscow at the beginning of the twenties the denial of gravity was a current issue. The best known examples are the Lenin tribune and El Lisickij's 'Wolkenbügel', but these are not the only ones. For example the students in Ladovskij's psychologically motivated classes on the theory of form at VKhUTEMAS were required to carry out studies into questions of 'mass and stability' or 'mass in balance', resulting in a series of daringly projecting constructions.[9] Right up to 1924 Mel'nikov, with Ivan Golosov, taught at VKhUTEMAS and was in contact with Ladovskij's group.
The traffic flow system for this version of the car park was based on the principle of a

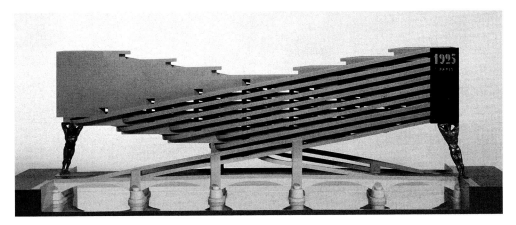

On page 144:
Leyland bus garage on Bakhmetevskaja street, 1926-1927

Project for a thousand-taxi garage in Paris, 1925

Views of the model (realised by R. Nottrot with B. Aslan, T. Budanceva)

Wender, Luckhardt & Anker garage in Berlin, 1924

V. Lavrov, central car park in Moscow (atelier Ladovskij), 1924

twofold double spiral ramp (two separate ascending and descending routes), though the ramps are not really shaped like spiral staircases but run diagonally in pairs along the frontages from bend to bend with spurs leading to the parking floors. The cars were to have parked diagonally, generally in groups of seven vehicles. Mel'nikov's design is startling and appears to be quite unprecedented, but this is not really the case. The car park had already turned up as a subject in Ladovskij's exercise 'realisation of a building in horizontal rhythm' (1924). Two examples of this are known, one project by V. Lavrov and another by Ju. Mušinskij. Both of them designed ramps running round the body of the building but in Lavrov's project the ramps also rise diagonally upwards across the frontage.[10] It seems that Mel'nikov was using a principle that was already known, but his own design unquestionably surpassed his model. In the design of a car park the use of diagonal ramps for ascending

and descending is mainly determined by practical considerations. But from an architectonic point of view things are different. For example the Wender garage by the Luckhardt brothers & Anker was designed with four striking horizontal 'traffic galleries' in the front elevation and ramps that were only visible through the side elevations. The view of moving vehicles showed the function of the building, but the designers put the emphasis on the horizontal stratification of the frontage. Their aim was to give an impression of dynamism by putting the diagonal lines clearly on display and using them as compositional elements. It is no accident that the student projects mentioned above had 'size, rhythm and dynamics' as their underlying themes. The use of a diagonal to suggest dynamism was a device much loved by the avant-garde in the twenties, and is also come across in architectural photography. It should be added that Mel'nikov used the diagonal as the organising principle for

his designs as far back as 1919.

The Reconstruction of the Second Version

Although at first sight Mel'nikov's drawings seem clear, on further examination it appears that a large number of differences can be detected between the drawing of the elevation and the perspective drawing. According to the drawing of the elevation there are nine diagonal ramps stacked above one another, but the perspective drawing only shows seven. To avoid any possible doubts created by these differences, it was decided that the first step would be to investigate the system for entering and leaving the car park. It was assumed here that the traffic was to move in one direction only, an assumption encouraged by Mel'nikov's principle that ascending and descending traffic streams should never intersect one another and the fact that the 4

metres width of the ramps is simply too narrow for two vehicles. The are a great variety of plausible answers to the question of which ramps were to take ascending traffic and which descending traffic. If all possible combinations are compared, there appears to be one system that would function better than all the rest. If someone turns right on to the bridge, the first ramp on his side goes down, which is safe because descending vehicles are able to see the right-hand traffic lane. The second ramp therefore goes up. If the same arrangement is also used on the other side of the bridge, this makes the ramps consistent on both elevations, alternately rising and falling, just as all openings on to the parking floors are alternately entrances and exits. The building therefore has two ramps carrying vehicles up from the bridge carriageway, each with five spurs serving fifty-two entrances. Two ramps each with four spurs carry descending cars from forty exits back to the bridge carriageway. The perspective drawing shows

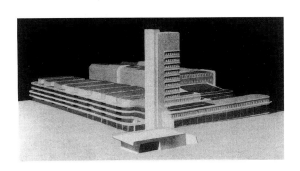

*Project for a thousand-taxi
garage to be built on a Seine
bridge in Paris, 1925
(reconstruction by R. Nottrot)
scale 1:2400 and 1:200*

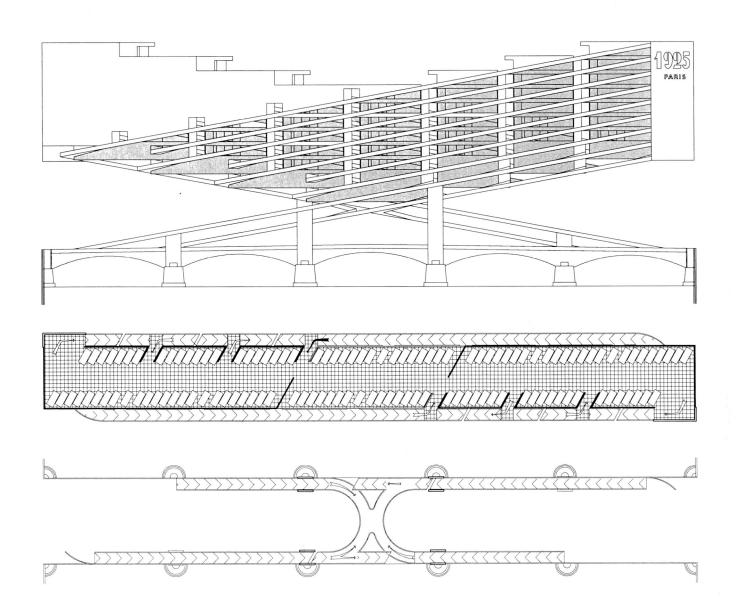

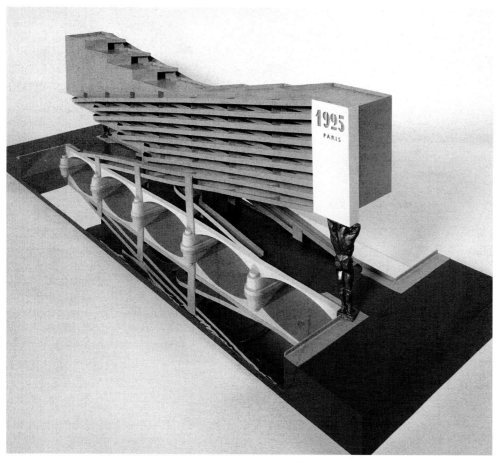

a further two ramps. These are located at each end of the bridge on the left side of the carriageway, and meet one another in the centre beneath the building, where they form an intersection with the two descending ramps. This makes it possible to make a hundred and eighty degree turn on the bridge by driving upwards on the right and then immediately down

again from a point above the centre of the bridge. Because all descending cars emerge on the 'wrong' side of the bridge, they are forced to cross over to the right side. This is perfectly acceptable if they are driving on in the direction of descent, but if they have to go to the right they can do better by going across the top and using the additional ramps to get back on to the

proper side of the road.

The gradients along which vehicles drive up or down are constant (approximately 10°), even round the bends. The bends in the pairs of ramps which run above one another through the building seem to cross the parking floors such a way that where this happens it is impossible to gain access to the floor. Thus the parts of the floors

which are situated between two bends are inaccessible to traffic. In the model walls have been added across the frontage by the entrances and exits. These walls are purely speculative. They do however define the parking spaces and turn out to give constructive help to providing stability along the length of the building.

Mel'nikov's drawing of the elevation seems to indicate that the frontage is open between the ramps. The perspective drawing on the other hand shows continuous vertical lines which more suggest an enclosed building. In the course of building the model a 'feeling' developed for the composition of the frontage. The choices that were made based on this feeling were concerned with the contrast between open and enclosed within the object itself but also in its capacity as an object in the centre of the city of Paris and more specifically above and across the Seine.

At first the basic requirement that the garage must be able to accommodate a thousand vehicles was taken quite literally. At the time it was quite usual for the Paris city council to have car parks designed for a thousand cars. How many parking places are actually provided in Mel'nikov's car park? If every floor of the building is it used to its maximum capacity, there are 970 parking places. But if the rule is followed that traffic along the ramps is all one-way, then

several parts of the floor can only be driven in to while others can only be driven out of. If these sections of the floor are excluded then it is only possible to provide parking space for 908 cars. And then we still have to exclude the spaces enclosed between two bends in the ramps, so that in the end there is only room for 848 cars. The more entrances and exits a floor has the more smoothly the system appears to function, but many of the floors have relatively poor accessibility. During the process of reconstruction the assumption was made that Mel'nikov's design was more a representation of a traffic system then a daring constructional experiment, though of course it was both of

these things. The drawings give insufficient information on the load-bearing techniques used, which makes it difficult to draw sensible conclusions. It did however turn out that the model was impossible to build (on a scale of 1:200) without the two telamones. The clay in which the two male figures were modelled conceals a strong metal rod. Mel'nikov wrote: "Two telamones at diagonally opposite corners will paralyse the wind"[11] as if the load-bearing capacity of these strong men was a matter of secondary importance. Perhaps the word 'wind' was intended metaphorically, referring to the criticism to which he was subjected for his over confident construction. This criticism was 'paralysed' by adding the

telamones to the drawing. Although the available drawings give no guidance in determining the colours of building, there were a few basic principles which could be used for the reconstruction. In the drawing of the elevation the surface at the end of the ramps above the telamon is very heavily shaded. From the perspective drawing (seen from the front) it seems that this surface is 'folded' round the corner of the building, but this time coloured white. The principle employed for the ramps might be expressed as a combination of positive and negative. One series of ramps conforms to another, and conversely, in a way analogous to the combined yin-yang symbol. To compromise between the two drawings and also to provide visual support for the parking system, it was decided that one corner should be black and that the diagonally opposite corner should therefore be white. In contrast to these two corners, the building between has become grey.
Otakar Máčel, Robert Notrott

[1] K.S. Mel'nikov, *Arkhitektura moej žizni. Tvorčeskaja koncepcija. Tvorčeskaja praktika*, Moskva 1985, p. 79.

[2] K.S. Mel'nikov, *Stroitel'stvo garažej*, typescript dated 29 October 1965, in: A.A. Strigalev, I.V. Kokkinaki, *op. cit.*, p. 180.

[3] See note 1

[4] For both versions see S.F.Starr, *Melnikov. Solo Architect in a Mass Society*, Princeton 1978, pp. 103-105; A.Ferkai, *Konstantin Melnikov*, Budapest 1988, pp. 24-25; S.O.Khan-Magomedov, *Konstantin Mel'nikov*, Moscow 1990, pp. 103-104. In Khan-Magomedov the sequence of the versions is reversed. Mel'nikov himself was not always consistent on the sequence in his writings.

[5] S.F. Starr, *op. cit.*, p. 104.

[6] Even Prof. L.A.G. Wagemans of the faculty of Civil engineering, Delft University of Technology, an expert on the subject of car parks, was unable to give a totally convincing explanation of the traffic flow along the ramps in this project.

[7] S.F. Starr, *op. cit.*, p. 104.

[8] See A. Wortman (ed.): *Melnikov. The Muscles of Invention*, Rotterdam 1990, p. 38. The photo comes from the collection of Gerrit Oorthuys, Amsterdam.

[9] See S.O. Khan-Magomedov, *Pioneers of Soviet Architecture*, London 1987, pp. 107-114.

[10] S.O. Khan-Magomedov, *Psichoanalitičeskij metod N. Ladovskovo vo Vkhutemase-Vkhuteine*, Moscow 1993, pp. 141-147; S.O. Khan-Magomedov 1987, *op. cit.*, p. 133.

[11] See note 1.

The Bus Garage on Bakhmet'ev Street

"Moscow has embarked on the construction of a huge depot for 'Leyland' buses from Britain. My beautiful creation has persistently ruled my life, demanding that I abandon construction and begin again. This was no fit of caprice on her part, but an audacious act of will by Beauty to forestall the spending of millions on eyesores. Before us stood a mountain of officially approved drawings, and a wall of intransigence from the road transport authorities. But the desire of an architect who had walked in off the street had proved more than a match for them. Without delay I had raced over to Ordynka, where I saw those foreign dandies being shunted to and from, as they were reversed, with much swearing, into their overnight bays. I began to lament the spending of all that gold. In my dreams, the "Leyland" appears to me as a thoroughbred steed which finds its own way into its stall. But what can buses do? If we take the sharp corners out of the street-plan, we shall have a smooth-flowing system. This brainchild of Art had gripped my heart, and on the 16th of March 1926 I entered into a contract for the construction of a depot of an oblique-angled form unfamiliar to Moscow, on a rectangular section of Bakhmet'ev, now Obrazcov, Street, from whose long threshold my Golden Period was born. The depot's trapezoid

building, 54 x 167 metres, covered the designated area in an oblique line, and the triangular cut-outs on the building's frontage area faced increasing flows of passing traffic."
K.S. .Mel'nikov, 1967[1]

The Suščevskij val Site Historical Developpement and the Bakhmet'ev Street Garage

The site allocated to the construction of the garage is located in the area of Suščevskij Val, which in the Twenties was on the fringe of the city. A large part of the district was not built on for a long time. The river Neglinnaja, which had a complex branched bed, flowed through here. Its low-lying characteristics and the complex fluvial landscape of the area did not favour residential construction. Fish- and mill-ponds were established along the river, and some of the adjacent land was under allotments. In the classical period, large suburban estates sprang up along the Neglinnaja's banks. Large public buildings gradually appeared in the unoccupied spaces: hospitals, institutes, colleges. Recreational gardens were laid out in the ponds which had been preserved along the river bed.
In the mid-nineteenth century the large green areas gradually began to shrink, as the network of streets began to form. The

new buildings here, however, were of timber construction, which gave the district a suburban appearance. Soon after 1910 the Neglinnaja's bed was enclosed in an underground manifold, along the route of which Novosuščev Street was built. It was planned that a wide avenue would be laid between this street and one other thoroughfare.
The decision to locate a depot here coincides with active town-planning measures in the block of land between Bakhmet'ev Street and Novosuščev Street. The new building of the depot is located in an environment made up of single- and two-storey timber—essentially rural—buildings. Exceptions to this are the buildings of the College of Engineering, which are adjacent to the new building then under construction.
In this project K. Mel'nikov elaborated a fairly detailed plan for providing the necessary ancillary buildings on the site: repair and maintenance shops, a fuel storage reservoir, an administrative building. At the time of construction, the original plan became somewhat amended. The garage building, the boiler- house and the storage facilities follow Mel'nikov's design, whereas other parts of the site are based on the plans of other architects. In the Thirties building proceeded apace in the areas adjacent to the Bakhmet'ev Street depot, and the district

began to take on an urban appearance. The garage has survived virtually unaltered up to the present, but the ancillary buildings designed by Mel'nikov have been completely rebuilt. The model replicates the situation at the time of planning and constructing the garage. At the time there were plans to lay a wide avenue as far as the Garden Ring and to build a thoroughfare to link it with Bakhmet'ev Street. Thus the garage complex was becoming a significant landmark in the district, set as it was diagonally facing two intersections.
The complex dynamic composition of the garage site is cunningly superimposed on the backcloth of the tranquil, long high-rise building of the College of Engineering (latterly the Road Transport Institute). The basis for the model was Mel'nikov's unrealised version of the project, which is highly representative of his creative philosophy at the time. The dynamics of the structures are underpinned by the logic of classical equilibrium. The unobtrusive scale of the entrances contrasts with the sharpness of their shape and their plasticity. The oblique attitude of the garage is finished off by the classical pediment of a gable roof. On the site, the diagonal stance is compensated by the elliptical arrangement of the repair shops and by the circle of the fuel reservoir, whilst the central transverse

Views of the Leyland bus garage on Bakhmet'evskaja street, 1926-1927

Reconstruction of the Bahkmet'evskij garage area before and after the construction of the project (Ju. Volčok, E. Nikulina)

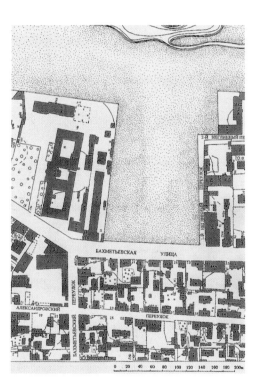

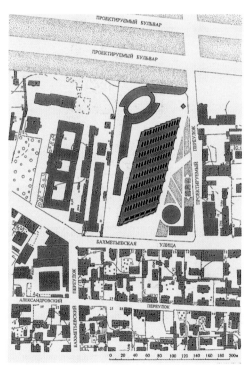

axis is marked by the hexahedron of the boiler-house with its chimney. The almost rural surrounding of single- and two-storey houses makes it easier to realise and to feel more keenly the progressive and visionary quality of the ideas at work in architecture and town planning at the time, as interpreted by Mel'nikov. The contrasting colours of the timber and stone buildings in the model help to show the unique flavour and mosaic quality of the expansion of Moscow in the Twenties. The blue colour of the roof of Mel'nikov's garage does not signify timber construction, and is used here only to emphasise the perceptual integrity of the city's expansion programme. Jurij Volčok, Elena Nikulina, Aleksandr Šadrin

Bakhmet'ev Street Garage Architecture

At the beginning of 1926 Moscow city council decided to build a bus depot for their newly acquired Leyland buses. Mel'nikov was not involved in this project. According to his own recollections work on the depot had already reached the stage of working drawings when he made a counter proposal. His counter proposal was accepted to the extent that the council decided to carry out experimental research into whether Mel'nikov design was indeed better than the plans that already existed. On 16 May 1926

the Leyland buses assembled on Arbuzovskaja square and their entry and exit times were measured with a chronometer. Mel'nikov got the commission.[2] What was so special about his proposal? It is not entirely clear precisely how the test of his system in the square was organised, but the principle is well-known: the buses drove in on one side and parked next to one another in diagonal rows. There was sufficient space between the rows for the buses to drive forward and then away to the side of. No sharp turns, no manoeuvring in reverse. In

the car parks of the day, vehicles usually had to reverse into the parking place.[3] Initially Mel'nikov drew a car park of five storeys, two of which were below ground. The total driving time needed for every bus to reach its parking place was reduced by deciding to locate an entrance at ground level. Available drawings show a large, elongated complex, crowned by a temple-like structure in the centre.[4] The internal traffic flow is not completely clear. According to Mel'nikov's abstract diagram it seems that the traffic flow was

organised diagonally around a central space, using ramps. The sketch of the interior suggests a difference in level of half a storey between the parking floor containing the buses and the exit lanes. This project was apparently too advanced for the clients, and was rejected. Mel'nikov therefore designed a second, single-level version of the depot, which was in fact built.[5] The floor plan of the bus park was shaped like an elongated parallelogram, 54 metres wide by 167 metres long. By choosing this shape Mel'nikov

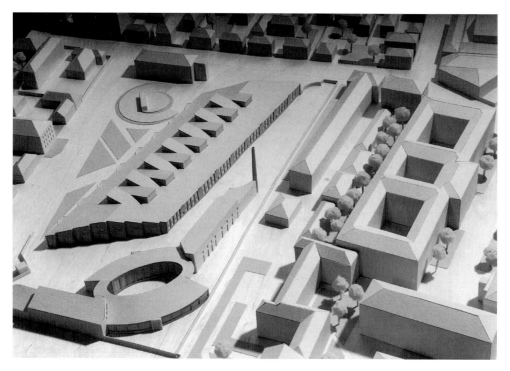

frames round the gates are provided with large asymmetric cannelures, rising on the left to two-thirds of the height and on the right to the full height of the gate. This might well be seen as a piece of art deco. Another striking feature is the lettering on the tympanum-like crown on the front elevation. Besides the name of the depot in the middle, the architect uses large letters to make the bus drivers and others aware of the fact that this is the side on which the vehicles drive in. The gates themselves are numbered with Roman numerals. The rear elevation is built entirely of brick, alternating with vertical window sections. Here too the gates are set at an angle, but this time facing up towards the roof, so that the whole elevation is rhythmically staggered. Above each gate is an 'oculus'. These round windows, like the staggered elevation, are frequently recurring features of Mel'nikov's architecture. The long side elevations are simply executed, with no special characteristics. The round windows reappear in one of the side elevations, and the exits in the long elevation through which the buses drive away are also set at an angle to the elevation, so that they face in the direction in which the vehicles are driving.

The roof, constructed of steel lattice trusses, is supported by two rows of columns, so as to leave the interior of the depot

retained two triangular pieces of 'spare space' on the short sides of the parallelogram, which provided sufficient driving space for incoming and outgoing buses. The buses can drive in through seven gates on the short side of the depot and park alongside one another in eight consecutive slanting rows. The distance between the rows of parked vehicles was chosen so that the buses could drive off forwards, turn right 127 degrees and so leave the depot via the long side elevation. Each row had its own exit door. Only the last row had to drive off through one of the seven doors in the

short rear elevation. This scheme enabled Mel'nikov to achieve an internal traffic flow which was actually very smooth, with no sharp turns or manoeuvring in reverse. The only question is whether in fact the seven gates in the front elevation did permanently act as entrances, as suggested by a global sketch of the piece of land on which the depot stood. It would seem more practical for the vehicles to have driven in through the leftmost door and then park in rows. Moreover the floor plan shows separate areas immediately behind the six other doors, which suggests

that there might have been facilities there for washing or lubricating the buses.

What we have here is a utilitarian building that still shows clear traces of the characteristic hallmarks of Mel'nikov's architecture. The front and rear elevations are treated differently, although there was no functional necessity for this. Part of the front elevation is executed in stucco, part in brick. The entrance gates are set at an angle (facing in the direction of the approaching buses), so providing more relief to the flat frontage. The sides of the

unobstructed. For the roof Mel'nikov sought the assistance of V.G. Šukhov, the well-known constructional engineer.[6] Despite Rodčenko's spectacular photographs of the roof, what we have here is not really anything extraordinary but rather a standard constructional engineering solution. What is interesting is the method used to allow light to penetrate the roof. The orthogonal dentition of the two surfaces of the roof enables them to intersect at the ridge and gives dynamism to the interleaved sections of the roof. Mel'nikov had already executed the roof of the Soviet pavilion in Paris in a similar way.

Next to the depot stands a boiler house with a tall chimney, also designed by Mel'nikov. The site also contains an administrative building, a workshop and a petrol station. Today the complex shows clear signs of restorations and repairs carried out with inadequate materials.

During the building of the model of the bus garage the question arose of why the model would be useful and in what form. The floor plan of the building was determined by the shape of the entrance and exit system used by the buses. This could perfectly well be

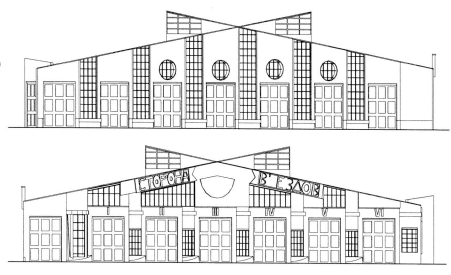

explained by means of a drawing. The real surprise is the roof of the building. In a model the distinctive shape of the roof can clearly be seen, and it is possible to get a better understanding of the entrance and exit gates, and the way in which the placing of these gates at an angle to the elevation ties in with the traffic flow system. The fact that Šukhov was involved in the design did not mean that the method of construction used for the roof was revealed. In fact the roof covering, the way it is covered,

reveals what the underlying technology was capable of. The model also shows Mel'nikov's boiler house. Only the rough shape of the workshop and the administrative building are modelled, because Mel'nikov's involvement has never been proved, and these buildings were only added to the site at a later date.
Because the building as ultimately executed differs only subtly from the preceding design drawings, it would not be particularly exciting to reconstruct an earlier phase.

The model represents the building in its undamaged state and this in itself is useful when one considers the present condition of the depot. The brickwork has been restored to its original colour[7] in the model and various openings have been reglazed.

[1] From K. S. Mel'nikov, *Arkhitektura moej žizni. Tvorčeskaja koncepcija. Tvorčeskaja praktika*, Moskva 1985, pp. 79-80.
[2] K.S. Mel'nikov, *Stroitelstvo garažej*, in K. S. Mel'nikov,

Arkhitektura moej žizni, cit., p. 178. See also the fragment "Kakoj garaž stroit'.Kak ispytyvalis' proekty garažej", in *Večernaja Moskva*, no. 111, 17.V.1926, *ibidem*. pp. 177-178.
[3] See the fragment from "Garažnaja sistema architektora Mel'nikova. Ispytanije proekta garažej", in *Nasa gazeta*, no. 118, 18 May 1926 in K.S. Mel'nikov, *Arkhitektura moej žizni*, cit., p. 177 and the fragment from Mel'nikov's patent application of 1927, *ibidem*, p.181.
[4] For a more concise description

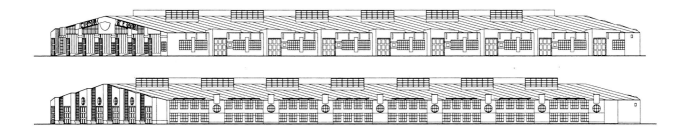

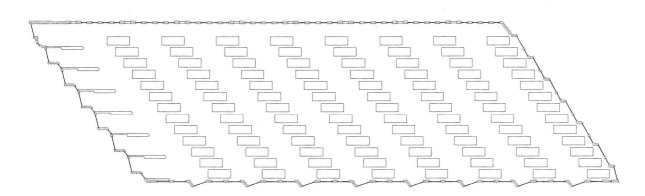

see "Pjatietažnyj garaž dlja
avtobusov v Moskve", in
Večernaja Moskva, no. 37, 15
February 1926 in c p. 176-177.
[5] See K.S. Mel'nikov, *Stoitelstvo
garažej*, in Idem, *Arkhitektura
moej žizni*, cit., p. 179; S.F. Starr,
op. cit., pp. 108-110; S.O. Khan-
Magomedov 1990, *op. cit.*, pp.
104-109. Khan-Magomedov
mentions another article on the
depot by the engineer V.

Buteskul in *Stroitelstvo Moskvy*,
1926, no. 10, p. 6.
[6] See R. Graefe, M. Gappoev,
O. Pertschi (ed.): *Vladimir
Grigorevic Sukhov. Die Kunst
der sparsamer Konstruktion*,
Stuttgart 1990, p. 72.
[7] K. S. Mel'nikov, *O pokrase
zdanija garaža*, in Idem,
Arkhitektura moej žizni, cit.,
pp. 181-182.

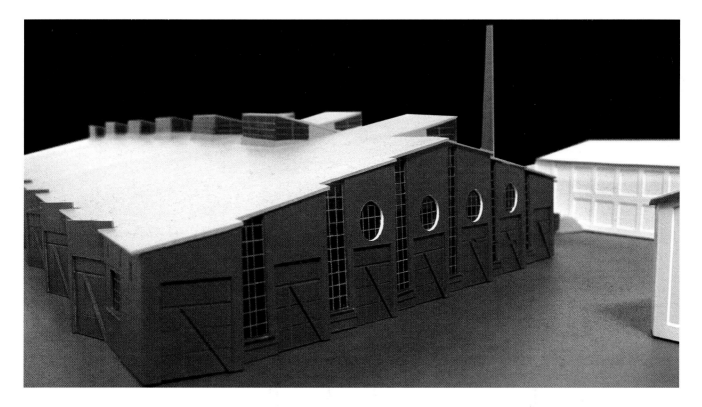

**Indoor Park
for Goods Vehicles
on Novo-Rjazanskaja
Street**

Even before the depot for the Leyland buses was ready, Moscow city council had asked Mel'nikov to design a park for goods vehicles. The available plot of land on Novo-Rjanskaja street was triangular in shape, which made it difficult to use the same system as used for the bus depot. To make the best possible use of the space available, Mel'nikov chose a semicircle for the shape of the floor plan.[1] In the illustration, published in Khan-Magomedov's monograph,[2] the semicircle appears to be precisely inscribed within the triangle formed by the plot. The space on the street side, within the semicircle, is largely taken up by a detached rectangular building, located immediately behind the building line, which contains offices and workshops. Given the choice of the floor plan, it was impossible to use the same system of traffic flow as in Bakhmetevskaja street. The goods vehicles can only enter and leave the car park at the two extremities of the semicircle, and park alongside one another in two rows, one on the outside of the semicircle and one on the inside. The space for traffic between the rows is needed not only to allow the traffic to flow but for the manoeuvres required when leaving a parking space. It is not clear whether Mel'nikov's original idea was to have one-way traffic within the car park,

because the actual building differs somewhat from the floor plan as drawn.
The execution shows a few differences. For example the two extremities of the semicircle did not end in a straight line but had a kink in the middle, with two gates on either side. This meant that the gates were set at an angle to the street, and according to Khan-Magomedov this solution was devised to simplify driving in from the street and back out on to it.[3] The angle through which the driver had to turn to execute these two manoeuvres was therefore less acute and presented fewer problems in coping with the heavy traffic on the street. Another difference can be seen in the way the office building was executed. In the floor plan as drawn, the corners are asymmetrical and the widths of the terminations of the corners are different. From a compositional point of view this ties in with the way the chimney is placed behind the office building, to the right of the central axis, offset in the direction of the narrower corner termination in the office building. The building as executed shows a symmetrical block, now located on the building line, with corner treatments of the same width and the same height. The chimney, which by now has vanished from the inner

courtyard, was originally built precisely on the central axis. It is impossible to put an unambiguous interpretation on the space formed by the office and workshop building and the semicircle of the park solely on the basis of the drawing of the floor plan. A detached boiler house is drawn in this space at the centre of the axis of the complex, with its chimney offset to the right. Behind the boiler house is an extension standing against the wall on the inside curve of the park building. It is difficult to form an impression of this part of the building, mainly because so far no drawings have been found of the elevations. Today the inner courtyard is built in such a way as to make it difficult to trace the original substance of the building, and access to the car park is denied to 'undesirable' visitors. What is certain is that as the building was renovated over the years no effort was made to carry out a proper restoration.
This park too shows clear traces of Mel'nikov's hand, even though some details are no longer to be found. The concept of the building as a whole is remarkable in itself. Although the arguments that Mel'nikov presented for the semicircular shape were based on practical considerations, the whole complex has a neo-classical look. This is even more pronounced when we look at the

version as executed, where every trace of asymmetry has vanished. It is quite impossible to avoid a comparison with the front elevation of Peter Behrens' AEG Turbinnenhalle: in both cases the classical idiom served to provide the architectonic design of a utilitarian building. The entire front elevation is dominated by vertical lines, both in the office building and by the entrances and exits. The large vertically structured glass surfaces alternate with a wall of plain brickwork. Once again round windows are placed above the projecting gates to the car park. The inner and outer rings of the semicircular park building are provided with a strip of windows directly under the roof. A striking feature of the elevation is the small stepped corbels under this strip of glass. The roofing of the car park is once again the work of V.G. Šukhov.[4] The constructional principle, riveted steel lattice trusses, is the same as that used for the bus depot on Bakhemetevskaja street. Impressive photos are available of this construction, once again taken by Rodcenko.
Long discussions, often on details which the scale of the drawings and models would make it impossible to reproduce and continuing right up to the deadline for the first exhibition, preceded each decision bearing on the five reconstructions. The

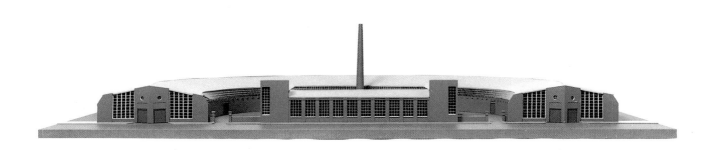

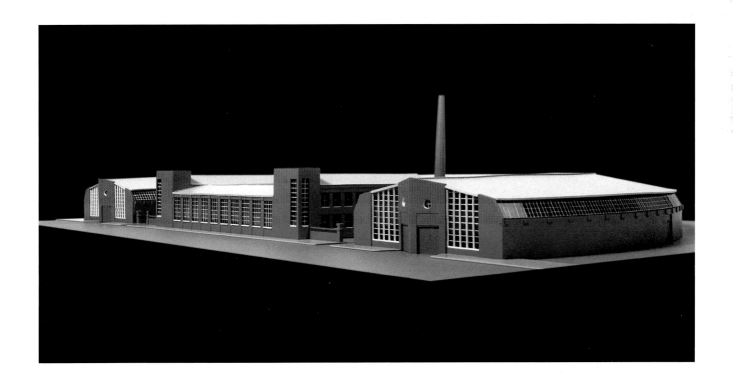

*Views of the model
(realised by R. Nottrot with
S. Bijker)*

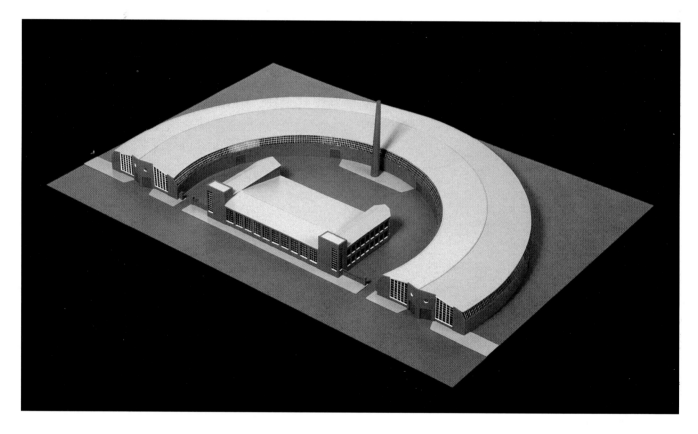

reconstructions themselves were carried out at the faculty of building at Delft University of Technology. Photos of the buildings in their present state were studied with a powerful magnifying glass.

The task of constructing a model of a building from drawings and sketches turns out to be quite different from that of giving back an existing building its former glory in a scaled-down reconstruction. Although the

people involved in both processes have no wish to speculate and go about their work conscientiously, it seems that in the case of a reconstruction each decision has to be considered by the generation of people who knew the building in its 'new' state. In the building of the model of the Novo-Rjazanskaja vehicle park decisions were taken which were not always supported by sufficient information. One gap

in our knowledge concerns the developments round the inner courtyard of the building. To emphasise the symmetry of the complex, the chimney has been placed at the original point in the centre behind the building used for offices and workshops, but the boiler house has been left out. The original boiler house must have been nothing like the boiler house in its present form. The extension shown in the drawings as

attached to the park building seems more likely to be a workshop, now housed in the same building as the offices. One interesting stage in the reconstruction involved the strips of windows along the lower edges of the depot's arched gabled roof. In contrast to the vertical position of the edges as they are now, these were originally executed on the slant, sloping more steeply than the enclosed roof surface. These

*Views of the truck garage
on Novo-Rjazanskaja street,
1926 (reconstruction by
S. Bijker) scale 1:600 and 1:300*

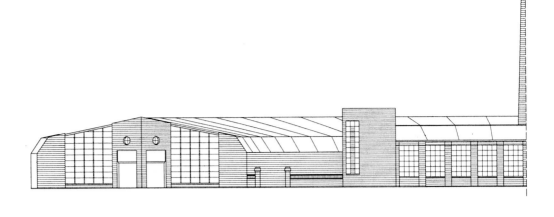

strips have been restored to
their rightful place. The
rebuilding of the long glass strip
reduced the amount of light
entering the building. The
windows, framed in concrete,
which are to be found all round
the building, seem to be a later
addition. This theory is
supported by the random way in
which the windows are placed.
Not surprisingly these windows
have been left out of the
reconstruction.

The central administrative
building was probably also a
workshop, allowing the vehicles
to drive in at the front and out
again at the back. In the model
the long elevations are provided
with large doors. In the elevation
fronting on the street these
doors are located precisely
where the building now has
windows. The roof of the
longitudinal section, which is
located between two higher
transverse sections, leads back
to a gabled roof so that the first
floor which is now built at the
back can not be original.

The building was put up in plain
brickwork, later painted. To
represent the plain brickwork the
same colour was chosen for the
reconstruction as was chosen
for the model of the
Bakhmetevskaja car park.
Perhaps to add a little style to
the building, the striking corbels
at the edge of the roof have in
the building's present state been
painted white, 'like pearls in a

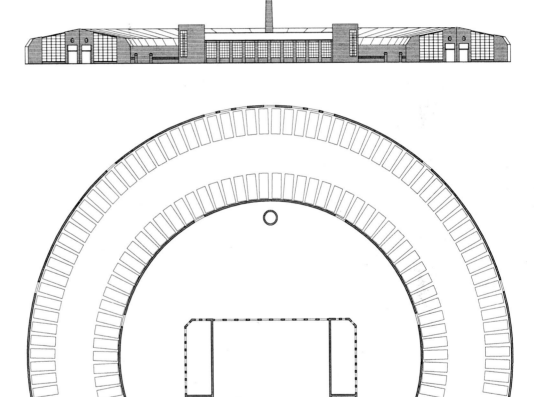

crown'. In the model they are
presented as brickwork, as was
originally the case, and so
painted red.

Otakar Máčel, Robert Nottrot

[1] K.S. Mel'nikov, *Arkhitektura
moej žizni. Tvorčeskaja
koncepcija. Tvorčeskaja praktika*,
Moskva 1985, pp. 179-180.
[2] S.O. Khan-Magomedov:
Konstantin Mel'nikov, Moscow
1990, p. 113.
[3] S.O. Khan-Magomedov, *op.
cit.*, p. 108.
[4] *Vladimir Grigor'evic Šukhov
1853-1939. Die kunst der
sparsamen Konstruktion*,
edited by R. Graefe, M.
Gapoev, O. Pertschi, Stuttgart
1990, p. 72.

Workers' Clubs, 1927-1929

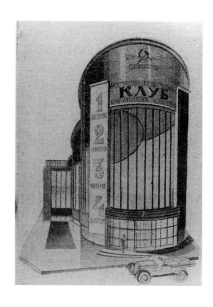

"The club—in our era I cannot find a purer architectural theme, as compared to others like, for example, the theatre, the cinema, or the Palace. During our Twenties this theme was assigned (at least in my opinion) the task of satisfying the most profound aspirations of the intellectual life of the individual, of the individual-person, and the club buildings should have been 'individualistic' objects in the overall scene of the construction of the city. The first two projects of this series of my buildings were for the Union of Municipal Workers: a triangle for the edifice of the Club Rusakov on Strominka Street, a sequence of five cylinders interpenetrating each other for a third of the diameter for the Club Zuev on Lesnaja Street. The outlandish look of the architecture of this project corresponded to the functioning of the interior of the edifice, consisting in a series of circular rooms that could be transformed by rolling divider walls for each of the cylinders. My idea of the architectonic interpenetration of the cylinders was utilised in a purely decorative way in the design by I. Golosov for the same club, and I have put it into practice in the design for my house."
K. Mel'nikov, 1965[1]

"The work of the club does not take place in an isolated room served by a corridor, without a door on which we might find the message 'do not enter' to prevent disturbance of the activities underway there. To teach people to be social, the work must be carried out in an open arena, in full view for the masses, and as a result in the club there must be a SYSTEM OF ROOMS. Different aspects of the work, as for example: politics, defence of the country, economic building, industrialisation, construction of socialism in a single country, production conferences, theatre, cinema, the neighbourhood, the factory, our *byt* and an infinity of other activities cannot be contained in any kind of single room. These requirements can only be fulfilled by the SYSTEM OF ROOMS. For the conducting of a work with an audience, it is necessary to have different volumes of rooms that can be grouped together—once again, this requirement can only be satisfied with the system of rooms. The system of rooms functions both in terms of the type of activity and the quantity of the participants, meaning that the architecture of the contemporary club consists in a mechanised forms (...) Design of the Edifice of Club Zuev in Moscow on Lesnaja Street. The form is of cylinders. With a normal cubic volume of rooms the structure develops upward on a vertical axis to the height of 20 meters. Four circular rooms, each for 200 persons, mechanised with the aid of cylindrical surfaces (*zestkoramnykh*), that roll up. The rooms for the pioneers and the reading room are located in a particular, separate form to the side of the rooms. The stage is a standard one with a rotating circle. The entire edifice of the club has a one-story base with a normal span. The dressing rooms are located in the base of the building..."
K.S. Mel'nikov, 1927[2]

Designed at the same time as the Club Rusakov and his own house, in the first months of 1927, the Zuev is the only one of the seven clubs designed by Mel'nikov that was not built. Nevertheless, this design contains a series of formal ideas, technical and typological solutions later used by Mel'nikov in different clubs and other works.
In particular, with respect to the use of the cylindrical volumes, apart from his own house, the system of interlocking with staggered floors was also used in other projects for community residence, and the solution of the closure of the spaces of the cylinders with mobile walls sliding on circular tracks was also envisioned for the first, unbuilt version of the Club Pravda in Dulevo, with two balconies contained in two cylindrical volumes facing onto the orchestra.
The system of rooms composed of spaces that can be grouped with one another while existing on different levels, and divided by mobile vertical diaphragms (mobile walls) proposed in this building is the also the solution adopted for the Rusakov, Pravda and Frunze clubs (in particular, the latter is the most comparable, due to its volume and size relationships), although adapted to other planimetric schemes (orthogonal).
In the model presented here—the reconstruction is based on a very small quantity of documentary material and literature, and includes all the information available on the design without the addition of arbitrary solutions where insufficient elements were available for a reconstruction (especially in the system of access to the lateral terraces, which appear to be inaccessible in the available drawings).
In the reconstruction of the frames of the large glazings the sizing is based on elements deduced from examination of the designs for other clubs by Mel'nikov (in particular, the solution for the large glazings in the tower edifice of Club Burevestnik).
Maurizio Meriggi

[1] From K.S. Mel'nikov, *Arkhitektura moej žizni. Tvorčeskaja koncepcija. Tvorčeskaja praktika*, Moskva 1985, p. 83.
[2] *Ibidem*, pp. 187-188.

On page 162:
*View of the Rusakov workers'
club (photo from the Thirties)*

*Project for the Zuev workers'
club, 1927; perspective view and
photomontage (S. Topuntoli)*

*I. Golosov, Zuev workers' club,
1927*

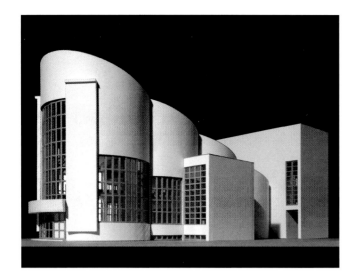

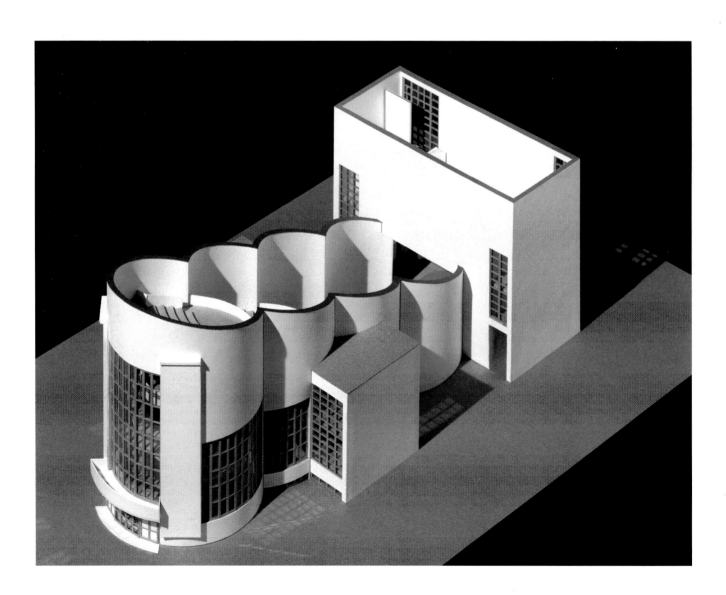

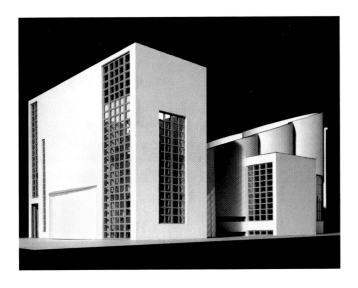

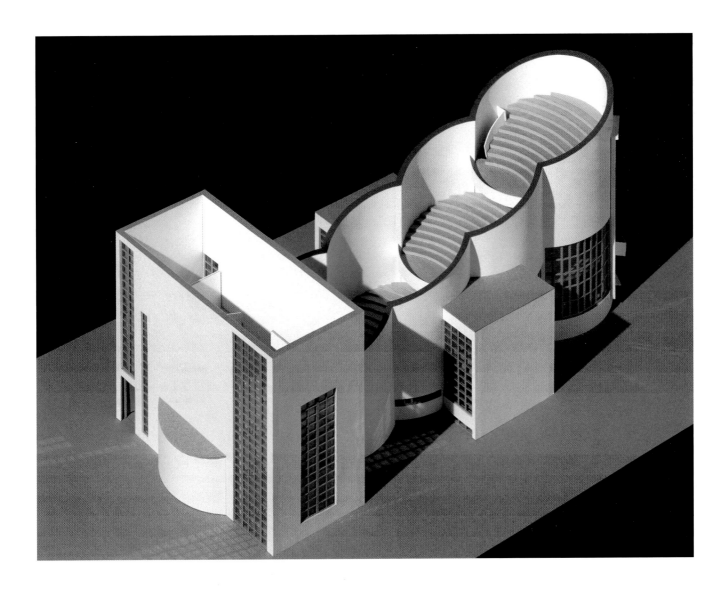

Project for the Zuev workers'
club, 1927
(reconstructed by A. Scaramuzzi,
re-drawn by R. Bazzani)
scale 1:600

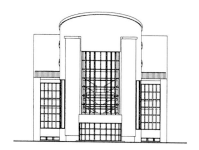

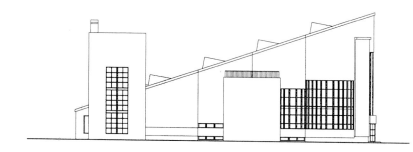

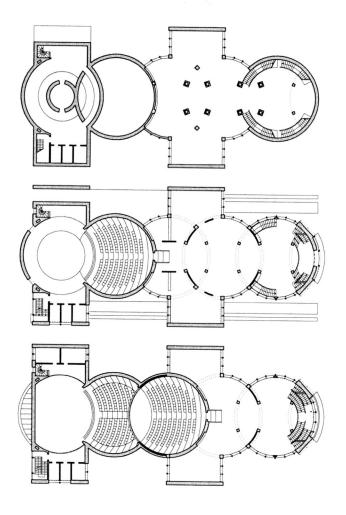

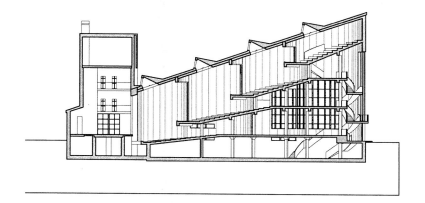

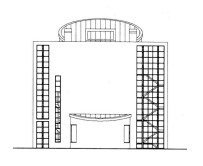

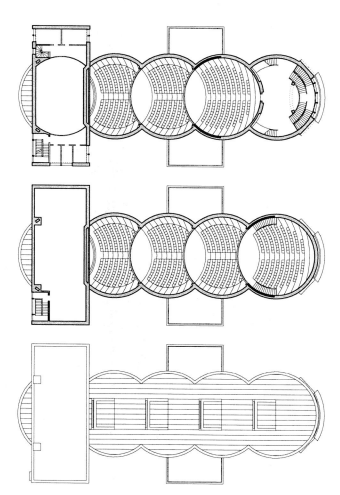

**The Rusakov
Workers' Club**

"It was immediately and forever decided that the project for the building of a club in the name of Rusakov should be a festal salute to Compressed Beauty, a volley aimed at the Future."
K. Mel'nikov, 1967[1]

"After many centuries of imitation Architecture stood out again in the innate beauty of its powerful muscles of cantilever tension, of resilient flight with aerial places for new spectators, in the impetuosity of the forms of the Rusakov club building, which was erected here with us, in Moscow, on Stromynka, in 1929. Since then the system of cantilever constructions has noticeably developed and spread throughout the globe. It is the best with regard to economy and strength. Besides, it has elegant forms that shaped style in the world treasury of styles. The Patriarch stands in rags, blinded by windows stuffed with bricks, and, like Homer, he irrepressibly attracts people to himself to this day through his hidden novelty."
K. Mel'nikov, 1927[2]

"The project for the building of the Rusakov club in Moscow on Stromynka. At the base is laid a triangle, like a figure of monumental dimensions in view of the small cubic content of the building. In the centre is a vestibule with two isolated staircases and a central staircase in the middle leading into two halls: the lower one can be used as a restaurant, and the upper

one—for meetings and sports practice. The side staircases serve the higher halls. The club has six (6) independent halls which come together into one hall with the aid of drop-gates situated between tiers. The two side halls each accommodate 120 people, and the three upper halls—190 people each, while the stalls have room for 360 people. Acoustical information for the building of the Rusakov club. The general shape of the building is such that if the source of sound is on the stage in the narrow part of the triangle, then the sound spreads through the halls, becoming louder on the principle of the megaphone. The back rows of the upper halls are, in terms of volume of sound, in almost the same conditions as the front row at the expense of reflecting the sound ray, by dint of the fact that the thicker net of reflected rays compensates for the direct wave which is weakened by its distance from the source. The inner walls which separate the halls are useful, since they increase the area for reflecting the rays, resonating and strengthening the sound. The resulting division of the common space into small halls aids the distinct transfer of the strengthened sound. The possibility of an echo arising falls away in view of the insignificant volume of air and the shortness of the path it has to traverse. One should point out that strenuous applause can drown out the orator, since the megaphone in

this case is turned into an ear-trumpet. On the other hand, this circumstance will be used to catch the comments coming from a certain place."
K. Mel'nikov, 1967[3]

Sokol'niki District Historical Development
The building of the Rusakov club was situated in a historical region of Moscow—Sokol'niki. In the sixteenth-seventeenth centuries this region, which was distinguished by a picturesque forest, was surrounded by royal out-of-town residences and was used for hunting. In the seventeenth century the forest was partly cut down, and in its place the spacious Sokol'niki field was formed, which was used for military manoeuvres and trade. A significant part of the forest was preserved—one of the biggest Moscow city parks was formed here in the nineteenth century. In the region of the park there arose many dachas; the locality had preserved its former out-of-town character. At the end of the nineteenth and beginning of the twentieth centuries different kinds of charitable institutions were built in the region: hospitals, workhouses, shelters, schools. There was some industrial development. At the end of the Twenties Sokol'niki was mentioned rather as a suburb than as a city region. As before, there was a predominance of small wooden building, over which there

towered the church of the Ascension of the Word and a fire observation tower. The observation tower building, thanks to its position at a sharp bend in the road, served as an important architectural accent. At the end of the nineteenth century the city authorities decided to preserve some fragments of Sokol'niki field which had not yet been built on as two city squares on both sides of Stromynka street. Here some large hospitals were built. However, on the whole the spaces occupied by the proposed squares remained unshaped for a long time. In the 1910s a part of the territory that had been preserved as Sokol'niki square was given over for use as a football field, and was gradually turned into a small open stadium. Later, a public garden was laid out next to the stadium. For a long time the north-western plot remained unbuilt-up. It was this plot that was given over for the building of the Rusakov club in 1927. Evidently, the siting of the building in a corner adjoining the red line of Stromynka street was connected with the still-existing intention to create Stromynka square, towards which the new building of the club was oriented. It is possible that the author also took into account the proximity of Sokol'niki park, which had an active influence on the structure of the region.
However, the square never came into being. Along the red line of

Stromynka street a hospital block was first built, and then some multi-storeyed residential houses. Nevertheless, the Rusakov club building continues to play an important city-building role to the present day; for it actively influences the organisation of the surrounding space.

The Rusakov Club and the Sokol'niki District

In the model the building is reproduced, including three main constructions—the club and its surroundings, the fire observation tower and the church. On looking at this composition, and also at the general plan of the park, the fundamental significance of the park for any planned building in this region becomes clear. The plan of the park represents a fan of alleys whose radii spread out from a central round area. It turned out that the observation tower and the club were axially oriented almost exactly towards the centre of the circle. The building in front of the park was low and both constructions, as well as the church, were perceived from the entrance as being dominant features, giving a big-city scale to the region, and being situated along the radii of the same circle. The club building crowned the highest point in the locality and completed the spatial composition of the region at that time. The city received a wonderful spatial ensemble on

the basis of a tri-axial fan. The First Polevoj pereulok, which goes out along a diagonal from the centre of the park, almost exactly coincides with the 'radius' of the club, while the building of the Ostroumovskaja hospital, which is now being reconstructed, did not close off this visual axis (earlier the side block was more compact and closer to the main block). In the siting of the club building and its (once again, fan-like) composition, which describes the spectator as going towards the park along the diagonal relative to the axis of Rusakovskaja street, we can again clearly see the Master's wonderful capacity to transform the compositional fabric (structure) of the city with a light hand, sharply and decisively introducing a diagonal which bounces off his buildings or is regenerated in their compositional generator like the ray of a hyperboloid.
Jurij Volčok, Elena Nikulina, Alexander Šadrin

Rusakov Club Architecture

The Rusakov Club for streetcar employees is situated on a corner lot on the broad Stromynka Street (no. 6). Set back somewhat from the street, sufficient space is available to allow an impressive perspective, which Mel'nikov made use of in a quite memorable way: three auditoriums projecting into the street area are the essential features of the overall

171

appearance of the building, which is laid out on a three-corner ground plan. The auditoriums, however, owe their existence not only to the desire to achieve a sculptural effect in the context of the urban landscape, but also to economic and functional considerations. Since little money was available, Mel'nikov eliminated the smaller conference rooms that were called for in addition to the large auditorium. Small conference rooms were created by means of revolving collapsible walls that separated the three parts of the auditorium located on the upper floor from the audience area on the ground floor. Like the seating area in front of the stage, the conference rooms were originally lighted naturally by high, narrow side windows; they could hence be used for discussion functions and meetings without consuming expensive electrical energy. The central vertical access behind the foyer leads to the lower level, which can be used as a restaurant, and up to the main audience area. Access is provided by two staircases between the projecting auditoriums lighted by long vertical rows of windows. These vertical elements contrast effectively to the horizontally oriented ground floor. There are exposed lattice girders above the audience area in front of the stage. Thus, not only the expressive design marked by the contrast between the smooth, undecorated white and grey plastered surfaces and the red brick of the tapering back

Views of the model
(realised by A. Šadrin,
A. Kuznecov)

View of the model
(realised by J. Appel, C. Lembke)

section but also technicistic interior details allude to the new future-oriented society. Lettering designed by Mel'nikov himself that pointed out not only the use of the building by workers of the communal administration ("Rabotnikov Kommunal'nogo" and later "Sojuza Kommunal'nikov") but also the ideological significance of the workers' club for the socialist society was installed on the front sides of the auditoriums: "Mošč proletariata" (Power of the Proletariat) and "Škola Kommunizma" (School of Communism). This lettering was later changed and eventually removed completely; the window openings were also walled in. The intention of the reconstruction, done on a scale of 1:100, was to depict, above all, these elements meant for effect.[4]

Dietrich W. Schmidt

Rusakov Club: Site Landscape and the System of Rooms

The triangular structure of Club Rusakov is positioned in the corner of a lot on one of the radial streets of the city—Ulica Stromynka. The facade looks toward the radial street, the right side toward an open field, concluded by the elevation of a factory, and the rear facade, placed at the top of the triangle, looks toward the municipal transport depot, whose union administered the club. The left side faces toward a residential area and a large hospital complex.

The device of the system of rooms arranged on a diagonal, with spaces that face onto one another though they are on different levels, and divided from one another by mobile vertical diaphragms, is organised in three spokes that emerge from the top of the triangle placed to the rear of the building. The facade toward the street is resolved by a classical giant ordering and a terrace with two imposing staircases, that function as a base, the alternation of volumes with rooms and glazed stairwells, that form the torso, and the top level of the system of rooms. The rear facade is composed of a stacking of similar volumes in brick, taking on the appearance of a construction in height with a smaller architectonic subdivision, alluding to the design of the facades in Russian wooden architecture. The two lateral facades reflect the internal structure of the building, or the section of the diagonal system of rooms, and in the original design a monumental staircase was included on one side, which from the field would have led into the building. In this way the different facades react, through both contrast and analogy, to the characteristics of the surrounding edification, making the device of the system of rooms contained in the building—directly represented in the volumes that compose the facades—the centre of the area, toward which horizontal routeways converge that continue inside the club, reaching the different spaces of the building along the vertical accessways.

The model presented here has been reconstructed on the basis of a comparative analysis of documents of different origins (drawings of the preliminary versions and from the worksite, photographs of the various phases of the life of the constructed facility), seeking above all to document the internal landscape of the building, so fully transformed today that it is unrecognisable with respect to the photographs from the 1920 (especially due to the closing of the lateral facades, whose glazings provided light for the system of rooms). Based on these considerations an open model has been chosen (without roofing, and without the central part of one lateral facade) in order to accentuate the transparency of the original building, thanks to which the internal device of the system of rooms (which in the completed building was graphically transcribed on the lateral facades through the play of reliefs and recessings of the opaque and glazed surfaces, and through the combination of white stucco surfaces and exposed brick surfaces) could be seen from the outside. The restoration, in the model, of this original quality of the building makes it easier to grasp how the architecture of the club tended to interact and construct itself within the system of relations defined by the presences of the surrounding context, reconstructed in the urban-scale model that opens the section on the clubs.

Maurizio Meriggi

[1] From K.S. Mel'nikov, *Arkhitektura moej žizni. Tvorčeskaja koncepcija. Tvorčeskaja praktika,* Moskva 1985, p. 80.
[2] *Ibidem*, p. 81.
[3] *Ibidem*, pp. 187-188.
[4] Hence, polystyrene was selected as the material corresponding to the smooth plaster surface, the lettering was included, and the original fenestration was depicted with acrylic glass. The roof was partially opened to allow a better impression of the interior spatial layout. The lattice girders were soldered from sectional brass tubes.

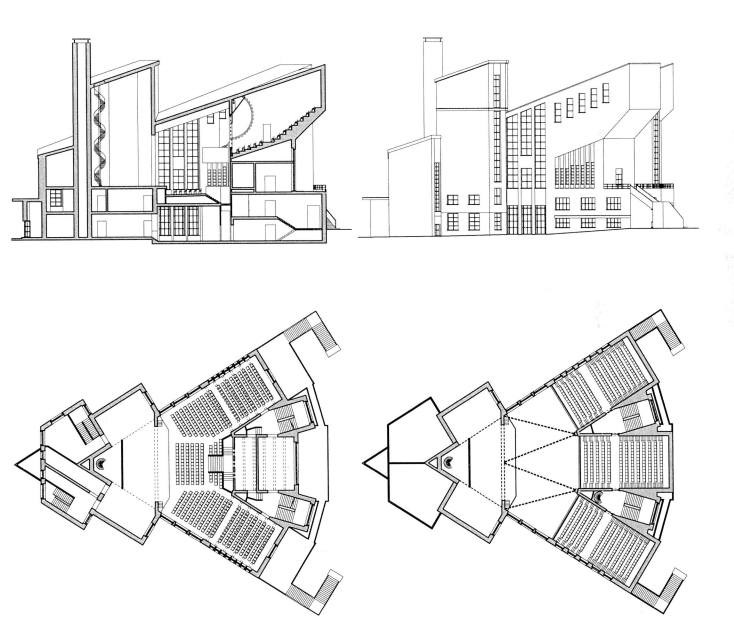

*Rusakov workers' club, 1927
(reconstructed by A. Scaramuzzi,
re-drawn by L. Gatti) scale 1:600*

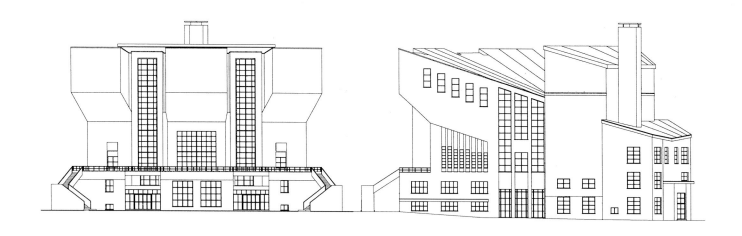

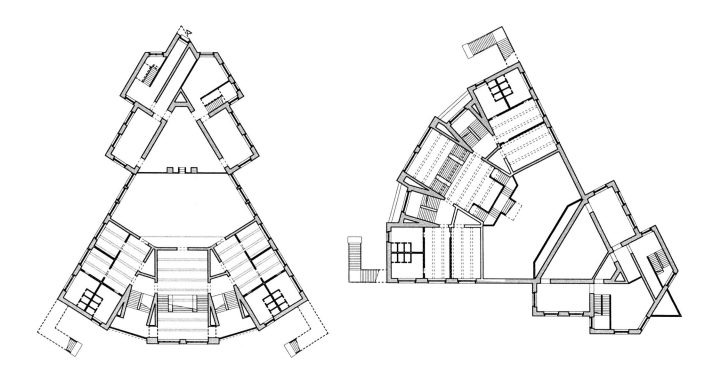

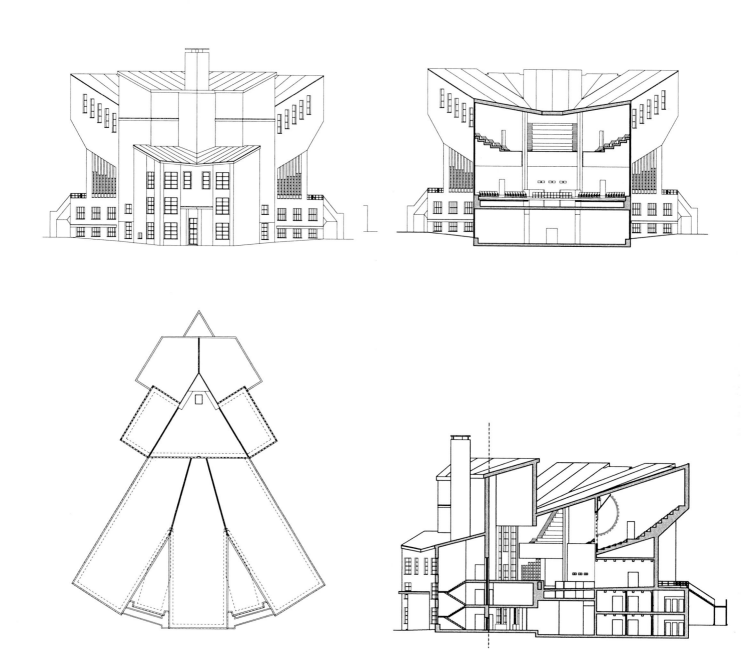

*Interior views of the model
(realised by R. Aiminio,
F. Montaldo)*

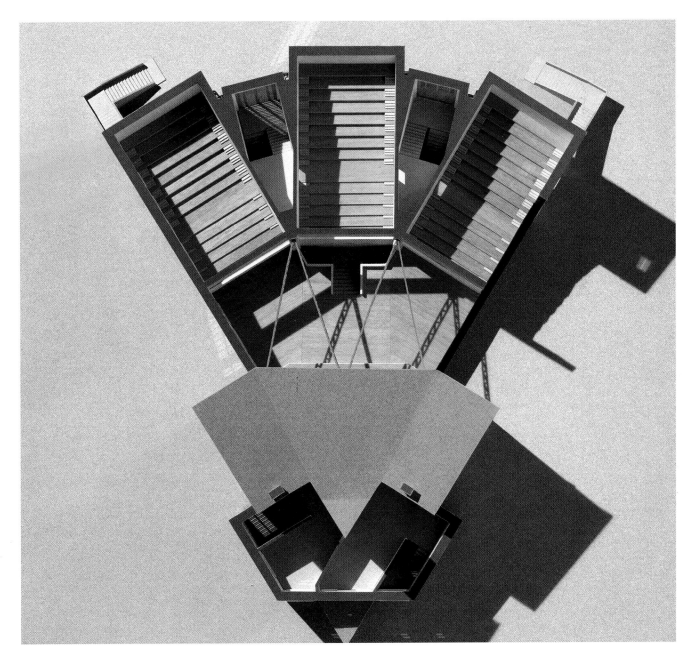

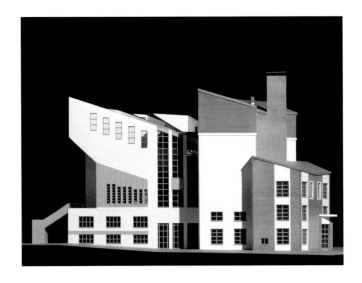

*Interior views of the model
(realised by R. Aiminio,
F. Montaldo)*

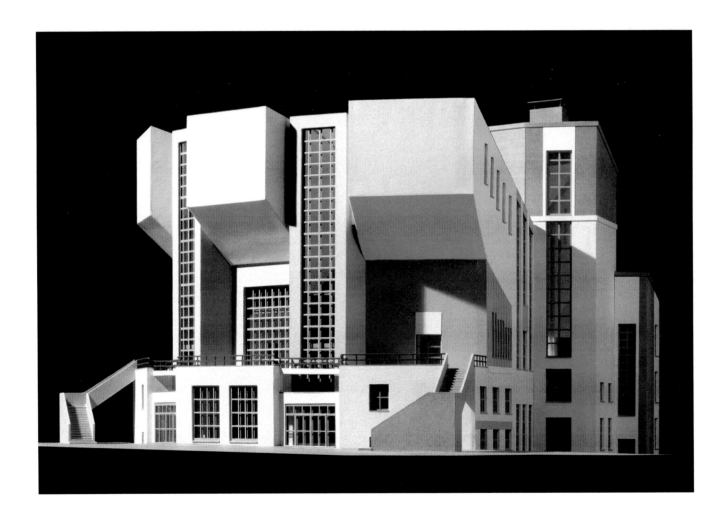

The Kaučuk
Workers' Club

"The wall of the 'Kaučuk' Factory Club curves round in an open area at the corner of the Devič'e Pole, on Pljuščikha. The auditorium of this club has three tiers of balconies integrated into one half-cylinder: their curves have the same radius and all of them are situated at the same distance from the wall of the stage. With this congruence in size, I designed the floor as an adjustable platform which could be raised or lowered from one balcony to the other, thus increasing or decreasing the number of seats in the hall itself. This concept allowed an auditorium with 800 seats to be integrated with a spacious gym and a number of rooms in an area of 13,500 m2. The vestibule with cash desks occupied a separate space, a design which is still copied today 40 years later."
K.S. Mel'nikov, 1967[1]

The Kaučuk Factory Club and Pljuscikha Street Site
The site allocated for the construction of the Kaučuk Rubber Factory Clubhouse was on the corner of Pljuščikha Street and Second Truženikov Lane. This was once the site of an urban estate with a complex layout organised according to classicist principles. The main estate house had been a single-storey timber structure facing towards Pljuscikha Street. Apparently, by the time of the building of the club it had already been demolished and

the site was vacant. The area of the former estate garden had been turned into a public park. Historically, the site where the Kaučuk Club was built used to be called Devič'e Pole. It stretched from Khamovniki to Novodevičij Monastery, which stands near the River Moskva. At the end of the eighteenth century Caricynskaja Street took shape on Devič'e Pole, but building was not begun here until the nineteenth century. At the turn of the century, health clinics, schools, an orphanage, and the Ministry of Justice archive were built. Up to 1911

Devič'e Pole had been a place of Shrovetide and Easter folk-festivities. In the Tenths it was turned into a park in the form of a triangle bordered by Kliničeskaja Street and Bol'šaja Pirogovskaja Street.
The vacant sites began to resolve into blocks of housing. Between 1894 and 1897 the Church of the Archangel Michael was built, to the design of architect A. Meisner. Its location was at the intersection of Pogodinskaja, Kliničeskaja, Malyj Voskresenskij (now Second Truženikov) Lane and Pljuščikha Street. The church

became an important planning feature in the layout of the district. Between 1909 and 1912 the lecture building for Women's Higher Courses was built on the corner of Malaja Pirogovskaja Street and Khol'žunov Lane. The building was designed by architect S. Solov'ev and engineer V. Šukhov. At the time of the construction of the Kaučuk Club, however, most of the surrounding buildings were of timber, which gave them a 'rustic' quality.
In laying out the clubhouse, Mel'nikov focused on the corner location of the site with its

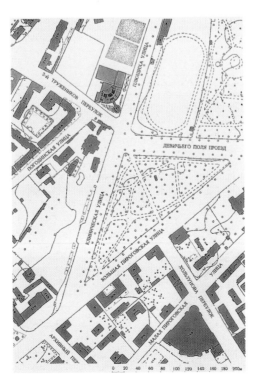

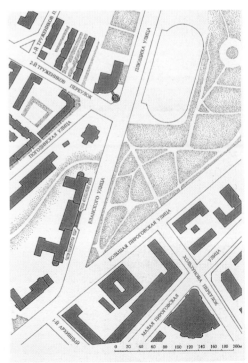

View of Trubeckoj pereulok from the side of the Devic'e pole (photo from the Tenths)

Reconstruction of the Kaučuk club area in the Thirties (Ju. Volčok, E. Nikulina)

Views of the Kaučuk club in the Thirties

accessibility to view from several streets and lanes. The complex was positioned to take account of an amendment made to the boundary lines on Second Truženikov Lane, where the siting of several multi-storey residential blocks had been planned.

In the following years the planned small-scale blocks were scrapped in favour of high-rise development. The park in Devič'e Pole has survived to the present day, and the Kaučuk Club building continues as before to be a milestone in the redevelopment of the district.

The urban-planning situation reproduced in model form to represent the layout of the place in the 1920's gives us a clear insight into the architect's intention. The entire stretch from the planned Frunze Academy to Pljuščikha Street square had not seen any significant redevelopment; therefore the four-storey club building is perceived from the square, amidst the greenery of the public gardens, as a large structure in immediate proximity to the church (as if completing it in the urban context; this was not the only example of mutual

complementarity of juxtaposed buildings in Mel'nikov's portfolio).

The low elevation of the sports complex from the direction of the green massif gives added upward dynamism to the central part of the club building.

The flat ground-level public garden in front of the square underscores the three-dimensional complexity of the composition of the club building against the background of the unobtrusive facades of the workers' apartment blocks with their gently regular rhythm.

A 'quarter' of the cylinder of the

club's central block is set diagonally to the axes of the square and orientated along the main path of the garden towards the existing building of the Women's Higher Courses, also comprising fragments of a dome-topped cylindrical structure.

These buildings share similarities not only of layout, but also between their pilaster designs, the rectangular extrusion of their stairways and the gradations of their stepped cladding.

This powerful visual diagonal, which includes an urban-planning 'dialogue' between two buildings, became particularly striking thanks to the model, as it has since been obscured by later building development. It may be imagined that this diagonal is orientated towards Lužniki, and this means that the 'endless thinness of the triangle' not only lies in the limits set by the walls of Mel'nikov's structures, but also extends to the compositional solution of inner city areas.

Jurij Volčok, Elena Nikulina, Aleksandr Šadrin

Kaučuk Workers' Club Architecture

Mel'nikov's approved construction application forms the basis for the reconstruction of the Kaučuk Worker's Club in Moscow (1927-1929) (reductions not drawn to scale). The specificity of detail was sufficient to build the model to a

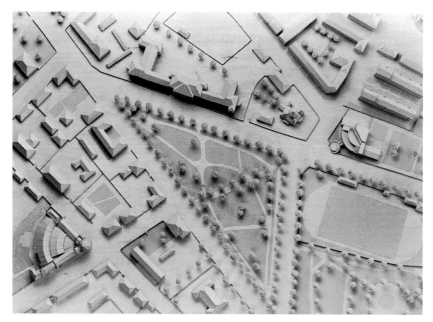

scale of 1:100. The guiding principle of the reconstruction was to reproduce Mel'nikov's original idea with as few changes as possible and not, for example, to copy the building as it was actually constructed, for in many aspects the completed structure deviated sharply from Mel'nikov's plans. A review of the literature yielded planning materials that were used, first of all, to draw new, complete plans to a scale of 1:100. This entailed in part the reconstruction of non-existing plans such as the floor plan of the top story and the elevations (except the south elevation). Upon reconstructing these plans, a few problem areas arose that were not a result of the original plans; there were also deviations from the structure as it was later completed.

For almost all staircases depicted in the original plans, there was a discrepancy between the floor plan and the cross section concerning the number of rises. The staircases were recalculated according to the height of the stories indicated in the cross section and altered to form staircases with functional rise and run ratios. The cross section and floor plans were correspondingly revised and adapted.

In the original plans, Mel'nikov provides for ramps accessing the main entrance instead of staircases. These ramps lead from street level to the round

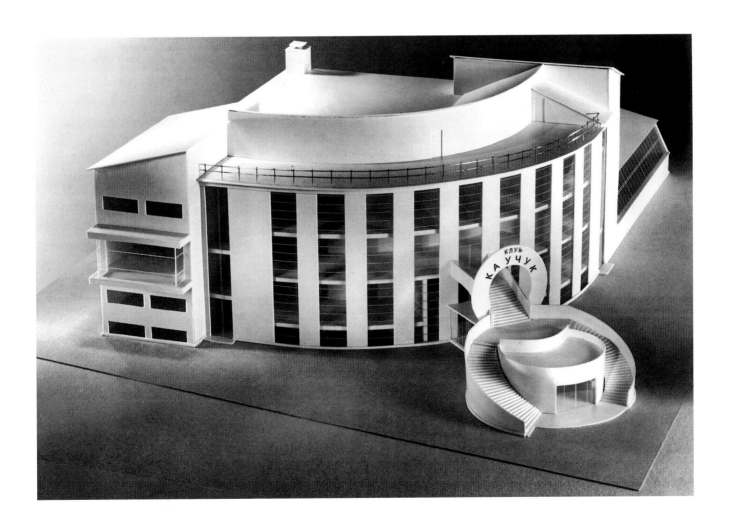

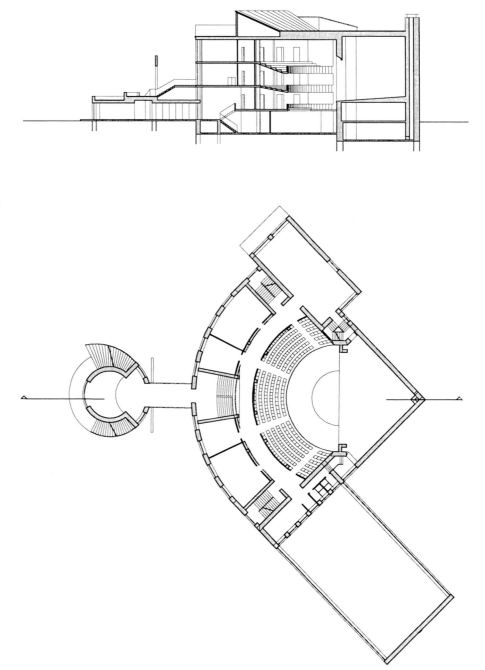

Kaučuk workers' club
(reconstruction by M. Gruhn,
Y. Maier) scale 1:600

entrance hall approximately one story high. This results in ramps that are so steep that they cannot possibly serve as access to the main entrance. Thus, the staircases used in the later construction were chosen here in place of the originally planned ramps. The shape of the left ramp, which becomes wider as it descends, was kept—in contrast to the actually completed variant—in order not to break up the basic form of the entrance area. The bent wall was made upright as in the realised version of the building, not sloped as in the original design. In the system cutaway of his design drawings, Mel'nikov provides for a raised roof structure in the area above the auditorium. There seems to be no clear aesthetic or functional reason for this, and the construction of the entire roof would be a highly complicated task if a reason were found to build this structure. At the most, this box set on top of the roof might be attributed the function of lighting and ventilation of the auditorium, since according to the system cutaway it possessed an encircling row of windows. Such a function, however, would be neither sensible as lighting for the auditorium nor sufficient as ventilation. After examining possible forms and dimensions using a working model of the room shape, the decision was made to use the completed variant of the roof, leaving out the roof structure. The cross

section was adapted to correspond to the changed situation.

After examining the functional situation, the newel-type spiral staircase planned by Mel'nikov for the north facade was left out and the roof access was changed to correspond to the actually completed variant, in which we find a simple steel ladder that better serves the function of roof access (for repairs). In addition, the originally planned spiral staircase structure directed far too much attention to itself, formally contradicting the sunken gymnasium, which as a compact annex to the actual building structure is pushed into the background

Mel'nikov actually planned a strict continuation of the alternation between pilaster-like wall panels and vertical rows of windows across the entire main facade in the south-east. He maintains this strict rhythm even in the middle, although in the entrance area on the lower level and ground floor the staircase walls end in the window (constructionally problematic). This is clearly to be seen in the depiction in the corresponding ground plans. Thus, for formal reasons Mel'nikov design idea was maintained here in contrast to the changes in the actually completed variant. This change in rhythm in the middle region of the facade of the completed construction creates a clearly different expression of the

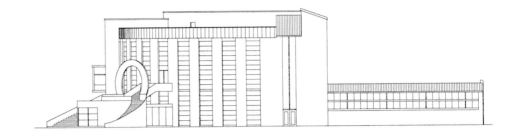

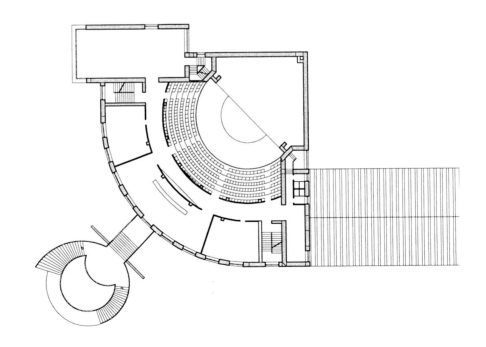

*Kaučuk workers' club
(reconstruction by M. Gruhn,
Y. Maier) scale 1:600*

*View of the hall (photo from
the Twenties)*

building from that found in Mel'nikov's original conception aimed at in the reconstruction. This original design idea is especially recognisable in the strong abstract perspectives and illustrations in which this alternation is emphasised by means of extreme contrasts in brightness (black and white bands).

No original plans or photos of the condition of the building after being built could be found for the rear (north and west) facades. In this case, the facades were reconstructed on the basis of information from the ground plans about the location and size of the windows. Balustrade heights and lintel heights are fitted to information from the existing plans, e.g. room function.

The side structures designated to be placed at the end of the quarter-circle extend through all floors in the plans of the architect. In contrast, the completed variant is one story lower. The model follows the design planning also in this case. Thus, the volume of the structure remains unchanged from Mel'nikov's original planning and deviates from the current Moscow Club in this regard.

Mel'nikov planned originally to extend only the staircase located to the right of the entrance all the way to the roof terrace; in the completed structure, however, both staircases were extended to the roof. Since,

however, there is no need for a second staircase leading to the roof terrace and since there are no spaces designated for the public on that level (only small, dark side rooms), the model once again corresponds to Mel'nikov's original design. The glass bay window on the second floor of the west side wing was not completed in 1929, as planned in 1927. Presumably, technical or economic factors that need not be taken into consideration for the reconstruction of an ideal design were decisive for the postponement. Since this section of the building was architecturally well-founded, having the functional and formal purpose of lighting and accentuation of the side hall, and since it represented no constructional difficulty, it too was completed in the model following the original design of the architect. In this manner, the structure receives a more sculpted quality, and the facade a striking formal accentuation.
Dietrich Schmidt

[1] From K.S. Mel'nikov, *Arkhitektura moej žizni. Tvorčeskaja koncepcija. Tvorčeskaja praktika*, Moskva 1985, p. 183.

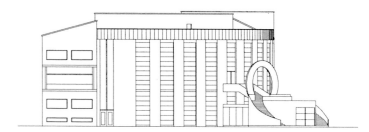

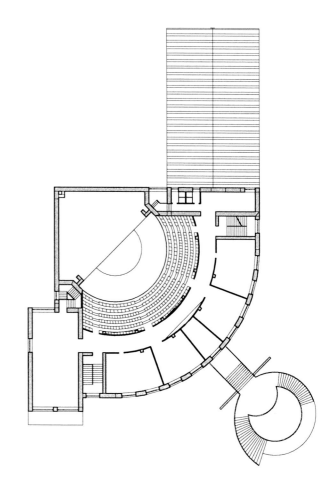

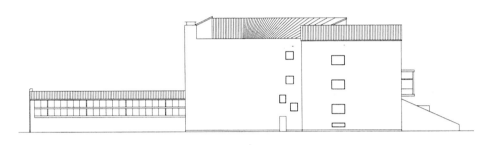

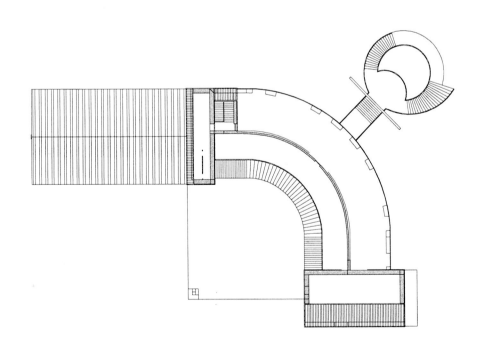

"The Club for the china factory in Dulevo, a town near Moscow, was to be built in parklands, and unlike its urban prototypes, this building was to be spread out and integrated into the surrounding landscape. But even it did not lack the architect's passion for architectural economy. The round foyer which joins all the buildings together can, if so desired, be turned into a large balcony for an auditorium, creating an area of 14,500 m^2 with 750 + 250 seats." K.S. Mel'nikov, 1967[1]

Undoubtedly the most characteristic feature of Mel'nikov's workers' clubs consists in his endeavour to find the most original and instantly recognisable building form possible. This is achieved through inscription, symbolism, and the spectacular arrangement of the building structures, particularly in their complete and partial cylindrical formation. In addition, these purely visual peculiarities of Mel'nikov's architecture are linked to a building type largely unknown in the West: the workers' club. All of these reasons make it especially appealing to reconstruct a model of this building. The analysis of the sources[2] revealed the existence of three building variants: the ground plans of two design variants were available in the sources. On the basis of slight constructional differences to variant B, the existing building in

Dulevo represents the third available variation of the building.

Given the only slight deviation of design variant 'B' from the constructed variant and the relative agreement of the cross sections and elevation drawings with the constructed variant, the plans of design variant 'B' were selected as the basis for constructing the model. The first of these deviations from the actual design is seen in the square in front of the building. In its real condition the square fortifications have never possessed a pattern. The design, however, provides for a black-white tile pattern fitting the function of the building as a club for the workers of the local ceramic combine. Further deviations are seen in the arrangement of the front facade: the first floor of the front wall, angled at 120 degrees, was moved back in the completed variant by a half-grid, thus creating a continuous building edge at the height of the roof terrace. This causes the front wall to be shorter on the whole; hence, it has only four *wide* windows—the original vertically-dominated organisation of the front facade with six *narrow* windows (variant B) was abandoned. In the completed building, the reduction of the front wall also resulted in a terrace angled at 120 degrees over the entrance area instead of the originally planned straight marquee. Functional

uncertainties regarding the original access to the roof terrace could not be cleared up using the existing source material: it could not be ascertained whether a photographically documented spiral staircase (source 2) behind the middle column of the front facade was the only ascent to the roof terrace or if the two structures attached to the large rotunda originally housed or still house staircases. In addition, it should be noted that the existence of these two structures is documented only by the MARKhI photos in the aforementioned literature and is not found in any of the plans. The situation is similar regarding the overall appearance of the main hall and the stage structure. The no doubt greatest deviation and hence greatest difficulty in completing the reconstruction was represented by the production of a sufficiently meaningful sectional drawing of these building parts: the hall and stage windows are not contained in the original sectional drawing and do not exist in the current condition of the structure; the parapet and window heights therefore had to be calculated from the difference between the plinth-attic measures and the overall wall height typical for buildings of that kind. The depicted heights and vertical form of the stage structure are based on ratio calculations based on the MARKhI photos, since this structure is not shown in the

original cross section.

At this point the analysis of the sources called for a decision for one of the three variations: variant 'A', an insufficiently documented design variant with fundamental differences from the two other variants (two rotundas); variant 'B', a second, relatively comprehensively-documented design variant with only one rotunda and, 'variant C', the completed variant with some uncertainties and constructional deviations from variant 'B'. The desire to reproduce the design intention of the architect resulted in a decision in favour of design variant 'B', since its deviations from the completed building are of a purely constructional nature and detract very little from the actual design idea. A scale of 1:100 was chosen in order to effectively depict the functional and spatial conception of the building . The interior situation in the hall between the partially cylindrical building elements typical for the architect is made visible by means of the transparent hall roof. For the depiction of the layered wall design, the model required slab-shaped materials; the presence of characteristically rounded building structures requires in turn that the material be sufficiently flexible.3

[1] From K.S. Mel'nikov, *Arkhitektura moej žizni. Tvorčeskaja koncepcija. Tvorčeskaja praktika*, Moskva 1985, p. 183.

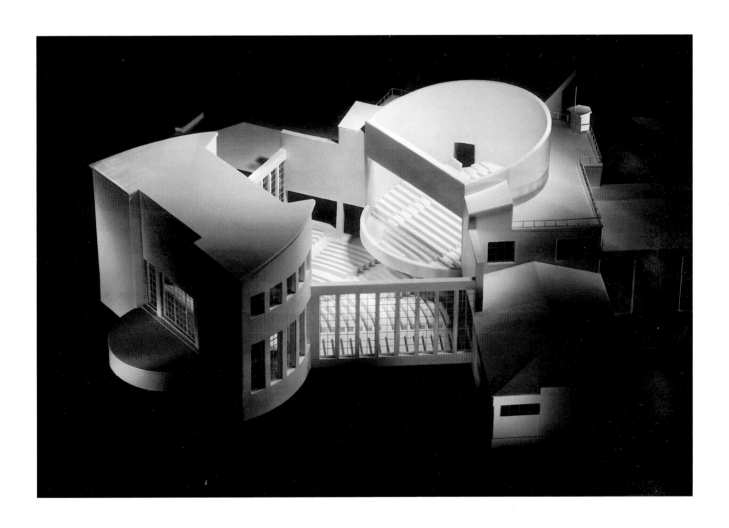

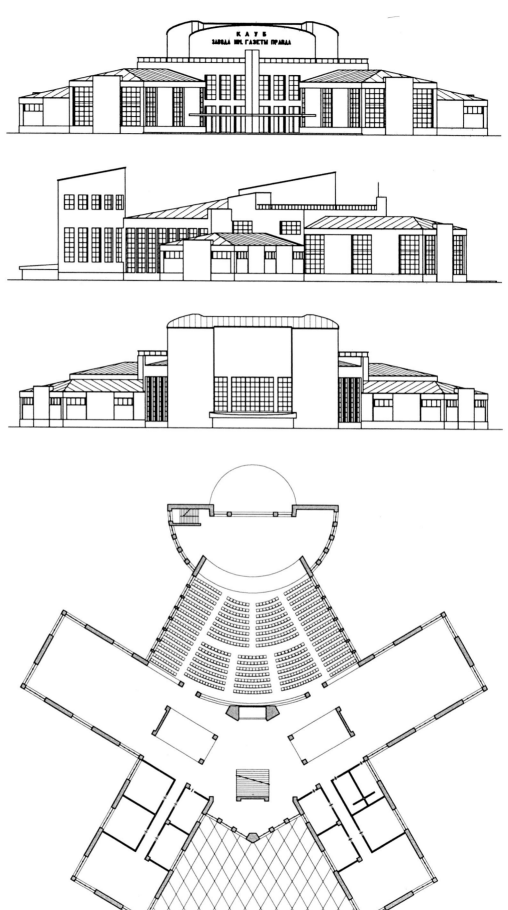

² The analysis of the aforementioned publications yielded ground plans for two design variants that differ primarily in the arrangement of the auditorium on the second floor. Variant 'A' calls for two identical rotundas situated next to one another, whereas variant 'B' contains only one large rotunda situated in the middle. The following individual original plans are available in the aforementioned literature: first and second floor plans for variant 'A' not drawn to scale (source 2); first and second floor plans for variant 'B', partly drawn to scale (source 1-3); 1 sectional drawing for variant 'B', incomplete and not drawn to scale (sources 2,3); 1 front view of variant 'B', not drawn to scale (source 2); 1 perspective view of variant 'B', not drawn to scale (source 3); diverse photos of the constructed variant (sources 1-3). In addition, 18 photographs of the constructed variant (in its current condition) were used for clarification of the aforementioned incomplete elements [source: MARKhI]).

3 Polystyrene was selected as construction material in order to obtain a sufficient degree of detail in the construction of the walls as well as an overall effect of unified whiteness approximating the effect of the actual building. In addition, this material allowed manual fabrication without use of machinery. The stabilising slabs made out of Kappa board were

*Pravda workers' club, 1928
(reconstruction by J.U. Goos,
P. Haffner) scale 1:600*

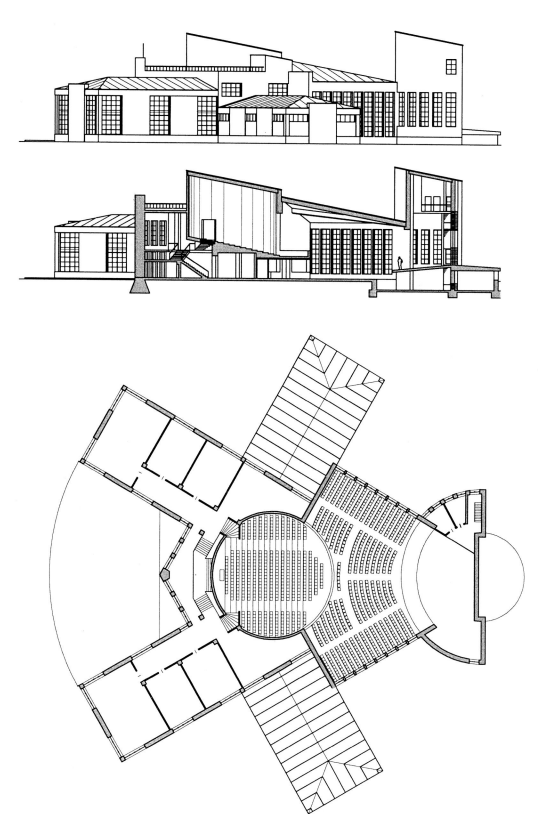

completely covered with
polystyrene. Inscriptions on the
rotunda were sprayed on with
black paint using a stencil,
suggesting a black and white
contrast for the overall
conception of the model. In
order to obtain a strong contrast
between the aforementioned
'whiteness' of the model, a black
millboard seemed to be an
appropriate covering for the
base plate; the formal elements
of the outside facilities, the tile
pattern of the forecourt, and the
spectator areas of the arena
were drawn on using white ink.
After thorough discussion of the
initial plan reconstruction and of
a test model with a scale of
1:200, the final model with the
scale of 1:100 was completed
through incremental
prefabrication: first, a
polystyrene base plate in the
shape of the building contour
was constructed; then it
equipped with rows of seats in
the area of the hall made out of
pre-warped 4 x 4 mm
polystyrene sectional tubes, and
a cavity for the orchestra pit was
also added. All windows
(plexiglas, scratched from the
back and coloured white,
polystyrene frames as window
reveal), the 5 mm Kappa layers
of the walls, as well as the
polystyrene wall panels were
prefabricated and fitted together
to form wall elements.

1927

Project for the Svoboda Workers' Club

"The Club for the 'Svoboda' Factory, now called the Gorkij Palace of Culture, is situated on Vjatskaja Street. Its compositional design appears to be opposite to the above-mentioned clubs. While the mechanical architectural form of the latter was based on integrated spaces, in the Palace on Vjatskaja Street the auditorium was designed in the shape of an oblong with an elliptical section which could be cut in two by a sliding wall, housing a cinema and a theatre with all its complicated stage equipment. The elliptical structure of the ceiling would also form the ceiling of the lower foyer that had no supporting columns: the open space between the supports was to be used as a swimming pool. However, this new structural concept (single ceiling structure for two rooms) won no support within the approving bodies and I, with pain in my heart, had to replace the ellipse with an angular shape and ramps with stairways.

In the Fifties, when the facade was renovated in the style of the day, bricks replaced all the glazed surfaces and the stairways and the concrete storage space for the sliding wall were all demolished; no one bothered to invite me, the architect. Another remarkable fact is that at this moment, in 1965, a huge stairway is being built, once again without me, to replace those demolished,

hopelessly disfiguring the facade of the building and the elegant architectural features of the initial project."
K.S. Mel'nikov, 1967[1]

The workers' club for the 'Svoboda' Factory for rubber boots was planned for the northern industrial area of Moscow, west of the railroad line to Dmitrov and the parallel Butyrskaja Street. As in the case of the Kaučuk and Pravda Clubs, the project was commissioned by the Union of Chemical Workers. On the basis of the preliminary design of 1927, a sharply altered plan was developed that was finally realised on Vjatskaja Street in 1929. The building was renamed 'Gor'kij Club', after the well-known writer, and altered to the point of unrecognisability in the Fifties and Sixties.
The originally dynamic design alluded in its symbolic language indirectly to the products of the factory workers: rubber boots for working in water. Mel'nikov hence designed an elliptical cylinder lying between two rectangles, which brought to mind the old Russian water wagons. Building such a structure with large vaulted glass surfaces was hardly imaginable other than with steel concrete ribs, which can be recognised in the sectional drawing. Technical specialists would have been necessary for the completion of this expensive plan. In this respect, Frederick

Starr's claim that Mel'nikov employed iinexpensive materials and simple techniques that semi-skilled and unskilled craftsmen could manage[2] must be contradicted. Thus, a primary economic reason for the changes made to the plans can be found in this construction, which required expensive material and advanced techniques. An additional constructional-functional reason seems to have been the problem of entrance areas. With an inviting gesture, two symmetrically curved ramps in the centre of the horizontal cylinder lead elegantly to the main entrance on the second floor, where, however, they run into the mighty lattice masts from which the heavy partitions of the auditorium could be lowered when required. The lattice mast makes the impression of an obstruction on the already small platform in front of the entrance. The design drawings are strangely unclear on this very point. Thus, the undoubtedly fascinating idea failed most likely not only due to technical difficulties but also as a result of the functional idea of situating the spacious entrance directly next to the large lattice mast that itself was a prerequisite for a decisive fundamental conception: the flexibilisation of the room sizes by means of a vertically movable partition. A possible psychological aspect that may have led to the ultimate solution

of using horizontal sliding doors is the unpleasant association of the vertical technique with a guillotine. Vertically sliding partitions had also been suggested by the architect for the Frunze Club but in considerably smaller dimensions.
Only incomplete planning documents were available for the construction of the model; these were supplemented with the help of parameters such as step measurements and realistic construction dimensions for walls and ceilings. Hence, the goal was to depict the basic conception of the spatial distribution of mass with a wood volume model made to a scale of 1:200. The essential structural elements meant for effect by the architect were emphasised as opposed to an elaboration of details. Nor was it necessary to depict the interior spatial conception, given the fact that the space distribution is recognisable from the outside. An additional detailed model made out of soldered sectional brass tubes with a scale of 1:100 depicts the cross section through the oval cylinder and illustrates the constructional aspect in the area of the oval main hall.
Dietrich Schmidt

[1] From K.S. Mel'nikov, *Arkhitektura moej žizni. Tvorčeskaja koncepcija. Tvorčeskaja praktika*, Moskva 1985, p. 183.

Project for the Svoboda club,
1927; perspective view

View of the model
(realised by H. Niemeyer,
B. Vogelmann)

[2] S.F. Starr, *Melnikov. Solo
Architect in a Mass Society*,
Princeton, 1978, p. 145.

*Views of the model
(realised by H. Niemeyer,
B. Vogelmann)*

Project for the Svoboda workers'
club, 1927
(re-drawn by A. Tomasi)
scale 1:600

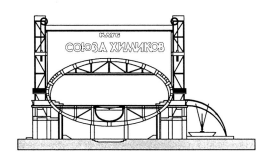

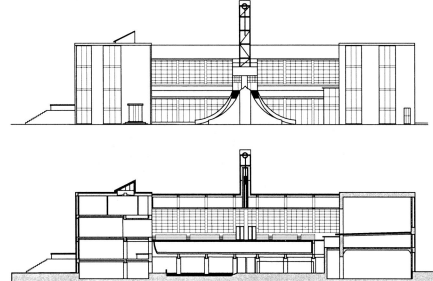

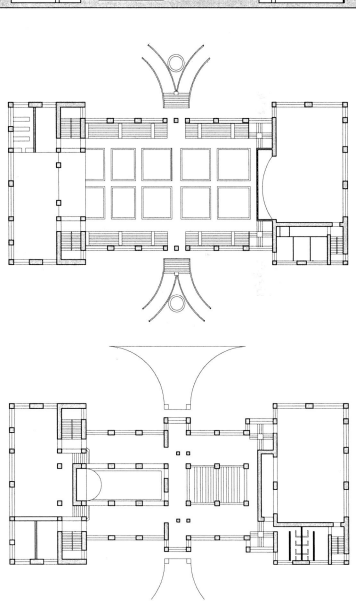

Design drawings and architectural plans for the original variant of the 'Svoboda' Club (1927) were often published, but only one floor plan of the upper floor could be found for the project completed in 1929. It may be assumed that any plans still in existence are in the possession of the club and that Mel'nikov, who was not satisfied with the completed variant (see Point 1, translation of the original text), did not publish any drawings or plans. Photographs of the building found in the various publications were often identical and showed only the street side. An additional problem was presented by the fact that many of these photographs showed the building during its construction phase or only at a much later point in time after the changes described by Mel'nikov. Further depictions showing the building from the side or from the rear could not be found. All together, seven different illustrations were available from the literature for the

reconstruction of the Gor'kij Club, one ground plan without indication of scale, as well as four slides from the private archive of Dietrich W. Schmidt of the Institute for the History of Architecture of the University of Stuttgart.
The reconstruction is based on Illustration 153 on page 146 of Frederick Starr's study. This photograph shows the building immediately after its completion in 1929. As indicated in the caption, the club was still called the 'Svoboda' Worker's Club at that time.
The main problem in drawing the floor plans and elevations was the lack of any sectional drawing as well as the fact that the only existing floor plan had no scale. A scale was approximated by means of a comparison of the staircases and door openings using common dimensions. In the following step, the height of the individual building segments could be determined from the reconstruction of the vanishing points of the photographs. The

access stairs served once again to verify the true dimensions. The control calculation yielded a rise of 17 cm and a run of 30 cm, i.e. completely realistic values. Based on the large number of symmetric conceptions in the work of the architect, the rear of the club was shaped to correspond to the front. The wall-openings indicated in the ground plan allow this step to be taken. In contrast to the front of the building, the access to the canteen is found in the middle rear of the building in place of the open staircases. No information could be found about this part of the building; hence it is indicated in the model by an unstructured cube that is cut off diagonally.
On the basis of the newly-drawn plans, a test model was made out of Kappa board in order to obtain an impression of the building's volume as well as to clarify connection points, e.g. in the roof region. The individual plans were checked once again against the test model. Like the model of the first design variant

of the Svoboda Club done in 1992, the model of the completed variant was fashioned in such a way as to allow for a good comparison: pear-wood was again selected as the material for the presentation model, and the same scale of 1:200 was used. Due to the dearth of sources, the wood volume model provides no information about the interior situation. As in the model of the first design variant, the goal was to portray the macrostructure produced by the exterior structural elements, e.g. staircases, hall building, stage block, and side rooms. Given the small scale used, details such as balcony railings and roof terraces could be left out.
Dietrich Schmidt

*View of the Gor'kij workers'
club, Thirties*

*Detail of the original model
(Twenties) with the access
staircase*

*Views of the model
(realised by Y. Jeong,
L. Mösche)*

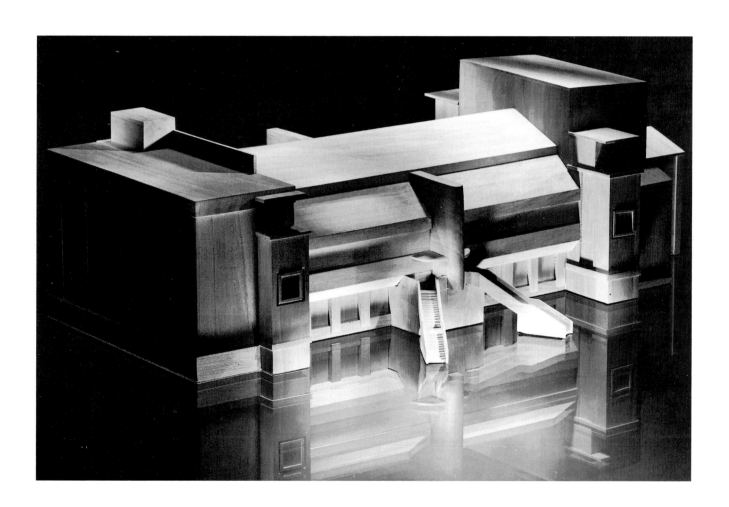

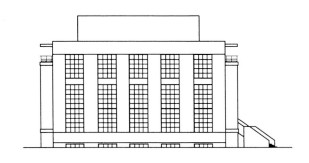

Gor'kij (formerly Svoboda)
workers' club, 1927
(reconstructed by Y. Jeong,
re-drawn by A. Tomasi,
L. Mösche) scale 1:600

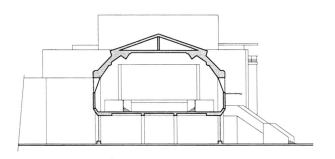

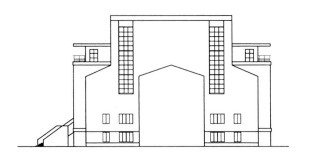

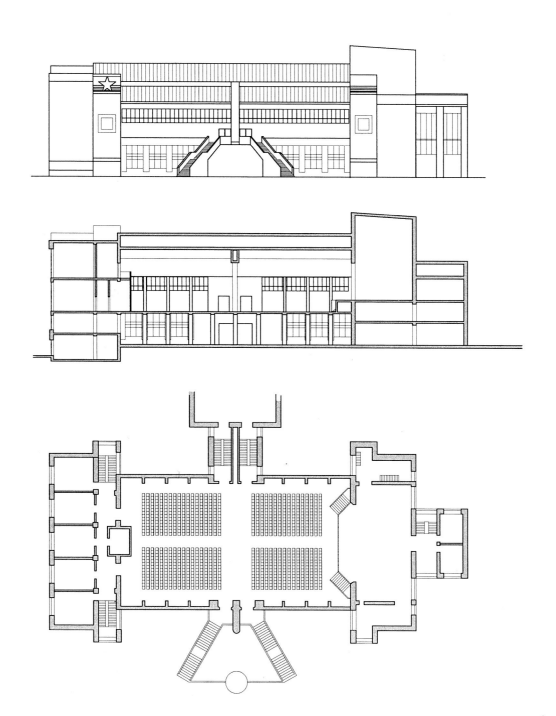

Frunze Workers' Club

"Then the Union of Chemical Workers got hold of me, so I had to build four more clubs for them. The Frunze factory club on the Moscow River embankment, opposite the Novodevicij convent, the smallest of all in terms of volume: 3,400 m³. Its tiny hall accommodates the spectators on three tiers, the lowest of which is lower than the stalls and can be used, when necessary, as a foyer. At the present time the building is surrounded by taller buildings and separated from the river by back yards."
K.S. Mel'nikov, 1967[1]

During the preparation of the ground plans and cross sections using, among other things, the presentation plans published in Starr's study, inaccuracies became apparent in the arrangement of the staircases; hence, they were not usable in the form presented.
Test models could not provide a definitive clarification. Even the sanitary facilities were not functional as designed. An additional difficulty was represented by the arrangement of the library window on the third floor: while Mel'nikov's original plan provided for only one horizontal opening divided by vertical mullions, the completed variant contains two additional smaller openings with horizontal formats underneath.
A definitive clarification of the interior layout could only be obtained through recourse to the plans of the MARChl. Since these plans provided for an arrangement of the sanitary facilities and staircases meeting functional requirements, they were ultimately consulted as the basis for the reconstruction. The three window openings completed in the library[2] were also taken up in the model, since they afford better lighting and most likely were incorporated into the plans by Mel'nikov himself on the basis of their superior functionality. A scale of 1:100 was selected not only to give sufficient expression to the cubic volume of Mel'nikov's smallest workers' club but also to allow for recognition of the facade articulation. The facade is marked not only by the alternation between vertical and horizontal openings but also by the graphic treatment of the large plain surfaces. In a typography typical of Mel'nikov, the function of the building is indicated not only by the signature 'Frunze' and a band of writing under the eaves of the main facade but also by the label 'Kino' and 'Tancy' on the right side of the facade. White polystyrene, an especially cool and functional-looking material, was selected for the right-angled, severely cubic building sculpture, which reveals Mel'nikov's rationalist[3] influence to a greater degree than many of his other buildings. The use of machines (e.g. CNC milling machine) was unnecessary. The individual wall segments were mounted on a foundation made out of Kappa board and welded together with chloroform. The windows made out of acrylic glass received the original, more elegant mullion arrangement of the ideal depiction through scratches made from the back.
Dietrich Schmidt

[1] K.S. Mel'nikov, *Arkhitektura moej žizni. Tvorčeskaja koncepcija. Tvorčeskaja praktika*, Moskva 1985, pp. 183-184.
[2] Compare Illustration 1191 in S.O. Chan-Magomedov, *Pioniere der sowjetischen Architektur*, Dresden, 1983, p. 444.
[3] For a short time Mel'nikov was a member of the rationalist association ASNOVA.

Frunze workers' club, 1927
(reconstruction by A. Giersch)
scale 1:600

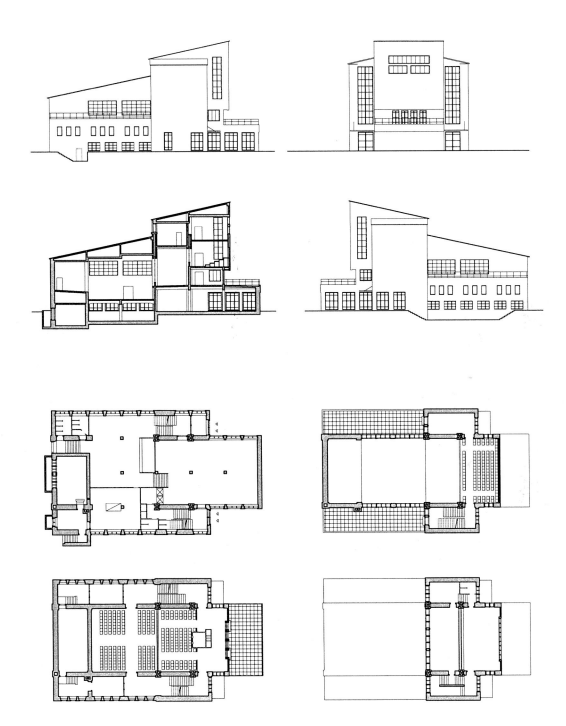

Burevestnik
Workers' Club

"The third Union—of Tanners—have commissioned me too, why do they all want me? During this period in the 1920s I have been commissioned to design two parking facilities, six club buildings, the renovation of the Kamernyj Theatre, and on top of that I had to dedicate much care and attention to building my own house. All the Moscow construction bureaux at that time were working on my projects … It is possible to explain the demand for one architect if one compares the product created by the joint collaboration of many architects with the product created by a single architect, but who has a variety of ideas. The site for the 'Burevestnik' Club of the Tanners' Union was rather narrow and at an angle to the road. Actually this angle was used to good effect: it allowed the creation of a triangular open space in front of the building, with a solid monolithic wall at its base; the crystal sculpture with the five leaves was placed at the vertex of triangle. In this way, what started off as a problem actually benefited the architectural design. The building, with a volume of 16,000 m3, housed an auditorium with 700 seats, which could be connected to a sports hall by moving away the sliding wall, and the sports hall was in turn connected, through an opening in the floor, to a swimming pool situated under the stalls, in the centre of the foyer. Having worked so enthusiastically on the clubs, intoxicated by rapidly changing ideas, now, when I am cooled down, I only regret that the technology needed to realise this fantastic passion was still going through a difficult infancy."
K.S. Mel'nikov, 1967[1]

The workers' club for the shoe factory 'Burevestnik' (petrel) is located in the north-western industrial sector of Moscow between the railroad line to Jaroslavl' and the Sokol'niki Culture Park on Rybinskaja 3ja Street. Opposite the factory is a once attractive Art Nouveau mansion.
Along with the Frunze Club, it is one of Mel'nikov's few workers' clubs that has a predominantly orthogonal ground plan. In this respect it resembles the designs of the rationalists and constructivists who saw functional advantages in this practical ordering principle. Mel'nikov, however, also discerned in its regular cuboid structures an instrument of order striving for the regimentation, supervision, and discipline of the individual, which the professed individualist rejected. Thus, not only formal concerns lay behind his efforts to indulge his preference for the circle: he also desired to give expression to his individualistic view of society. He accomplished this by means of a round tower composed of five glass cylinders dominating the main facade on the street. In this manner the otherwise simple structure with an auditorium and gymnasium attached at the rear obtains a sculptural dominant guaranteeing the unmistakability of the building and drawing attention away from the old carist Art Nouveau mansion to the new socialist construction. Technical and financial concerns undoubtedly explain why the completed structure turned out to be considerably clumsier than the elegant design drawing, which called for completely glassed-in cylinders and slender window frames: in the completed version the vaulted window areas were broken up by polygons, the thick wooden window frames did not attain the elegance of the thin steel frames, and the wide wall panels reduced the desired effect of transparency. Due to local conditions, facilities planned for the interior also had to be reduced: the swimming pool planned for underneath the auditorium did not materialise due to the lack of a sewerage system as well as for economic reasons.
The goal of the reconstruction completed to a scale of 1:100 was to show not only the structural organisation of the building but also its individualistic implications and the original elegance of the design. Thus, the glass cylinder housing the circular rooms for small groups was fashioned according to the design drawing: on the one hand, the slender glazing bars were merely indicated by scratches from the back; on the other hand, however, the wide wall panels correspond to the realised version of the building. Furthermore the expressive inscription 'Burevestnik' designed by Mel'nikov himself for the facade of the building was included, as well as the small sculpture on the landing in front of the main entrance. In order also to show the interior organisation, part of the roofing for the auditorium—originally lighted naturally by a row of skylights on each side—was left out. Wood was selected as the material in order to approximate the effect of the partially plastered brick structure in coloration and surface texture.

[1] From K.S. Mel'nikov, K.S. Mel'nikov, *Arkhitektura moej žizni. Tvorčeskaja koncepcija. Tvorčeskaja praktika,* Moskva 1985, p.185.

Views of the Burevestnik workers' club, Twenties

View of the model (realised by J. Ballreich, I. Hartmann)

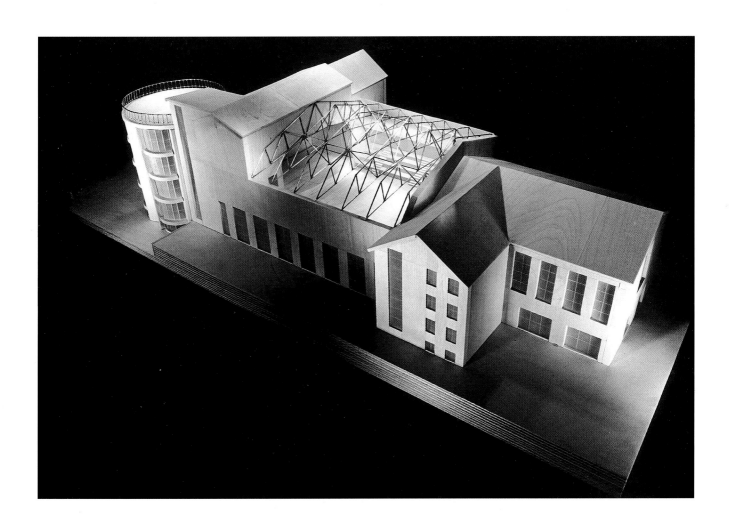

Burevestnik workers' club, 1929
(re-drawn by A. Tomasi)
scale 1:600

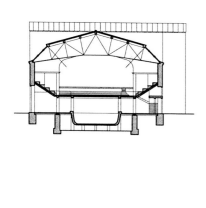

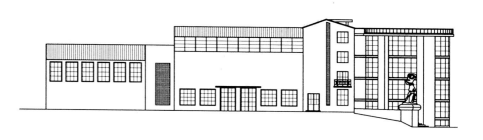

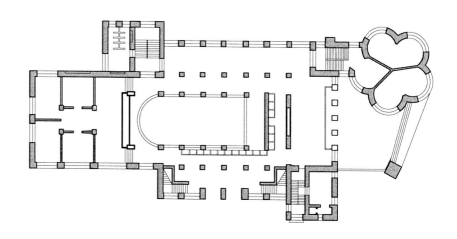

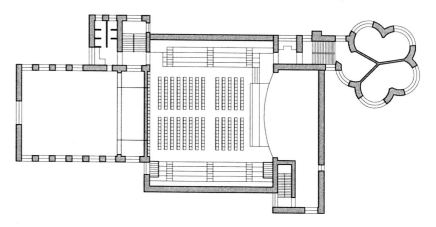

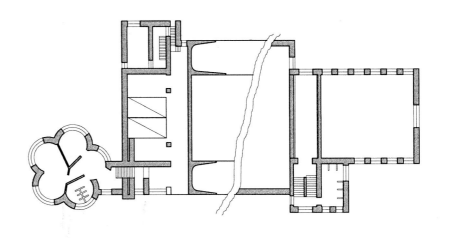

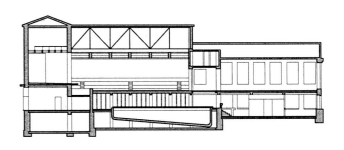

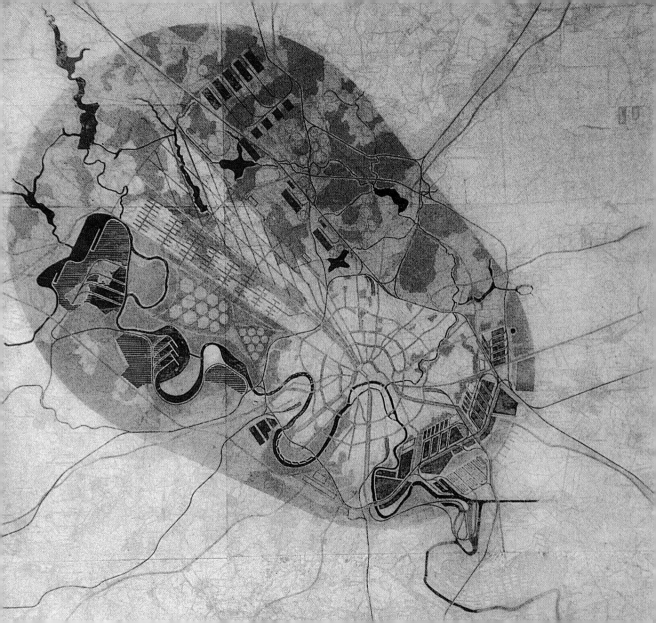

The Competitions for the "New City" and for the Major Monuments

The Competition for the 'Green City'.

The competition announced in 1929 by the limited company 'Green City' for the design of a large suburban *kurort*—a health resort for mass vacationing—to be built near Moscow, to offer rest and recreation for the workers of the capital, took place in a particular moment in the life of the city, a clear turning point both in terms of *design* and of *management*.

At the level of design the most evident aspect is a leap in scale: with the launching of the first five-year plan a debate began on the form of the socialist settlement, whose central theme was that of the plans for the new industrial cities, but which also concerned Moscow, for which proposals were developed, which although they were destined to touch on apparently partial or specific issues—the system of culture and vacation parks and the 'Green City'—nevertheless constituted, in practice, programs for the overall reorganisation of the capital.

At the level of management the launching of the planning led to a gradual marginalisation of the role of the trade union organisations in the government and the construction of the city. The unions, which had exercised a direct and nearly exclusive monopoly over the organisation of free time for the masses, through the promotion and construction of the workers' clubs from 1926 to 1929, seeking to accomplish the natural evolution of scale on this theme represented by the 'Green City', were not able to complete the initiative, due to the difficulties of inserting the project within the schemes of the planning. Work for the construction of this new settlement—which was to have been built in keeping with the management model already utilised in the preceding years for the reconstruction of the peripheries, namely a model based on the political support of the municipal administration, on the one hand, and the use of funds not only from the unions, but also from the co-operatives and other Moscovite social organisations, on the other—began in 1930-1931 with the production of a scale model, the tracing of the streets and the initial construction of a certain number of units, but the project was abandoned following the second debate on urban planning.

The Competition Guidelines
The idea for the construction of the city was advanced by the journalist Mikhail Kol'cov[1] (in *Pravda*, 1.30. 1929).

At a distance of 32 km to the north-east of Moscow, near the station of Bratovščina-Spasskaja, an area was identified with particularly good climate and landscape conditions, a zone 15,000 hectares, of which 11,500 were woodlands, crossed by two rivers (Vjaz' and Skalba) with a few small lakes, and by the Jaroslavskoe sosse highway.

The idea was to build a place for mass vacationing close to the workplace, with the substantial advantage of savings in terms of travel time. The vacation city would welcome workers for rest periods of one or two days, or for longer vacations, assigned in shifts. The area would be divided into different zones: one with actual sanatoriums, far from the rail line, in complete silence; a zone with rest homes and hotels; a zone for mass recreation activities, with parks, avenues, sporting facilities, stadiums, theatres, swimming pools. Another area was set aside to house a permanent population of about 3000 persons to staff the complex, along with an area for peasants featuring a model *kolkhos* for the growing of forage plants and grain. The 'Green City' called for maximum collectivisation of everyday life: dwellings, nourishment, cultural services, education. The suburban railway could transport up to 100,000 vacationers per day from Moscow to the 'Green City'.

The Social Organisations of Moscow joined forces in a limited company[2], which also included the participation of state agencies and co-operatives (for which a specific zone was set aside for dachas). A group of engineers and architects was formed to define in detail the single aspects, with a general project; in a second phase, an invitational competition was announced, with the participation of

On page 210:
*N. Ladovskij, Plan for the development
of Moscow, 1932*

*The area devoted to the construction
of the 'Green City'; masterplan and views*

*N. Ladovskij, Project for the 'Green City;
general plan and central hotel*

N. Ladovskij, K. Mel'nikov, M. Ginzburg, D. Fridman.
Although the guidelines presented, with a certain precision, a specific theme that in many ways was absolutely unprecedented, and which was to run a certain course throughout the architectural culture of this century in both the USSR and in different European contexts[3], the projects presented could not help but be influenced by the climate of the times and, in particular, by the debate in progress on the socialist city and by the socialist reorganisation of the *byt*.[4]

Ladovskij Project
In the project by Nikolaj Ladovskij the 'Green City'[5] was seen as a place of temporary residence, not belonging to one specific production sector, and therefore designed to house workers from different types of production.

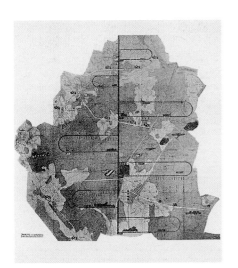

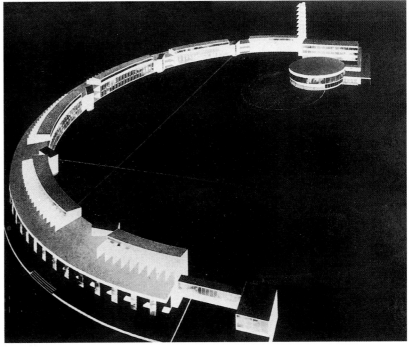

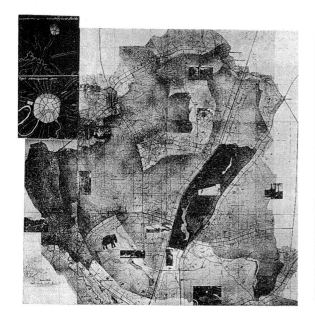

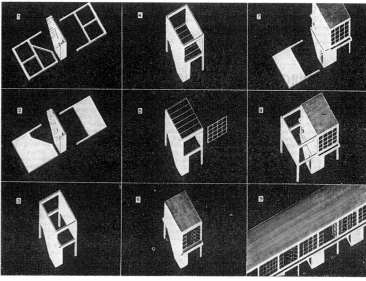

As a settlement, it would have to be combined with an agricultural city. A crucial question for the life of the 'Green City' is transport, and so the fundamental skeleton for the structure of the city is provided by a north-south highway that services a series of areas, attached like branches to the 'trunk' of the highway. Along this structure the zones of the future recreational city are arranged in a checkerboard pattern, east-west-east (with the possibility of extension, again like the branches of a tree), alternating with the zones of the agricultural city. For rail transport, the existing southwest-northeast line is maintained, with a central station near the intersection with the highway; the Jaroslavskoe sosse, temporarily maintained, was to be converted, in the future, only for freight transport.

Within the U-shaped areas serviced by the north-south highway the rest and recreation areas are placed, alternating with those of the *kolkhoz*, served by a street network that avoids, as far as possible, intersecting the vacation areas; the area of central services is located near the station; the area of victualling and commercial services, on the other hand, is placed in the strip between the rail line and the Jaroslavskoe sosse.

The typologies developed in depth for the city are: the 'district' hotels (capacity 144 persons each) placed in the vacation areas in different quantities; the central hotel (capacity

534) in the area near the station; the station-kursal, divided into two parts connected by a ramp, one for a club, the other for passenger services; several tourism pavilions.

Ginzburg Project
In the project developed by the team directed by Moisej Ja. Ginzburg and Mikhail O. Baršč (with consulting for macroeconomics matters by M. Okhitovič, and the collaboration of K.N. Afanas'ev, G.G. Sorinov, N.B. Sokolov, G.A. Zundblat) the 'Green City' constitutes a demonstrative example of a socialist city, defined as a settlement capable of reconciling and satisfying individual needs and collective organisation; the latter must reflect the system of standardised production, and the city must be organised in keeping with the core production activity; from this point of view, the particularity of the 'Green City' is that it is not primarily based on industry, though it is also designed for the workers in its own sector; therefore the city must rationally, organically organise repose, cultural production, sport, scientific and technical instruction, both for the temporary residents and the permanent ones. In the 'Green City', with a population of 100,000 inhabitants, a core industry will have to be activated, combined with a local industry, composed of the building sector (lumber, processing, furniture) and the food sector (vegetables, fruit, dairy). The other important activity of

the 'Green City' is recreation (with a culture and rest park equipped with two sports centres with stadiums, two large auditoriums, connected refreshment facilities, a zoo and a botanical garden). The settlement is built on linear segments of connection among various centres with stations, organised in bands, with residences placed at 200-400 meters from road and rail arteries, and organised in linear settlements. For the residential units, a basic individual cell is proposed, measuring 12 m2 or 3 × 4 m, for grouping in arrays of variable length; hotels are also proposed, for 100 persons, based on the model of the commune-house, and for 500 persons using the grouping of 500 cells, along with auditoriums, sports complexes, stations and tourism pavilions.

Mel'nikov Project
In the interpretation of K.S. Mel'nikov the 'Green City' is the 'city of rationalised repose', complementary to the city of production, and designed for the production of rest through slumber. The settlement is contained within an infrastructural ring with a diameter of about 10 km, composed of a rail line, a highway, a boulevard, a navigable canal. The existing rail line is maintained and cuts through the ring, while the Jaroslavskoe sosse is suppressed and deviated onto the ring highway; the rail ring can be connected to the centre by spokes

M. Ja. Ginzburg, Project for the 'Green City';
general plan and assemblage scheme
for the residential unit

D. Fridman, Project for the 'Green City';
general plan and central hotel

leading to the central sector and the
children's area, while all the zones for
rest are arranged along the perimeter,
with access from the infrastructural
ring. The circle is subdivided into
sectors for different purposes (woods,
kolkhoz, gardens and vegetable
gardens, zoo, central services, the
children's citadel); all these sectors
are served, inside, by the existing
road network (improved for the
circulation of bicycles and
automobiles); in the central sector
there are buildings of collective
interest (station, central hotel, staff
housing, stadium, scientific research,
entertainment, commerce), with the
Institute for the Change of the
Individual (a scientific centre for the
development of the 'new man') at the
centre. Along the infrastructural ring,
in the part of the wooded areas, the
rest settlements are concentrated (12,
with a capacity of 4000 persons each,
in 20 buildings with a capacity of 240
slumberers each).
The basic element that characterises
the entire settlement is the 'SONnaja
SONata' (a building with large
collective wards for repose); detailed
designs are provided for the rail
station-club, staff housing, district
hotels, the central hotel and two
different types of tourism pavilion.

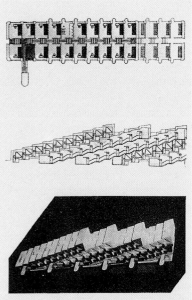

Fridman Project
The idea of the project by Danil
Fridman is based on certain
fundamental considerations: *from the
point of view of hygiene*—the city is

Le Corbusier, Scheme of the plan
for Moscow explained in the
'Response à Moscou', 1930

N. Ladovskij, 'Moscow parabola-city', 1932

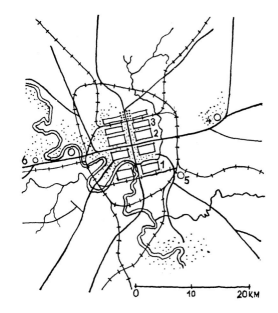

conceived as a large expanse of wooded areas between buildings and quarters, whose residential cells must be well-ventilated, filled with sunlight, protected from noise; *from the point of view of transport and connections*—the city is served by the existing rail line and sosse; *from the point of view of the physical plant*—it is not possible to resolve the problem of organised repose for all the inhabitants of Moscow; in this installation 100,000 inhabitants/visitors can be accommodated, while other 'green cities' will have to be created in the vicinity of the local Moscovite rail network; *from the social point of view*—the city is the result of the socialist reconstruction of the national economy, the very first experience of construction of a city of rest and recreation, and it must be developed in keeping with the most modern forms of organisation, both in terms of building and of transport; *from the technical/constructive point of view*—a massive application of standardisation and industrial technologies, using simple materials such as wood and brick; *from the architectural point of view*—just as Moscow is the city of work, the 'Green City' is the city of rest, and therefore the architecture must reflect the characteristics of this settlement, based on the natural landscape characteristics of the site, the environment, the topography and geography.

The various zones of the complex, each with a specially designed type of facilities (for the elderly, for children, hotels, sports, etc.) are positioned in keeping with the natural characteristics of the site; in the central area near the Bratovščina rail station the central hotel, administration and commercial services are located.

The basic design unit is a trapezoidal cell on pilotis, for different types of groupings and extensions, for the creation of hotels and residential structures of different sizes; the project also provided specific designs for district hotels and tourism pavilions.

Outcome of the Competition

The winning project was that of N. Ladovskij, although all four of the competitors were commissioned to experiment with prototype constructions of the buildings they had designed.

Nevertheless, the 'Green City' was never built.

Apart from the value of the projects themselves, this competition represented a crucial point in the development of the city of Moscow, precisely because of its ineffectual outcome, which was symptomatic of a series of structural phenomena that were to bring a definitive close to the experience of the Moscow of the Twenties.

An explicit theme of the 'Green City' is the design of a new settlement organism by means of a composition using natural landscape and new construction, which must not be created based on the model of the garden-city, nor on those of a city designed for production.[6]

The four proposals attempt to respond to the requirements by reworking and distilling the various experiences of their authors in Twenties Moscow, both in terms of the spatial organisational model of the settlement and in terms of the cultural orientation of the management and construction of the city. This is probably the starting point for the crisis of the avant-garde culture whose apogee coincided with the end of the NEP.

In the passage from the NEP to the Five-Year Plan the architects gradually found themselves lacking the support of institutional figures on the level of the cultural orientation of the management and construction of the city.

Two of the proposals were openly tendentious: the *disurbanistic* design by M. Ginzburg (one of the founders of the OSA) and the *dynamic structure* by N. Ladovskij (one of the founders of ARU), based on a theoretical reference framework[7] (although the latter does address, with a certain precision, the specific theme of the initiative), while the proposals of K. Mel'nikov and D. Fridman are apparently more pertinent with respect to the theme of the vacation city. But between the lines, in all four projects presented for

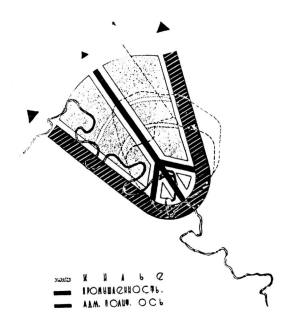

the competition for the 'Green City', we can observe, in a more or less explicit or accentuated form, an intention to make a demonstrative proposal for a possible future organisation of Moscow and of Soviet cities in general.

In any case, none of the four proposals appears to have been capable of interpreting the phenomena which the new cultural orientations of planning were producing, nor to meet the expectations of the administrative forces that rose to power in the Thirties.

Maurizio Meriggi

Competitions of Urban-Planning Concepts and the First Rounds of the Palace of the Soviets Competition

By 1929, i.e. by the start of the first state five-year economic plan, it was beginning to be felt that a new era was about to unfold in the architects' profession, with the reconstruction of Moscow, and indeed the whole of Soviet urban planning, awaiting its attention. It was time for the architects to move on from their dreams of transforming the capital, to face the down-to-earth concerns of urban construction. Building in Moscow was proceeding apace. Constructivism was becoming the main trend in architecture, with its methods and means of shape-designing, but by this time it was transforming itself more and more

from being a creative method of architecture to a modern style which was being imitated everywhere. During these years, buildings erected under the apartment-allocation system, and buildings in the so-called 'proletarian classic' style, were appearing alongside the constructivist designs which had created the whole fabric of Moscow's urban culture. An unsuccessful experiment which involved using a small number of trial commune-blocks showed that for the foreseeable future the apartment would remain the favoured form of housing. Architects began work on new types of economical and comfortable apartments employing industrial methods of construction. Moscow was expanding rapidly and it quickly became clear that the earlier schemes for its redevelopment under the new order could not be regarded as satisfactory. In the 'New Moscow' plan and the 'Greater Moscow' scheme the city's expansion was viewed in terms of adding new ring developments around a static centre which offered no scope for development.

In the years 1929-1932 a whole series of new reconstruction projects was offered by architects of various creative leanings. They were all fairly schematic but were accompanied by lengthy literary descriptions of Moscow's future. These were the first attempts to produce an overall purpose-driven scheme, to discover the basic principles necessary to

confront the complex town-planning challenge of no less a city than Moscow. At the same time, each project contained detailed attempts to solve practical problems of planning not only the city as a whole, but also its separate districts, the organisation of transport, communications and local services.

One of the first such projects was put forward in 1929 by N.A. Ladovskij, the leader of the urbanist school. As a result of several years of work already done on analysing various basic town-planning schemes, Ladovskij formulated a radically new approach to the problem of a flexible structure for the plan of the city and the role of the city centre. After comparing the advantages and disadvantages of the radial ring scheme, on the basis of which Moscow had been planned, and those of the linear scheme, which had by this time been quite thoroughly elaborated (by such architects as I. Leonidov, N. Miljutin and V. Lavrov), Ladovskij devised a scheme in the shape of a parabola; the social centre ran along its axis and was skirted by the residential, industrial and greenbelt zones. The centre had been given freedom to develop, without losing its dominant role over time. When a city grows as a whole, the growth of its separately functioning constituent parts is also guaranteed. The three-dimensional city was given a fourth dimension-time: it was developing along a dynamic axis, whilst retaining its

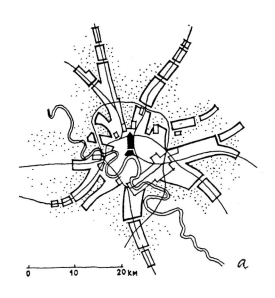

Schemes of competition projects
for the 1932 Moscow General Plan
by G. Krasin, E. May, V. Kratjuk

a

wholeness, an especially important fact from the creative viewpoint of the urbanists, who regarded the city's architecture as a "powerful means of organising the minds of the masses." It was not only in urban construction that a more profound approach to the problems of the relationship between time and space became the main characteristic of scientific quests and theoretical structures at the start of the Thirties. It was within literally a few months of each other in that same year (although, of course, quite independently of each other) that N. Ladovskij and the theoretical physicist Prof. Freedman proposed a graphically similar parabola of the 'Open Universe' and Prof. A. Gurevič devised the theory of embryonic shape-designing.

These theories, importantly, have not lost any of their validity or authority in architectural circles to this day. Ladovskij's 'Parabola' was 'rediscovered' in the Fifties European urban planning by K. Doxiadis and was dubbed 'Dynapolis', i.e. dynamic city.

The design projects for Moscow created in this period should not be viewed outside the context of the theoretical urban-planning debate which burst into life in 1929-1930, and which came to be known as the urbanist-deurbanist debate. The central focus of the discussion was such problems as the attitude to large cities, the dissolution of the town/country divide, and the

reconstruction of civic life. In the heat of the debate the urbanist side, led by the economist and sociologist L. Sabsovič, proposed the abolition of all the existing urban-planning structures as obstacles to social development. In place of these they proposed the creation of a symmetrical grid of 'ideal' settlements of 40-100,000 inhabitants with a socialised way of life and collective living arrangements-standardised living units organised on the principle of commune-houses.

The deurbanists were championed by M.Ja. Ginzburg, the constructivists' leader. They proposed a system of settlement in the form of a network of high-speed roads, along which individual dwellings, work places and social facilities complexes would be evenly distributed. While the urbanists conceived the future city as a territorial formation with defined—and even closed—boundaries, where transport and communications would only be tailored to the needs of the city, the deurbanists accorded to transport and communications a leading role, forming new attitudes in the individual towards everything around him: buildings, objects, other people. The development of transport decreases people's dependence on the home, and removes their attachment to a fixed place of abode. The economist and philosopher M. Okhitovič, also a protagonist for the deurbanists, wrote: "In these matters, space is measured as time. But even

this time is beginning to shrink." Perceptions of near and far, of solitude and social contact are changing.

The doctrine of deurbanism went to the heart of the 'Green City' project elaborated by M.Ja. Ginzburg and M. Baršč in 1929. The idea of creating a "city of relaxation" 30 kilometres outside Moscow was put forward by the journalist M. Kol'cov and immediately gained popularity. Its originators saw it as the first step towards de-concentrating the population of Moscow, reducing its numbers and locating the human habitat closer to nature. The concept of "unloading Moscow" led to a contest of commissioned design projects for the 'Green City', in which K.S. Mel'nikov took part.

The creation of a systematic scheme for the thinning of the population and the greening of the city was the objective of another competition in which Mel'nikov participated: the 'Central Leisure Park' project. This was at the same time a grandiose propaganda experiment, a specific kind of conceptual model of the future socialist city, a park-city which, according to the Moscow City Council's programme, was to "revolutionise the cultural life of worker and peasant and fill it with new meaning."

The striving to formulate the new social imperative—the political and ideological content of the Moscow reconstruction project—came to the

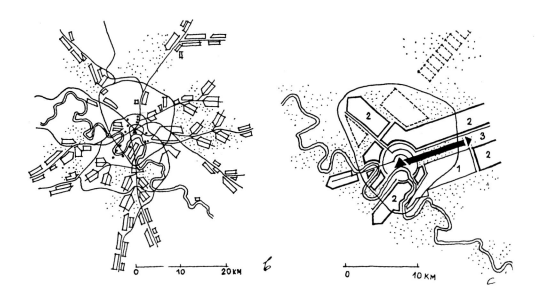

fore in the middle of 1930, when the competition to redesign the capital was announced. A special questionnaire-based opinion poll showed that concern for Moscow's spiritual role as the centre of the world's first worker-peasant state permeated even the most practical development issues.

Considerable influence was exerted on people's minds (not only those of the professional architects) by the ideas, already well known by this time, of Le Corbusier, who had also produced a reconstruction scheme for Moscow in 1930. As is well known, he envisaged Moscow as an ideal garden city with skyscraper residential estates filled with air and light. The previously enshrined radial-ring plan, and also most of the residential construction plan, were seen by Le Corbusier as a hindrance to the city's development, and he designated them for gradual replacement by the new scheme. Only a few of the park areas were to remain, for the preservation of the best architectural monuments. Many of those engaged in the public discussion of the problems of Moscow's reconstruction in 1930 agreed that the radial-ring scheme had had its day. V. Dolganov's scheme, for example—a response to Ladovskij's 'Parabola', envisaged giving the city freedom to develop eastwards, in the direction of the predominantly industrial districts. But the existing system of planning also had its adherents. The architect

D. Fridman argued for the interests of the "consumer of cultural values," who would become removed progressively farther away from the main cultural institutions as the linear development of housing provision continued. Professor B.V. Sakulin rejected the general centralism of the Moscow scheme, favouring the creation of new urban centres based on a 'planning spiral' and a rational road scheme.

The year 1930 saw the completion of 'The draft scheme for the replanning of Moscow' under the leadership of V.N. Semenov. The scheme incorporated many of the ideas generated by the current debate on socialist housing design as well as proposals from professionals. The plan was to divide the city into a system of complexes situated around the old city centre. Each of these 'town-complexes' would enjoy considerable autonomy, and would be encircled by a protective and recreational green zone. Many of the scheme's provisions, however, provoked criticism, not least concerning the scant attention paid by the design team to the aesthetic aspects of the housing project.

A new phase in Moscow's reconstruction planning began in the middle of 1931, with the enactment of the well-known law "On the urban economy of Moscow and the development of urban economy in the USSR." It provided for extensive civic and cultural construction, the

building of the capital's underground railway and the connection of Moscow to the water transport system by constructing the ship canal linking the River Moskva with the Volga. Criticism was targeted at the great-power approaches, as well as the small-minded parochialism, of the reconstruction schemes, and also at the 'ultra-left' proposals for the socialisation of civic life which did not take account of the real situation in the country at the beginning of the Thirties.

The Moscow City Council commissioned seven schemes for the reconstruction of Moscow, and they were presented for discussion early in 1932.

In the design proposed by G. Krasin, an engineer, the main focus was on the rational organisation of the transport system. He regarded the city plan primarily from the point of view of the time taken for a citizen to reach the city centre. His concept of 'the city of Moscow' embraced all the districts which were within one hour's travel from the centre.

Three reconstruction schemes were presented by well-known German architects E. May, G. Mayer and K. Mayer, who were working in the USSR. They all approached the task with a degree of caution, retaining the main radial-ring design, and worked through what they considered to be the most important issues related to housing people in satellite towns. K. Mayer proposed a static planning

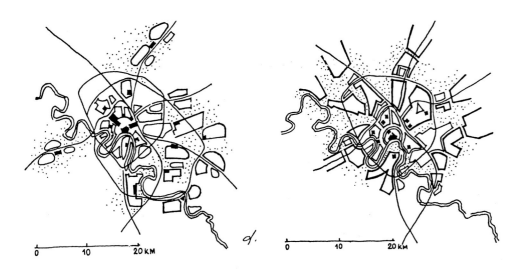

system in the form of a 'star city', in which the historical centre coincided with the political centre. The old centre of Moscow was to become a 'red forum', where the Soviet Union's main political and state institutions were situated. K. Mayer based his reasoning on the political role of the proletarian capital, which is its chief *raison d'être*; he considered that all other aspects of the city's life must be subordinate to this primary function. A little later, K. Mayer's scheme was counted among the most important, i.e. those which provided material for further work on Moscow's reconstruction.

Three other schemes were created by N.A. Ladovskij, by a team headed by V. Kratjuk and the 'proletarian architects' team under V.V. Baburov. Ladovskij's project, which developed further the 1929 idea, suffered criticism for excessive pandering to the interests of industry and understating "Moscow's importance as the world's only proletarian capital." In truth, the functional 'parabolic' scheme which expressed Ladovskij's creative vision provided every possible opportunity for the development of an architectural composition which made sense as an integral whole.

The designs by V. Kratjuk and V.V. Baburov in some measure incorporated techniques found by Le Corbusier and N.A. Ladovskij. V. Kratjuk's team proposed inserting breaks in the rings around Moscow in several directions, such as to divide the city into specialised 'district-towns' reminiscent of the mediaeval artisan districts in terms of their homogeneous social composition. The 'proletarian architects' team divided the city into five precincts which would be connected with the general urban industrial zone and the centre-line that accompanied it. The most promising part of the proposal related to transport: a new rectangular arrangement of streets would be superimposed on the existing network of main roads, to give easier access to the new districts. The results of the competition were decided in the middle of 1932, and a new stage in the planning of Moscow began, in the specially created Architectural Planning Authority, under the leadership of the city's Chief Architect V.N. Semenov. The preliminary draft project was completed at the end of 1932.

The years 1929-1932 saw a gradual transformation of ideas of the city, an awakening to the possibilities of the architectural expressiveness of the space which was being subjected to the dynamics of people moving *en masse*, and the overt symbolism drawn from the artwork of political propaganda and the theatre. The heroic revolutionary pathos and triumphal festivity of the city's public spaces were a distinguishing mark in particular of the projects for redesigning the city's old squares, which were being drafted in parallel with the city reconstruction plans (the Arbat Square project was being developed by K.S. Mel'nikov).

The new *zeitgeist* which was taking over from the spirit of the earliest years of the revolution made itself known in the increasingly frequent exhortations to give serious thought to the architectural aesthetics and appearance of the city. The discourse among architects and urban planners gradually reverted back to the 'academic' concepts which had long been out of fashion. New trends came into being, calling for the revival of 'the art of urban construction', of the concept of the city as a single organic ensemble, and of a switch of priorities away from open space to large-scale composition.

The first clear signs of a move to a new concept were the competition projects for the Palace of the Soviets which came to be seen as a symbol of the city of the future. For all their diversity, these projects had a common guiding principle: the aesthetic impact of the city, which arose out of the highly theatrical quality that the life of the capital had taken on, as least as far as the planners at the time were concerned. The designs for the Palace of the Soviets in effect amalgamated two themes which had, in the space of one and a half decades, already become traditional in Soviet architecture: the *leitmotif* of high-rise planning, a key principle of urban construction, and the search for a building form that

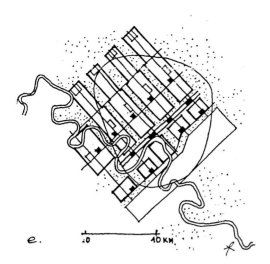

*Schemes of competition projects
for the 1932 Moscow General Plan
by G. Meyer, K. Meyer, VOPRA group*

e.   .0   10 KM.

symbolised the new era and embodied the idea of triumph of a new world social order. Attempts to design the country's 'main building', harmoniously incorporating the symbolic function and the reach towards the sky, had been made earlier, starting with the monumental tower for Petrograd by the artist V. Tatlin (1919), celebrating the Third International, and the gigantic lighthouse on Krasnaja Presnja in Moscow (1922).

The ideas behind the competition to design the Palace of the Soviets—the continuation of the series of design competitions—were first set out in the competition programme published in 1931, and were closely linked with the challenges involved in the creation of a new general plan for Moscow.

The purpose of the preliminary stage of the contest, in which 15 entries competed, was to present the complete spectrum of possible directions for the forthcoming contest and to refine the programme. The next stage would be to define the preferred options for developing the general idea, and to identify the detailed solution needed for the eventual design.

Most of the designs, at the preliminary stage, did not harmonise clearly the symbolic function of the building with the height requirement, although the high-rise criteria are featured in the drawings of B.M. Iofan, N.A. Ladovskij and others.

Despite the fact that the programme stipulated the construction of the Palace of the Soviets on the site of the Cathedral of Christ the Saviour, which was under demolition, the preliminary stage included other possible sites: the Vorob'evy Hills and Red Square. In general, architects had not yet come to see the Palace of the Soviets as a single construction, but were striving more to create a harmonious ensemble of complementary structures. The central focus in most of the designs was not the building itself, but the square for the staging of mass rallies. The solution for the artistic and symbolic functions did not pay very great attention to the facade; the designers gave more prominence to the 'business' character of the building.

At the All-Union Open Competition of 1931, in which 272 entries competed, some of the individual entries presented a linear graphic solution for the symbolic function, in the form of a tribune, or the head of a worker looking into the future. In the majority of the entries, however, it was the urban construction aspect that was given prominence, although the visual impact component was treated in various ways. Three of the entries—those of B.M. Iofan, I.V. Žoltovskij and the British architect George Hamilton—included the river Moskva in the complex spatial composition.

A number of designs encompassed

the high-rise criteria, but did not yet convey the sense of domination, but merely emphasised the dynamics of human movement *en masse* or the visual connection with the vertical lines of the Kremlin not far away. At this stage, the emphasis was still on creating a multi-structure ensemble, and the huge single facade was conceived more as a space for action, rather than as an object of contemplation. In many designs, the Palace of the Soviets was treated as a gigantic amphitheatre, a tribune, a 'city within a city' for the mass assembly of thousands of citizens. And yet it was here that the contours of that main idea were already beginning to form- the idea that was to develop, in rounds three and four of the competition, into a single, monolithic, artistically and symbolically self-sufficient structure (designed by G. Ludwig), an amalgamation into a single whole of the sacral impact of high-rise building crowned with an enormous dome.

The instructions of the Council for the construction of the Palace of the Soviets, enacted in February 1932 and defining the direction for the development of the project, marked a turning-point not only in the development of architecture and urban planning, but also for the whole of Soviet society. A decree was passed in April of that year "On the reconstruction of organisations in literature and the arts." It prescribed the formation of dedicated unions of

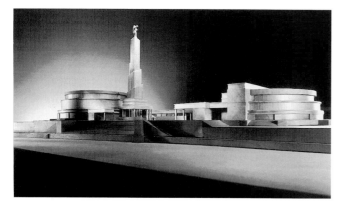

Palace of the Soviets: Project by B. Iofan
(model by K. Müller, S. Süs, 1994)

Project by A. and G. Perret
(model by B. Zonsius, 1994)

writers, composers, artists and architects to take the place of the existing diffuse and mutually competitive groups. In a creative *milieu* weary of politically aggressive phraseology, the creation of discrete unions was at first seen as a liberalisation of the situation.
In fact, what was slowly taking shape throughout the country was the preparation of the spiritual and organisational ground for the regulation of all the arts, the complete subordination of cultural processes to the political agenda.
This, in the years to come, would leave a clear imprint on architecture and urban planning, and, in particular, would greatly alter the treatment of the general plan for Moscow.
But in 1932 the euphoria generated by creative freedom had not yet departed from the architects and urban planners.
On the contrary, they approached their important role as integrators of the city's future formation with great zeal. V.N. Semenov wrote at the time: "Economists, statisticians, representatives of various disciplines—all impose their own sectional requirements in regard to the city … Only we, the planners, represent the interests of the city as a whole, and proceed on the basis of the data which the science of urban planning lays before us."
Jurij Volčok and Julia Kosenkova

The International Competition of 1931/1932 for the Palace of the Soviets: The Quest of Representing the Society of the Future

The Idea
In 1931, following its consolidation, the Soviet government in Moscow launched a Union-wide competition for the Palace of the Soviets, which reached international dimension by the invitation of foreign architects. A preparatory national competition[8] was held beforehand. These competitions, followed by further ones, stood for the true assignment to erect an ultimate building of the state, symbolising Soviet power. The idea of such an allegoric building of the 'State of Workmen and Farmers' arose soon after the bolshevist revolution and had numerous facets.[9] There were divergent ideas of the practical purpose of such a symbol, ranging from a multifunctional congress building up to a memorial.[10] The final result of 1933 was a national Lenin-Memorial on top of a congress hall. In the beginning, however, the path seemed not to be clear. In 1931, the competition papers described more a functional building for various meetings and mass demonstrations than an individual monument, and international participation was desired. Thus architects of a progressive profile from France, Germany, Italy and the United States were commissioned.[11]
Not before Stalin himself had

proposed to crown the building with the colossal statue of Lenin[12] instead of the statue of the 'liberated proletarian', the Palace building council declared it a Lenin-Memorial in 1933. This was to exceed two American superlatives: the Statue of Liberty (46 m) and the Empire State Building (381 m).
The location of this most important building of the state called for an important building site in the historic core of Moscow. Already in 1924 architects of the ASNOVA proposed a place south-west of the Kremlin near the attractive Moskva river embankment. It was the place of the huge Cathedral of Christ the Savior[13] symbolising the victory of 1812 over Napoleon. In August 1931, this church was blown up in order to be replaced by the Palace of the Soviets.

The International Part of the Competition (July-December 1931)
The second round of the now open competition had a clear program indicating the place of the cathedral as building site. Personal invitations received the Soviet architects Žoltovskij, Iofan and Krasin; but not Mel'nikov. Furthermore the western architects Perret and Le Corbusier[14] from Paris, Gropius, Mendelsohn[15] and Poelzig from Berlin, Hamilton, Lamb and Urban from United States and Brasini from Rome. The tremendous program of rooms unveils the volition of the people in power to instrumentalize the subjects in masses

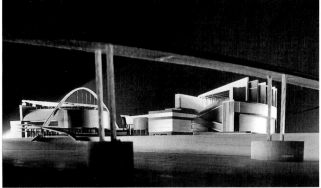

*Palace of the Soviets: Project by I. Žoltovskij
(model by Ch. Hepp, Chang Ju Kim, 1994)*

*Project by Le Corbusier
(model by U. Mork, P. Pietrasch, 1994)*

for their aims: two huge congress halls for 15,000 and 5900 people became the main parts of the whole complex. Gigantic demonstrations of thousands of people should be possible on the large stage. The stage of the smaller hall was to give room for not less than 500 people. Furthermore, the complex was to house exhibition space, a library, and 2000 m² for the administration.[16]

All together, 160 professional entries were counted, twelve of them commissioned and 24 from abroad. 112 unprofessional drawings came in, showing mostly a naive symbolism.[17] This most important second round of the competition is characterised by great differences of approaching the task regarding stylistics and structural composition. Three different groups can be discerned:

1. Complexes aiming simply at a monumental effect;
2. Neohistoristic designs aiming at the effect of familiar traditional forms;
3. Functional compositions, some of them expressing an abstract symbolism.

The jury awarded three first prizes *ex aequo*. As two of them belonged to the first group and one to the second group, this decision unveiled the tendency toward conventional values.

Monumental Complexes

Huge rotundas were proposed e.g. by Žukov & Čečulin, I. Golosov and V. Krinskij. Neither these stereometric designs nor the one of Hamilton (one

first prize) can express the different functions inside the building. Boris Iofan (one first prize) seems still open to modern ideas in this first plan, showing the two assembly halls clearly divided. The axial composition with a huge tower in the centre, however, owes much to classical order. This central monument topped by an 18 m high sculpture of the 'liberated proletarian', three times higher than the congress hall for the people, attracts much more the public attention than the building itself. The expression of movement and the demonstrations' dynamism, thus the functional idea is replaced by static forms of dignity and devotion to a person. The design's intention stresses more the proletarian cult than the very purpose of the building.

Neohistoristic Designs

Auguste and Gustave Perret were invited probably because of their modern and skilled utilisation of concrete. They designed an asymmetric ensemble of different geometric volumes placed around a rectangular forum, which is embraced by a neo-classical order of pillars. Orthogonal entrance pavilions on each side in the west and east function as a gate. The rectangular cube of the smaller auditorium is placed at Volconka street next to the Kremlin, whereas the semi-circular main auditorium with its impressive volume is effectfully placed in the south-west, next to the river

embankment. So despite the functional and asymmetric disposition of different volumes, the neo-classical order provided conventional forms of dignity for the main building of the state by means of historic values of expression.

Ščuko & Gel'frejkh designed a new Kremlin in the form of the Palace of the Doge in Venice and without any visible reference lost beside it, a huge Trajan's Column. The convinced neopalladian Žoltovskij and his disciple G.P. Gol'c (one first prize) aimed at the same gesture of a second Kremlin separated from the urban organism and elevated on a podest. The pattern of the smaller auditorium is the Teatro Olimpico at Vicenza, whereas the larger auditorium reminds us of the Coliseum at Rome. A sort of campanile facing the old Kremlin relates to its Borovickij tower.

On the whole, it bears the dark character of a closed and massive block, which does not invite the demonstrating masses. The practical functions of the building are not explained, so this new governmental centre of the state of future looks like and old Byzantine stronghold. The lack of transparency of the building reflects a typical part of every day reality in Soviet life: the rigorous renunciation of 'Glasnost'. Far beyond the competition, this meant the question of the future of Soviet art: eclecticism or creativity, imitation or innovation.

Palace of the Soviets:
Project by Van Loghem
(model by R. Hosie, K. Meyer-Bohlen, 1994)

Project by N. Vasil'ev
(model by St. Frick, F. Weisser, 1994)

Functional Compositions and Designs of Abstract Symbolism

This third group comprised mainly the Soviet avant-garde of rationalism and constructivism and the modernists from western Europe. The VKhUTEMAS trained architects Vainštein, Komarova and Mušinskij also belong to this group. Mel'nikov and his most remarkable design[18] may be mentioned here, because his composition incorporates not only a new symbolism, but also functional elements. The monumental impact, however, the combination of old and new features, and narrative elements anticipating in a certain way Socialist Realism, would rather give the Mel'nikov design an outstanding position.

Le Corbusier presented a rationalist organism showing clearly the disposition of masses and connections in between. The two great assembly halls with exquisitely engineered acoustics are composed as poles of an axis. From the large meeting field in the middle, ramps along this axis lead the demonstrating masses into the larger hall. Constructive elements like the great parabolic arch are converted into expressive elements thus gaining a representative meaning. As decorative elements (like in Iofan's design) are missing, the formal quality is based merely on the very structural elements. This architecture is characterised not by ornamentation but by organisation; being a sculpture itself it does not need sculptural

applications. The visibility of the load-bearing structure and the composition of particular functional components unveil the ideal relationship to Soviet constructivism. This idea of an axis in direction to the Kremlin is to be seen in most of the entries like in the ones of Poelzig, Lubetkin, or the brigade GIPROVTUZ, and others to be mentioned later; but also in those of Hamilton, Žoltovskij, Iofan, Žukov and of others. From the point of aesthetics and meaning, however, there is an enormous difference.

The Dutch architect Johannes Bernardus van Loghem put his assembly halls lighted from above in a similar way on an axis towards the Kremlin. The bent seat rows inside both auditoria articulate in the outside shape of their circular bent facades, facing each other; so the outside form depends of the function inside. As the fan-shaped load-bearing elements are visible, construction also contributes to the formal appearance. Around the smaller auditorium the secondary rooms are grouped, its stage is situated on the side to the Kremlin. In the architect's description, the building's form follows its functions, so the acoustic needs determine the shape of the auditorium, and the vertical accentuation of the overall horizontal building is based on the needs of the stage alone. The ten load-bearing beams of the larger auditorium, spanning over 125 m, are

constructed in the manner of bridging engineers.[19]

The St. Petersburg architect Nikolaj V. Vasil'ev had emigrated to New York, but like Naum Gabo, Berthold Lubetkin and others he thought it necessary to stay in contact with the modern architectural developments in his home country. His clearly divided building complex, a 'ship of the state', with the two assembly halls and a vertical accentuation in the middle like an ocean liner's smoke-stack, owes much to modern automobile design: The smooth and bent edges, as well as the large curved windows renounce any remembrance of historic features and symbolise the machine age. Regarding the up-to-date functional organisation of the plans, there are no important differences to the related entries of other functionalist or constructivist architects.

The Ukrainian architects Dodica & Duškin aimed at putting together the different functional units of the horizontal building. Between the two semi-circular halls of similar shape, in the centre of the building, a vertical wing is placed housing the library and rooms for the administration. In a similar way to van Loghem, the assembly halls have a flat spanning structure. The transparency of the large glass facades of the upper floors and of the 'pilotis' of the ground floor characterise the building as a modern congress centre.

Mendelsohn tried to combine the

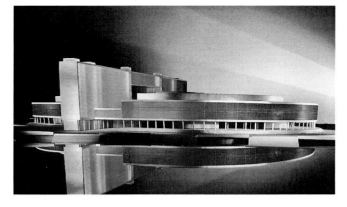

Palace of the Soviets:
Project by Ju. Dodica, A. Duškin
(model by R. Ambrosius, J. Kaiser, 1994)

Project by A.L. and V. Vesnin
(model by Yu Xie, Shoa Qun, 1997)

different volumes of the building to one single impressive volume. Two half cupolas topping the different assembly halls of varying sizes are connected in the centre by a slim box which houses the common stage and administrative rooms. Conference rooms and the library are grouped around the smaller auditorium. Horizontal stripes of windows provide on the one hand uniform daylight, and on the other hand they give the building the appearance of great serenity in front of the city's bustling backdrop. The clear and rational vocabulary renounces symbolism.

The Vesnin brothers designed a more differentiated volume of individual forms, owing much to their almost ten-year-old plan of the Palace of Labour (1923). The oval cylinder of the larger auditorium of 1923 is now converted into a classical circle, situated next to the Kremlin. The trapezoidal smaller auditorium on the opposite side has an annex for two conference rooms facing each other. According to constructivist principles, the different usages articulate in the architectural shaping. A square tower at Volconka street, partly of glass, is crowned by a Lenin statue. Despite this clear reverence for the taste of the officials, the constructivists were criticised by Molotov and the SOVNARKOM, as reported by Žukov.[20] After all, the former minister of cultural affairs, an important member of the palace

building council, had welcomed the crowning of the building by a sculpture of Lenin. Ikonnikov described this hypocrisy:
"…Lunacarskij hereby saw the direct expression of the idea that socialism put man above all."[21]
Walter Gropius based his design on a centralised symbol: in a single large circle the two main parts of the building face each other as sectors of a circle. The founder of the Bauhaus described his ideal starting point:
"the palace of the Soviets a new pole! A moment of the idea of the USSR: Therefore: one single mighty volume over the circle, a symbol of combining the people's masses to one human and political large unit."[22] The structure is formed by two sectors of a circle facing each other; in the centre they are connected by two circular wings on 'pilotis'. Inside auditorium and stage are melded together according the idea of the 'Totaltheater'[23]. The functional plan provides demonstrations to be moved over the stages as desired. Having in mind the symbolic call of the task to erect nothing less than the central building of the state, he designed a centralised structure to be covered with different sorts of natural stone of the vast land of the Soviet Union (granite, marble, porphyry). Noble material like copper roofing and window frames of bronze mouldings were added to express the dignity of the building.

Nikolaj Ladovskij already had

proposed in the preliminary round of the competition an enormous circular cupola surrounded by the slope of eight galleries. Inside this dome, the larger auditorium is grouped around a circular stage, which is reached by the demonstrations over a huge spiralled ramp. Next to the dome, a cylinder partly of glass, 35 stories high is erected to house other rooms, in addition to the smaller auditorium. This articulates the rationalist idea of perceiving the different functional elements of the building's organisation. The heavy criticism of this approach lead to dismissal of the professor by Molotov, Kaganovič and the SOVNARKOM.[24]
In a similar way Moisej Ginzburg and his partners S.A. Lisagor[25] and the Bauhaus trained Gustav Hassenpflug[26] from Germany had designed a huge glass dome. A large flat block on a square grid of 9 m served as substructure for the two assembly halls. A 15-storey wing of administration rooms with a terraced facade in the east reaches tangentially from the Moskva embankment to the two halls. Like Ladovskij, Ginzburg adapts the modern conception of a circular stage and equally sloping seat rows owing much to the 'Totaltheater'. The smaller auditorium on a trapezoidal plan, however, is built like a traditional theatre with four galleries. The all-around asymmetrical composition is dominated by the parabolic cupola of the larger auditorium. Four diagonal

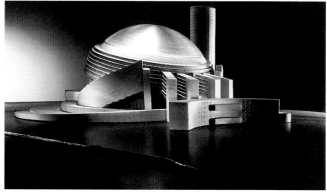

*Palace of the Soviets: Project by W. Gropius
(model by M. Kurfess, P. Mariosn, 1994)*

*Project by N. Ladovskij
(model by A. Fritz, B. Schorer, 1994)*

ribs with flat arches in between bear this cupola. Its surface mostly of glass articulates the basic idea of transparency and openness. This, however, was rejected by Molotov and Kaganovic, the men in power, who dismissed the professor on the same day, as Ladovskij.[27]

The Aftermath
The third round[28] is a national competition of twelve invited Soviet architects. The competition papers call for "monumentality, simplicity and the application of new and the best methods of classic architecture."[29] This, in short, is the outline of the new conviction of the so-called 'Socialist Realism'. Although Mel'nikov seemed to have understood quite well the now desired character of Soviet architecture, his monumental design, which incorporated modern concrete technology, symbolism of stereometric forms and classical means of expression by the allegoric atlases, was not taken in account by the officials. The forms of the Palace of the Soviets henceforth developed towards the reactionary taste of the commissioners. 'New methods' can be distinguished only in the field of engineering. The modern architectural approach, which understood the building as a forum for the republics of the Soviet Union, was replaced by the perception of a conventional palace like the Kremlin. The fourth round[30] of only five Soviet

collectives of architects is characterised by the tendency of converting the palace of the state into an enormous national monument. On May 10th, 1933 Boris Iofan's project, a 250 m high cylindrical structure, is chosen as "foundation of the design of the Palace of the Soviets." Jofan is appointed architect in chief on June 4th 1933. The building was to be topped by a sculpture of Lenin, 50-75 m high, "so that the Palace of the Soviets appears as the base of the statue of Lenin." Ščuko & Gel'frejkh become co-authors and Krasin engineer in chief. These decisions define the end of the competition. Three times the project is revised[31], and after a study tour to the United States in 1934 for consultation on the steel structure, foundation work is started on May 4th, 1937. On the lookout for modern American technology in order to overtower American world records with Soviet ones would fulfil a dream of Trockij: The victory of 'Soviet Americanism' over 'Capitalist Americanism'. The steel skeleton of the final project of 1939 should be finished by 1941. Scuko died in January 1939 at the age of 63. Lack of material and especially the beginning of the Second World War caused the end of construction[32] in winter 1941, when German tanks reached the borders of Moscow. This latest project—officially declared 'Monument to Lenin' by the Palace Building Commission—crowned by a Lenin sculpture of now 100 m had a

volume of 6.5 million cbm and an overall height of 539 m, thus overtrumping the Empire State Building. This world-record-attempt expresses one of the aims of the Soviets. This politically dazzled ideology of tonnage unveils the retrospectivism back to the funds of the age of the industrial revolution, which was just about to be realised in the Soviet Union by the Five-Year-Plan. It has nothing to do with the original aims of the social revolution. In 1957, a new competition for the Palace of the Soviets returns to the functional program of the competition of the Palace of Labour that Mel'nikov had participated in (1922/1923), stressing again the needs of the meetings of the soviets of the USSR and the RSFSR.[33] As none of the designs is realised, the highest executive congresses of the party and the state still have to renounce a modern assembly hall until the Palace of Congress is built in the Kremlin 1961 by Mikhail Posokhin, Mndojac et al. Meanwhile the desolate building pit is cleared by an architect of the second prize group: 1958-1960 D.N. Čečulin, V.V. Luk'janov and N.M. Molokov converted the foundations into a heated swimming pool.[34] So in an unusually profane metamorphosis, this meaningful place of the city is given back to the people of Moscow. However, this provisional sports facility is given a short duration: while the cathedral had existed 44 years and the foundations of the Palace of the

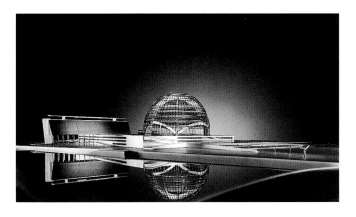

Palace of the Soviets:
Project by M.Ja. Ginzburg
(model by Th. Grühn, St. Moik, 1994)

Soviets almost three decades, the swimming pool had to give way for the remake of the cathedral after 34 years. The architect's name is the very same as the one of the Palace of Congress: Mikhail Posokhin.
D.W. Schmidt

The Competition for a Memorial to Columbus in Santo-Domingo (1929)

The idea of creating a majestic monument in the form of a lighthouse beacon that would immortalise the memory of Christopher Columbus was first expressed in a book published in Havana in 1852 by Don Antonio Del-Monte-i-Texada, *The History of Santo-Domingo*. In 1892, for the 400th anniversary of the discovery of America, the government of the Dominican Republic created a 'National Columbus Committee', entrusting it with the task of creating a worthy monument for Columbus. This Committee successfully continued its work after the formation of the Pan-American Union. At the fifth international conference of the American states in Santiago (Chili) in 1923 it was decided to immortalise the memory of Columbus with a monumental lighthouse. The temporary committee formed to create the monument (1927) suggested having a competition with the participation of architects from all countries. The expenses of the competition were assumed by the government of the Dominican republic.

It was decided that in the preliminary stage the competitors would be free to express their ideas, and then the authors of ten chosen projects would take part in a second round which would determine the Architect of the project. On September 1, 1928 the Pan-American union declared the International Competition for the Project of a Memorial Lighthouse to Christopher Columbus open. The entries had to be sent to Madrid before April 1, 1929. The international jury (chosen by the competitors themselves) included the president of Uruguay, Horacio Acosta Y Lara. He was chosen as president, while the architects were Eliel Saarinen (Finland) and Raymond Hood (USA).[35]

The complex, which was on a part of the Dominican coast with a suitable bay, had to include a Columbus museum, a chapel with his ashes and a lighthouse, as well as a large Pan-American park (1000 hectares), to which a government centre and airport had to be adjoined. According to the programme of the competition, the architect's task included the planning of this complex area and the creation of a noble monument filled with strength of spirit and bearing the symbolism and romanticism of past ages while at the same time including the achievements of contemporary architecture. According to the conception of the organisers of the competition, the memorial had to symbolise the greatness of America,

and by its monumentalism underline the strength and power of man, emphasising that the discovery of the continent was the greatest event in the history of mankind, exerting a huge influence on the development of world civilisation. Great attention was to be paid to the decision on how to light the memorial, since the monument had to be expressive both by day and by night. The height of the lighthouse was limited to 600 feet (182.8 metres). It was stipulated that all three elements of the memorial ensemble could be united into an integral structure, or they could be planned in the form of separate buildings creating the 'impression' of a simple composition. The memorial had to be on an embankment, terrace or terraces; it had to be visible from all directions and expressive both from close-up and at a distance; the structure was to contain a minimum of one large searchlight. The lighthouse was permitted to be constructed on a base of earthquake-proof steel or reinforced concrete, but the surface of the monument had to be completed from a good-looking material (the local stone, which was of a beautiful colour and texture and could be easily machined, was suggested).

Six pages of sketches on white paper were required for the competition: the facade and a cross-section of the lighthouse (on vertical 81 × 168-cm pages on a scale of 1:200), a general plan of the ensemble and of the site

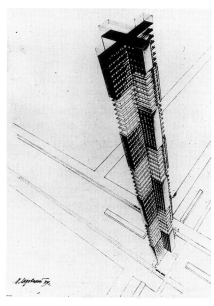

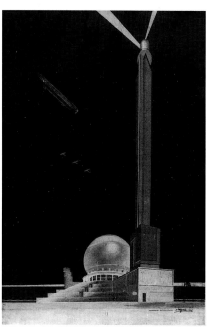

on horizontal 81 × 137-cm pages (scale 1:1000), a perspective and plans of the lighthouse at various levels on 1 page, details of the exterior and interior on 1 page. Soviet architects received invitations to take part in the competition in the summer of 1928. 23 projects were given in from the USSR: from Moscow – 9 (S.A. Vlasev; G.T. Krutikov in co-authorship with T.N. Varencov and A.V. Bunin; Krymskij; N.A. Ladovskij; I.I. Leonidov; K.S. Mel'nikov; A.A. Porokhovscikov; V.V. Tarasov; A.V. Ščusev); from Leningrad – 12 (A.E.Belogrud'; S.E. Brovcev; P.S. Duplicky; L.A. Il'in; E.I. Katonin in co-authorship with V.A. Vitman and V.V. Danilov; I.G. Langbard; N.E. Lansere – 2 variants, O.R. Munts; N.A. Orlovskij; V.G. Samorodov; M.S. Fedorov, and also A.M. Kasjanov (Kharkov) and G.I. Volosinov (Kiev). Besides, two projects were given in to the competition by Russian architects who were working at that time in the United States: V.K. Oltarževskij (who soon returned to the USSR) and N.V. Vasil'ev. The following also worked on projects, but did not present them at the competition: I.V. Žoltovskij with the sculptor S. Merkurov, V.F. Krinskij with A.M. Rukhljadev, L.M. Lisickij, G.M. Ljudwig, A.S. Nikol'skij, V.A. Ščuko and other architects.[36]

In all, for this, the biggest competition in the history of architecture, 455 projects (more than 3300 sketches) were received from 48 countries. The overwhelming majority of them were of a traditionalist orientation. Their exhibition was opened on April 28, 1929 in the palace in the park El Retro in Madrid, and then on August 7, 1929 in Rome. Most of the western projects contained a reference to the historical heritage: motifs from the Ancient East, from Greek and Roman classicism, from the Middle Ages and from Pre-Colombian America. Vertical solutions predominated in the compositions—variations of the skyscrapers that were typical for America at the time (mainly in neo-classical or art deco). In compositions with spread out volumes a powerful ray of light directed upward took the place of the missing vertical. One of the most interesting western works was the project of T. Garnier—a gigantic metal spiral of the lighthouse's tracery tower and included in it the glazed building of the memorial recalling the well-known Tatlin tower. The Soviet projects at the exhibition in Madrid and Rome were displayed as a separate section, since the jury put them into a special group of projects with special architectural qualities. In evaluating the results, the jury proceeded from the position that "the task of the competition was to find a symbol reflecting the basic qualities and significance of the great event in the history of mankind—the discovery of America by Columbus.

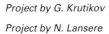

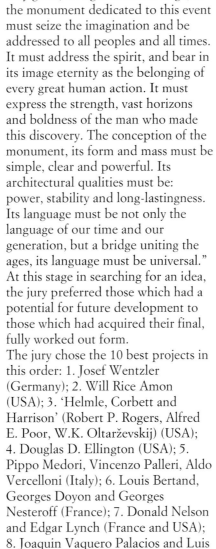

The influence of this discovery on the development of civilisation has been very great, its significance is huge, so the monument dedicated to this event must seize the imagination and be addressed to all peoples and all times. It must address the spirit, and bear in its image eternity as the belonging of every great human action. It must express the strength, vast horizons and boldness of the man who made this discovery. The conception of the monument, its form and mass must be simple, clear and powerful. Its architectural qualities must be: power, stability and long-lastingness. Its language must be not only the language of our time and our generation, but a bridge uniting the ages, its language must be universal."
At this stage in searching for an idea, the jury preferred those which had a potential for future development to those which had acquired their final, fully worked out form.
The jury chose the 10 best projects in this order: 1. Josef Wentzler (Germany); 2. Will Rice Amon (USA); 3. 'Helmle, Corbett and Harrison' (Robert P. Rogers, Alfred E. Poor, W.K. Oltarževskij) (USA); 4. Douglas D. Ellington (USA); 5. Pippo Medori, Vincenzo Palleri, Aldo Vercelloni (Italy); 6. Louis Bertand, Georges Doyon and Georges Nesteroff (France); 7. Donald Nelson and Edgar Lynch (France and USA); 8. Joaquin Vaquero Palacios and Luis Moya Blanco (Spain); 9. Théo Lècher, Paul Andrau, George Defontaine,

Maurice Gauthier (France); 10. J.L.Gleave (England). 10 more projects whose quality was recognised to be close to those of the prize-winners were awarded an honourable prize (in order of entering): 1. John Thomas Greasdale (USA); 2. Norris E. Krendall, Donald K.Kleen, George H. Riggs jr. (USA); 3. Nikolaj Lansere (USSR); 4. Nikolaj Vasil'ev (USA); 5. Abraham Gartfield (USA); 6. Enrico Minatti and Giovanni Masini (Italy); 7. Kamill Roskott (Czechoslovakia); 8. Maurice Gogoi, K.A. Dori (France); 9. Roger Cohen (France); 10. Jan Jelezovskij and Marcel Janin (France). The project of Oltarževskij (in the group of American architects) was awarded one of the first prizes, the projects of Lansere and Vasil'ev honourable prizes. The jury also found a way of marking the merits of other projects from Russia: those of Mel'nikov, Ladovskij, Tarasov, Kasjanov, Belogrud', the group of Krutikov. They were published, with interesting commentaries by the advisor to the Committee on erecting the monument Albert Kelsey, in a book (1930) on the results of the competition. A. Kelsey first reviewed the projects of the avant-gardists: "The struggle for that which is in principle new, and more powerful, simple and vital than has existed in architecture to the present time, is now taking place in many countries. This process is taking place with particular persistence in Russia. Architecture to the Communist is

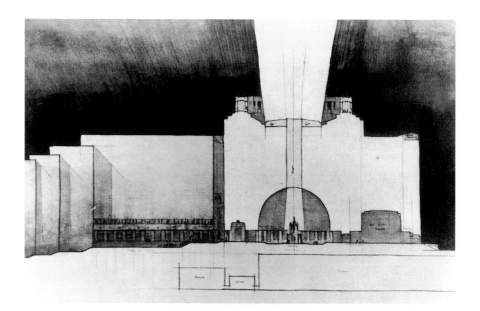

Monument to Christopher Columbus:
Project by J. L. Cleave

another revolutionary weapon, or it would be more just to say, another evolutionary medium of expression to serve both a practical purpose, and to spread, far and wide, the gospel of unadorned Communism. The Soviet architect is trying to express function in the most modern and scientific manner—to express mass-production, the electric age and above all the revolt against luxury and exclusiveness. 'One for all and all for one' is the Soviet slogan, and in its campaign against capitalism the Soviet is carrying on a social experiment of great interest, many an outside observer going so far as to believe that its ideas are as stimulating and uplifting as any that have guided mankind. However that may be, we confess ourselves old-fashioned, we still cling to old beliefs and old tradition, and for this reason perhaps are unable to fully appreciate every one of the twenty-three serious and thought-provoking designs submitted by Soviet Russia. That they are serious contributions we have no doubt, but judging them collectively they seem to lack that monumental, static and imperishable quality that is desired, and as some among them do not rivet attention on Columbus, or fire the beholder with an eager interest in things American, those therefore cannot be held up for emulation in the Second Competition. Without stimulating such thoughts, no design will be satisfactory."
For the avant-gardists the theme of

the monument was practically new. They were required to tear themselves away from the tasks of everyday life with its social-functional tasks and switch on to a new class of tasks— tasks that were in essence philosophical-ideological and grandiose in scale. Such an approach was particularly evident in Mel'nikov's project. Kelsey's commentary on this, the central Russian part of the competition, was laconic: "And that Mr. Melnikoff's extraordinary mechanical device, in particular, is both germane to Columbus and Pan-America. To do him full justice we must report that his conception was the most discussed design of the exposition in Madrid."
Mel'nikov's project was distinguished by a sharpness of conception, a multi-dimensional system of symbols, expressiveness of architectural forms, the application of new means of artistic expressiveness. The boldness of the spatial-constructive conception, the broad arsenal of methods and means used by the author for artistic expressiveness—his beloved diagonals, movement in opposite directions, 'symmetry outside symmetry' (one wing coloured black, the other red), the introduction of the physical movement of separate parts as a result of the immediate influence of forces of nature, the use of scripts, etc.—aided the birth of an original, expressive and memorable form of monument. There is no doubt

that, as with Garnier's project, Mel'nikov's project was based upon the image of the contemporary monument found by Tatlin in the Memorial of the IIIrd International (1920). But strictly speaking Mel'nikov's project (like those of Leonidov and a series of other Soviet architects) did not satisfy the conditions of the competition, since the height of the lighthouse proposed in it was more than 100 metres higher than the maximum height laid down by the programme.
Although the jury demonstrated a preference for projects in neo-classical and art deco styles, the participation of a large group of Soviet architects in the competition for the memorial in Santo Domingo turned out to be successful. Lansere's project, which was awarded an encouragement prize, presented him as a romantic brought up in classical traditions, but who still appreciated the achievements of contemporary architecture.
The representatives of the avant-garde in Soviet architecture, having created vivid, non-traditional images, demonstrated their readiness to provide solutions to artistic tasks through the means of new architecture; they broadened people's ideas of what was possible.
The prizes in the second stage of the competition were awarded in the following order: 1. J.L.Gleave (England); 2. Donald Nelson and Edgar Lynch: Bennett, Parsons and

Project by Helme, Corbett & Harrison,
R. P. Rogers & A. E. Poor, V. K. Oltarževskij

Project by J. Wentzler

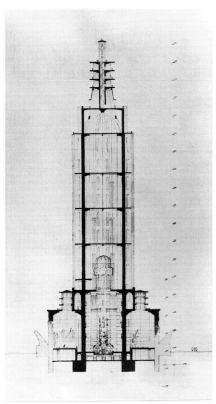

Frost (Associated Architects): Oskar
J.W.Hansen (Associated Sculptor)
(USA); 3. Joaquin Vaquero Palacios
and Luis Moya Blanco (Spain); 4.
Theo Lescher, Paul Andrau, Maurice
Gauthier (France).
Also singled out for a prize were: a)
Louis Bertand, Georges Doyon and
Georges Nesteroff (France); b) Josef
Wentzler (Germany); c) 'Corbett,
Harrison, MacMurray' (Robert P.
Rodgers, Alfred E. Poor, W.K.
Oltarzevskij) (USA); d) Pippo Medori
(Italy); e) Douglas D. Ellington
(USA); f) Will Rice Amon (USA).
That is, the project in which
Oltarzevskij was working on in
America was again picked out.
The jury based their choice of
Gleave's project as the leading one
was based on the fact that
"although expressions of new
resources in construction
characterising our twentieth-century
are absent, one design, making
wonderful use of light does take
refuge in a directness, simplicity and
force worthy of the great monuments
of the ages. This design is symbolic
but not to the point where symbolism
interferes with the simple beauty of
the work as architecture … The
whole has idea, unity and avoids by a
certain rational force the dull craze
for altitude and the persistent
erection of the 'post'."
However, Konstantin Mel'nikov's
Columbus project remains to this day
as an unexcelled masterpiece of
Russian architectural genius.

[1] Kol'cov Michail Efimovic, journalist, played
an important role in the Soviet contingent that
took part in the war in Spain. He was executed
by firing squad in 1939.
[2] The initial capitalisation of the limited company was ten million rubles, required for the
primary development phases. The initiative included participation of the factory collectives
and trade unions, the Central Committee of
the PCUS, the Regional Council of the Trade
Unions, the Moscow Soviet. These data, like
the other included in this article regarding the
contents of the project and the competition
guidelines, are found in N. Popov-Sibirjak,
"Zelenomu gorodu obscestvennoe vnimanie"
(Collective interest in the Green City), in
Stroitel'stvo Moskvy, n. 8, 1929.
[3] Of particular interest for comparison here is
the Spanish experience represented by the project, in 1932, for the 'Ciutad de repos' to be
built near Barcelona on the coast between the
mouth of the Llobregat and the breakfront of
Castelldefels. The project, sustained and developed by members of GATEPAC, was fully illustrated in the magazine of the group
'A.C.', n. 7, 1932, and n. 13, 1934. In the first
issue of the same magazine, January 1931, pp.
30-32, there is a lengthy article on the competition for the 'Green City of Moscow'. The
project for the 'Ciutad de repos' was also published in the Dutch magazine *De 8 OPBOUW*,
in the issue of June 1934. The project, after the
initial phase of land expropriation which was
not completed until 1937, was never built due
to difficulties caused by the spread of the civil war. For bibliographic reference see E. Do-
nato, "La città di riposo e vacanze", in *Hin-
terland*, n. 7/8, April 1979, offering a wide
range of sources. Another comparable project
with respect to the 'Green City' is the Italian
experience of the vacation colonies for children and adolescents, promoted by state
agencies and private companies for the children of their employees, and constructed for
the most part at the seaside or in the moun-
tains in Italy during the Twenties and Thirties.
These settlements became a very fertile theme

of study and work for Italian rationalist architecture. For bibliographic reference see: M. Labò, A. Podestà, *Colonie*, Editoriale Domus, Milano 1942; F. Monterisi, *Le colonie mariene e montane,* IRCE, Roma 1943; S. De Martino, A. Wall, *Cities of childhood. Italian Colonies of the 1930s*, Architectural Association, London 1988; ample coverage on the present state of conservation and the locations of these complexes is provided in *Domus*, n. 659, March 1985.

4 According to V.N. Simbircev, author of the essay "Cetere resenija" (Four solutions), that accompanied the publication of the competition results in *Stroitel'stvo Moskvy*, n. 3, 1930, the designs failed to resolve the most complex question, the most original theme, i.e. the question of the socialist city and the socialist reorganisation of the *byt* (everyday life), or "The architectural-technical synthesis of the different elements of the new forms of the *byt* [...] Among the forms of socialist reconstruction of life, of radical reorganisation of the *byt*, the idea of the green city is one of the most flexible and effective forms of wider reconstruction of the existing cities, of introduction of culture and the new collectivized byt in the masses of millions of workers, forced for the moment to make do with the old, individualistic [...] comfort of barbarous residential construction. [...] To rationalize and render intensive their repose, to utilize to this end all the moments of activity—nature, entertainment, architecture—these are the tasks of the builders of the city."

5 The synthetic description of the project by Ladovskij that follows, like the descriptions of the other three projects, is based on the descriptions that accompany the drawings published in issue n. 3 of *Stroitel'stvo Moskvy* in March 1930.

6 "This sanatorium will not simply be a garden-city, in keeping with the best-known examples from abroad, in which a city of single-family houses is created for isolated portions of the population. 'The Green City' has other aims. Our idea is that it should represent

the organisation of new cultural forms of repose, of care for workers through the healthfulness of local climate conditions, the introduction in the byt of the workers of hygienic living conditions, etc. Our 'Green City' will not resemble other cities [...] [because it will be] [...] a place of rest and health care." from N. Popov-Sibiriak, *Zelenomu gorodu obscestvennoe vnimanie*, cit.

7 The competition for the 'Green City' took place at the same time as other important competitions for the planning of new industrial cities under the first five-year plan, and in particular those for Magnitogorsk and Avtostroj, in which a confrontation took place, in substance, between two distinct disciplinary positions—the urbanists and the disurbanists. The results of these competitions were all published in the major architecture periodicals between January and April in 1930. In n. 1-2 of the magazine *Sovremmennaja Arkhitektura (SA)*, a constructivist publication guided by M. Ginzburg and the advocates of disurbanism (the OSA group—association of modern architects), the project for the 'Green City' of the members of OSA is published together with the project for Magnitogorsk, both based on a layout scheme of linear segments, and together with the polemical correspondence between Le Corbusier and M. Ginzburg on the theme of disurbanism. In issue n. 1 (1930) of *Stroitel'stvo Moskvy*, a publication of the municipality of Moscow which indiscriminately featured contributions from the widest range of architectural groupings, we find the publication of a project by N. Ladovskij for the development of Moscow with the title *O dinamiceskoj planirovocnoj strukture goroda* (On the dynamic planimetric structure of the city), whose principle of dynamic growth—through the identification of free settlement parts for development without modifying, in substance, the relations with the whole—is also applied to the project for the 'Green City', although with a completely different formal solution that the one formulated for Moscow. On this plan for Moscow, see the essay published

herein by Ju. Volčok, Ju. Kosenkova, *Competitions of Urban-Planning Concepts and the First Rounds of the Palace of the Soviets Competition*.

8 February-June 1931, 14 entries: Bronstein, Fidman, Jofan, Krassin & Kuzaev, Ladovskij, Ljudvig, Nikol'skij, Rosenblum, Ščusev, brigades of VOPRA, SASS, ARU, ASNOVA and MOVANO. Though invited the Vesnin brothers and Ščuko didn't submit designs in this first round.

9 E.g. the Tatlin tower 1919/1920 or the Palace of Labour competition of 1922/1923.

10 In 1924 Viktor Balichin called his Lenin-Memorial "headquarters of the world revolution."

11 Honorarium $ 2000 each

12 May 10th, 1933.

13 by K.A. Thon 1837-1887.

14 Architect of the Centrosojus building at Moscow.

15 Architect of the Krasnoe Znamja factory at Leningrad.

16 For more information about the program of rooms see: *Naum Gabo und der Wettbewerb zum Palast der Sowjets Moskau 1931-1933*, ed. by Berlinische Galerie, 1992, p. 202 ff.

17 The outline of one of the ground plans is the map of the USSR (motto: "one sixth of the earth"); other ones show the State's insignia, hammer & sickle, the Cyrillic letters 'SSSR' or 'LENIN'.

18 For further details about the Mel'nikov project see the description of the model.

19 Cf. "Oude en nieuwe architectuur in Sowjet-Rusland, van Verlosserskerk tot Sowjetpaleis", in *Bouwkundig Weekblad Architectura*, 1932, no. 16, p. 133 f.

20 They were given time to think over their architecture. Cf. Edgar Norwerth, "Architektura w ZSSR", in *Architektura i Budownictwo*, (Warsaw), no. 2, 1933, p. 50.

21 A.V. Ikonnikov, *Der Historismus in der sowjetischen Architektur*, in *Konzeptionen in der sowjetischen Architektur 1917-1988,* Berlin 1989, p. 88.

22 Manuscript in Bauhaus-Archiv Berlin, as

quoted by Probst/Schädlich, Walter Gropius, vol. 3, *Ausgewählte Schriften*, (translation by the author), Berlin, 1987, p. 150

[23] 1928 for Erwin Piscator in Berlin.

[24] Edgar Norwerth, "Architektura w ZSSR", in *Architektura i Budownictwo (Warsaw)*, no. 2, 1933, p. 50 [reported by the periodical of the German Werkbund, *Die Form*, no. 4, 1933, p. 102].

[25] He had his hands in the Politkatorzan housing at Rostokino and collaborated with Ginzburg since 1933 in the Giprogor; 1937 he was arrested and died 1938.

[26] Studied 1928-1931 at the Bauhaus in Dessau, worked with Marcel Breuer in Berlin and was familiar with the works of Gropius.

[27] As reported by the Soviet architect Žukov and quoted by the Polish critic E. Norwerth in: *Architektura i Budownictwo*, no. 2, 1933 [see notes nos 13 and 16].

[28] March-July 1932.

[29] Cf. *Sovetskoe iskusstvo*, no. 11, March 2, 1932.

[30] August 1932-June 1933.

[31] July 1933-February 1934, March 1934-March 1937 and April 1937-July 1939.

[32] Dekret of the SOVNARKOM of December 19, 1941.

[33] Cf. Dvorec Sovetov, *Materialy konkursa 1957-1959*, Moskva 1961, p. 12.

[34] Cf. *Sovetskaja arkhitektura. Ezegodnik 1960*, Moskva 1962, pp. 99-101 [For these information I have to thank Christian Schädlich].

[35] Here and further on factual data on the competition and quotations have been taken in the main from the publications: *Program and Rules of the Competition for the selection of an Architect for The Monumental Lighthouse which the nations of the world will erect in the Dominican Republic to the memory of Christopher Columbus*, issued by The Pan-American Union, 1928; *Program and Rules of the second Competition for the selection of an Architect for The Monumental Lighthouse which the nations of the world will erect in the Dominican Republic to the memory of Christopher Columbus*, issued by The Pan-American Union, 1930.

[36] State Archive of the Russian Federation, f. 5283, op. 2, d. 50, l. 12; op. 11, d. 53, l. 298; d. 58, ll. 33, 53.

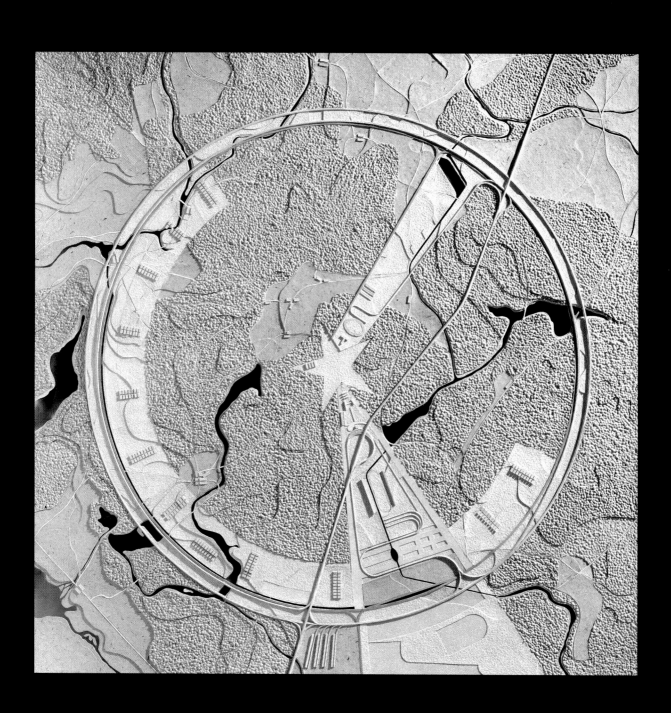

Works from 1929 to 1932

**Competition Project
for the 'Green City'**

The City of Rationalised Recreation

In the era of rationalisation of socialist cities, and of daily life, in the times of powerful cultural growth resulting from industrial progress, each architectural project, just like any other project directly related to any aspect of our everyday life, must incorporate the principles of rationalisation and take into account the overall cultural growth and future industrial development. Neither design nor construction must be irrational. The rationalisation should never be superficial. Rationalisation processes existing in the field of architectural design solutions must go as deep as the essence of the matter, to the root of things.

Major problems relating to the rationalisation of daily life have compelled us to adopt a similar approach to the general plan of the 'Green City'. The entire purpose of the 'Green City' is to provide recreation. Naturally, in this case the rationalisation must apply to those traditions and concepts which have the closest links to recreation in all its various forms. The main form, and the basis of recreation, is sleep. This means we are confronted with the problem of how to rationalize sleep, which means the rationalisation of one third of a human lifetime, when we take into account that people sleep an average 8 hours a day. Thus the rationalisation of sleep has become the basic problem

in the development of a general plan for the 'Green City', which is as follows.

The entire area of the 'Green City' is enclosed within a perfect circle formed by special lines: electric railway lines, roads, boulevards, and even a canal in one part of the circle. The circle gives the City a sense of unity, a fact that is not only important because it provides a theoretical basis for the whole system of public recreation, but also (and primarily) because it provides a practical solution to the design problem. To solve the problem in practice a strict and well-defined concentration of all the elements is required.

The circular area is split into sectors: the forest sector, the collective farmlands sector, the garden sector, the zoo sector, the collective sector and the children's town sector. The Institute for the Transformation of Humankind will occupy the central zone.

The forest area, the collective farmlands, and the zoo will be provided with all sorts of permanent roads, lanes, paths and trails, suitable for cars and bicycles. Special mobile restaurants, mobile libraries, mobile platforms with sporting gear etc. will serve the promenading public.

The areas to be used for exhibitions, the airfield, and the military field are located next to the southern part of the circle. The existing local highway comes as far as the peripheral

ring, but will not go on into the City. Railway stations will be built linking this highway with the buildings housing public facilities. The utilities, such as water, heating etc., will be also placed in the north, at the top of the Green City, outside the peripheral ring. Their location will allow the use of wind energy on a large scale. The south-western sectors outside the ring (so called "entertainment camps") are designed for promenades and festivities. At this point in time, the land available to the City outside its ring is relatively small. Nevertheless, these zones can be used in the future for the construction of public facilities, co-operative housing etc.

I have already pointed out what the principal nature of the recreation system in the 'Green City' would be. Its practical solution is indicated in the general plan as a number of buildings spread out round a circle with a circumference of 10 kilometres. These buildings, located mainly in the forest sector, are to be used exclusively for sleep. The residents will spend the rest of the time in the numerous facilities of the Green City meant for daytime recreation. The design and architectural solution should not be based on the concept of feeding a human body with extra hours of slumber. Unlike nutrition, feeding in this case can not be measured in a number of hours.

The point here is not to prolong the sleep but to increase its curative powers. To this end, the buildings are to be equipped with special facilities to make slumber comfortable, and, when necessary, these facilities must have a distinct clinical character. We are talking here not only about mechanised beds, but also about special chambers with condensed or rarefied air, chambers filled with ethers, or chambers where the intensity and, subsequently, the quality of sleep can be regulated by suitable music chosen by specialists using scientific research.

The design and layout of the buildings, the house regulations and routines within their walls are very closely linked to the organisation of daytime recreation, or, in other words, to all facilities which provide the common forms of modern recreation. These facilities will be located in the collective sector of the 'Green City'. The Skalba River running through this sector will be straightened into an open canal so it passes through the stadium and various other public buildings. In addition to water transport, electric trains will run through the sector stopping at different buildings and winter gardens. Buildings of this sector are to be divided in 4 types or groups. The first group includes all sorts of sports centres, the second includes buildings used for research and education, the third

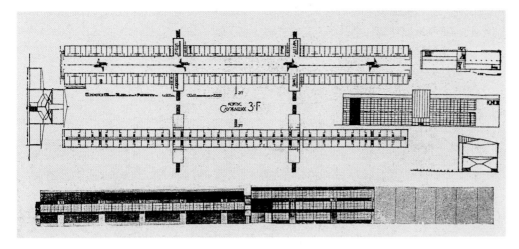

On page 234:
Plan for the 'Green City', 1929
(model by F. Salvarani)

Plan for the 'Green City'

Personnel's dwellings: plans,
elevations, sections; gallery

group houses entertainment centres, and finally the fourth group represents a limited number of trade and commercial premises. The last group is supposed to have a slightly original character, as in the 'Green City' the major part of pure commercial activities will be replaced by distributive activities.

The collective sector will be directly adjacent to the centre of the city, marked on the plan with a star. This site is designated for the construction of the Institute for the Transformation of Humankind. The area is covered with natural forest specially pruned so as to provide free sunlight penetration essential for the growth of flowers and fragrant shrubs.

To the north-east of the centre lies the children's town sector. Its layout will depend on the age of the children residing in the 'Green City'. An open swimming pool with flowing water will be constructed in this sector.

The purpose of dividing the 'Green City' into sectors is to improve the organisation of everyday collective life. The task of improving this system relates closely to the public order which will be established in the 'Green City' from the very first day. The city is not large enough to allow different objects to be scattered far apart, even in a more or less ordered way. In this respect the most rational layout would be a strict geometrical shape. I have chosen the most convenient (in

this particular case and in other cases) shape: a circle. The circle manifests itself not only in the planning of the whole city system but also in pure functional aspects of each building, from public facilities to special sleeping hotels. In the immediate future we will have to set up 12 such hotels each being able to house up to 4000 guests at a time. Treatment in these hotels requires clear-cut procedures. These procedures can be established by the relevant health care authorities of the City itself and of the other cities which will send their residents to the 'Green City' for treatment or rehabilitation.

Railway Station

The contemporary station is not only a place where people get on and off trains; it has an important social function too. The station is, to some extent, a place for public meetings and possesses cultural and welfare functions characteristic of a public building.

Our task has been to meet those functional requirements, systematising them to some extent through the use of an architectural structure. The general positioning of functions within the building's layers creates the situation in which a passenger can find his way at ease; the layout of different elements allows a perfect view over the whole premises.

The cubic space of the building is 27,000 m³. The rostra are

designed to accommodate 500 people. In total the building can hold 2000 people.

Service Staff Building

When designing the building our architectural task has been the creation of such an architectural structure as would allow the most simple and immediate transition from separate individual housing forms - being the most common and stereotyped dwelling units as regards architecture—to collectivist forms.

To this end, I have split the main composition into continuously repeating spaces, with a regular occurrence of architectural elements, and also extended the space to be designed, i.e. the lower gallery, to a length of 200 metres.

It should be noted, that this solution has made possible the arrangement of the gallery without increasing the total volume of the building.

Total rooms/units amount to 150, the lower level (double) rooms measure 32 m², the upper level 16 m² each. Overall volume of the building is 30,000 m², i.e., exactly according to the assignment.

District Hotel Building

The popularity of the cottage in the capitalist economy refers to a number of positive traits inherent in this architectural type. A cottage offers: firstly, perfect ventilation, secondly, perfect sunlight conditions (as

its all four sides are open to sunlight), and, finally, a cottage is a standardised and perfectly detached dwelling unit. Though meeting all these requirements, a cottage is still absolutely unacceptable for our housing owing to its class character and organisation of life processes. Being a kind of a villa, a cottage must contain service spaces required for individual household and housekeeping, such as a kitchen, different pantries and the like. Therefore, our task has been to preserve the mentioned positive sides of a cottage offering the possibilities for complete utilisation within our communal housing schemes.

The proposed project of a two-storey hotel building envisages only one corridor which will receive natural light from outside. Dwelling units—or rooms—will be situated on two levels. The floor in each room will be terraced into three levels, each of those organising housing processes in pure territorial terms.

The privacy of units is guaranteed by entrance design. The entrance door opens into a landing of a small staircase, connecting the room with the corridor, which remains separated from every unit.

The construction of one corridor instead of two (which used to be inevitable in traditional plans of similar buildings) bears certain economic advantages. The terraces, which organise

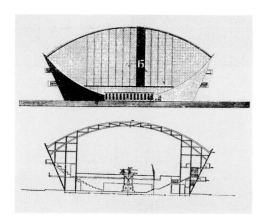

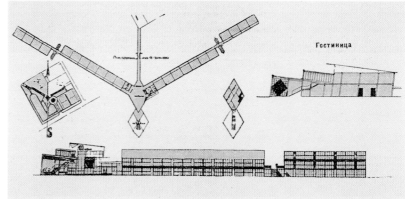

Гостиница

housing processes by territorial distribution of dwelling functions, offer the most advantageous conditions for the equipment of units with built-in furniture. At the moment, the problem of built-in mechanised furniture, organically embedded in an architectural structure, seems insoluble only because this problem—although solved in principle—clashes in practice with old architectural patterns, namely, with perfectly ordinary things as floors and walls. Here, as we see, the built-in furniture forms an integral part of the architectural structure, and here, in a manner of speaking, we have created the economic basis for solving the problem of built-in furniture with maximal qualitative effect.

Tourist Pavilions

Two types of tourist pavilions have been designed. The first type differs from the second one by having a gallery on the ground floor (while the second type has a roof gallery). The purpose of this difference is to provide a choice, depending on the individual characteristics of each particular site.

Central Hotel

The hotel complex consists of two main groups. The first group comprises the building with communal spaces, while apartment buildings are assigned to the second group, subdivided, in turn, into two parts. On the way from the main entrance, with adjacent lobby and cloakroom, different spaces are planned: the hotel office, the watchman's room, the hairdresser's room, luggage rooms, and several bathrooms. Further on our way we see waiting rooms, game halls, and the dining hall for 240 people to eat a meal at the same time. The dining hall has two sources of lighting. The passageways leading to the library and the reading room are suspended from girders.

To allow 240 people to dine simultaneously a mechanised (to a certain degree) food-serving and table-cleaning system has been designed, consisting of a row of rolled conveyor tables.

The communal dormitory is architecturally the simplest, the most cost-efficient and widespread type of collective apartment. From the socialist point of view, as far as collectivisation and socialisation of dwelling functions are concerned, such an architectural structure is above any criticism. In principle it is perfect; but, principles aside, the common dormitory has lots of inconveniences.

The main disadvantages of this architectural type are: noise when the room is being filled, roommates passing to their beds, talking, humming and snoring. All these negative phenomena have one source: noise. This can be eliminated in two ways: by means of sound insulation, which is more difficult, or by muffling unorganised sounds by organised sounds, having not a negative but a positive effect on a human body. These organised sounds belong to the artistic form we call music.

With these factors in mind we propose a barrack-type structure housing a dormitory, to be built collectively, by joint efforts and knowledge of different specialists: musicians, doctors, architects etc.

Based upon those collective efforts and knowledge in different technical fields we have produced the architect's part, which is represented by the proposal for a sleep-concert building called 'SONnaja SONata'.[1]

The design of the building takes account of every acoustic detail. The building consists of two wings of 2 halls each. The wings are connected by a central corpus, housing service rooms (rooms for undressing, showers, toilets and bathrooms). Either end of the building contains special acoustic booths which will transmit symphonies and sound effects such as the rustle of leaves, the babble of a brook and other sounds of nature to the sleeping halls.

It should be mentioned that transmission of sounds, aimed at improving of the most vital human need—a sound and healthy sleep—is an absolutely new domain. To master it we should not limit ourselves by

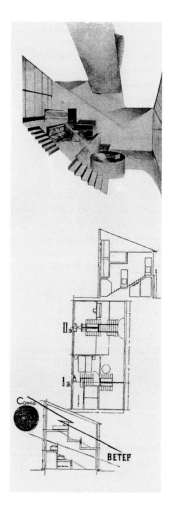

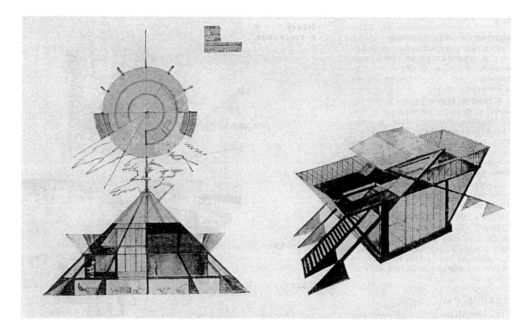

only recruiting musicians for such construction work. The work of medical specialists who have researched the impact of sound on sleep is absolutely indispensable.
K. S. Mel'nikov, 1929[2]

The 'Green City' – Rest and Vacation City: A Reconstruction

In the reconstruction of the design for the settlement - conducted beginning with the existing iconographic documentation published in the monographic issue of the magazine *Stroitel'stvo Moskvy* on the competition[3]—it has become clear that the circular graphic layout with sectors that supports the assembly of the panel manifesto illustrating the plan of the city, when transferred onto the map of the area, corresponds to a clear planning logic for the territory. The landscape of the territory involved in the competition was lacking in geographical features based on a logic of settlement: the area was dominated by a large zone of forest, with small villages scattered within a

sprawling network of small roads; the area is crossed by two rivers (the Skalba, to the west, and the Vjaz' to the east) with a few villages on their banks, and crossed on a southwest-northeast by the Moscow-Jaroslavl' rail line with the parallel sosse; only in the centre of the area is there a territory with different characteristics, with the village of Petuškij and two other settlements positioned at the centre of an agricultural zone.

By superimposing Mel'nikov's design on this geography we can see that the apparently spontaneous arrangement of the villages is actually the result of a clear, recognisable scheme: the villages in the forest at the edge of the territory of the competition are connected to the circumference created by the rail line and sosse in the design; those in the fields form a sort of ring around the centre of the same circumference; those outside the circumference, instead, are identified as centres of complementary activities to those of the Green City (places of recreation, wind power

generators).

In substance, the reconstruction of the model has shown that Mel'nikov's project was the result of a painstaking analysis of the existing settlement characteristics, and that the functional subdivision in sectors was based on an intent to best exploit the characteristics of the landscape as they appear in the different locations.

Among the various buildings for the 'Green City' designed by Mel'nikov, models have been reconstructed for: the main residential building ('SONnaja SONata'—in the version for 240 guests), the railroad station (the VOKsal-KURsal volume), and the two variations for the tourist pavilions (built with different forms, but using the same construction elements).
Maurizio Meriggi

[1] *SON* is the Russian word for sleep.
[2] Published in *Stroitel'stvo Moskvy*, n. 3, 1930, pp. 20-25.
[3] The cartographical base used for the reconstruction is published in N. Popov-Sibiriak, *Zelenomu gorodu*

obscestvennoe vnimanie, cit. herein reproduced in the text by M. Meriggi, *The competition for the "Green City"*. Others topographical information of the site had been derived by the official State Map of Russian Federation in scale 1:200.000.

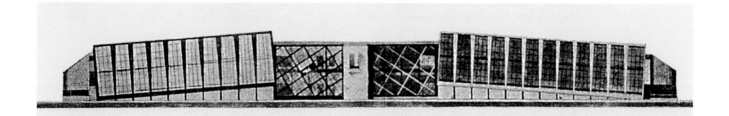

Plan for the 'Green City', 1929
(reconstruction by M. Meriggi)
scale 1:100.000

Legend
A   Wooded park
B   Pasture park or Kholkoz
C   Agricultural park
D   Zoological park
E   Central services sector
E1 Exhibition
E2 Scientific institutes
E3 Sport facilities
E4 Stations
F   Children park

G   Municipal services
H   Aerodrome
I   Training field
L   Boundary of the hotel
    residence
L1 SONnaja and SONata
    settlements
M   Tower of the winds
N   Recreation park
O   Institute for the new Man
a. Hydraulic system of the
    Skalba river
b. Hydraulic system of the Vjaz
    river

Plan for the 'Green City'
(model by F. Salvarani);
views of the city from South,
East and West

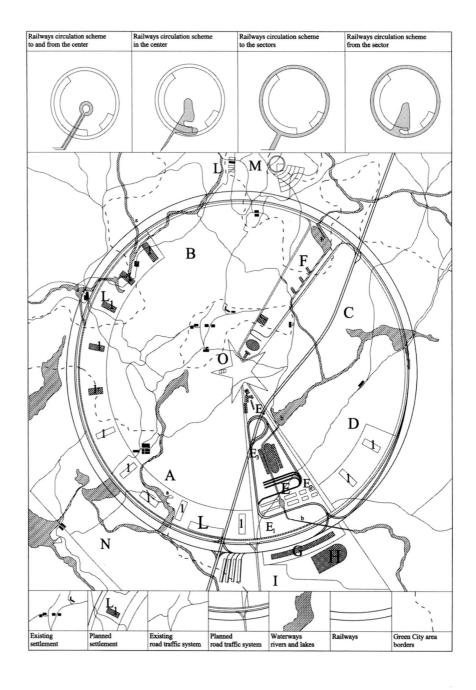

Railways circulation scheme to and from the center	Railways circulation scheme in the center	Railways circulation scheme to the sectors	Railways circulation scheme from the sector

Existing settlement	Planned settlement	Existing road traffic system	Planned road traffic system	Waterways rivers and lakes	Railways	Green City area borders

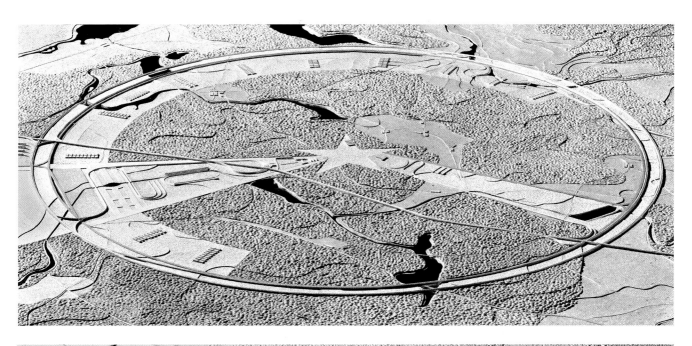

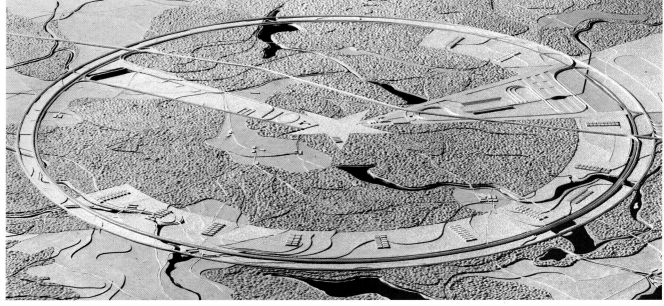

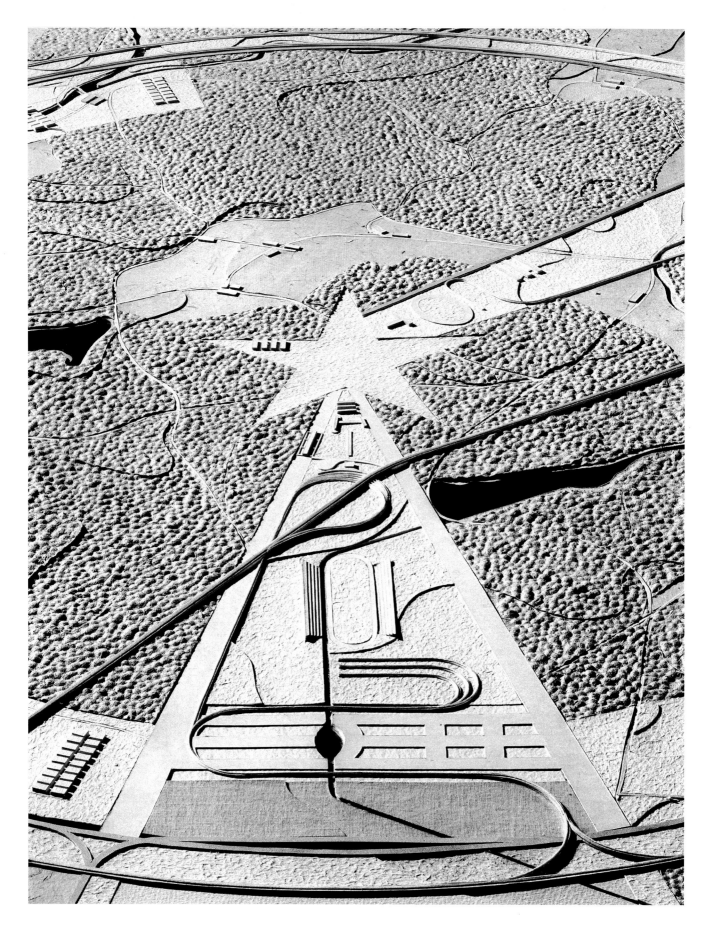

Plan for the 'Green City'
(model by F. Salvarani);
detail of the central sector

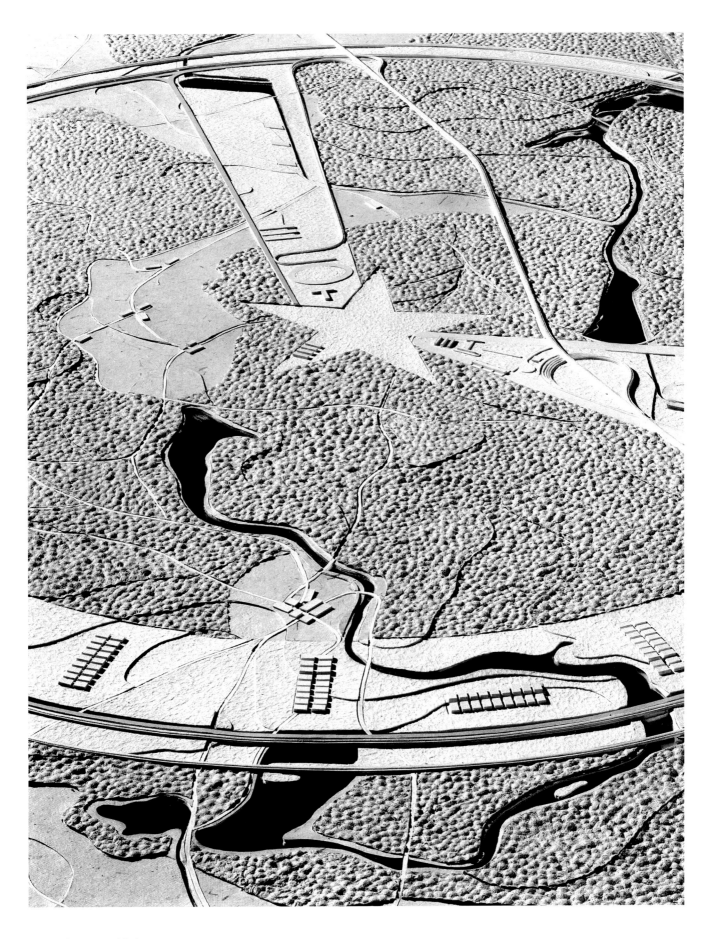

*Detail of the area with the
wooded park and the SONnaja
and SONata buildings*

Railway station
(model by A. Belotti)

Railway station of the 'Green
City', 1929
(reconstructed by A. Belotti,
re-drawn by L. Gatti)
scale 1:600

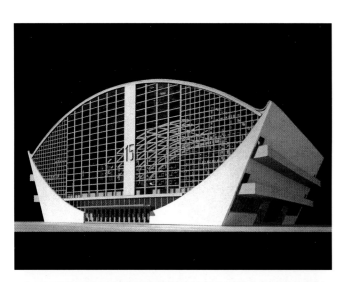

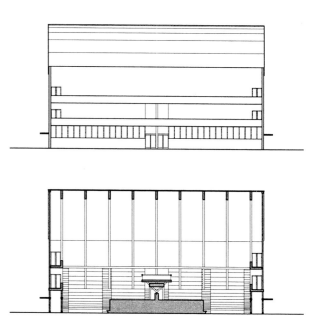

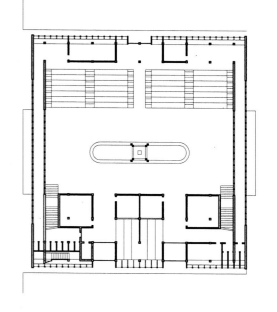

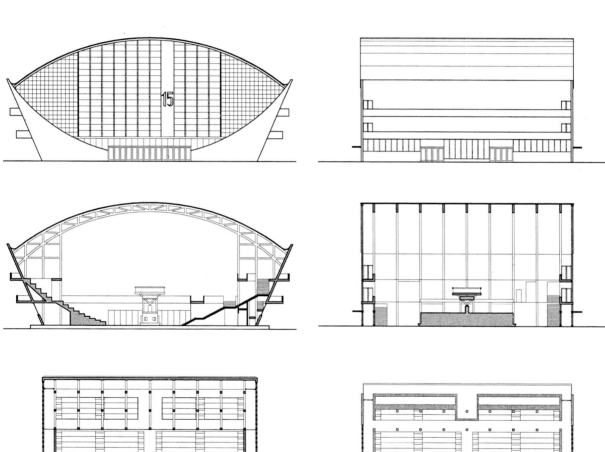

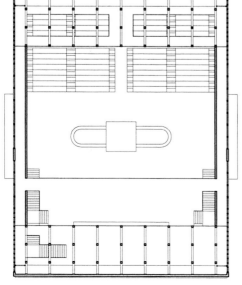

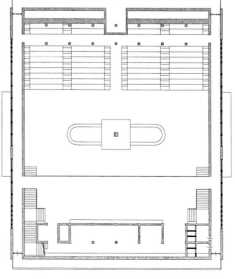

SONnaja SONata
(model by E. Salvadé)

SONnaja SONata, 1929
(reconstruction by E. Salvadé,
R. Rizzi) scale 1:600

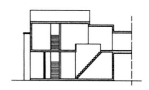

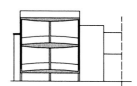

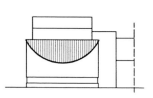

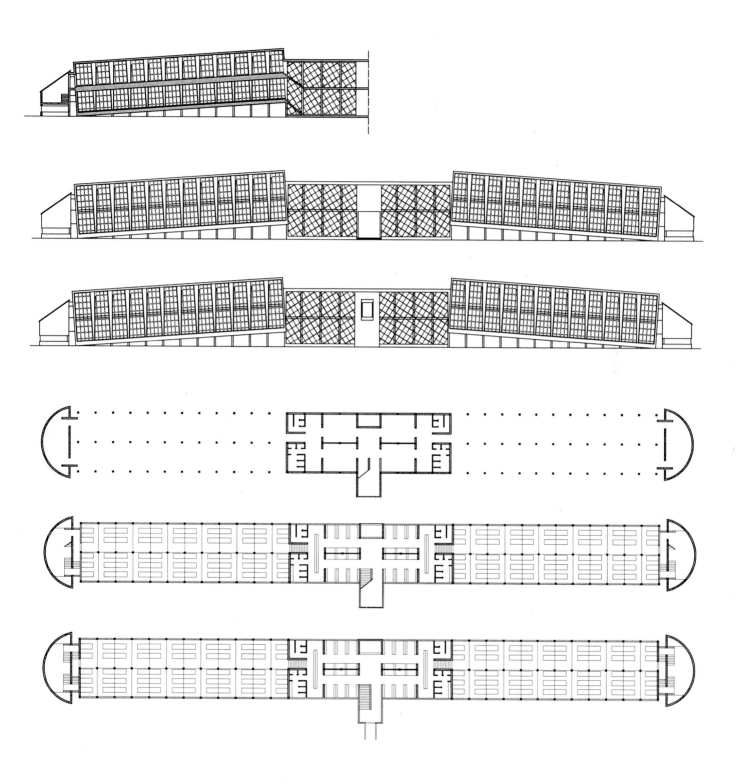

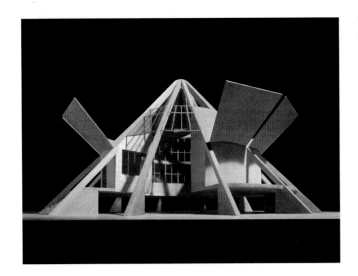

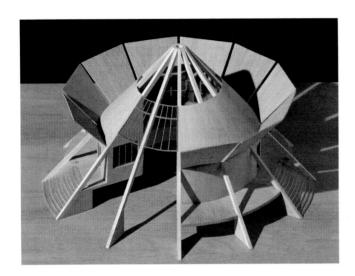

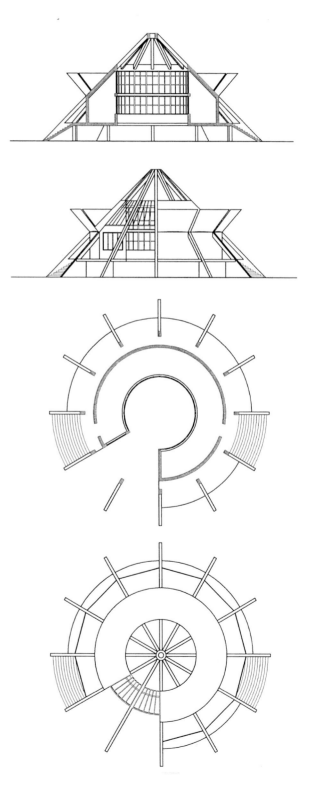

*Tourists' pavilion – Solarium
(model by A. Colzani)*

*Tourists' pavilion – Solarium,
1929
(reconstruction by A. Colzani)
scale 1:300*

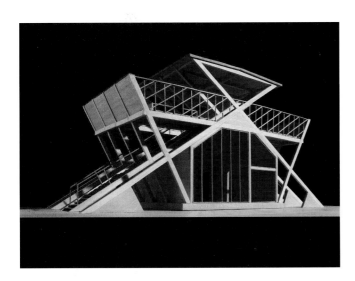

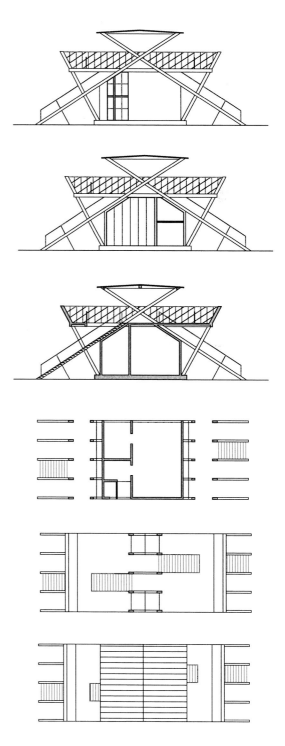

Tourists' pavilion – Solarium
(model by G. Camagni)

Tourists' pavilion – Solarium,
1929
(reconstruction by G. Camagni)
scale 1:300

**Competition Project
for the Monument
to Columbus
at Santo Domingo**

"Two worlds [two systems], the one supporting the other. In the midst of the two worlds the monument to Columbus, who, in uniting them, aroused the life force of America.

Created on the basis of European civilisation, the culture of America has continually increased in independence and creative originality. The buttress of the Old World (the lower cone) has been replaced by new and powerful buttresses in the form of two unfurled wings. These mechanised buttresses cut through the wind and are favourably placed to keep the cupola in equilibrium, thereby creating a new image each time to impress the inhabitants of Santo Domingo.

The greatness of Columbus' discovery of a whole new world, and the enormity of its significance, can in no way be squeezed into a constant, whatever that may be. Therefore the limitlessness of the architectural effect of the memorial in honour of Christopher Columbus can only be realised by bringing the elements into the composition of the project.

In the present project the monument in honour of Columbus can turn on its base; if the diametrical direction of the wings coincides, and at the same time a defined quantity of rainwater appears on the peak of the cone, - so that one wing will shut off the tap washing the monument, while the other wing will turn on the lower tap—then all the water, having the necessary pressure, will be directed onto the turbine under the floor, and the monument will slowly, slowly...

A telegram:
San Domingo. On the night of March 12th the statue of Christopher Columbus turned 38°8′ to the north-east;
London. On the night... (in English);
Paris. On the night... (in French);
Moscow. On the night... (in Russian);
Tokyo. On the night... (in Japanese).
And so on.
This could happen once in a hundred years. The wings take up the cone on seven rings (gamma), and on unfurling send their waves out over the whole surface of the earth, stirring up humanity day and night to the unceasing performance of great works and exploits, like Christopher Columbus."
K. S. Mel'nikov, 1929[1]

**Description of the Project
and Rebuilding the Model**
In 1892, 400 years after the second discovery of America a decision was made to plan a "monument of the immortality of Columbus" in Santo Domingo. In the following years the conception of a monumental lighthouse came into being. In 1928/1929 the Pan American Union organised the first round of an international competition specifying the following criteria:

a tower at least 600 ft. (185 m) high made out of reinforced concrete (in order to withstand earthquakes and hurricanes) covered with noble material; a chapel sepulchre; buildings for the president and the government; a museum; apartment houses and an airport. 455 entries from 48 countries were submitted before the deadline (April 1, 1929 in Madrid), among them 27 designs of Soviet architects; the most striking of them was Mel'nikov's kinetic proposal. In this first round of the competition none of the Soviet designs was ranked among the top ten; the first prize was awarded to the German Josef Wentzler from Dortmund, and the 10th prize to the British student Joseph L. Gleave. On April 28, 1929 no less than 3300 plans submitted in the competition were put on display in Madrid; an exhibition in Rome follows on August 7, 1929.
In 1931 the ten prize winners were invited to participate in the second round of the competition, which would determine the plans to be used for the realisation of the project. The winner now was Joseph L. Gleave (1907-1965), who symbolically portrayed the Christianisation of the continent with a huge cross serving as the basis for the ground plan. Foundation work was begun in 1939, but construction ceased within a short time. Gleave revised his plans between 1950

and 1952; he died in 1965. It was only between 1986 and 1992 that Teófilo Carbonell could complete the construction according to Gleave's plans in the Eastern Park of Santo Domingo.
On the contrary to this metaphor of Christianisation, Mel'nikov's design, with its kinetic implications, owed much to the widespread belief of the time in technical sciences, but it was by no means earthquake-proof and would hardly have resisted the tropical hurricanes of the region. This no doubt caused the rejection of Mel'nikov's bold competition entry; but there were additional reasons as well. The Soviet architect had neglected the covering with noble material and, above all, had failed to add some symbols of Christianisation to this monument designed for a Catholic country. Not at all being a piece of personal cult for the Christian conqueror, rather one of idolising the genius of invention, this design unveiled the Russian belief in American technology. This outstanding structure was hence clearly a symbol of technical progress and architectural creativeness. As in his design of the Palace of the Soviets Mel'nikov used two cones to symbolise the Old and the New World.
Sources in the literature for reconstructing Mel'nikov's design are rather scanty: one section, one sectional perspective, one elevation, one

Competition project for the monument to Christopher Columbus, 1929

View of the model (realized by R. Wied, J. Kübler, F. Reichardt, 1993)

perspective, three floor plans and one site plan; in addition the description of the architect. The dimensions of the 195-meter-high monument with a diameter of 85 meters and the dearth of information (no measurements) about detailing as well, made the scale of 1:500 seem reasonable. The intention was to show the impressive macro structure of the futurist design along with the mechanised character. Therefore, acrylic glass and metal were the materials chosen.
Dietrich Schmidt

[1] K.S. Mel'nikov, *The Project for a memorial to Christopher Columbus in a Global Competition.* 1929, in *Mastera sovetskoj arkhitektury ob arkhitekture*, Isskustvo, Moskva 1975, pp. 166-167.

Competition project for the
monument to Christopher
Columbus, 1929
(reconstruction by R. Wied,
J. Kübler, F. Reichardt)
scale 1:200

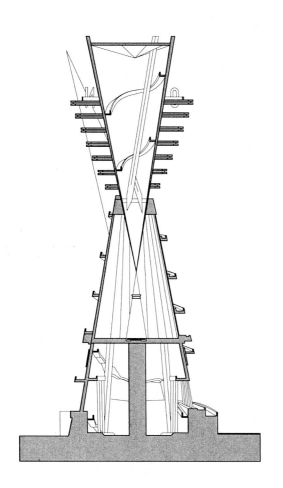

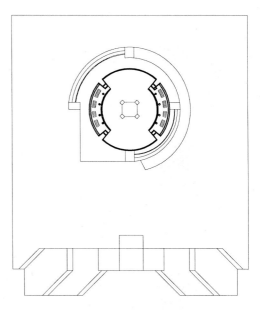

**Project for the
Reconstruction
of the Arbat Square**

"The fifth—a pure and sincere love for the city manifested itself in 1931, in the reconstruction proposal for Arbat square. My desire was to illuminate, through the rays of architecture, the great power of art which does not die—not even when it lies in ruins."
K. Mel'nikov, 1967[1]

Arbat Square Architecture
"The architecture of Arbat Square is designed to form a long isosceles triangle, with the Nikitskij Boulevard at the base, while the Gogol' monument forms the focal point at the vertex. The curved end of Vozdviženka has been straightened, and its new direction brings it to the junction of Molčanovka and Vorovskij Street. A closer look at the entire network of streets flowing into the square, allows us to divide them into clearly defined groups: Exactly the same number and size of streets fan out from each corner of the triangle: 4 streets at the eastern corner, 4 streets at the western corner, and finally 4 streets at the vertex.
It goes without saying that the shape and the size of the square must be suited to meet the service requirements of the city's arterial roads, and therefore it is quite obvious that a square with greater number of connecting streets requires a larger area to accommodate them, and [...] in the case of Arbat Square [...] a triangle

fulfils this purpose with an even distribution, leaving no empty spaces.
The triangle, although it has a small surface area, is nonetheless rather long, as a consequence of which a large number of streets can enter directly onto the Square itself. A rectangular design, for example, prevents many streets from joining onto it. In fact, a square in a big city functions as a relay switch, directing and re-directing the city traffic circulation (in this case from Frunze Street to Vorovskij Street etc.)
Of course, performing this function is a high-priority task in the reconstruction of the socialist capital. The more feasible and concrete the project, the sooner it will be accomplished.
From this point of view a triangle, as opposed to any other shape, offers the most efficient plan for demolishing the existing structures (in the proposal, the Arbat Street side is shown with an estimated number of demolition when this side is straightened). The triangle forms the basis of the entire composition, its elongated form created by the junction of the main Frunze, Vozdviženka, and Vorovskogo Streets …
However, [...] Arbat Street cuts through the pattern, breaking into it to become the geometrical centre of gravity. The proposal, which sees Arbat Street as the centre of the whole city system, emphasises its

unique quality by letting it flow into the centre of the Square. Other aspects of the proposal are [...]:
1. The Square serves as a collective transportation hub (starting with tram and bus lines, automobiles, and, finally, the metro) and then;
2. The Square serves as centre for mass rallies, and finally;
3. The Square is equipped with all conveniences for the technical service of the street life.
These features are all to be concentrated in the centre of the Square, some on and some under the surface. The underground structures will be covered up with vegetation. An incline is required for the car access ramp to the garage; the incline faces south to provide the vegetation with more sunlight.
The widest part of the Square is rounded out to ease the traffic flow; this will also make room for the amphitheatre, offering the perfect shape for the tribunes for mass rallies, the tiers of which will shield the public against street noise. Thanks to this curved shape, recreation areas and playgrounds will be filled with sunlight and protected against the sound of traffic. Subways will lead down to the station and the garage, in which there will also be toilets and showers.
For direct pedestrian access from the boulevard side we propose to use the existing structure, which will be equipped with as many public facilities (café's,

etc.) as possible. In general, pedestrians are not supposed to cross the road to get to the centre of the Square. To this end bridges and tunnels are designed at the corner of Arbat Street and the corner of Frunze Street.
I cannot conceive of planning open public spaces without a clear architectural method. For me, there is no architecture without space. That is why the choice of shape for the square is so important.
Every space designed must be strictly substantiated and prominent in itself.
Therefore I have designed a sloping (receding) building profile which would not block out the sun and let the eye freely pass through to the centre of the Square.
Since Arbat Street breaks up the triangular composition, its junction with the side of the Square will be completely hidden, allowing the long angle to set the Gogol' monument in an even better focal point at the vertex of the triangle.
K. Mel'nikov, 1931[2]

Arbat Square Site Historical Development
The modern Arbat Square, situated at the junction of Kalinin Prospekt and the Boulevard ring road, is a result of the many transformations that have effected this large city hub, originally formed as early as the sixteenth century. Its emergence was mainly caused by the ancient road routes that lead to

Competition project for the arrangement of Arbatskaja square, 1931

Views of the area of Arbatskaja square in the Tenths

Reconstruction of the competition area in the Twenties and localization of the project in the area (Ju. Volčok, E. Nikulina)

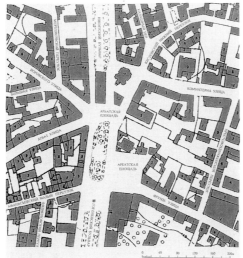

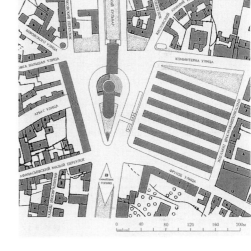

the Kremlin. These roads fan out westwards from the gate of the Belyj Gorod (White Town), one of the Moscow fortifications. The gate area was called Arbat, the name which was later given to one of the streets, and, subsequently, to the square. This city hub was characterised by the proximity of the Arbat gate to the large estates of dukes, craft and military settlements, churches, and market places. All this resulted in a picturesque development of random composition, far removed from the regularity inherent in city planning.

The forming of the square at the Arbat gate dates back to the Classical period of the late eighteenth, early nineteenth century, when Moscow experienced major changes in city planning aimed at adjusting the city layout to a new understanding of spatial interconnections.

In this period the walls of the Belyj Gorod (White Town) and other parts of the city, including entire quarters in the Arbat gate area, were demolished. The resulting empty space was to be used for a large market place surrounded by new buildings of Classical design. A wide boulevard replacing former city fortifications was to join the Square from the north and from the south.

In the nineteenth century, the planned changes were only partially carried out. The size of the Square was significantly

reduced; the Square itself never received the full treatment characteristic of the Classical concept and retained many features of a medieval city. The large space was utilised for trade, often serving as a city market. The decision to erect a monument to Gogol' in the square was an attempt to unite buildings of different character, and an underlying desire to enhance the status of this complex architectural formation. However, in 1909, the monument was erected not in the square itself but at the end of Prečistenskij Boulevard.

In the early 1900's architect F. Šekhtel elaborated a concept for redeveloping Arbat Square. He proposed the construction of a cultural, sports and entertainment centre—The Moscow Sport Palace—

enclosing the existing Khudozestvennyj cinema, a restaurant and a huge oval skating rink. An *Arc-du-Triomphe* type arch was designed to serve as the entrance to the centre.

The square started to function as a major transport hub as early as the end of the nineteenth century. In the 1880's a tramline was laid and pavilions for tram stops were built. In the early 1920's the decision was taken to tear down the Church of Saints Boris and Gleb, which was hindering the flow of traffic.

Mel'nikov's project

The Arbat Square reconstruction plan proposed by architect Mel'nikov was an attempt to give adequate solutions to the existing problems: to organise rational traffic management; to

furnish the square with new facilities offering comfortable recreation to the city's inhabitants; to develop a comprehensive composition which would take into account the main street directions and connect the boulevards; to visually increase the compositional significance of the Gogol' monument and integrate it into the design of the Square.

In order to solve the transport issue a number of streets were to be enlarged and their routes adjusted. For example, the plan provided for enlargement of Arbat Street and Malyj Afanas'evskij Pereulok, and alteration of the route of Kominterna Street (formerly Vozdviženka) in order to streamline traffic in the direction of Bol'šaja Molčanovka Street.

The building line on the Nikitskij Boulevard was to be straightened. The district between Frunze Street, Kominterna Street and Krestovoždvizenskij Pereulok was to be demolished and completely rebuilt. The new square would integrate, as an essential element of composition, the large building of the former Alexandrovskij school, built in Classical style in 1792 from a design by the architect F. Camporese, and bordered by the building line on Znamenka (later Frunze Street). Mel'nikov's plan was never implemented. However, in the following years the old buildings in the area where, according to Mel'nikov's proposal, new houses were to be built, were gradually pulled down. The re-routed Kominterna Street became an elongation of the new Kalinin Prospect, and a traffic tunnel was built under the Square. The Square has in fact become nothing more than a transport junction. The historical composition of a square noted for its picturesque appearance and exceptional greenery was lost forever while a new composition was never actually created.

The proposal for the redevelopment of Arbat Square is one of the least elaborate and detailed architectural works of Konstantin Mel'nikov. Plans and perspectives show various designs for parallel residential

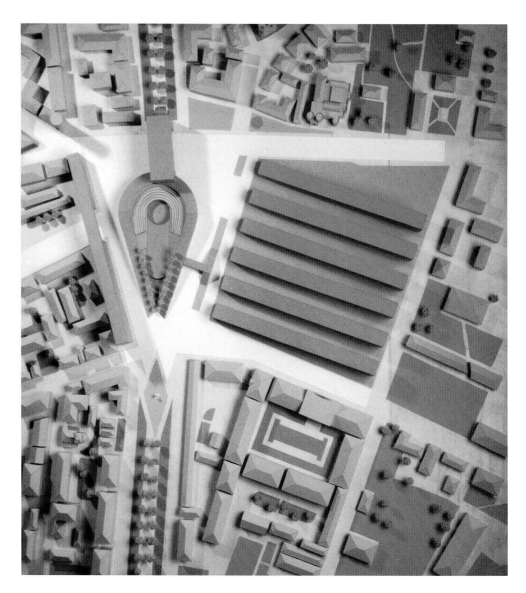

buildings situated in the eastern part of the complex. The buildings themselves are represented in a schematic way, so that the plan does not provide a reliable idea of their borders and positioning. The general plan, clearly showing the main compositional axis between the boulevards, forms the basis of the model. The building lines of long blocks run parallel to the sides of the central triangle. Six apartment blocks are placed perpendicular to the building line and bordered at the far end by the existing street. In Mel'nikov's proposal, the boulevard axis splits into two prongs, both of which seem to be important transport arteries. Together with the planned transverse main road, leading eastward towards the Kremlin, the new Arbat Square would become a vital factor in urban life and a transport hub for this part of Moscow, forming a link between it and the other districts in the city. For the composition of the Square, Mel'nikov has chosen a dynamic and well-balanced design based on contrast and contraposition. A long sheer-faced building forms an almost monolithic screen between the city and the Square, while the apartment blocks on the other side offer a broad perspective of the Kremlin and the churches. The layout is full of contrast as the buildings slope upwards in different directions. The horizontal axis, radiating from the triangle sides,

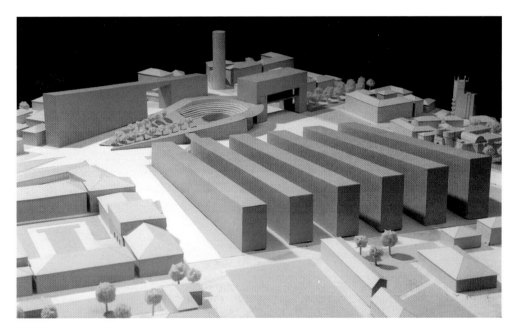

is marked with "empty spaces", while the central axis of the boulevard is distinguished by a robust cafÈ building with a central arch. Quite unexpectedly, the colossal edifices which are in sharp contrast to the old Moscow landscape prove to be commensurate in significance with the relatively small Gogol' monument, situated at the vertex of the compositional triangle. In this manner the three-pronged composition, a classic in the history of urban planning, has found an absolutely original solution in Mel'nikov's proposal. In the model, the planned buildings and roads are colour-coded, and the shapes are simple and rough as they are in author's sketches; the idea is to

emphasise the new scale in urban planning and architectural modernism inherent in the proposal.
Jurij Volčok, Elena Nikulina, Alexander Šadrin

[1] From K.S. Mel'nikov, *Arkhitektura moej žizni. Tvorčeskaja koncepcija. Tvorčeskaja praktika,* Moskva 1985, p. 84.
[2] *Ibidem*, pp. 213-215.

**Competition Project
for the MOSPS
Theatre**

"The cinema can rage in the perfection of natural illusions, but the theatre will touch us—wounded, deformed, exhausted by the demanding artificiality—on a much deeper level.

The reality of all art forms—fiction, painting, sculpture, architecture, music—is only a part of the total, mighty, immensely active, living in FLESH-THEATRE.

The aesthetics of theatre is not beauty but the power of its maximum potential. What people dream about becomes reality on stage. To witness a transfer of action happening at incredible speed and remain safe and sound at the same time—this will be the aim of modern theatre performance.

Building theatres is currently a primary theme for architecture. The task of the theatre is to express the idea of moment in the strongest way, so that the spectator, regardless of his individual will, is imbued, together with the rest of the audience, by one, forged together, thought. The theatre should be convincing to all its visitors, otherwise, if the message can be misunderstood and interpreted in different ways, it will not be theatre.

The essence of my architectural design lies in the fact that theatre should be considered a dynamic art form: the actor is in motion, his voice is in motion, acts change, the lighting moves. So, in order to bring the spectator closer to the theatre he should also be in motion.

Subjecting the audience to extraordinary, rapid, performances—this is the future of theatre.

The auditorium is designed as an IMMENSE CHAIR ON SEVEN TIERS, FOR THREE THOUSAND PEOPLE.

[In order to] bring spectators closer to three separate stages, I have designed not the horizontal movement of the giant body [of the auditorium] but its ROTATION. Therefore, from the point of view of technical possibilities this form of mechanical movement is the most simple—the easiest to realise, as well as to operate. In the truncated cone of the auditorium, the seats will have the shape of a sickle, sloping towards the stages.

The stage equipment and their number (three) is defined by the three types of mechanical movement: horizontal, rotational and vertical. *Rapid* movement, and *abundance* of movement and a *variety* of movement - these are, in essence, the three objectives of theatrical action. Lifting mechanisms, being cumbersome, do not allow swift changes of scenery. Therefore a rotating mechanism, equipped with prefabricated scenery, can quickly transform the set in front of the public. No theatre at all would probably be better than a theatre without 'live' water. *Sadko, Loengrin, Rusalka, Tsar Saltan* and other new plays would then emerge when it is known that there is such a theatre for fantastic reality...
K.S. Mel'nikov, 1931[1]

The additional sources indicate that this project was a design for a competition organised by the Moscow Regional Soviet of Trade Unions (MOSPS)[2] in 1931.[3] Although Mel'nikov was not able to realise the construction of a single theatre,[4] with the exception of the renovation of the Moscow Chamber Theatre (in 1930), he had already been able to gain experience with this type of building by designing his workers' clubs, all of which contained a stage. In this task Mel'nikov was concerned with achieving the greatest possible flexibility, above all in the interior space of the theatre. Thus, both the rotating auditorium and the four different stages could be moved into different positions. This is most clearly demonstrated by a stage that is suspended from a *Ferris wheel* and that can be opened both toward the street and the interior.

Mel'nikov's basic ideas was that the theatre is a *dynamic art* in which everything is in motion: the actors, the lights, the stages, etc. The ultimate consequence of this for Mel'nikov is to set the audience in motion as well. The auditorium can hence be turned toward each of the stages. By means of the design of the building, which resembles a movie camera and hence directly alludes to its use in a kind of *architecture parlante*, the interior functions are also readable from the outside. This was an essential demand of

functionalism, to which the rationalists of the ASNOVA were receptive. Even passers-by seeing the theatre by chance were supposed to come under its spell.

The architectural origin of the variable connection between stage and auditorium can be traced to the Total Theatre designed by Walter Gropius for Erwin Piscator in 1927, a model of which was exhibited at the Werkbund Exhibit in Paris in 1930.

The goal of the reconstruction was to portray the macrostructure of the differentiated building form and the proportions in the total ensemble; therefore, a presentation format emphasising overall form was selected. The complicated interior structure was taken into consideration only to the extent that it determined the exterior. The materials selected, wood and acrylic, were best suited to express the design of a composition made up of many strongly differentiated individual volumes that fit together to form a harmonious whole. This combination also made it possible to effectively reproduce the interplay between reinforced concrete and glass, the materials selected by Mel'nikov.

Based on various parameters, e.g. stair rise and run, constructionally realistic measurements for distance between supports, wall thickness, and story heights, a

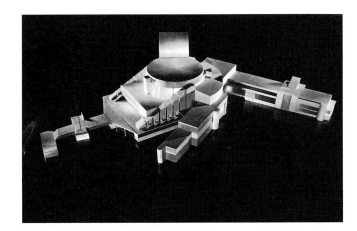

*Competition project for the
MOSPS Theatre, 1931*

*Views of the model
(realised by St. Birk, F. Friedrich,
L. Heilmeyer, 1998)*

*View of the model
(realised by St. Birk, F. Friedrich,
L. Heilmeyer, 1998)*

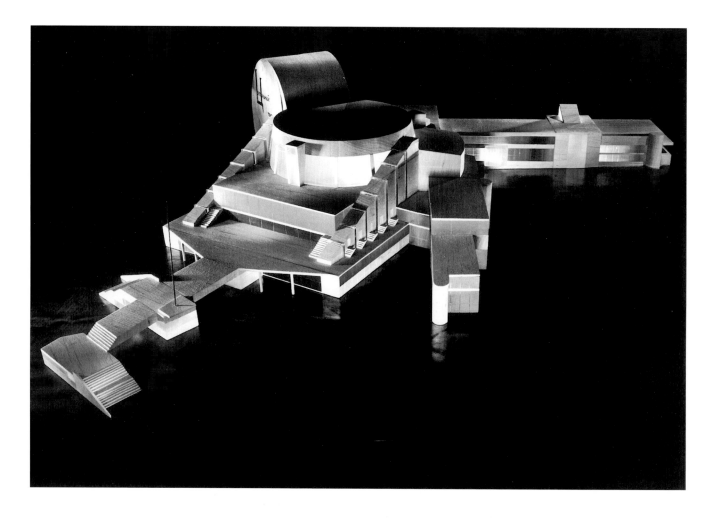

scale was figured for the existing
plans. On this basis new sketches
for the reconstruction were
drawn to a scale of 1:333.3.
These provided the basis for
initial test models that would
clarify problems concerning
connecting points as well as
overall stereometry. Since the
planning material did not provide
information about all facades,
the missing ones had to be
reconstructed with the assistance
of the ground plan. It seemed
reasonable to take symmetrical
considerations as a basis, since
they predominate in numerous
designs of Mel'nikov.
Traditional machines (band-saw,
circular saw, belt sanding
machine) were used to produce

the various individual parts as
well as to treat the materials:
wood and acrylic. In cases where
a finer differentiation was
necessary, a veneer was
produced from the same wood,
moistened and fitted to the
round structures. Finally, the
individual parts were fitted
together to form the complete
composition. The available
literature contains no indications
as to the surroundings of the
theatre; therefore, the
reconstruction model also makes
no statements regarding the
cityscape context. The grounds
are depicted in the model with
sheet lead and therefore contrast
in colour to the building.
Dietrich Schmidt

[1] From K.S. Mel'nikov,
*Arkhitektura moej žizni.
Tvorčeskaja koncepcija.
Tvorčeskaja praktika,* Moskva
1985, pp. 212-213.
[2] Moskovskij Oblast Sovetov
Professionalnij Sojuz.
[3] According to F. Starr, 16 entries
were turned in, among them
those of V. Ščuko, V. Gel'frejkh,
N. Ladovskij, B. Taut.
[4] His last architectural design,
completed in 1967, was a
children's theatre for Moscow.

Competition project for the
MOSPS Theater, 1931
(reconstruction by St. Birk,
F. Friedrich, L. Heilmeryer)
scale 1:1200

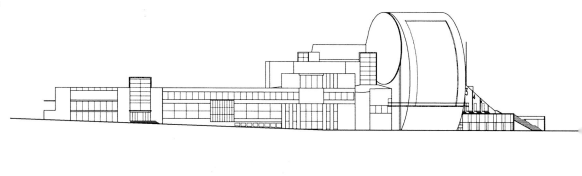

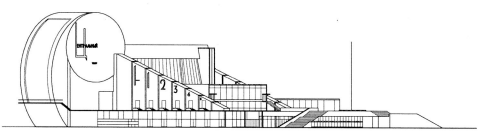

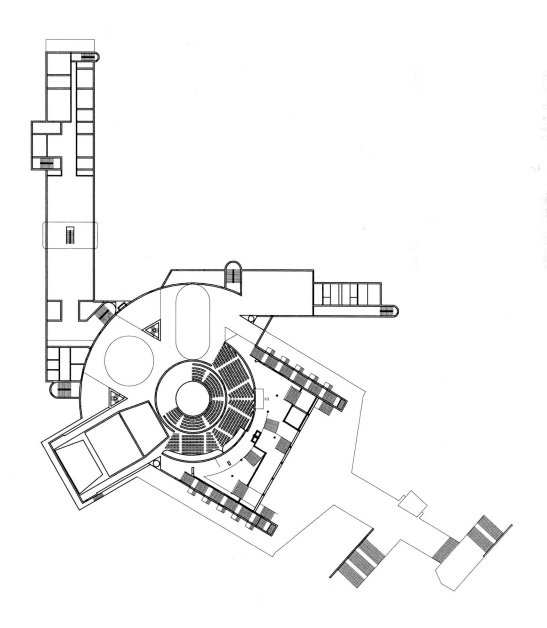

**Out of Competition
Project for the Palace
of the Soviets**

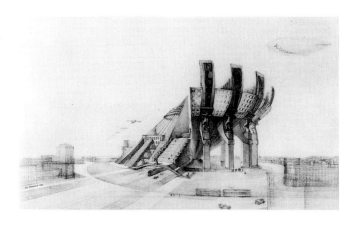

"The project expresses the struggle between old and new forms of architecture. The triumph of the new forms is expressed by means of contrast between a living and constantly developing form of the flower and the finished static form of the pyramid…"
K.S. Mel'nikov, 1933[1]

Unlike some of his colleagues, Mel'nikov was not invited by the State Construction Administration to participate in the first competition for the Palace of Soviets on April 17, 1931. As Strigalev writes, this angered him and he submitted a design labelled significantly "Dvorec Narodov" in the second, international round held between July 13 and December 1, 1931. In the momentous decision of February 28, 1932 Mel'nikov's entry was rejected. In the following years, three additional variants of this competition entry came into being: in 1932, 1933, and 1934/35. From among these designs, which are quite similar in macrostructure, the 1932 variant was selected for the model reconstruction, since the published drawings document it in greatest detail. However, one can hardly regard these drawings not done to scale as plans in the strict sense, for they provide only quite incomplete information about the interior functions, construction, and formal details.
Given the immense size of the

structure resting on a circular ground plan with a 200 m diameter and a height of 112 m, a scale of 1:1000 seemed to be justified. Changes in formal details found in the various design variants therefore play a minor role. The goal of the depiction was to show Mel'nikov's basic conception of two cones symbolising the old and the new social orders: paraphrasing the pyramid as the traditional metaphor for death, the cone resting on its base served as a symbol of the old carist hierarchy. Building on the broad base of workers and serfs the hierarchy continued up to the lesser nobility, the aristocracy and clergy, and finally led to the autocratic ruler at the top.
By standing the second cone on its head, which housed the 80 m high plenary chamber, Mel'nikov turned the underclass into the upper class that was now to guide the fortunes of the state. The small class of former rulers is now destined for the role of the disfranchised.
This construction, which was originally planned as a multifunctional congress centre for the representatives of the people and only later degenerated to a symbol of the Soviet central authority (respectively Lenin monument), was also, according to Mel'nikov's ideas, supposed to symbolise the federal structure of the Soviet Union. Thus, the seven supporting elements of

the cone became symbol-bearers: as 17-meter-high Atlases they support the federation and represent the then seven Soviet Republics, whose abbreviations appeared on the plaques mounted above the Atlas figures. As vertical access elements, the supports also fulfil a functional purpose. In addition to these seven, as it were, concealed staircases, a monumental flight of stairs between the two halves of the cone serves as access to the plenary chamber. On this flight of stairs, the demonstration parades of the proletarian masses are, so to speak, guided toward heaven under the red star mounted above, the symbol of the socialist ideal state. Mel'nikov's architectural language—with its geometric expressivity, synthesis of old and new elements, impressive dimensions, and utilisation of figural sculptures—becomes an *architecture parlante* that, strangely enough, foreshadows essential features of socialist realism.
The building for the People's Commissariat of Heavy Industry designed two years later also used this vocabulary. Wood was the most appropriate reconstruction material for an architecture of this type, which can hardly be imagined in the technicistic materials of the rationalists and/or constructivist avant-garde but in concrete covered with natural stones.
Dietrich Schmidt

[1] From K.S. Mel'nikov, *Arkhitektura moej žizni. Tvorčeskaja koncepcija. Tvorčeskaja praktika,* Moskva 1985, p. 215.

*Non-competing project for the
Palace of the Soviets, 1932*

*View of the model
(realised by Ch. Von Buchwald,
K. Müller, 1994)*

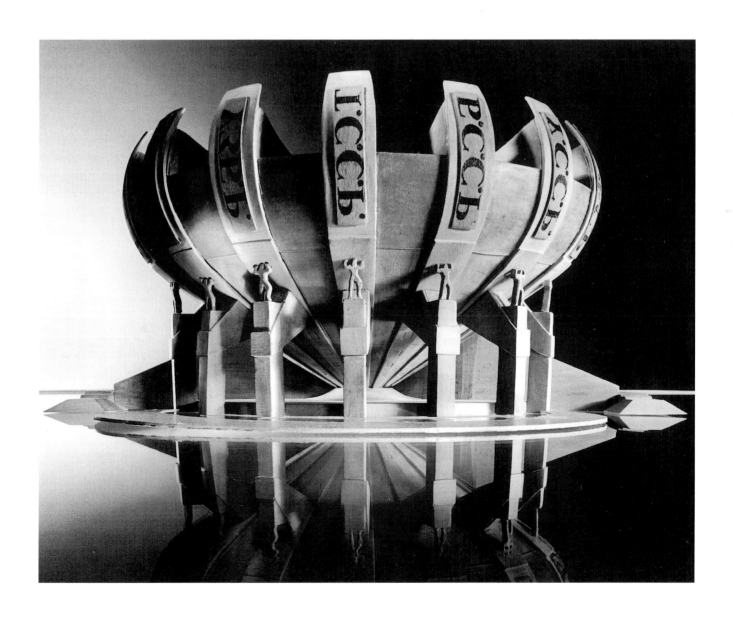

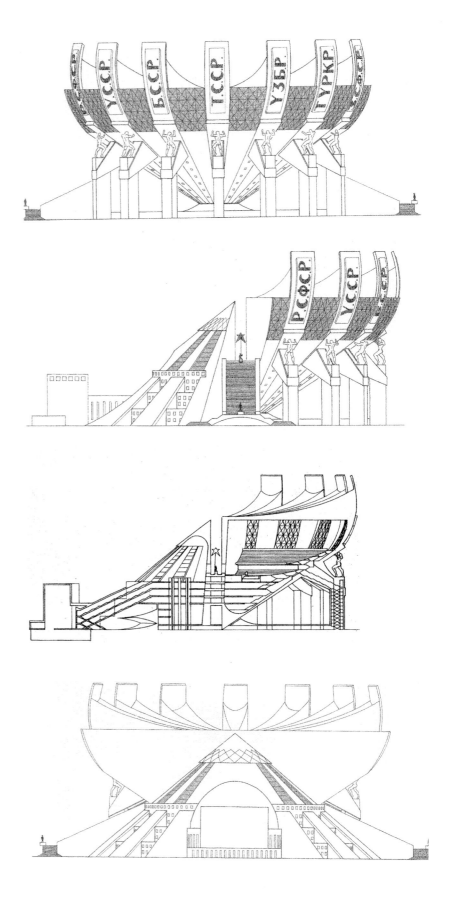

*Non-competing project for the
Palace of the Soviets, 1932
(reconstruction by Ch. Von
Buchwald, K. Müller)
scale 1:2400*

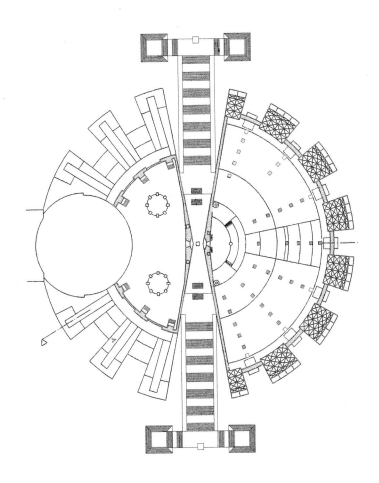

The Construction
of the Capital City

The background to the 1935 General Plan for the socialist reconstruction of Moscow

The change in direction in Soviet architecture which became apparent in the early Thirties arose mainly out of the replacement of the utopian model of socialism which the state ideology had created. The experimental search for the model society of the future which characterised the Twenties was superseded by the subordination of the country's economic, social and artistic life to a unified plan which was supposed to regulate it right down to the last detail and obliterate from people's minds the dividing line between reality and the imagined future.

'Socialist realism', which in 1932 was proclaimed the guiding creative principle in Soviet literature, gradually gained a hold in the non-verbal arts. Architecture became an increasingly semiotic, symbolic counterpart to the main political slogans of the time, recreating in its forms the eternal prosperity of the imminent 'Golden Age'. Not only did the formal and artistic priorities change, but also the language, which was now in the service of interpreting the classics. Even so, the permeation of the architecture of 'socialist realism' with utopian fervour in no way pales alongside the avant-garde of the Twenties. It also seeks to transform the world, to change man's nature and impose on him a 'better future'. In reality, what had been an attempt to reorganise life was

becoming a desire to influence hearts and minds by the power of artistic images.

Whereas in the Twenties society's expectations were mainly linked to a belief in the power of technology, the focus was now on faith in the enormous potential of the human spirit, which was inspired by the creation of a socialist future. The organisation of life in accordance with the intended unified plan, and the banishment from it of any hint of the chaos or disorder which characterised the structure of urban life in earlier times, were seen as merely the visible manifestation of the internal powers of its creator.

The dawning of a new era in architecture was most clearly manifested during the final stages of the design competition for the Palace of the Soviets (1932-1933). Among the wide-ranging design entries, B.M. Iofan was singled out for special recognition. It had become, by that stage, transformed into a monolithic structure on top of which a stepped tower reached heavenwards, a beacon to mark the centre of Moscow. This was exactly the kind of centre-marker that, in the view of the government Council for the Construction of the Palace of the Soviets, could symbolise the new era, by expressing it through a "strong and bold reach skywards." This image, however, was felt to be lacking sufficient power, and the Council issued a supplementary instruction to complete the building

with a powerful sculpture of Lenin, 50-75 metres tall, so that the Palace of the Soviets should be a pedestal for the figure of the leader. The creation of the final version of Jofan's design was achieved with the help of V. Sčuko and V. Gelfrejkh as co-designers, and, in February 1934, the Palace of the Soviets design project received the go-ahead.

The Palace of the Soviets was regarded not only as a symbol of the new society, but also as the conceptual centre of Moscow—the capital of the world's only proletarian state. Therefore the designing of the Palace of the Soviets and of the general plan of Moscow was, essentially, a single process: the search for a large-scale structure for the city that would create the perception of its wholeness The city's wholeness, in turn, was inseparably connected with the concept of 'metropolity'—the image of Moscow as a capital of world significance. The gigantic building of the Palace of the Soviets, over 400 metres tall, marked the culmination of the centre-focused planning of the capital, which was adopted as the basis for the general plan. It brought together vast areas of the city's space into a single symbolic system.

The main characteristic feature of the work on the general plan of Moscow in the Thirties was the desire to see the city as the sum total of large-scale complexes under construction simultaneously. A shift from designing and constructing separate buildings to

On page 266:
*Moscow general plan of 1935;
axonometric view of the center*

*Final solution of the project for the Palace
of the Soviets (B.B.M. Iofan, V.G. Gelfrejkh
with Ja.B. Belopol'skij, V.V. Pelevina), 1936*

*Planimetric scheme of Moscow general plan,
1935*

creating integrated ensembles was
being announced as the paramount
concern of Soviet architecture. The
creative thinking of V. Semenov and S.
Cernysev, the designers of the new
general plan, was moving from the
general towards the particular, from
the city as a whole to its component
parts. For Semenov the new starting
point was the image of the city, its
holistic apprehension. "The design of
a city is not a two-dimensional, but a
three-dimensional image," he wrote.
What Černyšev was looking for in the
ensemble was that important
ingredient which could distinguish
Moscow, the capital of a socialist state,
from the world's other cities: "A
socialist city is not the mechanical
amalgamation of separate fragments
which are in competition with each
other and which often cause each
other harm … but an urban complex,
designed and executed as an entity."
The main challenges which faced the
designers of the unified ensemble—the
new Moscow—was the creation of an
expressive city skyline which conveyed
its internal artistic structure, the
reconstruction of the centre, the
placing of buildings along the urban
highways and around the squares, the
provision of restored and new parks
and lakes.
The confirmation of the need to create
a new look for Moscow was combined
with another vital principle—
recognition of the importance of the
planning structure of the city which
had coalesced in earlier times. It was

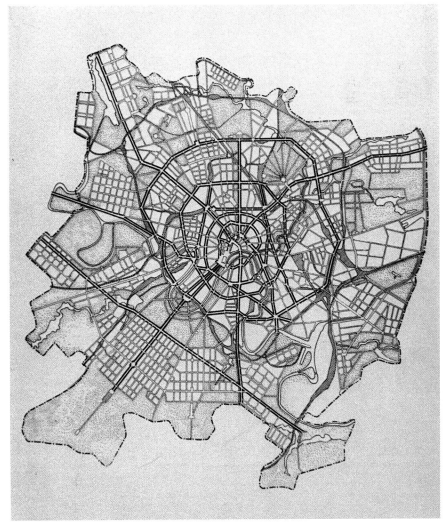

this that dictated its preservation as a major monument of urban design culture. The coupling of these two principles presented the designers of planning 'knots' of Moscow with considerable challenges.

The elaboration of architecturally important sections of the city plan had begun during the drafting of the general plan itself. In connection with this a whole series of competitions for

the design of large public and administrative buildings was held during the first half of the Thirties. Their purpose was, on the one hand, to provide design support for the Palace of the Soviets project (an idea that subsequently fed into the post-war high-rise construction programme), and, on the other- to become free-standing centres, around which the space of large sectors of the city would

crystallise.

The most significant of these, as it transpired, was the design competition for the building of the People's Commissariat of the Heavy Industry (Narkomtjažprom). This building, which was to embody the idea of industrialisation of the country at large, was to be erected right on Red Square, in immediate proximity to the Kremlin. This was in 1934, and K.S.

Mel'nikov was one of the entrants. Just as the planning of the Palace of the Soviets had entailed the re-planning of a large area adjacent to it, so the Narkomtjazprom scheme involved the redesigning not only of Red Square, but also of the whole central area. The results of this major competition showed that the construction of this huge building on Red Square would have been a mistake, and a new site was found for it.

Actual work on reconstruction commenced while the general plan was still on the drawing board. The year 1932 saw the completion of the planning schemes which launched the reconstruction of Theatre Passage, Sverdlov and Okhotnyj Rjad Squares and Mokhovaja Street. Even before the general plan received approval, many buildings were started which encompassed images of the grand scheme of the city: the Red Army Theatre, which had a stepped high-rise construction and a five-pointed star configuration (the building was referred to as "a rehearsal for the building of the Palace of the Soviets"), and the first line of the Moscow Metro, the significance of which went far beyond the scope of the usual technological project. It was as if the Metro continued the theme of a dream city of the future existing in a subterranean world in conventional time and space. Isolated from the real city, the Metro became a kind of projection into the present of the festive beauty and harmony of the

architectural ensembles of the future, whilst at the same time being a convincing symbol of the technological potential of the state.

The general plan of Moscow, approved in 1935, presupposed that the population of Moscow in the coming ten years would reach 5 million. Accordingly, it was planned that the city would expand by means of annexing to itself new districts, the most promising of which was thought to be the south-western district. The preservation of the radial-ring layout demanded the replanning of the streets which followed the line of Kamer-Kolležskij Val, and the creation of a new park ring. The centre would have to undergo substantial replanning, to provide for new radial urban highways and relief-roads. Existing squares would be transformed, and new ones built. Even before the general plan had been finalised, Moscow City Council had special design workshops in place, to cope with the huge redesigning tasks; they were initially geared towards tackling the aesthetic challenges which the project presented.

The daunting task set by the authorities—to concentrate the main body of housing construction along the major urban highways and embankments—threw up a number of problems related to the formation of an integrated street plan. The model for the correct approach to street design at this time was seen to be the work recently begun on the

reconstruction of Gor'kij Street (now Tverskaja), planned as a street for triumphal processions. This was where the most advanced methods of design and reconstruction of the time were being tested and put into practice. Residential blocks were being erected using rapid-construction methods devised under the leadership of architect A. Mordvinov. Old buildings were extended upwards, and some were even repositioned so as not to impede the widening of the street. Major residential construction was also under way on Bol'šaja Kalužskaja Street (now a part of Lenin Avenue), on Možaisk Sosse (now Kutuzov Avenue) and elsewhere.

Bridges were also a highly important element in the 'new look for Moscow' scheme. Between 1936 and 1938 alone, five bridges were built across the River Moskva, three across Vodootvodnyi Canal, and one over the River Jauza. Moscow's top architects and engineers were involved in their design and construction, since bridges were accorded special importance, as the links which would bind the whole city-centre ensemble together.

Another key element of the 1935 general plan for Moscow was the 'Garden City' concept, which had by then progressed very far from its original idea. The idea of a blossoming garden which would penetrate throughout the entire aesthetic structure of the new general plan, was based on a reconstructive and transformative approach to nature.

A.V. Vlasov, Project for the building of the Lenin Higher Institute, atelier n. 1, 1931

A.V. Ščusev, A.K. Rostovskij, Project for the Rostovskij and Smolenskij riverside, atelier n. 2, 1934

L.S. Teplickij, access pavilion to the ìArbatskajaî metro station, atelier n. 2, 1934

I.A. Fomin, project for the entry building from the city to the Science Academy, atelier n. 3, 1934

The Moscow of the future was envisioned as a luxuriant man-made oasis. The free harmony of the emerging new society was inextricably linked with the conquest and harnessing of nature's essence. Conversely, the spontaneity, haphazardness and uncertainty of untamed nature were associated with lack of freedom, and with man's dependence on ungovernable forces. The general plan evinced a desire to harmonise the historical with the natural, through a unified concept of order in our world.

The emerging culture of the future was particularly dependent on water, as a symbol of revitalisation and transformation of the environment. Therefore, water and vegetation, which permeated the whole expanse of the city, not only fulfilled a pragmatic, climate-enhancing function, but were a vital component of the image of the future Moscow. The opening of the man-made Moskva-Volga canal in 1937 was a crucial event not only for our society, but also for the life of the architectural profession.

The general plan provided for a major programme of irrigation work, as a result of which Moscow would acquire two 'rings' of water. The smaller of these—the inner-city ring—would come into being after the joining of the Jauza and the Khimki Reservoir by the Likhoboryj canal. The plan envisaged the connecting of the River Moskva with the outer ring at Južnyj (Southern) Port, beyond Izmajlovo Park. Water flowed towards the centre in the form of small aquifers, streams, cascades and fountains. Moscow was seen as a series of uninterrupted landscape compositions, where the verdant streets and decorative water-fountains merged into the system of city parks, which in turn fan out into the outer—suburban woodland parks. Many of the urban highways were planned as tree-lined radii. The main tree-lined canal would run from Tjoplyj Stan in the south-west to Pogonno-Losinov Island in the north-east. Its central section would form the Palace of the Soviets Avenue, which was planned as the city's main landscaped thoroughfare.

The main urban-planning elements at that time—the urban highways and the squares—often resembled rivers that flow into a lake. However, free space would be needed to create such a grandiose and festive artificial environment. Free-style landscape compositions were sometimes conceived which would cut swaths through the historical fabric of the city and even uproot existing greenbelt areas. The paradoxical nature of the Moscow reconstruction scheme manifested itself in the fact that, despite the declared general appreciation of the value of their heritage, the architects, in giving free rein to their visualisations, paid very little heed to the existing urban environment. The logistics of a living city were somewhat alien to them, and the continuing legacy of the past was often seen merely as an obstacle to the development of the new. In their striving for the ideal artistic expression of the form of an urban highway, embankment or square, the designers hardly reckoned with the practicability or otherwise of its execution. For this reason, most of the designs of the

Thirties remained on the drawing board. World War II also played its part, setting the boundary to both the development of Soviet society and to the vision of architectural and urban construction.

Nevertheless, at the end of the Thirties the architecture of Moscow, which had grown up during the execution of the general plan, had gained the approval of the public at large. It had begun to be regarded as a cultural phenomenon artistically on a par with the monuments of classical architecture; at the same time it was seen as a pledge of the feasibility of the dreams of the future.

The general plan for Moscow was itself an influential factor in Soviet culture from the Thirties to the Fifties; it claimed to embrace "absolutely every aspect of the city's life." There was a gradual shift, in the late Thirties, towards abstractionism in architectural thought, a move away from functional definitions of the elements of city life towards a focus on the city's image-bearing and symbolic role, which was to explain the ideas of socialist construction. This shift was turning the general plan of a particular city into a universal methodological tool which, according to the convictions of the time, could be used for the redesigning and construction of any city in any part of our vast country. At the 1940 plenary session of the Union of Soviet Architects, which was specially dedicated to the architectural issues of redesigning Moscow, one and

the same message was echoed in the Moscow architects' speeches: a unified ensemble had yet to be achieved for the city; whereas the provincial architects spoke of the first examples of misapplication of Moscow's construction experiences to completely dissimilar conditions. In the post-war years, however, the dividing line between what was planned and what was done in the actual reconstruction of Moscow was to prove barely noticeable to the general populace, and the general plan for Moscow will long remain as a milestone in the development of Soviet architectural thought.

Jurij Volčok, Julia Kosenkova

The Architectural Planning Workshops of Moscow City Council (MOSSOVET)

From August 1932 to September 1933, preparatory work was carried out for the creation of a new organisational system for architectural planning in Moscow.

The impulse for this change came from three areas:

– In June 1931 a resolution was passed to equip the country's urban centres with services and utilities. In fact, the works completed in July 1935 started with the decision to work out a general plan for the reconstruction of Moscow.

– On 23 April 1932 a party resolution was passed to remould the activity of the country's literary and artistic organisations. Based on this resolution

creative unions of writers, artists, composers and architects were formed.

The previous informal creative groups stopped their activity. In their place came thematic commissions of a single creative professional Union. In our case, the Union of Architects of the USSR.

– Also in June 1931, a decision was taken to build a metro in Moscow. Work was started in 1932, and on 14 May 1935 the opening of the first Moscow metro line (from the Gor'kij Park to Sokol'niki) was triumphantly celebrated.

These three decisions had a real and significant impact on the professional activity of architects and urban planners in Moscow, substantially reshuffling the priorities within various aspects of the internal city dialogue. Most importantly, it created a perception of the city as an object to which professional effort could be applied.

"The general initial working methods and principles [of the newly created architectural workshops—Ju. V.] can be reduced to the following: we have moved on from the previous archaic development and haphazard growth to a planned construction and design, not only of separate buildings and structures, but also of whole quarters, streets, squares and embankments, in order to create architectural ensembles."[1]

This paved the way for the abolition of Moscow City Council's architectural

planning section, which had been responsible for all kinds of planning activities in Moscow, and for the establishment of a Planning Department in its place, subordinate both to the Moscow City Council and the Moscow City Executive Committee. These institutions were charged with managing the creative work of 10 design and 10 planning workshops, each responsible for a particular urban district. In practice there were fewer workshops. In the beginning, around 1934-1935, there were 10, but by the end of 1935 workshop number 12 had been closed down.

Detailed here is the composition of the first 10 architectural design workshops called into being.

Workshop no. 1 – Leader: I.V. Žoltovskij; senior professionals: L.O. Bumažnyj, A.V. Vlasov, G.P. Gol'c, S.N. Kozin, M.P. Parušnikov, I.N. Sobolev, M.O. Baršč, M.I. Sinjavskij, K.N. Afanas'ev, G.A. Zunblat.

Workshop no. 2 – Leader: A.V. Ščusev; senior professionals: A.K. Rostkovskij, D.N. Čečulin, A.F. Žukov, A.V. Kurovskij, V.F. Krinskij, A.M. Rukhljadev, V.S. Birkenberg, L.S. Teplickij, E.G. Černov.

Workshop no. 3 – Leader: I.A. Fomin; senior professionals: P.V. Abrosimov, A.P. Velikanov, M.A. Minkus, L.M. Poljakov, A.F. Khrjakov, Z.O. Brod, N.G. Bezrukov, A.G. Mordvinov, K.I. Solomonov, K.N. Duškin, I.E. Rozin, G.G. Krutikov, V.S. Popov, L.N. Davidovič, A.K. Arkin, Ja. G.

Likhtenberg.

Workshop no. 4 – Leader: I.A. Golosov; senior professionals: P.P. Antipov, A.A. Zuravlev, V.M. Kusakov, A.T. Kapustina, D.D. Bulgakov, N.K. Markuze, B.F. Rogajlov, K.I. Dzus, I.V. Gokhman, S.F. Kibirev, M.K. Kostandi, S.A. Kozlovskij, S.A. Alimov, G.K. Jakovlev.

Workshop no. 5 – Leader: A.F. Fridman; senior professionals: L.O. Greenspoon, A. Lurçat, A.I. Kaplun, P.A. Aleksandrov, L.N. Pavlov, E.A. Iokheles, I.A. Dlugac.

Workshop no. 6 – Leader: N.Ya. Kolli; senior professionals: S.G. Andrejevskij, F.N. Sammer, T.I. Makarycev, N.A. Selivanov, V.P. Sergeev, A.N. Fedorov, M.G. Kupovskij, V.B. Vol'fenzon, I.N. Kastel', V.N. Kutukov.

Workshop no. 7 – Leader: K.S. Mel'nikov; senior professionals: V.N. Kurockin, T.M. Kuz'menko, N.I. Tronkvilickij, D.V. Razov.

Workshop no. 10 – Leader: V.D. Kokorin; senior professionals: V.D. Vladimirov. M.V. Andrianov, G.I. Ležava, M.M. Curakov, M.T. Bazilevic, B.N. Žoltkevic, I.A. Zvezdin, E.V. Sakharov, A.I. Nosov, F.I. Mikhajlovskij, A.A. Ulbrikh, A.B. Varsave, A.I. Antonov, A.M. Sevcov.

Workshop no. 11 – Leader: M.V. Krjukov; senior professionals: N.F. Visnevskij, G.P. Vorob'ev, A.A. Kessler, I.Z. Weinstein, B.N. Blokhin, A.G. Turkenidze, A.N. Zemskij, A.K. Burov, Ju. N. Emel'janov.

Workshop no. 12 – Leader: N.G. Borov; senior professionals: G.S. Zemskij, Ju.A. Revnovskij, N.V. Bogoslovskij, S.K. Zabaluev, A.V. Ivanov, A.E. Lopukhin, I.A. Young. This list of architects speaks volumes to anyone even slightly acquainted with the history of Muscovite architecture in the twentieth century. It is interesting to see how the participants in the creative groupings of the Twenties and the graduates of VKhUTEMAS chose their own workshop leaders. It is also important to draw attention to the fact that K.S. Mel'nikov became one of the youngest architects to be given his own workshop (no. 7). It should also be mentioned that it was here that he

revealed his quest for individuality and independent creativity. Judging by all the data, his workshop was the smallest, and it did not contain any 'big name' architects of the day except the leader himself.

With the reorganisation of city's design activities the new workshops were essentially multi-discipline. They not only had to deal with architectural design problems, but also with other (engineering, constructional, economic) aspects of design.

The centralisation of the workshop management allowed their creative tasks to be structured: from designs for large sections of the city (embankments, the project for the Central park of culture and recreation

(Gor'kij Park), the town of the Academy of Sciences, big public and residential complexes, theatres, metro stations, etc.) to designs for street kiosks, areas for public services and utilities, and interior design.

Needless to say, the theoretical preference for centralised planning dominant at that time was also applied in a much broader context, i.e. to the organisation of the country and the political system as a whole. In this context it was quite logical that the architectural workshops of Moscow City Council gradually began to receive commissions for large-scale projects in other cities: Arkhangel'sk, Alma-Ata, Nal'cik, Novosibirsk, Stalinsk, Tbilisi, etc.

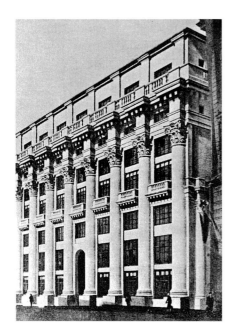

Right from the beginning, the architectural studies of Moscow City Council also had an additional, clearly political, function. Besides designing for other cities, they had to promote the high quality of the capital's architecture in the rest of the USSR. The interest in it—or, more precisely, the feeling of the necessity of such an interest—was also expressed by the fact that the book containing a collection of articles about the activities of the workshops was published with title pages, headings and captions in two languages—in Russian and French.

Today, these features, together with excellent presentation of the explanatory notes, subject and geographical indexes, etc., can be taken as evidence that a professional publication was considered important. But the decision of the editorial board to publish the book in two languages stemmed from a broader range of concerns, which included their opinion that there was a growing interest in Muscovite architecture abroad.

Thus in the first year of activity (1934) two opposed, and in many ways mutually exclusive tendencies, began to take shape in the architectural workshops. However, these tendencies complemented each other in other areas and lead to the creation of new directions in architectural form and style.

On the one hand workshops were being established so as to increasingly 'tie' architectural creativity to the actual city itself, to the particular building site, and on the other hand there appeared a new and quite important criterion for evaluating the activity of the workshops: the 'capital style' of architecture, in which the concrete location of the project, its individuality and the building's 'function' naturally all become of secondary importance.

At this point it is important to recognise a very essential detail for understanding architecture in Moscow towards the middle of the Thirties: the design work of the workshops is presented in the collection without a linear scale. This facet of its work significantly complicates the understanding and interpretation of the volume/spatial and architectural/planning specifics of the authors' proposals, but also makes the concepts more universal and somewhat impersonal.

This criterion (the 'capital style' of architecture) became so important that it also influenced the workshop organisation principles. Their newly appointed leaders were given the opportunity to invite people who shared a similar spirit or view on architecture. This in a certain sense helped to relieve the problems of the transfer from architectural practices to the new approach to architectural design. But this opportunity also allowed the workshop management to make strict demands in relation to the quality of design work. It should also

be mentioned that in the collection "The Work of Architectural Workshops", which is mostly a summary of the workshop activities in 1934, it was not the creative credo of the workshop leaders that was published, but the architectural creativity principles of the workshop collective as a whole. This observation is quite important, since it allows a definition of the emerging qualitative change in the mutual relations of 'I' and 'We' (individual, personal and collective, en masse) in architectural design.

It goes without saying that in the "principles of architectural creativity" a significant role is played by I.V. Žoltovskij (the leader of workshop no. 1) with his attentive interest and immense knowledge about the heritage of architecture and Renaissance culture, the influence of A.V. Ščusev (leader of workshop no. 2) whose personal professional experience can be easily read between the lines, and the ideas of A.I. Fomin (leader of workshop no. 3) concerning creative approaches to the development of forms and the relationship between the modern and the classic.

However, it is not these differences that matter here, but the common points that unite the "principles of architectural creativity." Perhaps the creative credo of Scusev's studio articulated this more exactly and completely than the others. "The workshop strives to base its activities

A.V. Vlasov, Project for the Gor'kij central park of culture and rest, atelier n. 1, 1934

A.K. Burov, Ju.N. Emel'janov, Project for the middle school n. 55 in the Krasnopresnenskaja section of popular education, atelier n. 11, 1935

on the principles of teamwork, in every way assisting the creative development of each individual."[2] In an analogous document by workshop no. 3 this thought is developed as follows: "With this aim in mind, some of the commissions are fulfilled by the leader together with one or two young authors on the basis of equal authors' rights, and the others, by young authors individually, and finally, creative collectives are put together from the more experienced and less experienced authors. All the work is carried out under the general supervision of the workshop leader."[3] The architectural creativity principles of K.S. Mel'nikov's workshop (workshop no. 7) were devised in a qualitatively different manner. Here, as had been the case in the past, there was no discussion of the principles of collective creativity in architecture. On the contrary, greater emphasis was given to the problems of personal talent and the skills of each architect who worked in the workshop. "…It is just as incredible to allow an architect who has had his creativity depersonalised to get down to practical construction as it is to see a painter who is not able to draw with his own hand…" And again: "The genuine talent of an architect, his great skill and the high level of knowledge, culture and artistic feeling of our critics and the people responsible for approving the designs, the high qualifications of the design execution team and the high quality of the

building materials, construction technology and the construction industry must all contribute to the abolishing of architecture's backwardness on the general front of socialist construction."[4] "Only the genuine creative talent of the artist/author gives his work the right to life. Meanwhile among us architects the quantity of collective work, which is often brilliant in form, has reached enormous proportions. This work, in our opinion, will soon be depreciated by life itself."[5] This text gives expression not so much to the creative principles of the collective work of workshop no. 7 as the professional credo of its leader.

This was also obvious to the compilers of the report. Only once in its 10 issues did the editors consider it necessary to make a small insertion of their name, where first of all they note that they are of course publishing the personal beliefs of the architect K.S. Mel'nikov and not the creative work principles of workshop no. 7, and secondly, they not only disown Mel'nikov's words, but also his creative endeavours, adding the reservation that they "were subjected and are being subjected" to criticism, including the project for the House of the Narkomtjažprom [People's Commissariat of the Heavy Industry], which was included in the issue, "with the abstractly conceived drawing of its plan, its 63-metre-deep excavation in front of the building and the 16-storey-high external staircases."[6]

The editors hinted that Mel'nikov had received a State workshop as an 'advance' as it were, with the reckoning that "reconstruction on the basis of socialist realism" would lead to a genuine flowering of his gift. But one could draw another conclusion from this thesis: that by 1933 K.S. Mel'nikov's professional authority was so great that it was impossible to pass him by in deciding on the formation of the State architectural workshops and the choice of their leaders.

Jurij Volčok

[1] *Rabota arkhitekturnykh masterskikh. Sbornik otdela proektirovanija Mossoveta*, Moskva, 1936, p. 17.
[2] *Ibidem*, Workshop no. 2, p. 3.
[3] *Ibidem*, Workshop no. 3, p. 4.
[4] *Ibidem*, Workshop no. 7, p. 4.
[5] *Ibidem*.
[6] *Ibidem*.

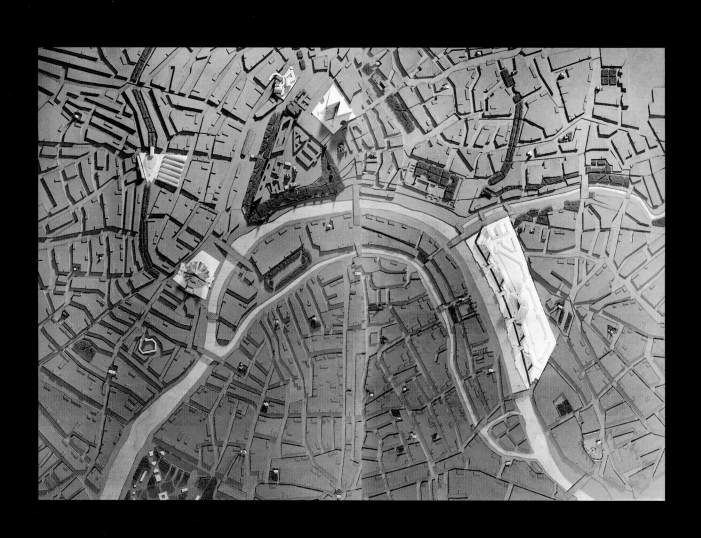

Works from 1932 to 1936

1923-1935

**The Large Scale Designs
of K.S. Mel'nikov
for the City Centre**

"The city of the future

All the city streets will be green and completely pedestrianised. The roads will be underneath (to keep them free of snow and protected from the sun); beneath the roads will be moving pavements, and lower still, rapid inter-city transport. There will be sloping houses; their sloping roofs will be used to suspend roads in the sky, while transport machines will be moored at their side.

There will be a city of hospitals [...] on the snowy peaks the city of heroes, the pantheon city, the city of ethnography, each state will construct its own national city, its capital…"

K.S. Mel'nikov, 1944[1]

**"The interior design
of the street**

What belongs to the sphere of interior design?

Why not develop the idea of 'The interior design of the street', which would be especially interesting considering the multiple functionality of city streets together with their virtually insoluble problems.

The typical city street has a continuous line of buildings on both sides. In many cities—and particularly in Moscow—these buildings have no uniformity in terms of their individual size, which tends to give the streets a temporary character and a multitude of protruding surfaces. The exterior finishing of the buildings is also haphazard and characterised by a total lack of

principle, giving the street a mixed appearance.

This 'artistic' chaos of our cities can in some cases be made picturesque by giving the streets some sort of interior design. But our main reason for considering it vital to cultivate an interior design concept for city streets is that general and unbending law by dint of which any architectural structure, even of the most excellent style, will not escape the deformity given to it by foreshortening when the object exceeds the limits of aesthetic understanding…

A beaming smile on the facade of a house (if such can be produced by an architect), as on a living face, can, when a passer-by moves closer, change and be transformed into a grimace, sometimes a terrible grimace. This transition from beauty into deformity is inevitable, and is constantly repeated in the conditions of street traffic, and is impossible to correct—only distracting the attention by creating a sort of 'interior' can change it.

The following elements would make up the entire compositional structure of this interior:

(a) the physical proportions between the various street elements;

(b) the seasons;

(c) the lighting arrangements;

(d) the architecture of the street itself.

(a) When there is so little space for traffic it is impermissible to

introduce yet more objects that take up even more space. In these conditions the architectural design makes use of horizontals - the roadway and its pavements - and also the elevations of the existing buildings.

Streets with their abundance of transverse intersections are embellished with both a range of architectural objects (fountains, masts) and by trees and grass. Greenery must be employed to the maximum of its potential, starting with the planting of large trees and ending with flowers, either in the form of bright flowerbeds or in the form of separate bouquets delivered round the streets by cars every morning in standard containers, just as rubbish is removed now."

K.S. Mel'nikov, 1948[2]

The design activity of Mel'nikov, which was developed in the context of a specific city, coincided with an extremely dynamic and contradictory era in the development of Moscow, the groundwork for which was to a great extend prepared by its entire history.

During its growth, Moscow became the product of various urban development ideas, each of which strove to realise a concept of the ideal city characteristic for that particular historical period.

The layout of the city centre was formed over the course of several centuries. Throughout this historical process, two development tendencies became

interwoven: the uncontrolled, 'natural' development, concentrated around the numerous local centres which gradually began to consume the gaps in the landscape; and the purposeful, planned activity that strove to subordinate the structure of the city to one centre and establish a strict hierarchy of city districts within an integrated system.

One can confirm that these phenomena affected the development of Moscow during Mel'nikov's active period; but there are also other two key issues that at that time affected the transformation of the city and its core: the restoration of Moscow to the status of capital and the abolishment of private land ownership opened up previously unprecedented opportunities for the comprehensive reconstruction of the city which so many architects deemed necessary.

It is well known that a great variety of ideas were proposed for the reconstruction of Moscow in the Twenties. These ideas pleaded both for an attempt to plan the city as a whole, and for a reconstruction of the separate city districts. This was most vividly demonstrated in the architectural competition plans of the Twenties, where, alongside a search for new methods of project development and a new architectural language, one can also see a unique emotional attachment to the space of the ancient city.

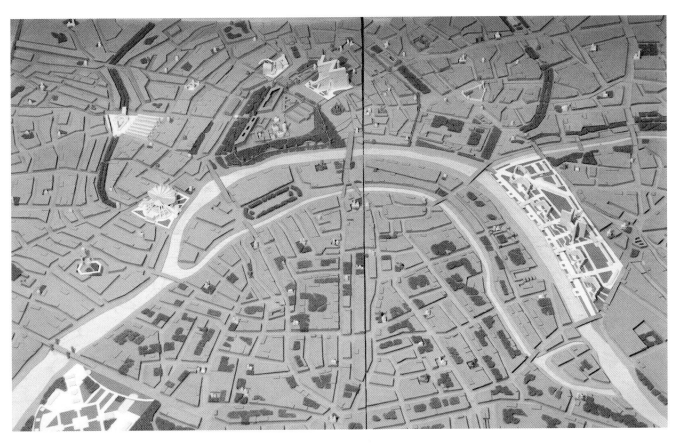

Even today, many people are shocked by the projects of this era, but there is no doubt that most of them came about because of Moscow's extraordinary character and spatial variety, and because the obvious 'compositional incompleteness' of the city as an architectural whole presented the opportunity for the creation of new design concepts.

The sites chosen for the competitions were often the most important urban development priorities of the time. These were mainly squares or embankments. However, certain city districts, or parts of districts, were chosen to be rebuilt with a new type of housing.

In the Twenties and Thirties Mel'nikov contributed to the urban development proposals for many Moscow districts. These included: the projects for the central squares—the project for the Palace of Labour in Okhotnyj rjad and the project for the reconstruction of Arbat Square; Red Square—the project for the Narkomtjazprom (People's Commissariat of the Heavy Industry) building; the embankments of the Moscow River, which give the city centre its particular shape, redesigning of the Kotelničeskaja and Gončarnaja embankments; the Central city park—the project for the fountain in the Central park of culture and recreation. This is far from a complete list, so that all his projects put together give an idea of the "Mel'nikov Moscow" which would have been created had all his designs been put into practice.

In practically all his work, in spite of his call for innovation and his display of creative intentions, Mel'nikov remained sensitive to the urban context in which any project was being realised.

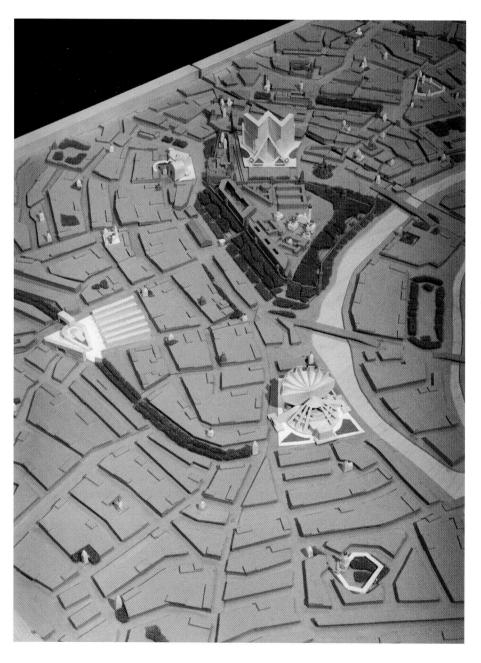

*Views of the model
(realized by A. Šadrin with
E. Gončarova, A. Pankratova,
A. Romanov)*

It seems that the master's creativity was greatly nourished by his keen perception of urban reality; he even tried to solve local problems as if they were urban development problems. Mel'nikov's participation in the formation of Moscow city centre extended over more than ten years, and coincided with an active search by architects for new solutions for urban development problems.

If we chronologically review Mel'nikov's projects, then in spite of their originality they reveal a tendency generally characteristic of the Moscow reconstruction process of the Twenties and early Thirties: the scale of reconstruction intervention and the vastness of the planned transformations gradually turned design into an almost abstract occupation. The construction of the ideal city required one to completely renounce the existing context. It is possible that precisely because this way of solving urban development problems was predominant in architectural practice in that era that further design activity of the master was finally curtailed.

The model of the centre of Moscow was created to show the development of the Kotelničeskaja and Gončarnaja embankments in the context of the city as a whole. The scale of the model was therefore fixed at 1:2500, which has obvious consequences for the character of the model.

We have decided to reproduce

This car-park for the national tourist office and the Gosplan car park dating from the same year are the last two of Mel'nikov's works ever to be built. For both car parks the architect limited himself to sketching the exterior elevations. The parking section and the ramps were designed by his colleague, V.I. Kurockin.[1] The reasons for this are not clear, but it can be assumed that it was a consequence of the way work was shared out in Moscow's city project office, where Mel'nikov was working at the time.
In the Intourist garage complex it is possible to make a distinction between high-rise and low-rise. The high section contains mainly parking facilities for private cars, while the lower section is for larger vehicles such as buses. In plan the two high sections of the building (the car park and the office building) combine with the lower gateway building and an interior courtyard to form a right angle, enclosed on the side and at the back by a low-rise building (the bus park and workshops). The rearmost half of this right angle is taken up by the car park, with access provided by means of a Humy ramp system. The gateway building is located on the axis running through the centre of the garage at the front of the right angle. The square that lies between the car park and the gateway building is bounded on one side (the north) by the low-rise bus park and on

the opposite side (the south) by the high-rise administration building.
The low rise building which contains the parking places for buses is not terribly interesting. Two elevations are however important: the front elevation containing the gateway building and so the entrance side, and the long side elevation formed by the walls of the administration building and the car park. The front elevation is asymmetrical, varying in height from one end to the other. Each separate function has its own clearly distinguishable location. Similarly, in the long high side elevation the functions of parking and administration are each individually designed with asymmetry as a characteristic.

Mel'nikov was responsible for both these elevations at least.[2] The building as executed differs in a number of ways from the architect's drawings. The most striking difference is in the design of the long side elevation, where Mel'nikov used a diagonal to weld the two heterogeneous volumes of the car park and the office building into a single unit. The main vertical features of the section containing the car park are two dissimilar bays of windows, with a large round window at one end. The office building contains horizontal bands of windows. The bottom of the circle formed by the round window runs on into a diagonal which rises along the full length of the elevation up to the roof where,

as it were, it breaks away from the elevation at the corner. Below the rising diagonal the appearance of the wall is determined by a rhythmic alternation of vertical narrow glass surfaces and abstract pilasters, contrasting with the broader division into bays of the otherwise relatively flat surface of the wall above the diagonal, behind which lies the car park. Mel'nikov justified the idea of the diagonal line as symbolising travel: "…the path of the tourist is represented as infinite, starting with a curving sweep [round the circular window - O.M.] and then aiming to move off at high speed into space."[3] The design as drawn also shows a car driving up along the diagonal. This may have been a

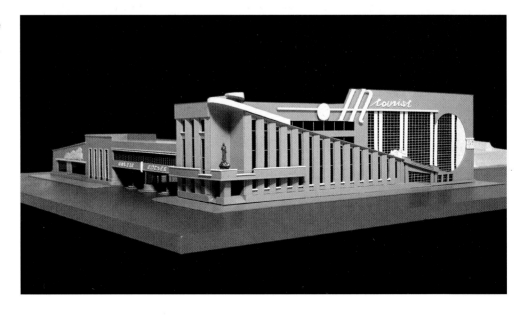

View of the Inturist garage (photo from the Fifties)

Views of the model (realised by I. Klevering)

suggestion for a sculptural decoration for the building, because the upward moving diagonal band was merely a symbolic route: it was simply too narrow for a real motor vehicle. It should be noted here that for Mel'nikov the diagonal, although applied symbolically here, had for years been a tried and tested design feature, a characteristic of his work since the end of the twenties. For example, in his design for the MOPS theatre (1931) the entrance is also flanked by two diagonally rising volumes.

The composition of the facade for the Intourist car park provides an interesting solution at the corner marking of the start of the front elevation. The volume of the corner is deeply indented and crowned by the spiralling end of the diagonal. At first floor level the corner is held together by a balcony-like canopy with a piece of sculpture at its centre. Mel'nikov combines all these design elements to produce a dynamic composition, which however in contrast to most of his work has a rather decorative appearance. All sorts of small details contribute to this effect, for example fragments of frames and the continuation of the top of the wall of the car park above the roof, which also forms a decorative element in the composition. In contrast to most of Mel'nikov's projects, which generally involved a composition of abstract stereometric volumes, his

design for the Intourist car park is a decorative wing.

The design as executed is however much simpler. The diagonal discussed above ends halfway, i.e. at the beginning of the body of the office building, the surface of which is divided up in its own way by double abstract pilasters, all of the same height. The idea of linking the two volumes into a single wall was abandoned. This also meant that the solution for the corner became conventional: an open indented corner with four balconies. No doubt changes in the Soviet Union's cultural policy left their traces here too. Since the car park as executed clearly has nothing like the power of the earlier design drawings, it was decided to build a model of the design with the diagonal continuing along the side elevation. After all, the purpose of this catalogue and exhibition is to bring out as much as possible everything that Mel'nikov could do. If one looks at the architect's whole body of work, this car park is a special case. In no other case does a decorative approach come so strongly to the fore. There still remain a number of distinct versions of the design with the complete diagonal. In one version the low-rise building containing the bus park in the front elevation is provided with decoration in the form of a draped piece of material, in another the same elevation is decorated with statuary

representing a row of three buses. The fact that the three buses provide an immediate indication of the function of the part of the building to which they are applied, made this the obvious choice. The choice also made the model easier to interpret correctly.

In the construction of the Bakhmetevskaja bus depot and the Novo-Rjazanskaja goods vehicles park, glass is represented by plastic with black paint on the back. The same principle is also applied in this reconstruction, except in the frontage of the car park. It was essential to make visible the fact that the slope of the symbolic diagonal is the same as the slope of the ramps ascending behind the glass.

The low-rise building in which buses were parked and which provided accommodation for the workshops is coloured white, mainly because this part of the building was reconstructed on the basis of too little information. For the same reason part of the frontages to the inner courtyard have also been left white and have not been worked out in any greater detail. In particular we know nothing about openings in these frontages. The model places particular emphasis on the two elevations in which we recognise Mel'nikov's hand, the front elevation and the long side elevation containing the diagonal band. Both elevations are relatively simple to

understand from the drawings and so were straightforward to reconstruct. A long time was spent choosing the colour for these elevations. Nowadays the building as executed is painted light green and white. It cannot be assumed with any certainty that these are the original colours. Although sufficient justice is done to the powerful plasticity of the elevations by executing the model entirely in white, it was decided to try to achieve contrast by the use of colour, the colour being represented by grey. The difference in plasticity below and above the diagonal is so intense that it was decided to keep the colour of both parts of the elevation the same. The effect of light and shade produced by the rhythmic alternation of windows and pilasters below the diagonal has a powerful influence on the colour. The lack of deep shadows in the flat treatment of the portion of the elevation above the diagonal provides its own contrast.

It might be supposed that, as in the present-day building, the grey sections of the elevations were interspersed with white elements. It was precisely to do justice to these white elements that the choice was made to have a model in which a single colour, in this case grey, provides all the contrast necessary. The frontage as it is today was used as a model to enable a consistent set of rules

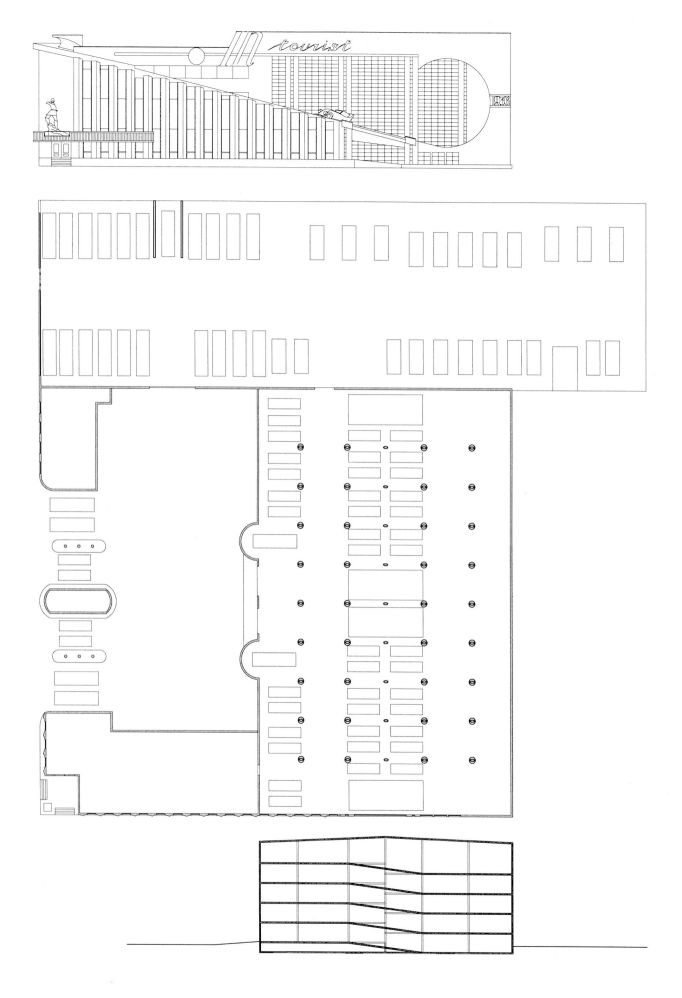

Inturist garage, 1933-1936
(reconstruction by I. Klevering)
scale 1:600 and 1:300

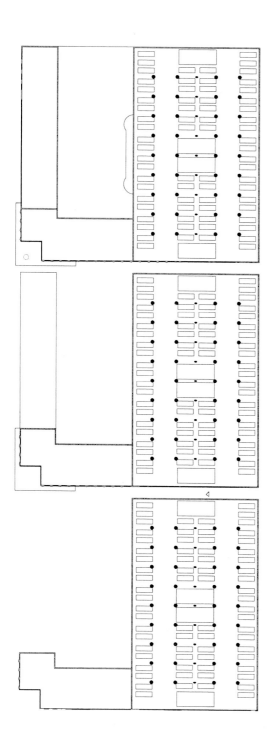

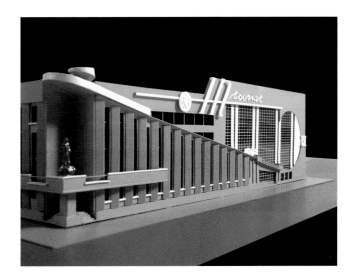

to be followed in the painting of
the white elements.
Otakar Máčel, Robert Notrott

[1] K.S. Mel'nikov, *Arkhitektura
moej žizni. Tvorčeskaja
koncepcija. Tvorčeskaja praktika*,
Moskva 1985, p. 18; Ju.Ja.
Gercuk, A.A. Strigalev,
*Konstantin Mel'nikov. Risunki i
proekty*, Moscow 1989, p.37.
[2] See F.S. Starr, *Mel'nikov. Solo
Architect in a Mass Society*,
Princeton 1978, pp. 190-193; A.
Ferkai, *Konsztantyin Melnyikov*,
Budapest 1988, p. 25, figs. 30-31;
S.O. Khan-Magomedov,
Konstantin Mel'nikov, Moscow
1990, pp.114-117.
[3] K.S. Mel'nikov, *Arkhitektura
moej žizni*, op.cit., p. 180.

1934

**Competition Project
for the Commissariat
of Heavy Industry
(Narkomtjažprom)**

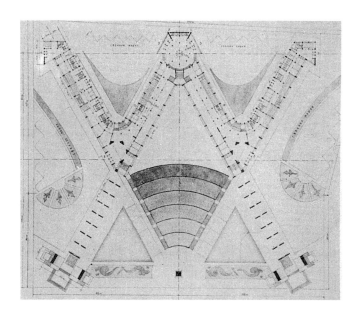

"Socialism is based on heavy industry. The Commissariat of Heavy Industry (Narkomtjažprom) should therefore be housed in a building of monumental proportions.

The spatial solution shown in the design is a concertina structure subordinated to the main axis of Red Square. External staircases, which lead from Red Square to the centre of the building over a deep excavation, create astounding depth which reinforces the monumental character of the building. The staircases can also be used during mass rallies held in Red Square.

The sharp composition of the diamond-shaped excavation, 16-storeys deep, emphasises the monumental scale.

If the October revolution festivities are held at night, this excavation will allow the creation of extremely powerful lighting effects, such as the spotlighting of the rallies and the total perspective of the Square.

The building facades embody the industrial theme in general, while different parts of the building contain compositions on this theme.

The plan of the building is set out in the form of two Roman numeral V's placed side by side, their vertexes pointing towards Red Square. The building lies on the same axis as the Lenin Mausoleum. From a planning and compositional point of view,

a 16-storey diamond-shaped excavation is to be dug out in the central area between the two V's. To reach the bottom, visitors will use stairways leading down from Red Square (departments), Il'inka Street (the library) and Sverdlov Square (the hotel). Courtyards with car parks, porches (entrances) and other service areas for the building, adjoining the Bljukher Lane, will fill the internal space of the V's.

Entrances to the various departments of the Commissariat will be generally situated in the central part of the building facing Bljukher Lane. The building will be accessible from all sides with the planned use of traffic signs and parking facilities.

Because it keeps within the confines of the site the project can be realised without demolishing the GUM building or any other large buildings. The main facade faces Red Square; the Sverdlov Square and Il'inka facades play a subordinate role, without, however, disrupting the general composition and without losing their intensity.

Being completely integrated, the Bljukher Lane facade reflects its 'main entrance' character and serves as the fixing point for the main road to Lubjanka Square. In the design, all entrances to the Narkomtjažprom House shown on the ground floor level are divided according to the function of the department.

The offices for cultural and household services will have its entrance on the Bljukher Lane side; the entrance will have its own internal courtyard with a car park.

Each group of offices will have a separate lobby and cloakroom for employees and visitors, as well as its own staircases and lifts. Bathrooms, toilets, smoking rooms etc. are shown on each floor.

The ground floor divides the volume of the building into two main areas:

a) the area above ground level,

which will house the chief commissar's office, the departments and sections, a large public restaurant and a group of offices for cultural services;

b) the area below ground level, which will house 'trusts' (enterprise groups with centralised management), various service areas, such as the library, pantries, kitchens and an exhibition hall/museum. This part of the building will still receive natural light because of the excavation.

The main entrance lobby is

located on floor 0 [the ground floor] facing Red Square. The stairways leading to the entrance will be equipped with escalators. In total the building will have 41 floors above ground level and 16 floors below ground level.

The chief commissar's offices are located on floor +1. The chief commissar and members of conference presidiums will access the building through a special entrance with a lift. Functional departments and management boards will be located in the central area of floors +2 – +13 and on the whole area of floors +14 – +38, and they will be vertically connected to each other and with the chief commissar's offices. The offices of associations and 'trusts' will occupy the floors below ground level (–16 to –1) along both sides of the diamond-shaped cavity. The hotel with its main entrance on Sverdlov Square will occupy 13 above ground floors in the left wing of the first 'V'.

The same left wing of the first 'V' will also house the hospital clinics (on 7 floors) with separate lobbies for visitors, staff and a children's ward on the Bljukher Lane side. The staircases of the hospital clinics and hotel ending on the floor +13 will separate these areas from the upper floors (the offices of the commissariat). Floors +39, +40 and +41 in the right wing of the second 'V' are planned for the workers social club (large hall), which will have

its main entrance on the ground floor level. The workers social club can be connected to the commissariat offices by means of internal staircases.

The library will occupy 13 floors of this right wing, some rooms on the first 3 floors of the library will face Il'inka Street.

The first three floors below the hospital clinics (right wing of the first 'V') will be given to the nursery.

The large public restaurant with all its rooms will be situated on floors +39 – +40 in the left and right wings of the first 'V'. The lifts (floor +39) will connect the distribution area of the central kitchen with satellite distribution areas in the centre of the building, which in turn are connected to the dining halls.

The construction materials: metal framework and reinforced concrete. The foundations will be of reinforced concrete. Staircases will be made of fireproof materials, supported by steel strings. Floor panels will be made of reinforced concrete and iron (structure), with (wooden) parquet flooring. Service room floors will be covered with cement or tiles."
K.S. Mel'nikov, 1934[1]

According to Starr, the design was influenced by, among other things, the atmosphere of the cultural revolution and the first Five-Year Plan, which was to completely industrialise the Soviet Union. A decisive role was played in this by the

People's Commissariat of Heavy Industry. Since the commissariat urgently needed a new building, a competition was announced in 1934.

With its overproportionate size, Mel'nikov's monumental design completely dominates Red Square, which also undergoes a shift in orientation from the Kremlin to the People's Commissariat Building—a shift in significance also in Moscow's cityscape, as it were, from the old political centre of power to the new industrial administration. An architectural and, at the same time, symbolic connection between the Kremlin on Red Square and the seat of the industrial administration so important for the underdeveloped country is created by two gigantic staircases leading from the level of the square up to the 16th floor. The stairs are accessed through portals shaped like giant roller bearings and equipped with (no doubt unfeasible) escalators, which are to show clearly the ascent of the Soviet Union via industrialisation. Ascending the staircase, the gaze of the observer is directed to allegorical figural sculptures. Once again, after the design of the Palace of Soviets completed three years earlier, Mel'nikov demonstrates his passion for the *architecture parlante*: the visual representation of meaning becomes the basis for the entire design.

With this design foreshadowing socialist realism, Mel'nikov celebrates both heavy industry and the first Five-Year Plan of the Communist Party.

Available Plans

Since this design represents a preliminary draft that was never elaborated further, there is very little planning material in existence. The following was available: a greatly reduced floor plan of the ground floor; a building cross section; two elevations and two perspective views.

Except for the height of the building no measurements were present, and there were often great differences between drawings, e.g. in the elaboration of the figures, the wheels, the top of the building, or the arrangement of the windows. There were absolutely no statements regarding the north-east elevation.

A smaller test model served to clarify differences of level, staircase connections, and building structure. CAD plans with more exact measurements were then reconstructed on the basis of existing depiction. A scale of 1:500 was selected because of both the enormous size of the building and the dearth of statements about the elaboration of detail. This scale allows, however, along with the depicted Kremlin wall and Lenin mausoleum (1929-1930 by A.V. Ščusev) an impression to be given of both the effect made in

*Views of the model
realised by K. Filbert,
M. Ledermann)*

the cityscape and the desired symbolic effect of the 'speaking' elements of the design, e.g. the Roman 'five' of the ground plan and the insignias of industrialisation. Since, however, the goal was to create a building model rather than an urban development model, a conscious decision was made to forego

depiction of the buildings bounding Red Square. Thus, solely the north-west edge formed by the Historical Museum of Sherwood and Semenov (1874-1883) was indicated on the baseplate. Following extensive discussions, the two allegorical monumental sculptures at the top of the

building were depicted only schematically. The material used was maple, mainly solid, but also as multiplex board and as veneer. In this manner the sculpted parts could be adequately shaped and the surface structure of the natural stone siding could be expressed. This material, which is warmer

than the smooth polystyrene, also reflects Mel'nikov's turn away from the cold rationalism of his constructivist contemporaries. The principle tools used were the circular saw, sanding machine, and CNC milling machine. The north-east facades were not given further detail, since absolutely no

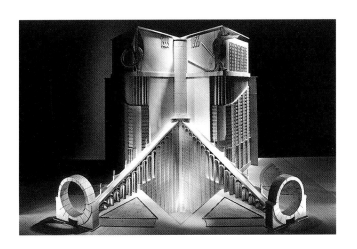

information exists about them; in
any case, since they were most
likely supposed to correspond to
a large degree to the south-west
facades, an elaboration of these
facades would have brought no
new information to light.

[1] Published in *Arkhitektura
SSSR*, no. 11, 1934, pp. 16-17.

*Competition project for the
popular Commissariat of Heavy
Industry, 1934
(reconstruction by K. Filbert,
M. Ledermann) scale 1:2400*

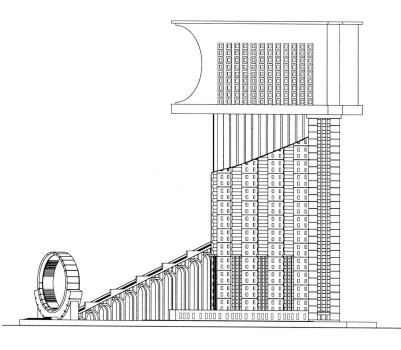

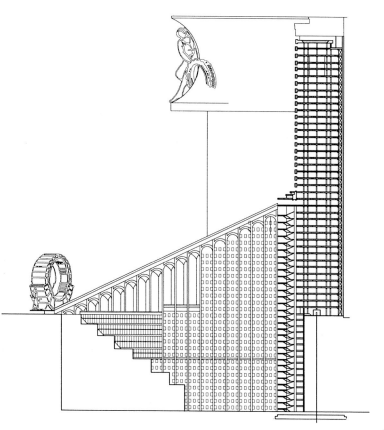

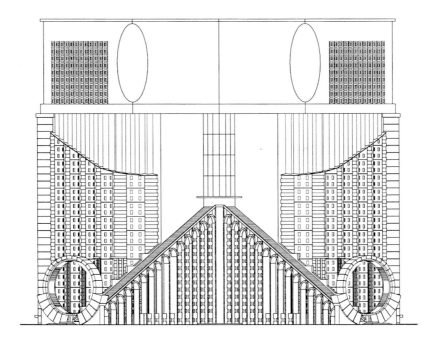

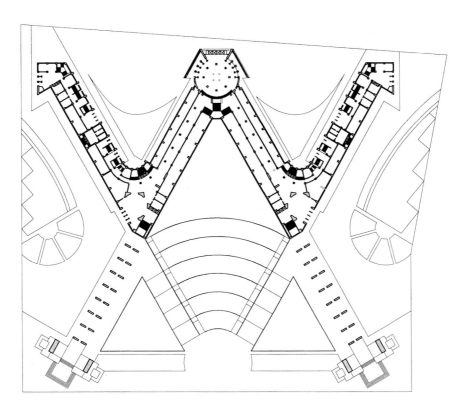

**Proposal for the
Development
of Kotel'ničeskaja
and Gončarnaja
Embankments**

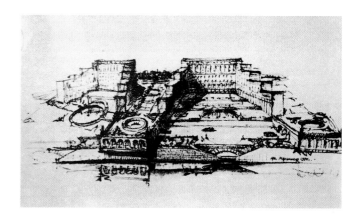

"The site along the
Kotel'ničeskaja and Gončarnaja
Embankments proposed for
housing development is
bordered by the line of the
Moskva River.
Enrichment of the river basin
resulting from construction of
the Moskva-Volga channel raises
the significance of the
embankment as an element of
architectural and artistic
waterway design.
The Proletarskij district where
the embankments are situated
belongs to the industrial zone of
Moscow. Therefore special
attention has been given to the
task of linking the district to the
centre. One should not consider
the embankments separately,
outside of the context of the
entire network of the district. The
millions of cubic metres to be
developed in the city centre and
along the riverbank offer the
solution to the essential
architectural issues: to raise
housing and cultural standards
of workers and to transform the
embankments into most scenic
places of the capital serving as a
model and example for the entire
city development.
The composition of the housing
estates on the embankments has
to express not only a creative
enthusiasm, but also the
keenness to develop a new way
of life. Maximal utilisation of the
aesthetic riverside perspective
constitutes one of the essential
conditions for the performance
of this task. Thanks to the way
they fold out, the apartment

blocks extend (visually) up the
full height of the embankment
giving the architectural form a
rich means of expression.
With several wide, green
boulevards running over, parallel
and perpendicular to the river's
edge, the proposal emphasises
the favourable natural conditions
of the embankments, i.e., their
high profile.
The boulevards are a
continuation of the Il'ic Allée,
and with their greenery and
fountains, they hold the whole
composition together at the
river's edge.
A new highway will be built in
order to improve the
infrastructure within the
proletarian centre of Moscow. Its
direction will closely follow the
line of the Moskvorečkaja
Embankment and the Palace of
Labour situated on it.
This planned road, offering a
number of convenient transit
shortcuts, will go through the top
(and thus the most spectacular)
point of the Svivaja hill, from
which a view over the
surrounding landscape—
Taganskaja Square, the Palace of
Labour, the Kremlin—is opened
up.
The boulevards will run up to the
river's edge ending by hanging
gardens and restaurants, which
will further accentuate the
intimate and cosy character of
the neighbourhood and also
differentiate the longitudinal and
transversal traffic.
To preserve existing housing and
also for compositional reasons

the Sadovoje Kol'co (Garden
Ring) will be moved somewhat
aside in the direction of the
Kremlin.
The main Radiščevskaja road will
remain intact. Volodarskogo
Street will be straightened and
built up with residential houses
with arcade outlets to the
boulevards and the riverbank.
The embankment will be
furnished with spectacular
terraced quay-sides. The building
line is set at 10 meters.
The overall area of the district is
235,000 square metres, the
development area—24,000
square metres, the site coverage
is 11%, the building density—850
man/hectare.
The proposed residential
housing will have a trapezoid
shape, the longest side aligning
the waterfront.
With the topographical features
of the site in mind the houses are
designed to fold out in two
layers down the slope. Each
layer will feature rooftop solaria
and cascading fountains.
Number of storeys: 5 to 10.
Compass point orientation:
south, south-west, south-east.
The way the apartment buildings
fold out will allow the residents
to see the river, feel the air, sun
and space.
The line of Volodarskogo Street
will contain apartment buildings
of 6-8 storeys. The internal area
of these buildings will be utilised
for interior courtyards, a sports
ground, household yards etc.
Child welfare institutions and
shops will occupy the ground

floors. The embankment will
accommodate refreshment
facilities—cafés and
restaurants—which will form a
part of the composition along
with boulevards and hanging
gardens.
Total development volume:
937,000 cubic metres. Total living
space: 180,000 cubic metres.
With a norm of 9 square metres
per person the total occupancy
of the embankment quarter will
be 20,000 people.
In this way the embankments
will become some of the most
spectacular parts of the capital.
Their design will complete the
major arterial road which will
pass by the Palace of Labour on
its way to the Palace of Soviets.
The embankments will present
the central show points of
socialist Moscow to be admired
from the riverside. Natural
environmental resources—such
as air, space, cleanness, beautiful
wide perspectives, vegetation:
parks, boulevards; sun: rooftop
solaria, proper compass point
orientation, grounds; water: the
central river feature, pools,
fountains, cascades—are
perfectly located for use by the
residents of the district.
The scheme presents a solution
for the arrangement of the
development as a systematic
whole: Taganskaja Square, the
embankments, the Palace of
Labour, the centre. It also
permits a clear-cut distinction
between different types of traffic
and communication,
emphasising and arranging the

Project for a complex on the Kotl'ničeskaja and Gončarnaja riverside, 1934

parade/public side of it. And last but not least, the project is feasible and cost-efficient because: 1) metro and underground communication lines remain intact; 2) the project can be phased in a planned way, each phase being a complete element; 3) new construction is possible without demolishing old houses; 4) the landscape profile is optimally utilised which guarantees minimal excavation.

Proposal for the Development of Kotel'ničeskaja and Gončarnaja Embankments by architect K.S. Mel'nikov, with participation of architects Volod'ko, V.M. Lebedev, D.V. Razova and Trankvilickij."

K. S. Mel'nikov, 1934[1]

The area bounded by the Jauza River and Sadovoje Kol'co lies on the high bank of the Moskva River. Its structural layout started to take shape in the period when the city of Moscow did not exist as such. The steep slope and ancient roads influenced the layout. As was common in Moscow at the time, numerous craft communities, churches, monasteries, and vast private estates all joined on to each other in this one area. The most prominent sites, from the compositional point of view, were assigned to the churches. The churches stuck out against the background of low buildings that descended down to the river, thus creating a scenic panorama of the left riverbank.

The steep slopes were the breeding grounds for many small districts divided by narrow winding lanes. The Moskva River embankment had no architectural design in the traditional sense of the word, and was used merely as a back exit for large estate gardens and small craftsmen's courtyards. The nineteenth century saw the coming of small industrial enterprises which used the river for goods transportation. The development of respectable estates took place mainly along Gončarnaja (Volodarskogo) Street which ran along the crest of the hill. The medieval character of the area was somewhat altered in the Classical period: ancient buildings were reconstructed in a new style, at times becoming a full embodiment of Classical *château* canon. The hierarchical planning principles for particular compositions, and the urban landscape in general, remained unchanged up until the first decades of the twentieth century.

Due to its elevated position, which made it visible from quite a distance, the area has always played an important part in the shape of urban development in Moscow. For many years its panorama as seen from the Jauza Bridge has been considered one of the most spectacular views of the city. The 'New Moscow' proposal envisaged active reconstruction of the right bank, to the west of

the Jauza River mouth. However, in the early Thirties, urban development policy changed: the Kotel'ničeskaja and Gončarnaja Embankments received the status of active reconstruction zones. The underlying reason for the decision was the idea of laying a new highway from the city centre to Taganskaja Square and putting an end to the prevalence of small wooden houses no longer of any further use. Obviously, the role of the area in the urban development structure of Moscow was also an important factor, as the new development was to embody the image of a new socialist city.
In 1934-1935 various architects presented draft proposals for the development of the Kotel'ničeskaja and Gončarnaja Embankments.
A. Ščusev as well as the Vesnin brothers in collaboration with M. Ginsburg proposed their own variants, as did the Mossovet Architect's Office directed by K.S. Mel'nikov.
In the proposal of this office the main compositional accent was shifted from the hilltop, featuring a couple of churches and a tall ch,teau with a belvedere, to the mouth of the Jauza River. The idea was to make the area a kind of gateway for the highway to Taganskaja Square. Residential buildings were set facing towards the river, in broad terraces down the slope. The author used the full extend of the sloping landscape for the development of various

sophisticated facilities such as systems of stairs and walkways suspended over one of the highways running parallel to the river bank. The development principle as proposed by the author was to a certain extent analogous to the picturesque structure of the old lanes, which were to be modified and thus completed in terms of composition and meaning. These lanes, running down to the embankment, would receive a new aesthetic quality. Retaining the main compositional scheme, Mel'nikov sketched two possible solutions for a new system of spaces and facilities, one being presented as a model, the other being presented with graphics. As we all know, the proposal was never implemented. Later, the principle use of apartment blocks would prevail in the development of this area: the multi-storey apartment blocks would be set along the river, their interior areas serving as convenient courtyards. In the early Fifties the Jauza mouth was marked by the construction of a Moscow skyscraper designed by the architect D. Čečulin.
The concept for the development of the embankments' area was not put into practice either. New blocks are still standing next to left over fragments of the historical city, preserving in many ways a medieval structure. The vast dimensions of the planned development area meant it was necessary to produce a model on a very small

scale if the whole area was to be included.
The development proposal given shape in the model is also represented in the general model for the development for Moscow city centre. This shows the significance of the project for the urban reconstruction programme, as well as its influence on the composition and on the perception of large city districts.
The large model clearly illustrates Mel'nikov's dialogue with the principles and design tools of the Classical heritage. Post-1923 Soviet architecture aimed to utilise this heritage to create large urban developments. The tempered rhythm of the housing units splits the whole site into several autonomous complexes. In this way, the complete symmetry of the housing units and symmetry in the classical sense of integrity and balance, became the main principles of the proposal. Repetition in the terrace layout, round shaped facilities, square spaces on the embankment pavilion level, and parks situated behind the matchbox-shaped housing units, a repeating rhythm of pilasters and stairs - as well as many other details— correspond exactly to the 'utilisation of the Classical heritage'.
However, this well-balanced and calm character only applies to the planning system of the whole development, and not to its spatial composition, which is set

out according to Mel'nikov's dynamic scenario. The matchbox-shaped apartment blocks look like a staircase when seen from the side, and their perspective can ultimately be perceived as expressive. Central prismatic towers oppose each other with sharp edges, creating tension in the centre of the whole development, their diverging sides forming diagonal rays, which possess such a compositional power that they hold the whole Zamoskvoreč'e and the north-western segment Moscow city centre together. Space cascades down from the upper terraces of the staircase boulevards, leaping down to the river, and crossing the channel with ease, before opening out towards Zamoskvoreč'e on the horizon. Mel'nikov's perspectives are full of expression. The model clearly demonstrates the significance of the whole development as a pivotal factor in the urban composition. Thanks to its openness towards the city and the diagonal location of the matchbox-shaped apartment blocks, the whole development, rising up from the low plateau of Moscow city centre, spans both riverbanks without dominating the surrounding buildings.
According to the concept of the proposal, the whole embankment development, with its scale matching the Kremlin and the Saviour's Temple, would become another important city feature which would push the

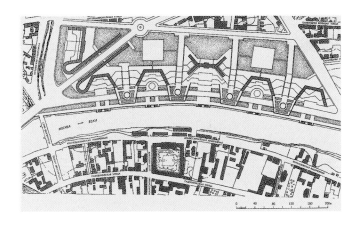

Reconstructions of the area of the Kotel'ničeskaja riverside in the Thirties and localization of the project in its first version (Ju. Volčok, E. Nikulina)

Masterplan and elevation in the second version of the project (re-drawn by P. Nozdračeva)

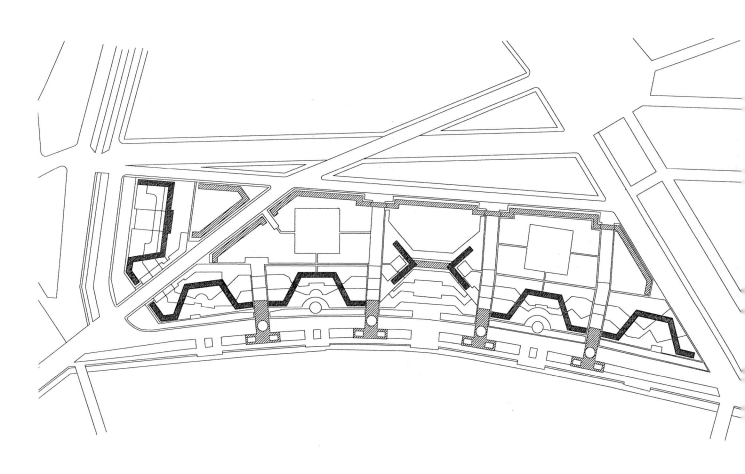

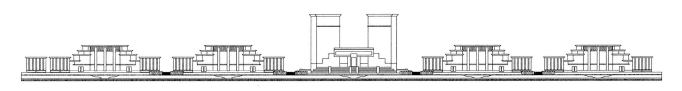

*Views of the model
(realised by A. Šadrin with
A. Pankratova)*

development of the city eastwards.

The proposal also puts forward a solution for the organisation of the east-west traffic links. For instance, the diagonal highway running from the Jauza side would connect Taganskaja Square (the eastern transportation hub) through the city centre to Arbatskaja Square in the west.

In his proposal Mel'nikov offered a solution of another difficult problem for Moscow, namely the problem of being a river city. Embankments occupied by traffic would cut the residents off from the water. In the proposal, provision is made for flyovers suspended over the highway, open spaces leading from the apartment blocks to a green pedestrian embankment and to the river itself. Many ideas expressed in the proposal are still relevant today.

The development proposal for the embankment is included in the model of the centre of Moscow.

Jurij Volčok, Elena Nikulina, Aleksandr Šadrin

1 Published in *Arkhitektura SSSR*, 1934, no. 4, p. 26-27.

"The buildings on Bol'šaja Dmitrovka Street, parallel to the boulevards, form an angle in the sky with the broad and gently sloping staircase that leads to the front yard. In the middle of the yard there is a flower bed surrounded by a restaurant, games rooms, offices, and other essential domestic facilities. The buildings consist of separate areas connected by a common ground floor; the side facing the boulevard has a row of mirror-plated windows. All residents will use one common entrance by going up a monumental staircase at the corner. Every flat, including those that look on to the yard, will have three aired walls and large, open balconies with a view of the street below. Architecture combines imaginative design and a natural living form for the dwellings themselves; the form is created by air, which circulates between the buildings through gaps in the cornice, and is enriched by the sun falling on the fluffy petal-shaped balconies."
K.S. Mel'nikov, 1935[1]

The following changes were made in Mel'nikov's design sketches[2]: the balcony form had to be altered for functional reasons so that the balcony door of the floor below it could be opened; the exotic-looking ornaments of the roof area were consistently applied to the adjoining facade design underneath; formal considerations were the decisive factor for the change; the western and southern facade had to be adapted to fit the ground plan; functional and constructional considerations were decisive in this case. A reconstruction scale of 1:200 was chosen: firstly, in correspondence to the low level of detail exactness in the existing plans; secondly, in order to obtain a defensible size for the entire complex that would also preserve the effect desired by the architect. In order to enable the most precise depiction of the roof ornaments and facade arrangement with a defensible expenditure of time and resources, polystyrene was chosen as the material. These polystyrene parts were sprayed with a matte white spray paint in order to create the effect of concrete slabs, which assumably would have been used if the plans had been realised.[3] The individual facade segments were routed with a CNC milling machine according to CAD plans, bent under hot air, and then welded together with chloroform. In order to obtain a lively contrast and weak reflections, glossy photographic paper exposed in various shades of grey was

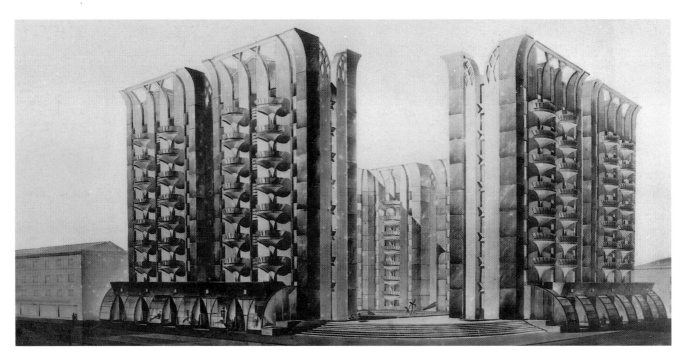

*Project of a housing complex
for Izvestija employees, 1934*

*Views of the model
(realised by B. Frenzel,
St. Ruping, A. Saile)*

pasted behind the window
openings. The blossom-shaped
balconies of pear-wood were
made individually at the lathe
using a template, manually
sanded, and then painted and
glued on. The baseplate was
routed with the CNC milling
machine and glued onto a wood
foundation.
The glass bodies of the shops
consist of dull-cut solid acrylic
glass.

[1] From K.S. Mel'nikov,
Arkhitektura moej žizni.

*Tvorčeskaja koncepcija.
Tvorčeskaja praktika*, Moskva
1985, pp. 225-226.
[2] The available plans are the
followings: 1. ground plan of the
complex without inner courtyard,
shops, and relationship to street
ink plan drawn to scale, partially
furnished, with length and width
of building unit; 2. floor plan of a
living module ink plan drawn to
scale, partially furnished, without
dimensions; 3. view from the
north of a segment of the
complex sketch drawn to scale,
surfaces drawn in, collage-like; 4.

*Project of a housing complex
for Izvestija employees, 1934
(reconstruction by B. Frenzel,
St. Ruping, A. Saile) scale 1:600*

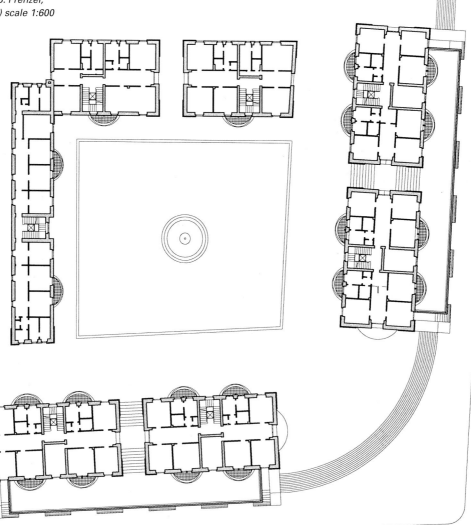

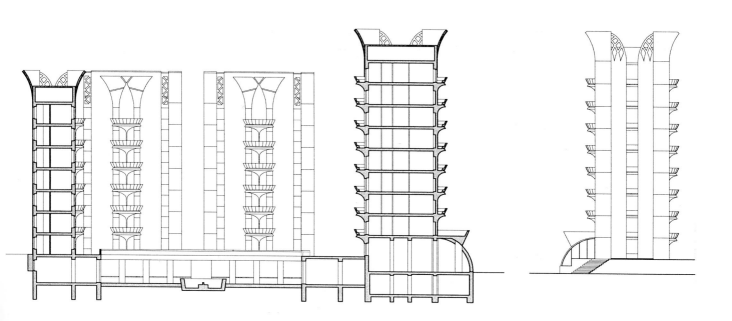

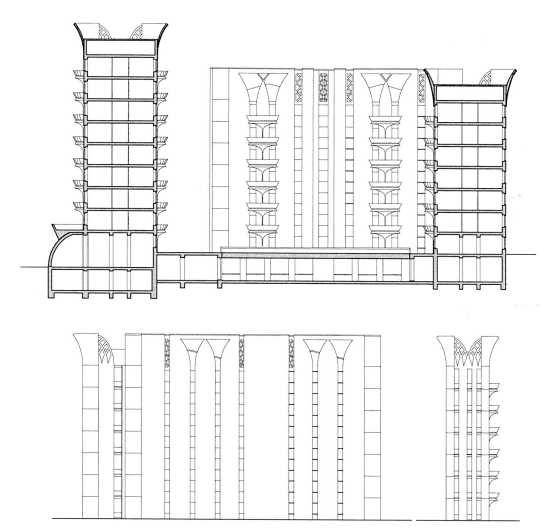

cross section of the complex from the east sketch drawn to scale, depth and facade arrangement of the inner courtyard, sketch of part of the facade; 5. perspective from the north-east earlier sketch not drawn to scale with staircase outline, shops, faÁade arrangement ; 6. perspective from the north-east later sketch not drawn to scale with detailed plan of staircase, shops, facade arrangement; 7. bird's-eye perspective earlier sketch not drawn to scale with ideas for the arrangement of the interior courtyard, fragmentary.

Plans 1, 2, 4, and 6, which were used as the basis for the reconstruction, represent the most reliable and informative sources that do not contradict one another. Plans 3, 5, and 7 have a comparatively small amount of information and contradict one another in the facade arrangement, position of the balconies, dimensions, etc.

[3] Ornamental concrete slabs with large surface areas were used, for example, in 1940 for the Moscow Apartment House on Leningrad Avenue no. 25 (A. Burov, B. Blokhin, A. Kučerov, G. Karmanov).

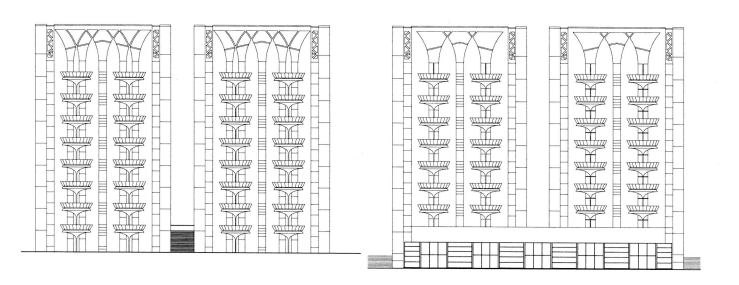

Resume of Works of K.S. Mel'nikov
by Anatolij Strigalev

The following resume has been published in the book K.S. Mel'nikov, Arkhitektura moej žizni. Tvorčeskaia koncepcia. Tvorčeskaia praktika, edited by A.A. Strigalev and I.V. Kokkinaki. Moscow: Iskusstvo, 1985.
This revised version has been updated concerning the archives where the drawings are stored, as well as names of places and institutions that have changed in the last 15 years. Drawings and projects for wich no indication is provided, are contained in the Mel'nikov's family archives.

1914
Vestibule in the Roman Style
Student project
1914
Café-restaurant in the Renaissance style
Student project
1914-1915
House in the Romanesque style
Student project
1915
Service corpus for a railroad station (Railway pavilion for important figures in the Romanesque style)
Student project
1915
Two-storied building for visitors in the Renaissance style
Student project
1915
Dwelling for rent in the Renaissance style
Student project
1915
Artistic-industrial school in the Elisabethan Baroque style
Student project

1915
Provincial church in the Russian style
Student project
1916
Military museum in the classical style
Student project
1916-1917
AMO automobile factory in Moscow (now Likhacev factory, Tjufelev forest). Practical test (exercise) for the diploma, guided by the engineer A.F. Lolejt and by the engineer A.V. Kuznezov. Facade of the main administration block (realisation 1916-1917, ulica Avtozavodskaja, 23). Facades of the Litejt unit, facades of the Kuznezov unit, facades of the press unit (realisation 1916-1917, renovated).
1917
Sanatorium for the officials (officers) injured in Crimea in Empire Style of Zar Aleksandr. Unfinished project for the diploma. Family archive, incomplete.
1918-1919
Ensemble for the Alekseev psychiatric hospital in Moscow (dacia Kanatcikov). Project for the Arkhitekturnaja Planirovočnaja Masterskaja Mossoveta (AMP – Mossovet). Family archive, incomplete.
1918-1922
One family dwelling (sketches of the personal house),1918-1922. Variants with the perpendicular (right angle) disposition of the rooms. Variant with the rectangular plan, divided along the diagonal. Variant with the circular plan. Variant with the oval plan.

1919
Wooden dwelling for three working families. Project for the APM – Mossovet.
1918-1922
The plan for the Butyrskij district of Moscow, (project for the plan ìNew Moscowî). Definition of the limits of the built environment of Butyrskij district according to the regulations of 1918. Preliminary design to the plan of the district.
1919
A workers' communal settlement, 1919. Project for the APM.
1919-1920
Crematorium-columbarium. Competition design for the APM – Mossovet.
1919-20
Palace of People. Competition design for the APM – Mossovet.
1920
Workers' housing. Competition design for the APM – Mossovet.
1922
Plan for the area of Khodynskij field, (design for the plan 'New Moscow'). In collaboration with A.L. Poljakov and I.I. Fidler. MIRM (Museum of History and of Reconstruction of Moscow).
1922-23
Workers' model housing in Moscow (between Serpukhovskaja Street and the first and the second Ščipovskij lane). First level competition design (pseudonym 'Atom', second prize), 1922-23. Second level competition design, 1923.
1923
Palace of Labour in Moscow (plot between the Squares Teatral'naja e Revoljucii e the Tverskaja Street).

Competition design (pseudonym "Nerv").

1923

Makhorka Pavilion at first All-Union Agricultural and Cottage Industries Exposition in Moscow (Neskucnyj park, Moscova riverside). Project on commission. Project of the pavilion. Family archive, incomplete. Built in 1923, the pavilion is dismantled at the end of the exposition. Projects of the exposition-display window, of the manifest, of the emblem of the workers' union of the Makhorka factory for the "Makhorka" pavilion (realised in 1923, no longer existing).

1923

Reconstruction of the Square of Soviet in Moscow. Counter-proposal to the plan "New Moscow". Sketch. Family Archive, a sheet of paper.

1924

Offices of the Moscow unit of Leningradskaja Pravda in Moscow (Strastnaja Square, now Puškin Square). Design for competition on invitation. GNIMA. (Ščusev State Museum of Architecture), a sheet of paper.

1924

Sarcophagus of V.I. Lenin in the Mausoleum on the Red Square. Design for the competition on invitation. February 1924. First prize. Project on commission. Variants nn. 1-4 of June 1924 and n. 5 of 26 June 1924. Realised in July 1924, has remained in the Mausoleum of Lenin until the reconstruction of the interior according to the project of A.V. Ščusev in the Forties. Project n commission. Variants nn. 6-7 of June 1924, n. 8 of 1st of July of 1924.

1924

Headquarters for "Arkos" (anonymous) stock society in Moscow (angle of Il'inka Street and of B. Čerkasskij Lane). Competition design (pseudonym "Vajen Dong"). Variant with the round courtyard. Variant with a rectangular courtyard. Family archive, incomplete.

1924-1926

Sukharevka Market in Moscow (B. Sukharevskij Lane, 9), 1924-1926. Project on commission. Project for the site plan and for the built environment on the market, 1924. Realisation 1924-26. Dismantled in the Thirties. Project for the main building, 1924. Realisation 1924-1926. It has been preserved with

relevant modifications of the facades and with interior alterations. Project of sign for the buildings of the market, 1925. Realisation 1926. No longer existing.

1924-1925

Soviet Pavilion at the "Exposition Internationale des Arts DÈcoratifs et Industriels Modernes" in Paris (Cours la Reine). Project for the competition on invitation, 1924. First prize. Definitive project December 1924 – January 1925. Family archive, incomplete. At the GNIMA, two sheets of copies done in the Sixties following K. S. Mel'nikov's indications. Realisation 1925. The pavilion was dismantled and reconstructed in 1926 on the Avenue Moreau in Paris and used as factory club. No longer existing.

1925

Commercial sector (?Display kiosks) at the Exposition Internationale des Arts Décoratifs et Industriels Modernes" in Paris. (Esplanade des Invalides). Sketches of the project, selected from the competition of 1925. Definitive project 1925. Realisation 1925. No longer existing.

1925

Garage for one thousand cars over Seine. Project on commission. Project of a garage above the bridges of Seine. Project of multistorey garage of cubic shape.

1925

Crematorium in Moscow (Donskaja Street), 1925. Design for competition on invitation for the reconstruction of a church. Second prize. MIRM, two sheets.

1926

Soviet Pavilion at the International Fair in Salonika (Greece), 1926. Project on commission. Realisation 1926. No longer existing.

1926

Baldachin for funeral of L. B. Krasin. Project on commission. Realisation 1926. No longer existing.

1926

Bus garage in Moscow (in the Bakhmetevskaja Street, now Obrazov Street, 19a). Counter-projects on commission. Project of a five-storey garage, 1926 (unknown location). Variant of the project in two blocks, 1926. Family archive, incomplete. In the CANDT, there are drawings made by collaborators of Mel'nikov. Realisation 1928. It has been preserved with some transformations. General layout

and design of the building for mechanics' workshop 1927. Family archive, incomplete. At the Moskovskij Istorico-Arkhitekturnyj Arkhiv, there are drawings done by collaborators authorised by Mel'nikov. Realisation 1928.

1926-1927

Project of the maintenance shops and of the offices of garage. Three variants. Family archive, incomplete. At the Moskovskij Istorico-Arkhitekturnyj Arkhiv, there are drawings done by the collaborators authorised by Mel'nikov (the project has been realised by another architect).

1926-1929

Garage for trucks in Moscow (Novo-Rjazanskaja Street, 27). Project on commission. General layout designs, 1926; variants: A for 100 places; B for 98 places; C for 97 places; D for 106 places; variant for 104 places; E for 93 places; variant for 99 places. General layout designs, 1926, variants n. 3 for 101 places; variants 4-8; horseshoe shaped plan, 1926. Family archive, incomplete. At the Moskovskij Istoriko-Arkhitekturnyj Arkhiv, there are drawings produced by collaborators of Mel'nikov. Realisation 1926-1929. It has been preserved with significant modifications.

1927

House of K.S. Mel'nikov (Krivo-Arbatskij Lane, 10). Family archive, incomplete. Moskovskij Istorico-Arkhitekturnyj Arkhiv. Realisation 1927-1929. It has been preserved with slight modifications (the furniture, the finishing of the bedroom have been lost, and the plan of the ground floor has been partially modified).

1927

Project of the Club Rusakov. Family archive, incomplete. Moskovskij Istorico-Arkhitekturnyj Arkhiv. Realisation 1927-1929, with modifications of the original design. It has been preserved with alterations (some windows have been closed, the sign on the facade and the mechanism which separated the halls have been eliminated, the colours, the finishing have been changed, and more). Project with location of the same project in Novo Rjazanskaja Street, 1926-1927. Family archive, incomplete.

1927

Zuev factory workers' club (Lesnaja

Street). Project on commission. Family archive, incomplete.

1927

Frunze factory workers' club (Berežkovskaja Embankment, 28). Project on commission. Project of the building of the club, 1927. Family archive, incomplete. At the Moskovskij Istoriko-Architekturnyj Arkhiv there are drawings of collaborators of Mel'nikov, four sheets. Realisation with modifications. Project of the canteen of the club, 1928, three sheets. Realisation 1928. No longer existing. Project of reconstruction of the gym of the club. Beginning of the Sixties. Family archive, incomplete.

1927

Svoboda factory workers' club (now Gor'kij Palace of Culture) in Moscow (Vijataskaja, 41). Project on commission. Family archive, incomplete. GNIMA, four sheets. Project of the building, version with the transversal section of the ecliptic hall. Project of the building, version with the transversal section of the polygonal hall. Realisation 1929-31, with modifications of the original design. It has been preserved, but completely modified. Project of the canteen of the club, 1928.

1927-1928

Club of the China factory Pravda in Dulevo (now Likino-Dulevo, zone Orekovo-Zuevskij, region of Moscow, 8). Project on commission. Family archive, incomplete. Realisation 1928-1930, with insignificant modifications.

1927-1929

Club of Municipal Union of Moscow (Stromynskaja Square, 10 and Novo-Rjazanskaja). Project on commission.

1927-1970

Kaučuk factory workers' club in Moscow (Pljuščkha Street, 64). Project on commission. Project of the building of the club, 1927. Family archive, incomplete. At the Moskovskij Istoriko-Arkhitekturnyj Arkhiv, there are drawings of the collaborators of Mel'nikov, four sheets. Realisation 1927-29. It has been preserved with insignificant modifications. Project of the canteen of the club, 1928. Realised in 1928. No longer existing.

1928

Administrative Centre in Ul'janovsk. Counter-project. In collaboration with G. V. Jurghenson (responsible for the organisation and for the scientific part of the project).

1929

Monument to Christopher Columbus, Santo Domingo (Dominican Republic). International competition design. First level.

1929

Burevestnik factory workers' Club in Moscow (Ogorodnaja Street, now 3rd Rybinskaja Street, 17). Project on commission. Family archive, incomplete. In the Moskovskij Istoriko-Arkhitekturnyj Arkhiv there are drawings of Mel'nikov's collaborators. Realisation 1929-1932, with modifications of the original design. It has been conserved with insignificant alterations.

1929

Reconstruction of ZPKiO (Central Park of Culture and Rest) in Moscow (Park Neskučnyj). Project on commission, preserved in the archive of the office of ZPKiO. Location of the project unknown. Plan for the area of ZPKiO. Partial realisation of the project at the beginning of the Thirties. Preserved only partially. Project for the fountain located at the entrance to the ZPKiO.

1929

Project of the dwellings in row (communal house?). Project on commission. Variants with disposition based on central layout and with round shaped cells in plan. Variant with block disposition and circular cells. Family archive, incomplete. Variant with rectangular module.

1929-1930

Green City, near Moscow (in Puskin area). Project on commission in the competition on invitation. Family archive, incomplete. General plan for the "Green City". Project of the station-kursaal (garage). Partially realised as experimental project in 1930. No longer existing. Project for the district hotel. Realisation of the dwelling cell in 1930. No longer existing. Project of the central hotel. Project of the employees' block. Project of the tourist pavilion (conical variant). Project of the tourist pavilion (flat roof variant).

1930

Reconstruction of Moscow Chamber Theatre (Tvereskoj Boulevard, 23). Project on commission. Family archive,

incomplete. Realisation in the beginning of the Thirties. Partially preserved.

1930

Maintenance shop of the bicycle factory in Khar'kov, 1930. Project on commission. In collaboration with G. V. Jurghhenson. Private house of the architect I. K. Zaporožez in Moscow. Project on commission.

1930-1931

Frunze Military Academy in Moscow (Devic'e Pole). Project on commission for the competition on invitation. GNIMA, one sheet.

1931

Theatre of the Moscow Regional Council of Professional Unions (MOSPS) in Moscow (Karetyj District). Project on commission for the competition on invitation.

1931

General plan for the Park of Culture and Rest (ZPKiO) in Moscow (area of Neskučnyj garden, Lenin and Lužnikov hills). Project for the competition on invitation.

1931

Reconstruction of the Arbat Square in Moscow. Project on commission.

1931-1933

Palace of Nations in Moscow (Prečistenskaja Riverside). Project based on the program for the competition reserved for the designers of the Palace of Soviets.

1932

Reconstruction of the Sverdlov Square in Moscow (now Teatral'naja). Project on commission.

1932

Military School for the pupils of the VZIK in Moscow (Kremlin). Project on commission.

1932-1933

Palace of Labour in Taskent. Project on commission for a competition on invitation. First prize, 1932. Project on commission 1932-1933.

1933

Personal Exposition of K. S. Mel'nikov at the Fifth Triennial of Milan (Palace of Arts). Project of the exhibition layout.

1934

School-model in Moscow (Sukharevskij Lane). Project worked out in the atelier of architectonic and urban design n. 7 of Mossovet. Co-author A.A. Sil'cenkov.

1934

Replanning of Kotel'ničeskaja and

Gončarnaja Embankments in Moscow. Project on commission for the competition on invitation, worked out in the atelier of architectonic and urban design n. 7 of Mossovet. Family archive, incomplete.

1934

People's Commissariat of Heavy Industry in Moscow (Red Square). Project on commission for the competition on invitation. Project worked out in the atelier of architectonic and urban design n. 7 of Mossovet. Collaborators: V. M. Lebedev, N. I. Trankvilickij, N. A. Khorjakov. GNIMA, 8 sheets.

1934-1936

Intourist Garage in Moscow, (Suscevskij Val, 33). Project worked out in the atelier of architectonic and urban design n. 7 of Mossovet. Co-author V.I. Kurockin. Family archive, incomplete. There are some documents at the Moskovskij Istoriko-Arkhitekturnyj Arkhiv. Partially realised (the right half of the facade) in the first half of the Thirties. It has been preserved.

1935

"Izvestia" living quarters in Moscow (corner between the Strastnyj Boulevard and B. Dmitrovka Street), 1935. Project worked out in the atelier of architectonic and urban design n. 7 of Mossovet.

1935

Replanning of Lužniki district in Moscow. Project worked out in the atelier of architectonic and urban design n. 7 of Mossovet.

1935-1936

Soviet Pavilion at the "Exposition Internationale des arts Décoratifs et Industriels Modernes" of Paris. Champs de Mars. Banli embankment). Project on commission for the competition on invitation. Family archive, incomplete.

1936

Plan for the south-western region of Moscow, 1936. Project worked out in the atelier of architectonic and urban design n. 7. Collaborators: V.E. Bykov and V.I. Byckov.

1936

Dwelling with several apartments in Moscow (1st Mescanskaja Street, now Prospect Mira). Project worked out in the atelier of architectonic and urban design n. 7 of Mossovet. Family archive, incomplete.

1936

Quarters of Hydrometereological service of Moscow, Mid–thirities, Family archive, incomplete.

1936

Gosplan Garage in Moscow (Aviamotornaja Street, 44). Project worked out in the atelier of architectonic and urban design n. 7 of Mossovet. Co-author V. I. Kurockin. Location of the project is unknown. Partially realised in the second half of the Thirties. It has been preserved with modifications.

1937

Municipal hospital n. 39 in Moscow. Project worked out in the atelier of architectonic and urban design n. 7 of Mossovet.

1938

Pedestrian crosswalks of Novinskij Boulevard in Moscow. Project worked out in the atelier of architectonic and urban design n. 7 of Mossovet.

1941

Main gate of estate of Sukhanovo, near Moscow. Project on commission .

1941

Wall candlestick for the estate of Sukhanovo, near Moscow. Project on commission. Family archive, incomplete.

1944

"City of the future". Architectonic fantasies.

1944

Building-model for the "Russian bath". Project on commission.

1945

Free-standing "dacha" of wood (cottage). Project on commission. Family archive, incomplete.

1945

General layout and buildings project nearby the Lopasnaja station (Moscow Region). Family archive, incomplete.

1945

Facade design for the four-storey dwelling-model. Project on commission. Family archive, incomplete.

1947

Mjasokombinat Building decorations (kombinat of the meat) Mikojan in Moscow (Mikhailovskij, 4). Project on commission. Project of the gate and of the enclosure fence. Project for the colouring of the building of Mjasokombinat. Partial realisation at the end of the Forties. Haven't been preserved.

1947-1948

Bust of the Hero of the Soviet

Union S. A. Kosak, twice the natural size, in the Iskorost' village (Korosten' city, Zitomir region). Sculpturer S. D. Saposnikov. Realised in 1949.

1949

Central'nye Univermagi interior design in Saratov. Project on commission. Realised with modifications of the project of 1950. No longer existing.

1959

General layout and buildings project of the Vjasovka district, in the Saratov region. Project on commission. Students and professors of Saratovskij Avtozavodskij Institute have collaborated in the design of the buildings.

1951

Reconstruction of the Kirov Square in Saratov. Competition design, second prize.

1951

Railway station of Novosibirsk. Competition design (pseudonym "Deviz"). Family archive, incomplete.

1954

Project of the Masino-Traktornaja Stanzija of Volokolamsk of Moscow region. Project completed with the support of Masino-Arkhitekturnyj Institute. Family archive, incomplete.

1954

Lenin's monument in the electrical station of the Kasinno village (kolkhoz dedicated to the memory of Il'ic) in the Volokolamsk district of Moscow region. Family archive, incomplete.

1954

Monument in honour of the thirtieth universakry of reunification of Ukraine and Russia in Moscow (Square of the Station Kirovskaja, 4). Competition design (pseudonym "Kristall").

1955

Pantheon of the USSR in Moscow (Lenin Hills). Competition design (pseudonym "Svet"). Palace of Congress in Moscow (Lenin hills), 1959. Competition design (pseudonym "Rasnoravnoe").

1962

Soviet Pavilion for the World Fair in New York. Counter-project presented at the competition. Family archive, incomplete. GNIMA, nine sheets.

1967

"Mel'nikov Street", architectural fantasies, 1964. Movie Theatre for children in Moscow (Arbat). Competition design (pseudonym

"L"). Consolation prize.

1967-1973

Universe of architecture, architectural fantasies on the theme of Palace of People (1931-1933) and the Palace of Soviet (1958-1959).

Bibliography

by Maurizio Meriggi and Jurij Volčok

**Principal Guides and Sources
on Moscow Architecture
During the Twenties and Thirties**
I. Antonova, I. Merkert eds.,
Moscau-Berlin, 1900-1950.
Munich- New York-Moscow:
Prestel-Galart, 1995.
V.N. Aruin, A. Manina,
K. Murasov, V. Quilici,
D. Taurina eds., *Architettura nel
paese dei Soviet 1917-1933. Arte di
propaganda e costruzione della
città*. Milan: Electa, 1983.
I.L. Buseva-Davydoviva,
M.V. Nasokina, M.I. Astaf'eva-
Dlugac, *Moskva. Arkhitekturnyj
putevoditel'* (Moscow.
Architectural guide). Moscow:
Strojizdat, 1997.
J.L. Cohen, M. De Michelis, M.
Tafuri, *URSS 1917-1978. La città,
l'architettura – URSS 1917-1978.
La ville, l'architecture*. Rome-Paris:
Officina-L'Equerre, 1978.
C. Cooke, *Russian Avant-garde.
Theories of Art, Architecture and
the City*. London: Academy, 1995.
C. Cooke, I. Kazus', *Soviet
Architectural Competitions 1920s-
1930s*. London: Phaidon, 1992.
A. De Magistris, *Mosca 1900-1950.
Nascita di una capitale*. Milan:
Clup, 1994.
A. De Magistris, *La costruzione
della città totalitaria*, Milan: Clup,
1995.
M. De Michelis, E. Pasini, *La città
sovietica. 1925-1937*. Venice:
Marsilio, 1976.
R. Graefe, Ch. Schädlich, D. W.
Schmidt eds., *Avantgarde I. 1917-
1923. Russisch-sowjetische
architektur*. Stuttgardt: DVA,
1991.
A.V. Ikonnikov, *Arkhitektura

Moskvy XX vek* (Moscow
architecture of the XX century).
Moscow: Moskovskij rabocij,
1984.
S Ju. S. Jaralov ed., *Moskva*
(Moscow). Moscow: Strojizdat,
1979.
S.O. Khan-Magomedov, *Pioneers
of Soviet Architecture*, New York:
Rizzoli International, 1987.
A. Koop, *Ville et revolution.
Architecture et urbanisme
sovietiques des années vingt*. Paris:
Editions Anthropos, 1967.
A. Kopp, *L'architecture de la
période stalinenne*. Grenoble:
Presse universitaire de Grenoble,
1985.
A. Latour, *Mosca. Guida
all'architettura moderna, 1890-
1991*. Bologna: Zanichelli, 1990.
V. Quilici, *Città russa e città
sovietica. Caratteri della struttura
storica. Ideologia e pratica della
trasformazione socialista*. Milan:
Mazzotta, 1976.
V. Quilici ed., *Mosca capitale
dell'utopia*. Milan: Mondadori,
1991.
Ch. Schädlich, D. W. Schmidt
eds., *Avantgarde II. 1924-1937.
Sowjetische architektur*. Stuttgart:
Hatje, 1994.
Several Authors, *Moscou-Paris*.
Paris: Centre George Pompidou,
1979.

**Moscow 1900-1929
The 'New Moscow' Plan
The Moscow Competitions
of 1922-1923**
M.I. Astaf'eva-Dlugac, *Razvitie
teoretičeskoj mysli i principov
sovetskogo gradostroitel'stva v
pervye poslerevoliucionnye gody.

1917-1925* (The Development of
Theoretical Thought and the
Principles of Soviet Urban
construction in the First Post-
Revolutionary Years (1917-1925).
Architectural candidate's
dissertation. Moscow, 1971.
M.I. Astaf'eva-Dlugac, Ju.P.
Volcok, *Moskva stroitsja. Sem
novell ob arkhitektura Moskvy*
(Moscow is being Built. Seven
novells on Moscow architecture).
Moscow: Moskovskij Rabocij,
1983.
*Iz istorii sovetskoj arkhitektury
1917-1925 gg. Dokumenty i
materialy* (From the History of
Soviet Architecture, 1917-1925.
Documents and materials).
ed. K.N. Afanas'ev, compiler,
author of articles and footnotes
V.E. Khazanova. Moscow:
Izdatel'stvo Akademii Nauk SSR,
1963.
*Iz istorii sovetskoj arkhitektury
1926-1932 gg. Dokumenty i
materialy.* (From the History of
Soviet Architecture, 1917-1925.
Documents and materials). ed.
K.N. Afanas'ev, compiler, author
of articles and footnotes V.E.
Khazanova. Moscow: Nauka,
1970.
V.E. Khazanova, *Sovetskaja
arkhitektura pervykh let Oktjabrja.
1917-1925* (Soviet Architecture in
the First Years of the October
Revolution. 1917-1925). Moscow:
Nauka, 1970.
Ju.L. Kosenkova, *Sovetskoe
gradostroitel'stvo kak cast' proekta
"bol'sogo obscestva"* (Soviet Urban
construction as Part of the Project
of "the Great Society"), in *Obrazy
istorii otecestvennoj arkhitektury.*

XX vek (Images of the History of Home Architecture. 20th Century. Moscow: NIITAG, 1996.
Several Authors, *Mastera sovetskoj arkhitektury ob arkhitekture* (Masters of Soviet architecture on architecture). Volume 1. Moscow: Iskusstvo, 1975.

Urban Landscape and City Management.
B.E. Bykov, I.P. Domslak, Ja.A. Kornfel'd, V.L. Kulaka, I.E. Mal'cin, S.Z. Ostrovskaja, N.G. Umanskij, *Arkhitektura rabočikh klubov i dvorcov kul'tury* (Architecture of Workers' clubs and Palaces of Culture). Moscow: Gosudarstvennoe Izdatel'stvo literatury po stroitel'stvo i arkhitekture, 1953.
M.I. Astaf'eva-Dlugac, *Die Erste Allruische Landwirtschafts-ausstelung*, in R. Graefe, Ch. Schädlich, D.W. Schmidt eds., *Avantgarde I. 1917-1923 ...*, op. cit.
W. Benjamin, *Moscau (1927)*, in Id. *Stadtbilder* (Frankfurt on Main: Suhrkamp Verlag, 1955).
T.J. Colton, *Moscow. Governing the Socialist Metropolis*, Cambridge Mass.-London: Belknap Press of Harvard University Press, 1995.
Iz istorii sovetskoj arkhitektury 1926-1932 gg. Dokumenty i materialy. Rabočie kluby i dvorcy kul'tury (From the History of Soviet Architecture, 1917-1925. Documents and materials. Workers' clubs and paleces of Colture). ed.
K.N. Afanas'ev, compiler, author of articles and footnotes
V.E. Khazanova. Moscow: Nauka, 1984.
V.S. Kemenov ed.,*10 rabočikh klubov Moskvy* (10 Workers' clubs in Moscow). Moscow: 1932.
V.E. Khazanova, *Klubnaja žizn' i arkhitektura kluba* (Club life and club architecture). Moscow: Rossijskij Institut Iskusstvoznanija, 1994.
N. Lukhmanov, *Arkhitektura kluba* (Architecture of the Club). Moscow: 1929.
D.W. Schmidt, *Der sowjetische Arbeiterklub als Paraphrase des deutschen Volkhauses. Konzeptionelle Verbindungen bei der Entwicklung eines Bautyps fur die Arbeierbildung*, in Ch. Schädlich, D.W. Schmidt eds., *Avantgarde II. 1924-1937...*, op. cit.
V. Tolstoj, I. Bibikova, C. Cooke, *Street Art of the Revolution*. London: Thames and Hudson, 1990.

Moscow 1929-1932
The Competition for
the 'Green City'
V.E. Khazanova, *Sovetskaja architektura pervoj pjatiletki* (Soviet architecture of the First Five Years Plan). Moscow: Nauka, 1980.
M. Kol'cov, *Dača tak Dača* (Daca so daca)*, in *Pravda*, 30 genuary 1929.
M. Kol'cov, *Zelennyj gorod* (The Green City), in *Revoljucia i kul'tura* 2, 1930.
D.F. Fridman, *Socialističeskij lesnoj kurort* (Socialist resort in the woods), in *Stroitel'stvo Moskvy* 3, 1930.
M.Ja. Ginzburg, *Zelenyj gorod – opyt socialističeskogo rasselenija* (The Green city – an experience of socialist settlement), in *Stroitel'stvo Moskvy* 3, 1930.
M.Ja. Ginzburg, M. Barsc, *Zelennyj gorod. Socialističeskaja rekonstrukcija Moskvy* (The Green City – Socialist reconstruction of Moscow), in *Sovremmennaja Architektura* 1-2, 1930.
La ciudat verde de Moscu, in *A.C.* 1 , January-March 1931.
N. Ladovskij, *Gorod otdycha i socialističeskogo byta* (The city of rest and of socialist *byt*), in *Stroitel'stvo Moskvy* 3, 1930.
Le Corbusier, *Commentaires relatifs à Moscou et à la "Ville Verte", Moscou 12.3.1930*, in J. Cohen, *Le Corbusier et la Mystique de l'URSS. Theories et projets pour Moscou 1928-1936*. Liège: Mardaga, 1987.
K.S. Mel'nikov, *Gorod racionalizirovannogo otdykha* (The city of razionalised rest), in *Stroitel'stvo Moskvy* 3, 1930.
K.S. Mel'nikov, *Avtovokzal "Zelonogo goroda"* (The Bus station of the Green City), in *Zelenyj gorod* 5, 1930.
N. Popov-Sibiriak, *Zelenomu gorodu obscestvennoe vnimanie* (Collective interest in the Green City), in *Stroitel'stvo Moskvy* 8, 1929.
V.N. Simbircev, *Četerie rešenija* (Four solutions), in *Stroitel'stvo Moskvy* 3, 1930.
O.Ju. Smidt, *Cto rešila rabočaja obščestvennost' o planach "zelennogo goroda"* (The decision of the Workers society on the Green City projects), in *Stroitel'naja promyšlennost*, May 1930.

Competitions of Urban-Planning Concepts and the First Rounds of the Palace of the Soviets Competition
M.I. Astaf'eva-Dlugac, Ju. P. Volcok, *Stanovlenie obraza Moskvy*

v proektakh i zamyslakh (The Development of the Image of Moscow in Projects and Concepts), ed. Ju. S. Yaralov Moscow. Moscow: Strojizdat, 1979.
Ju.P. Bocarov, N.F. Guljanickij eds., *Arkhitektura SSSR 1917-1987* (Architecture in URSS. 1917-1987), Moscow: Strojizdat, 1987.
Ju.P. Bocarov, E.A. Sirenko, *Preobrazovanie planirovki Moskvy po General'nomu planu 1935 g.* (The replanning of Moscow according to the General Plan of 1935), in *Arkhitektura v istorii russkoj kul'tury* (Architecture in the Russian Cultural History), issue 2, The Capital city. Moscow: URSS, 1998.
A.V. Ikonnikov, *Utopia e realtà*, in *L'Arca* 27, 1989.
A.I. Morozov, *Konec utopii. Iz istorii iskusstva v SSSR 1930-kh godov* (The End of the Utopia. From the History of Art in the USSR of the 1930s). Moscow: Galart, 1995.
Moscow: V.L. Khajt, *Otečestvennaja arkhitektura v mirom arkhitekturnom processe XX veka* (Home Architecture in the Global Architectural Process of the 20th century) in *Obrazy istorii Otečestvennoj arkhitektury XX vek* (Images of the History of Home Architecture. 20th Century). Moscow: NIITAG, 1996.
S.O. Khan-Magomedov, *Gradostroitel'stvo 1917-1932* (Urban Construction 1917-1932), in *Vseobšaja istorija arkhitektury* (General History of Architecture), vol. 12, part 1. Moscow: Izdatel'stvo Literatury po Stroitel'stvu, 1975.

The International Competition of 1931/1932 for the Palace of the Soviets
E. Norwerth, *Architektura w ZSSR*, in *Architektura i Budowinictwo (Warsaw)* 2, 1933.
A.V. Ikonnikov, *Der Historismus in der sowjetischen Architektur*, in *Konzptionen in der sowjetischen Architektur 1917-1988*, Berlin 1989.
Oude en nieuwe architectuur in Sowjet-Rusland, van Verlosserskerk tot Sowjetpaleis (Old and new Architecture in Soviet Russia, from the Redeemer's church to the Palace of Soviet), in *Bouwkundig Weekblad Architectura* 16, 1932.
Sovetskoe Iskusstvo 11, march 1932.
Several Authors, *Dvorec Sovetov. Materialy konkurs 1957-1959* (The Palace of Soviet. Materials of the

1957-1959 competition). Moscow, 1961.
Several Authors, *Naum Gabo und der Wettbewerb zum Palast der Sowjets Moskau 1931-1933*. Berlin: Berlinische Galerie, 1992.
Several Authors, *Sovetskaja arkhitektura. Ežegodnik 1960* (Soviet architecture 1960 yearbook). Moscow, 1962.

The Competition for a Memorial to Columbus in Santo Domingo
Program and rules of the Competition for the selection of an Architect for the Monumental lighthouse which the nations of the world will erect in the Dominican Republic to the memory of Christopher Columbus. Pan-America Union, 1928.
Program and rules of the second Competition for the selection of an Architect for the Monumental lighthouse which the nations of the world will erect in the Dominican Republic to the memory of Christopher Columbus. Pan-America Union, 1930.
I. Kazus, M. Velikanova, *Storia del concorso per il monumento-faro a Cristoforo Colombo. Santo Domingo. 1929*, in P. Cavellini ed., *Architetti russi per Cristoforo Colombo. Santo Domingo, 1929*. Brescia: Nuovi Strumenti, 1993.

Moscow 1932-1940
The Background to the 1935 General Plan for the Socialist Reconstruction of Moscow
The Architectural Planning Workshops of Moscow City Council (MOSSOVET)
Arkhitekturnye voprosy rekonstrukcii Moskvy. Materialy VII Plenuma pravlenija SSA SSSR. 8-12 ijulja 1940 g. (Architectural issues of the redesigning of Moscow. VII Plenary Meeting of the Soviet Union of Architects SSA SSR, 8-12 July 1940). Moscow: Gos. Izd. Akad. Arch. SSR, 1940.
M.I. Astaf'eva-Dlugac, *Oblik Moskvy buduscego v general'nom plane 1935 goda* (The image of Moscow in the General plan 1935), in *Stroitel'stvo i Arkhitectura Moskvy* 6, 1985.
M.I. Astaf'eva-Dlugac, Ju.P. Volcok, *O professional'nom vosprijatii celostnosti Moskvy* (The professional comprehension of the integrity of Moscow), in *Stroitel'stvo i Arkhitectura Moskvy*, 1, 1983.
B. Grojs, *Utopia i obmen* (Utopia and Exchange). Moscow: Znak, 1993.